D0843068

The
Origins
of the
Koran

The Origins of the Koran

Classic Essays
on Islam's
Holy Book

Edited by **Ibn Warraq**

Prometheus Books

59 John Glenn Drive
Amherst, New York 14228-2119

Published 1998 by Prometheus Books

Inquiries should be addressed to
Prometheus Books
59 John Glenn Drive
Amherst, New York 14228–2119
VOICE: 716–691–0133, ext. 210
FAX: 716–691-0137
WWW.PROMETHEUSBOOKS.COM

16 15 14 13   15 14 13 12

Library of Congress Cataloging-in-Publication Data

The origins of the Koran : classic essays on Islam's holy book / edited by Ibn Warraq.
    p.   cm.
Includes bibliographical references.
ISBN 13: 978-1-57392-198-5
ISBN 10: 1-57392-198-X   (alk. paper)

    1. Koran—History. I. Ibn Warraq.
BP131.O74   1998
297.1'221—dc21   98–6075
                                                    CIP

Printed in the United States of America on acid-free paper

Contents

5

PART ONE

Introduction

1.

Introduction

Ibn Warraq

THE STEREOTYPIC IMAGE OF THE Muslim holy warrior with a sword in one hand and the Koran in the other would only be plausible if he was left-handed, since no devout Muslim should or would touch a Koran with his left hand which is reserved for dirty chores. All Muslims revere the Koran with a reverence that borders on bibliolatry and superstition. "It is," as Guillaume remarked, "the holy of holies. It must never rest beneath other books, but always on top of them, one must never drink or smoke when it is being read aloud, and it must be listened to in silence. It is a talisman against disease and disaster."[1]

In some Westerners it engenders other emotions. For Gibbon it was an "incoherent rhapsody of fable,"[2] for Carlyle an "insupportable stupidity,"[3] while here is what the German scholar Salomon Reinach thought: "From the literary point of view, the Koran has little merit. Declamation, repetition, puerility, a lack of logic and coherence strike the unprepared reader at every turn. It is humiliating to the human intellect to think that this mediocre literature has been the subject of innumerable commentaries, and that millions of men are still wasting time absorbing it."[4]

For us in studying the Koran it is necessary to distinguish the historical from the theological attitude. Here we are only concerned with those truths that are yielded by a process of rational enquiry, by scientific examination. "Critical investigation of the text of the Qur'an is a study which is still in its infancy,"[5] wrote the Islamic scholar Arthur Jeffery in 1937. In 1977 John Wansbrough noted that "as a document susceptible of analysis by the instruments and techniques of Biblical criticism [the Koran] is virtually unknown."[6] By 1990, more than fifty years after Jeffery's lament, we still have the scandalous situation described by Andrew Rippin:

> I have often encountered individuals who come to the study of Islam with a background in the historical study of the Hebrew Bible or early Christianity, and who express surprise at the lack of critical thought that appears in introductory textbooks on Islam. The notion that "Islam was born in the clear light of history" still seems to be assumed by a great many writers of such texts. While the need to reconcile varying historical traditions is generally recognized, usually this seems to pose no greater problem to the authors than having to determine "what makes sense" in a given situation. To students acquainted with approaches such as source criticism, oral formulaic compositions, literary analysis and structuralism, all quite commonly employed in the study of Judaism and Christianity, such naive historical study seems to suggest that Islam is being approached with less than academic candor.[7]

The questions any critical investigation of the Koran hopes to answer are:

1. How did the Koran come to us?—That is the compilation and the transmission of the Koran.

2. When was it written, and who wrote it?

3. What are the sources of the Koran? Where were the stories, legends, and principles that abound in the Koran acquired?

4. What is the Koran? Since there never was a *textus receptus ne varietur* of the Koran, we need to decide its authenticity.

I shall begin with the traditional account that is more or less accepted by most Western scholars, and then move on to the views of a small but very formidable, influential, and growing group of scholars inspired by the work of John Wansbrough.

According to the traditional account the Koran was revealed to Muhammad, usually by an angel, gradually over a period of years until his death in 632 C.E. It is not clear how much of the Koran had been written down by the time of Muhammad's death, but it seems probable that there was no single manuscript in which the Prophet himself had collected all the revelations. Nonetheless, there are traditions which describe how the Prophet dictated this or that portion of the Koran to his secretaries.

THE COLLECTION UNDER ABU BAKR

Henceforth the traditional account becomes more and more confused; in fact there is no one tradition but several incompatible ones. According to one tradition, during Abu Bakr's brief caliphate (632–634), 'Umar, who himself was to succeed to the caliphate in 634, became worried at the fact that so many Muslims who had known the Koran by heart were killed during the Battle of Yamama, in Central Arabia. There was a real danger that parts of the Koran would be irretrievably lost unless a collection of the Koran was made before more of those who knew this or that part of the Koran by heart were killed. Abu Bakr eventually gave his consent to such a project, and asked Zaid ibn Thabit, the former secretary of the Prophet, to undertake this daunting task. So Zaid proceeded to collect the Koran "from pieces of papyrus, flat stones, palm leaves, shoulder blades and ribs of animals, pieces of leather and wooden boards, as well as from the hearts of men." Zaid then copied out what he had collected on sheets or leaves (Arabic, *suhuf*). Once complete, the Koran was handed over to Abu Bakr, and on his death passed to 'Umar, and upon his death passed to 'Umar's daughter, Hafsa.

There are however different versions of this tradition; in some it is suggested that it was Abu Bakr who first had the idea to make the collection; in other versions the credit is given to 'Ali, the fourth caliph and the founder of the Shias; other versions still completely exclude Abu Bakr. Then, it is argued that such a difficult task could not have been accomplished in just two years. Again, it is unlikely that those who died in the Battle of Yamama, being new converts, knew any of the Koran by heart. But what is considered the most telling point against this tradition of the first collection of the Koran under Abu Bakr is that once the collection was made it was not treated as an official codex, but almost as the private property of Hafsa. In other words, we find that no authority is attributed to Abu Bakr's Koran. It has been suggested that the entire story was invented to take the credit of having made the first official collection of the Koran away from 'Uthman, the third caliph, who was greatly disliked. Others have suggested that it was invented "to take the collection of the Quran back as near as possible to Muhammad's death."[8]

THE COLLECTION UNDER 'UTHMAN

According to tradition, the next step was taken under 'Uthman (644–656). One of 'Uthman's generals asked the caliph to make such a collection because serious disputes had broken out among his troops from different provinces in regard to the correct readings of the Koran. 'Uthman chose Zaid ibn Thabit to prepare the official text. Zaid, with the help of three members of noble Meccan families, carefully revised the Koran comparing his version with the "leaves" in the possession of Hafsa, 'Umar's daughter; and as instructed, in case of difficulty as to the reading, Zaid followed the dialect of the Quraish, the Prophet's tribe. The copies of the new version, which must have been completed between 650 and 'Uthman's death in 656, were sent to Kufa, Basra, Damascus, and perhaps Mecca, and one was, of course, kept in Medina. All other versions were ordered to be destroyed.

The version of events is also open to criticism. The Arabic found in the Koran is not a dialect. In some versions the number of people working on the commission with Zaid varies, and in some are included the names of persons who were enemies of 'Uthman, and the name of someone known to have died before these events! This phase two of the story does not mention Zaid's part in the original collection of the Koran discussed in phase one.

Apart from Wansbrough and his disciples, whose work we shall look at in a moment, most modern scholars seem to accept that the establishment of the text of the Koran took place under 'Uthman between 650 and 656, despite all the criticisms mentioned above. They accept more or less the traditional account of the 'Uthmanic collection, it seems to me, without *giving a single coherent reason* for accepting this second tradition as opposed to the first tradition of the collection under Abu Bakr. There is a massive gap in their arguments, or rather they offer no arguments at all. For instance, Charles Adams after enumerating the difficulties with the 'Uthmanic story, concludes with breathtaking abruptness and break in logic, "Despite the difficulties with the traditional accounts there can be no question of the importance of the codex prepared under 'Uthman."[9] But nowhere has it yet been established that it was indeed under 'Uthman that the Koran as we know it was prepared. It is simply *assumed* all along that it was under 'Uthman that the Koran was established in its final form, and all we have to do is to explain away some of the difficulties. Indeed, we can apply the same arguments to dismiss the 'Uthmanic story as were used to dismiss the Abu Bakr story. That is, we can argue that the 'Uthmanic story was invented by the enemies of Abu Bakr and the friends of 'Uthman; political polemics can equally be said to have played their part in the fabrication of this later story. It also leaves unanswered so many awkward questions. What were these "leaves" in the possession of Hafsa? And if the Abu Bakr version is pure forgery where did Hafsa get hold of them? Then what are those versions that seemed to be floating around in the provinces? When were these alternative texts compiled, and by whom? Can we really pick and choose, at our own will, from amongst the variants, from the contradictory traditions? There are no compelling reasons for accepting the 'Uthmanic story and not the Abu Bakr one; after all they are *all gleaned from the same sources,* which are all exceedingly late, tendentious in the extreme, and all later fabrications, as we shall see later.

But I have even more fundamental problems in accepting any of these traditional accounts at their face value. When listening to these accounts, some very common-sensical objections arise but which no one seems to have dared to ask. First, all these stories place an enormous burden on the memories of the early Muslims. Indeed, scholars are compelled to exaggerate the putatively prodigious memories of the Arabs. Muhammad could not read or write according to some traditions, and therefore everything depends on him having perfectly memorized what God revealed to him through His Angels. Some of the stories in the Koran are enormously long; for instance, the story of Joseph takes up a whole chapter of 111 verses. Are we really to believe that Muhammad remembered it exactly as it was revealed?

Similarly the Companions of the Prophet are said to have memorized many of his utterances. Could their memories never have failed? Oral traditions have a tendency to change over time, and they cannot be relied upon to construct a reliable, scientific history. Second, we seem to assume that the Companions of the Prophet *heard and understood* him perfectly.

VARIANT VERSIONS, VERSES MISSING, VERSES ADDED

Almost without exceptions Muslims consider that the Quran we now possess goes back in its text and in the number and order of the chapters to the work of the commission that 'Uthman appointed. Muslim orthodoxy holds further that 'Uthman's Quran contains all of the revelation

delivered to the community faithfully preserved without change or variation of any kind and that the acceptance of the 'Uthmanic Quran was
all but universal from the day of its distribution.

The orthodox position is motivated by dogmatic factors; it cannot be
supported by the historical evidence....

Charles Adams[10]

While modern Muslims may be committed to an impossibly conservative
position, Muslim scholars of the early years of Islam were far more flex-
ible in their position, realizing that parts of the Koran were lost, perverted,
and that there were many thousand variants which made it impossible to
talk of *the* Koran. For example, as-Suyuti (died 1505), one of the most
famous and revered of the commentators of the Koran, quotes Ibn 'Umar
al-Khattab as saying: "Let no one of you say that he has acquired the entire
Koran for how does he know that it is all? Much of the Koran has been lost,
thus let him say, 'I have acquired of it what is available'" (As-Suyuti, *Itqan*,
part 3, page 72). 'A'isha, the favorite wife of the Prophet, says, also
according to a tradition recounted by as-Suyuti, "During the time of the
Prophet, the chapter of the Parties used to be two hundred verses when
read. When 'Uthman edited the copies of the Koran, only the current
(verses) were recorded" (73).

As-Suyuti also tells this story about Ubai ibn Ka'b, one of the great
Companions of Muhammad:

> This famous Companion asked one of the Muslims, "How many verses
> in the chapter of the Parties?" He said, "Seventy-three verses." He (Ubai)
> told him, "It used to be almost equal to the chapter of the Cow (about
> 286 verses) and included the verse of the stoning." The man asked,
> "What is the verse of the stoning?" He (Ubai) said, "If an old man or
> woman committed adultery, stone them to death."

As noted earlier, since there was no single document collecting all the
revelations, after Muhammad's death in 632 C.E., many of his followers
tried to gather all the known revelations and write them down in codex
form. Soon we had the codices of several scholars such as Ibn Mas'ud, Ubai
ibn Ka'b, 'Ali, Abu Bakr, al-Aswad, and others (Jeffery, chapter 6, has listed
fifteen primary codices, and a large number of secondary ones). As Islam
spread, we eventually had what became known as the metropolitan codices
in the centers of Mecca, Medina, Damascus, Kufa, and Basra. As we saw

earlier, 'Uthman tried to bring order to this chaotic situation by canonizing the Medinan Codex, copies of which were sent to all the metropolitan centers, with orders to destroy all the other codices.

'Uthman's codex was supposed to standardize the consonantal text; yet we find that many of the variant traditions of this consonantal text survived well into the fourth Islamic century. The problem was aggravated by the fact the consonantal text was unpointed, that is to say, the dots that distinguish, for example, a "b" from a "t" or a "th" were missing. Several other letters (f and q; j, h, and kh; s and d; r and z; s and sh; d and dh, t and z) were indistinguishable. In other words, the Koran was written in a *scripta defectiva*. As a result, a great many variant readings were possible according to the way the text was pointed (had the dots added).

Vowels presented an even worse problem. Originally, the Arabs had no signs for the short vowels: the Arab script is consonantal. Although the short vowels are sometimes omitted, they can be represented by orthographical signs placed above or below the letters—three signs in all, taking the form of a slightly slanting dash or a comma. After having settled the consonants, Muslims still had to decide what vowels to employ: using different vowels, of course, rendered different readings. The *scripta plena*, which allowed a fully voweled and pointed text, was not perfected until the late ninth century.

The problems posed by the *scripta defectiva* inevitably led to the growth of different centers with their own variant traditions of how the texts should be pointed or vowelized. Despite 'Uthman's order to destroy all texts other than his own, it is evident that the older codices survived. As Charles Adams says, "It must be emphasized that far from there being a single text passed down inviolate from the time of 'Uthman's commission, literally thousands of variant readings of particular verses were known in the first three (Muslim) centuries. These variants affected even the 'Uthmanic codex, making it difficult to know what its true form may have been."[11]

Some Muslims preferred codices other than the 'Uthmanic, for example, those of Ibn Mas'ud, Ubai ibn Ka'b, and Abu Musa. Eventually under the influence of the great Koranic scholar Ibn Mujahid (died 935 C.E.), there was a definite canonization of one system of consonants and a limit placed on the variations of vowels used in the text that resulted in acceptance of seven systems. But other scholars accepted ten readings, and still others accepted fourteen readings. Even Ibn Mujahid's seven provided fourteen possibilities since each of the seven was traced through two different transmitters, viz,

1. Nafi of Medina according to Warsh and Qalun
2. Ibn Kathir of Mecca according to al-Bazzi and Qunbul
3. Ibn Amir of Damascus according to Hisham and Ibn Dhakwan
4. Abu Amr of Basra according to al-Duri and al-Susi
5. Asim of Kufa according to Hafs and Abu Bakr
6. Hamza of Kuga according to Khalaf and Khallad
7. Al-Kisai of Kufa according to al-Duri and Abul Harith

In the end three systems prevailed, those of Warsh (d. 812) from Nafi of Medina, Hafs (d. 805) from Asim of Kufa, and al-Duri (d. 860) from Abu Amr of Basra. At present in modern Islam, two versions seem to be in use: that of Asim of Kufa through Hafs, which was given a kind of official seal of approval by being adopted in the Egyptian edition of the Koran in 1924; and that of Nafi through Warsh, which is used in parts of Africa other than Egypt. As Charles Adams reminds us:

> It is of some importance to call attention to a possible source of misunderstanding with regard to the variant readings of the Quran. The seven (versions) refer to actual written and oral text, to distinct versions of Quranic verses, whose differences, though they may not be great, are nonetheless substantial. Since the very existence of variant readings and versions of the Quran goes against the doctrinal position toward the Holy Book held by many modern Muslims, it is not uncommon in an apologetic context to hear the seven (versions) explained as modes of recitation; in fact the manner and technique of recitation are an entirely different matter.[12]

Guillaume also refers to the variants as "not always trifling in significance."[13] For example, the last two verses of surah LXXXV, Al-Buraj, read: (21) *huwa qur'anun majidun;(22) fi lawhin mahfuzun/in.* The last syllable is in doubt. If it is in the genitive -*in*, it gives the meaning: "It is a glorious Koran on a preserved tablet"—a reference to the Muslim doctrine of the Preserved Tablet. If it is the nominative ending -*un*, we get: "It is a glorious Koran preserved on a tablet." There are other passages with similar difficulties dealing with social legislation.

If we allow that there were omissions, then why not additions? The authenticity of many verses in the Koran has been called into question by Muslims themselves. Many Kharijites, who were followers of 'Ali in the early history of Islam, found the sura recounting the story of Joseph offensive, an erotic tale that did not belong in the Koran. Hirschfeld[14] questioned the authenticity of verses in which the name Muhammad occurs; there being something rather "suspicious in such a name, meaning 'Praised', being borne by the Prophet." The name was certainly not very common. However the Prophet's name does occur in documents that have been accepted as genuine, such as the Constitution of Medina.

Most scholars believe that there are interpolations in the Koran; these interpolations can be seen as interpretative glosses on certain rare words in need of explanation. More serious are the interpolations of a dogmatic or political character, which seem to have been added to justify the elevation of 'Uthman as caliph to the detriment of 'Ali. Then there are other verses that have been added in the interest of rhyme, or to join together two short passages that on their own lack any connection.

Bell and Watt carefully go through many of the emendments and revisions and point to the unevenness of the Koranic style as evidence for a great many alterations in the Koran:

> There are indeed many roughnesses of this kind, and these, it is here claimed, are fundamental evidence for revision. Besides the points already noticed—hidden rhymes, and rhyme phrases not woven into the texture of the passage—there are the following: abrupt changes of rhyme; repetition of the same rhyme word or rhyme phrase in adjoining verses; the intrusion of an extraneous subject into a passage otherwise homogeneous; a differing treatment of the same subject in neighbouring verses, often with repetition of words and phrases; breaks in grammatical construction which raise difficulties in exegesis; abrupt changes in length of verse; sudden changes of the dramatic situation, with changes of pronoun from singular to plural, from second to third person, and so on; the juxtaposition of apparently contrary statements; the juxtaposition of passages of different date, with intrusion of late phrases into early verses;
>
> In many cases a passage has alternative continuations which follow one another in the present text. The second of the alternatives is marked by a break in sense and by a break in grammatical construction, since the connection is not with what immediately precedes, but with what stands some distance back.[15]

The Christian al-Kindi (not to be confused with the Arab, Muslim philosopher) writing around 830 C.E., criticized the Koran in similar terms:

The result of all this (process by which the Quran came into being) is
patent to you who have read the scriptures and see how, in your book,
histories are jumbled together and intermingled; an evidence that many
different hands have been at work therein, and caused discrepancies,
adding or cutting out whatever they liked or disliked. Are such, now, the
conditions of a revelation sent down from heaven?[16]

SKEPTICISM OF THE SOURCES

The traditional accounts of the life of Muhammad and the story of the
origin and rise of Islam, including the compilation of the Koran are based
exclusively on Muslim sources, particularly the Muslim biographies of
Muhammad, and the Hadith, that is the Muslim traditions.

The Prophet Muhammad died in 632 C.E. The earliest material on his
life that we possess was written by Ibn Ishaq in 750 C.E., in other words, a
hundred twenty years after Muhammad's death. The question of authenticity becomes even more critical, because the original form of Ibn Ishaq's
work is lost and is only available in parts in a later recension by Ibn Hisham
who died in 834 C.E., two hundred years after the death of the Prophet.

The Hadith are a collection of sayings and doings attributed to the
Prophet and traced back to him through a series of putatively trustworthy
witnesses (any particular chain of transmitters is called an *isnad*). These
Hadith include the story of the compilation of the Koran, and the sayings
of the companions of the Prophet. There are said to be six correct or
authentic collections of traditions accepted by Sunni Muslims, namely, the
compilations of Bukhari, Muslim, Ibn Maja, Abu Dawud, al-Tirmidhi, and
al-Nisai. Again it is worth noting that all these sources are very late indeed.
Bukhari died 238 years after the death of the Prophet, while al-Nisai died
over 280 years after!

The historical and biographical tradition concerning Muhammad and
the early years of Islam was submitted to a thorough examination at the
end of the nineteenth century. Up to then careful scholars were well aware
of the legendary and theological elements in these traditions, and that
there were traditions which originated from party motive and which
intended "to give an appearance of historical foundation to the particular
interests of certain persons or families; but it was thought that after some
sifting there yet remained enough to enable us to form a much clearer

sketch of Muhammad's life than that of any other of the founders of a universal religion."[17] This illusion was shattered by Wellhausen, Caetani, and Lammens who called "one after another of the data of Muslim tradition into question."

Wellhausen[18] divided the old historical traditions as found in the ninth- and tenth-century compilations in two: first, an authentic primitive tradition, definitively recorded in the late eighth century, and second a parallel version which was deliberately forged to rebut this. The second version was full of tendentious fiction, and was to be found in the work of historians such as Sayf b. 'Umar (see above). Prince Caetani and Father Lammens cast doubt even on data hitherto accepted as "objective." The biographers of Muhammad were too far removed from his time to have true data or notions; far from being objective the data rested on tendentious fiction; furthermore it was not their aim to know these things as they really happened, but to construct an ideal vision of the past, as it ought to have been. "Upon the bare canvas of verses of the Koran that need explanation, the traditionists have embroidered with great boldness scenes suitable to the desires or ideals of their particular group; or to use a favorite metaphor of Lammens, they fill the empty spaces by a process of stereotyping which permits the critical observer to recognize the origin of each picture."[19]

As Lewis puts it, "Lammens went so far as to reject the entire biography as no more than a conjectural and tendentious exegesis of a few passages of biographical content in the Quran, devised and elaborated by later generations of believers."[20]

Even scholars who rejected the extreme skepticism of Caetani and Lammens, were forced to recognize that "of Muhammad's life before his appearance as the messenger of God, we know extremely little; compared to the legendary biography as treasured by the faithful, practically nothing."[21]

The ideas of the Positivist Caetani and the Jesuit Lammens were never forgotten, and indeed they were taken up by a group of Soviet Islamologists, and pushed to their extreme but logical conclusions. The ideas of the Soviet scholars were in turn taken up in the 1970s, by Cook, Crone, and other disciples of Wansbrough.

What Caetani and Lammens did for historical biography, Ignaz Goldziher did for the study of Hadith. Goldziher has had an enormous influence in the field of Islamic studies, and it is no exaggeration to say that he is, along with Hurgronje and Nöldeke, one of the founding fathers of the modern study of Islam. Practically everything he wrote between

roughly 1870 and 1920 is still studied assiduously in universities throughout the world. In his classic paper, "On the Development of Hadith,"
Goldziher "demonstrated that a vast number of Hadith accepted even in
the most rigorously critical Muslim collections were outright forgeries
from the late 8th and 9th centuries—and as a consequence, that the meticulous isnads [chains of transmitters] which supported them were utterly
fictitious."[22]

Faced with Goldziher's impeccably documented arguments, historians
began to panic and devise spurious ways of keeping skepticism at bay, by,
for instance, postulating ad hoc distinctions between legal and historical
traditions. But as Humphreys says, in their formal structure, the Hadith
and historical traditions were very similar; furthermore many eighth- and
ninth-century Muslim scholars had worked on both kinds of texts. "Altogether, if hadith isnads were suspect, so then should be the isnads attached
to historical reports."[23]

As Goldziher puts it himself, "close acquaintance with the vast stock of
hadiths induces sceptical caution,"[24] and he considers by far the greater
part of the Hadith "as the result of the religious, historical and social
development of Islam during the first two centuries." The Hadith is useless as a basis for any scientific history, and can only serve as a "reflection
of the tendencies" of the early Muslim community.

Here I need to interpose a historical digression, if we are to have a
proper understanding of Goldziher's arguments. After the death of the
Prophet, four of his companions succeeded him as leaders of the Muslim
community; the last of the four was 'Ali, the Prophet's cousin and son-in-
law. 'Ali was unable to impose his authority in Syria where the governor
was Mu'awiya who adopted the war cry of "Vengeance for 'Uthman"
against 'Ali (Mu'awiya and 'Uthman were related and both belonged to the
Meccan clan of Umayya). The forces of the two met in an indecisive battle
at Siffin. After 'Ali's murder in 661, Mu'awiya became the first caliph of the
dynasty we know as the Umayyad, which endured until 750 C.E. The
Umayyads were deposed by the 'Abbasids, who lasted in Iraq and Baghdad
until the thirteenth century.

During the early years of the Umayyad dynasty, many Muslims were
totally ignorant in regard to ritual and doctrine. The rulers themselves had
little enthusiasm for religion, and generally despised the pious and the
ascetic. The result was that there arose a group of pious men who shame-
lessly fabricated traditions for the good of the community, and traced them

back to the authority of the Prophet. They opposed the godless Umayyads but dare not say so openly, so they invented further traditions dedicated to praising the Prophet's family, hence indirectly giving their allegiance to the party of 'Ali supporters. As Goldziher[25] puts it, "The ruling power itself was not idle. If it wished an opinion to be generally recognized and the opposition of pious circles silenced, it too had to know how to discover a hadith to suit its purpose. They had to do what their opponents did: invent and have invented, hadiths in their turn. And that is in effect what they did." Goldziher continues:

> Official influences on the invention, dissemination and suppression of traditions started early. An instruction given to his obedient governor al-Mughira by Muawiya is in the spirit of the Umayyads. "Do not tire of abusing and insulting Ali and calling for God's mercifulness for 'Uthman, defaming the companions of Ali, removing them and omitting to listen to them (i.e. to what they tell and propagate as hadiths); praising in contrast, the clan of 'Uthman, drawing them near to you and listening to them." This is an official encouragement to foster the rise and spread of hadiths directed against Ali and to hold back and suppress hadiths favoring Ali. The Umayyads and their political followers had no scruples in promoting tendentious lies in a sacred religious form, and they were only concerned to find pious authorities who would be prepared to cover such falsifications with their undoubted authority. There was never any lack of these.[26]

Hadiths were liable to be fabricated even for the most trivial ritualistic details. Tendentiousness included the suppression of existing utterances friendly to the rival party or dynasty. Under the 'Abbasids, the fabrications of Hadiths greatly multiplied, with the express purpose of proving the legitimacy of their own clan against the 'Alids. For example, the Prophet was made to say that Abu Talib, father of 'Ali, was sitting deep in hell: "Perhaps my intercession will be of use to him on the day of resurrection so that he may be transferred into a pool of fire which reaches only up to the ankles but which is still hot enough to burn the brain." Naturally enough this was countered by the theologians of the 'Alids by devising numerous traditions concerning the glorification of Abu Talib, all sayings of the Prophet. "In fact," as Goldziher shows, amongst the opposing factions, "the mischievous use of tendentious traditions was even more common than the official party"[27]

Eventually storytellers made a good living inventing entertaining Hadiths, which the credulous masses lapped up eagerly. To draw the crowds the storytellers shrank from nothing. "The handing down of hadiths sank to the level of a business very early. Journeys (in search of hadiths) favored the greed of those who succeeded in pretending to be a source of the hadith, and with increasing demand sprang up an even increasing desire to be paid in cash for the hadiths supplied."[28]

Of course many Muslims were aware that forgeries abounded. But even the so-called six authentic collections of Hadiths compiled by Bukhari and others were not as rigorous as might have been hoped. The six had varying criteria for including a Hadith as genuine or not—some were rather liberal in their choice, others rather arbitrary. Then there was the problem of the authenticity of the texts of these compilers. For example, at one point there were a dozen different Bukhari texts; and apart from these variants, there were deliberate interpolations. As Goldziher warns us, "It would be wrong to think that the canonical authority of the two [collections of Bukhari and Muslim] is due to the undisputed correctness of their contents and is the result of scholarly investigations."[29] Even a tenth-century critic pointed out the weaknesses of two hundred traditions incorporated in the works of Muslim and Bukhari.

Goldziher's arguments were followed up, nearly sixty years later, by another great Islamicist, Joseph Schacht, whose works on Islamic law are considered classics in the field of Islamic studies. Schacht's conclusions were even more radical and perturbing, and the full implications of these conclusions have not yet sunk in.

Humphreys sums up Schacht's theses as[30]: "(1) that isnads [the chain of transmitters] going all the way back to the Prophet only began to be widely used around the time of the Abbasid Revolution—i.e., the mid-8th century; (2) that ironically, the more elaborate and formally correct an isnad appeared to be, the more likely it was to be spurious." In general he concluded, "NO existing hadith could be reliably ascribed to the prophet, though some of them might ultimately be rooted in his teaching. And though [Schacht] devoted only a few pages to historical reports about the early Caliphate, he explicitly asserted that the same strictures should apply to them." Schacht's arguments were backed up by a formidable list of references, and they could not be dismissed easily.

Here is how Schacht himself [31] sums up his own thesis:

It is generally conceded that the criticism of traditions as practiced by the Muhammadan scholars is inadequate and that, however many forgeries may have been eliminated by it, even the classical corpus contains a great many traditions which cannot possibly be authentic. All efforts to extract from this often self-contradictory mass an authentic core by "historic intuition"... have failed. Goldziher, in another of his fundamental works, has not only voiced his "sceptical reserve" with regard to the traditions contained even in the classical collections [i.e., the collections of Bukhari, Muslim, et al.], but shown positively that the great majority of traditions from the Prophet are documents not of the time to which they claim to belong, but of the successive stages of development of doctrines during the first centuries of Islam. This brilliant discovery became the corner-stone of all serious investigation...

    This book [i.e., Schacht's own book] will be found to confirm Goldziher's results, and go beyond them in the following respects: a great many traditions in the classical and other collections were put into circulation only after Shafi'i's time [Shafi'i was the founder of the very important school of law which bears his name; he died in 820 C.E.]; the first considerable body of legal traditions from the Prophet originated towards the middle of the second [Muslim] century [i.e., eighth century C.E.], in opposition to slightly earlier traditions from the Companions and other authorities, and to the living tradition of the ancient schools of law; traditions from Companions and other authorities underwent the same process of growth, and are to be considered in the same light, as traditions from the Prophet; the study of isnads show a tendency to grow backwards and to claim higher and higher authority until they arrive at the Prophet; the evidence of legal traditions carries back to about the year 100 A.H. [718 C.E.]...

Schacht proves that, for example, a tradition did not exist at a particular time by showing that it was not used as a legal argument in a discussion which would have made reference to it imperative, if it had existed. For Schacht every legal tradition from the Prophet must be taken as inauthentic and the fictitious expression of a legal doctrine formulated at a later date: "We shall not meet any legal tradition from the Prophet which can positively be considered authentic."[32]

    Traditions were formulated polemically in order to rebut a contrary doctrine or practice; Schacht calls these traditions "counter traditions." Doctrines, in this polemical atmosphere, were frequently projected back to higher authorities: "traditions from Successors [to the Prophet] become traditions from Companions [of the Prophet], and traditions from Companions become traditions from the Prophet." Details from the life of the Prophet were invented to support legal doctrines.

Schacht then criticizes isnads which "were often put together very carelessly. Any typical representative of the group whose doctrine was to be projected back on to an ancient authority, could be chosen at random and put into the isnad. We find therefore a number of alternative names in otherwise identical isnads."

Schacht "showed that the beginnings of Islamic law cannot be traced further back than to about a century after the Prophet's death."[33] Islamic law did not directly derive from the Koran but developed out of popular and administrative practice under the Ummayads, and this "practice often diverged from the intentions and even the explicit wording of the Koran." Norms derived from the Koran were introduced into Islamic law at a secondary stage.

A group of scholars was convinced of the essential soundness of Schacht's analysis, and proceeded to work out in full detail the implications of Schacht's arguments. The first of these scholars was John Wansbrough, who in two important though formidably difficult books, *Quranic Studies: Sources and Methods of Scriptural Interpretation* (1977) and *The Sectarian Milieu: Content and Composition of Islamic Salvation History* (1978), showed that the Koran and the Hadith grew out of sectarian controversies over a long period, perhaps as long as two centuries, and then was projected back onto an invented Arabian point of origin.[34] He further argued that Islam emerged only when it came into contact with and under the influence of Rabbinic Judaism—"that Islamic doctrine generally, and even the figure of Muhammad, were molded on Rabbinic Jewish prototypes." "Proceeding from these conclusions, *The Sectarian Milieu* analyses early Islamic historiography—or rather the interpretive myths underlying this historiography—as a late manifestation of Old Testament 'salvation history.' "

Wansbrough shows that far from being fixed in the seventh century, the definitive text of the Koran had still not been achieved as late as the ninth century. An Arabian origin for Islam is highly unlikely, the Arabs gradually formulated their creed as they came into contact with Rabbinic Judaism *outside* the Hijaz (Central Arabia, containing the cities of Mecca and Medina). "Quranic allusion presupposes familiarity with the narrative material of Judaeo-Christian scripture, which was not so much reformulated as merely referred to.... Taken together, the quantity of reference, the mechanically repetitive employment of rhetorical convention, and the stridently polemical style, all suggest a strongly sectarian atmosphere in which a corpus of familiar scripture was being pressed into the service of as yet unfamiliar doctrine."[35] Elsewhere Wansbrough says, "[The] challenge to produce an identical or superior scripture (or portion thereof), expressed five times in the Quranic text can be explained only within a context of Jewish polemic."[36]

Earlier scholars such as Torrey, recognizing the genuine borrowings in the Koran from Rabbinic literature, had jumped to conclusions about the Jewish population in the Hijaz (i.e., Central Arabia). But as Wansbrough puts it, "References in Rabbinic literature to Arabia are of remarkably little worth for purposes of historical reconstruction, and especially for the Hijaz in the sixth and seventh centuries."[37]

Much influenced by the Rabbinic accounts, the early Muslim community took Moses as an exemplum, and then a portrait of Muhammad emerged, but only gradually and in response to the needs of a religious community. It was anxious to establish Muhammad's credentials as a prophet on the Mosaic model; this evidently meant there had to be a Holy Scripture, which would be seen as testimony to his prophethood. Another gradual development was the emergence of the idea of the Arabian origins of Islam. To this end, there was elaborated the concept of a sacred language, Arabic. The Koran was said to be handed down by God in pure Arabic. It is significant that the ninth century also saw the first collections of the ancient poetry of the Arabs: "The manner in which this material was manipulated by its collectors to support almost any argument appears never to have been very successfully concealed."[38] Thus Muslim philologists were able to give, for instance, an early date to a poem ascribed to Nabigha Jadi, a pre-Islamic poet, in order to "provide a pre-Islamic proof text for a common Quranic construction." The aim in appealing to the authority of pre-Islamic poetry was twofold, first to give *ancient* authority to their own Holy Scripture, to push back this sacred text into an earlier period, and thus give their text greater authenticity, a text which in reality had been fabricated in the later ninth century, along with all the supporting traditions. Second, it gave a specifically Arabian flavor, an Arabian setting to their religion, something distinct from Judaism, and Christianity. Exegetical traditions were equally fictitious and had but one aim, to demonstrate the Hijazi origins of Islam. Wansbrough gives some negative evidence to show that the Koran had not achieved any definitive form before the ninth century:

> Schacht's studies of the early development of legal doctrine within the community demonstrate that with very few exceptions, Muslim jurispru-

dence was not derived from the contents of the Quran. It may be added that those few exceptions are themselves hardly evidence for the existence of the canon, and further observed that even where doctrine was alleged to draw upon scripture, such is not necessarily proof of th earlier existence of the scriptural source. Derivation of law from scripture ... was a phenomenon of the ninth century.... A similar kind of negative evidence is absence of any reference to the Quran in the Fiqh Akbar I.[39]

The latter is a document, dated to the middle of the eighth century, which was a kind of statement of the Muslim creed in face of sects. Thus the Fiqh Akbar I represents the views of the orthodoxy, on the then prominent dogmatic questions. It seems unthinkable had the Koran existed that no reference would have been made to it.

Wansbrough submits the Koran to a highly technical analysis with the aim of showing that it cannot have been deliberately edited by a few men, but "rather the product of an organic development from originally independent traditions during a long period of transmission."

Wansbrough was to throw cold water on the idea that the Koran was the only hope for genuine historical information regarding the Prophet; an idea summed up by Jeffery,[40] "The dominant note in this advanced criticism is 'back to the Koran.' As a basis for critical biography the Traditions are practically worthless; in the Koran alone can we be said to have firm ground under our feet." But as Wansbrough was to show: "The role of the Quran in the delineation of an Arabian prophet was peripheral: evidence of a divine communication but not a report of its circumstances.... The very notion of biographical data in the Quran depends on exegetical principles derived from material external to the canon."[41]

A group of scholars influenced by Wansbrough took an even more radical approach; they rejected wholesale the entire Islamic version of early Islamic history. Michael Cook, Patricia Crone, and Martin Hinds writing between 1977 and 1987

regard the whole established version of Islamic history down at least to the time of Abd al-Malik (685–705) as a later fabrication, and reconstruct the Arab Conquests and the formation of the Caliphate as a movement of peninsular Arabs who had been inspired by Jewish messianism to try to reclaim the Promised Land. In this interpretation, Islam emerged as an autonomous religion and culture only within the process of a long struggle for identity among the disparate peoples yoked together by the Conquests: Jacobite Syrians, Nestorian Aramaeans in Iraq, Copts, Jews, and (finally) peninsular Arabs.[42]

The traditional account of the life of Muhammad and the rise of Islam is no longer accepted by Cook, Crone, and Hinds. In the short but pithy monograph on Muhammad in the Oxford Past Masters series, Cook gives his reasons for rejecting the biographical traditions:

> False ascription was rife among the eighth-century scholars, and... in any case Ibn Ishaq and his contemporaries were drawing on oral tradition. Neither of these propositions is as arbitrary as it sounds. We have reason to believe that numerous traditions on questions of dogma and law were provided with spurious chains of authorities by those who put them into circulation; and at the same time we have much evidence of controversy in the eighth century as to whether it was permissible to reduce oral tradition to writing. The implications of this view for the reliability of our sources are clearly rather negative. If we cannot trust the chains of authorities, we can no longer claim to know that we have before us the separately transmitted accounts of independent witnesses; and if knowledge of the life of Muhammad was transmitted orally for a century before it was reduced to writing, then the chances are that the material will have undergone considerable alteration in the process.[43]

Cook then looks at the non-Muslim sources: Greek, Syriac, and Armenian. Here a totally unexpected picture emerges. Though there is no doubt that someone called Muhammad existed, that he was a merchant, that something significant happened in 622, that Abraham was central to his teaching, there is no indication that Muhammad's career unfolded in inner Arabia, there is no mention of Mecca, and the Koran makes no appearance until the last years of the seventh century. Further, it emerges from this evidence that the Muslims prayed in a direction much further north than Mecca, hence their sanctuary cannot have been in Mecca. "Equally, when the first Koranic quotations appear on coins and inscriptions towards the end of the seventh century, they show divergences from the canonical text. These are trivial from the point of view of content, but the fact that they appear in such formal contexts as these goes badly with the notion that the text had already been frozen."[44]

The earliest Greek source speaks of Muhammad being alive in 634, two years after his death according to Muslim tradition. Where the Muslim accounts talk of Muhammad's break with the Jews, the Armenian has another version of the events.

> The Armenian chronicler of the 660s describes Muhammad as establishing a community which comprised both Ishmaelites (i.e., Arabs) and Jews, with Abrahamic descent as their common platform; these allies then set off to conquer Palestine. The oldest Greek source makes the sensational statement that the prophet who had appeared among the Saracens (i.e., Arabs) was proclaiming the coming of the (Jewish) messiah, and speaks of the Jews who mix with the Saracens, and of the danger to life and limb of falling into the hands of these Jews and Saracens. We cannot easily dismiss the evidence as the product of Christian prejudice, since it finds confirmation in the Hebrew apocalypse [an eighth-century document, in which is embedded an earlier apocalypse that seems to be contemporary with the conquests]. The break with the Jews is then placed by the Armenian chronicler immediately after the Arab conquest of Jerusalem.[45]

Although Palestine does play some sort of role in Muslim traditions, it is already demoted in favor of Mecca in the second year of the Hegira (Arabic *hijra,* or exodus from Mecca) when Muhammad changed the direction of prayer for Muslims from Jerusalem to Mecca. Thereafter it is Mecca which holds center stage for his activities. But in the non-Muslim sources, it is Palestine which is the focus of his movement, and provides the religious motive for its conquest.

> The Armenian chronicler further gives a rationale for this attachment: Muhammad told the Arabs that, as descendants of Abraham through Ishmael, they too had a claim to the land which God had promised to Abraham and his seed. The religion of Abraham is in fact as central in the Armenian account of Muhammad's preaching as it is in the Muslim sources; but it is given a quite different geographical twist.
>
> If the external sources are in any significant degree right on such points, it would follow that tradition is seriously misleading on important aspects of the life of Muhammad, and that even the integrity of the Koran as his message is in some doubt. In view of what was said above about the nature of the Muslim sources, such a conclusion would seem to me legitimate; but it is only fair to add that it is not usually drawn.[46]

Cook points out the similarity of certain Muslim beliefs and practices to those of the Samaritans (discussed below). He also points out that the fundamental idea developed by Muhammad of the religion of Abraham was already present in the Jewish apocryphal work called the Book of Jubilees (dated to c. 140–100 B.C.E.), and which may well have influenced the formation of Islamic ideas. We also have the evidence of Sozomenus, a Christian writer of the fifth century who "reconstructs a primitive Ishmaelite monotheism identical with that possessed by the Hebrews up to the time of Moses; and he goes on to argue from present conditions that Ishmael's laws must have been corrupted by the passage of time and the influence of pagan neighbors."[47]

Sozomenus goes on to describe how certain Arab tribes who, on learning of their Ishmaelite origins from Jews, adopted Jewish observances. Again there may have been some influence on the Muslim community from this source. Cook also points out the similarity of the story of Moses (exodus, etc.) and the Muslim *hijra*. In Jewish messianism, "the career of the messiah was seen as a re-enactment of that of Moses; a key event in the drama was an exodus, or flight, from oppression into the desert, whence the messiah was to lead a holy war to reconquer Palestine. Given the early evidence connecting Muhammad with Jews and Jewish messianism at the time when the conquest of Palestine was initiated, it is natural to see in Jewish apocalyptic thought a point of departure for his political ideas."[48]

Cook and Patricia Crone had developed these ideas in their intellectually exhilarating work *Hagarism: The Making of the Islamic World* (1977). Unfortunately, they adopted the rather difficult style of their "master" Wansbrough, which may well put off all but the most dedicated readers; as Humphreys says, "their argument is conveyed through a dizzying and unrelenting array of allusions, metaphors, and analogies."[49] The summary already given above of Cook's conclusions in *Muhammad* will help nonspecialists to have a better grasp of Cook and Crone's (CC, henceforth) arguments in *Hagarism*.

It would be appropriate to begin with an explanation of CC's frequent use of the terms "Hagar," "Hagarism," and "Hagarene." Since a part of their thesis is that Islam only emerged later than hitherto thought, after the first contacts with the older civilizations in Palestine, the Near East, and the Middle East, it would have been inappropriate to use the traditional terms "Muslim," "Islamic," and "Islam" for the early Arabs and their creed. It seems probable that the early Arab community, while it was developing its own religious identity, did not call itself "Muslim." On the other hand, Greek and Syriac documents refer to this community as *Magaritai,* and *Mahgre* (or *Mahgraye*) respectively. The *Mahgraye* are the descendants of Abraham by Hagar, hence the term "Hagarism." But there is another dimension to this term; for the corresponding Arabic term is *muhajirun;* the *muhajirun* are those who take part in a *hijra,* an exodus. "The 'Mahgraye' may thus be seen as Hagarene participants in a hijra to the Promised Land; in this pun lies the earliest identity of the faith which was in the fullness of time to become Islam."[50]

Relying on hitherto neglected non-Muslim sources CC give a new account of the rise of Islam, an account, on their admission, unacceptable to any Muslim. The Muslim sources are too late, and unreliable, and there are no cogent external grounds for accepting the Islamic tradition. CC begin with a Greek text (dated c. 634–636), in which the core of the Prophet's message appears as Judaic messianism. There is evidence that the Jews themselves, far from being the enemies of Muslims, as traditionally re-counted, welcomed and interpreted the Arab conquest in messianic terms. The evidence "of Judeo-Arab intimacy is complemented by indications of a marked hostility towards Christianity." An Armenian chronicle written in the 660s also contradicts the traditional Muslim insistence that Mecca was the religious metropolis of the Arabs at the time of the conquest; in con-trast, it points out the Palestinian orientation of the movement. The same chronicle helps us understand how the Prophet "provided a rationale for Arab involvement in the enactment of Judaic messianism. This rationale consists in a dual invocation of the Abrahamic descent of the Arabs as Ish-maelites: on the one hand to endow them with a birthright to the Holy Land, and on the other to provide them with a monotheist genealogy."[51] Similarly, we can see the Muslim *hijra,* not as an exodus from Mecca to Medina (for no early source attests to the historicity of this event), but as an emigration of the Ishmaelites (Arabs) from Arabia to the Promised Land.

The Arabs soon quarreled with the Jews, and their attitude to Chris-tians softened; the Christians posed less of a political threat. There still remained a need to develop a positive religious identity, which they pro-ceeded to do by elaborating a full-scale religion of Abraham, incorpo-rating many pagan practices but under a new Abrahamic aegis. But they still lacked the basic religious structures to be able to stand on their two feet, as an independent religious community. Here they were enormously influenced by the Samaritans.

The origins of the Samaritans are rather obscure. They are Israelites of central Palestine, generally considered the descendants of those who were planted in Samaria by the Assyrian kings, in about 722 B.C.E. The faith of the Samaritans was Jewish monotheism, but they had shaken off the influence of Judaism by developing their own religious identity, rather in the way the Arabs were to do later on. The Samaritan canon included only the Pentateuch, which was considered the sole source and standard for faith and conduct.

The formula "There is no God but the One" is an ever-recurring refrain in Samaritan liturgies. A constant theme in their literature is the unity of God and His absolute holiness and righteousness. We can immediately notice the similarity of the Muslim proclamation of faith: "There is no God but Allah." And, of course, the unity of God is a fundamental principle in Islam. The Muslim formula "In the name of God" (*bismillah*) is found in Samaritan scripture as *beshem*. The opening chapter of the Koran is known as the *Fatiha*, opening or gate, often considered as a succinct confession of faith. A Samaritan prayer, which can also be considered a confession of faith, begins with the words: *Amadti kamekha al fatah rahmeka*, "I stand before Thee at the gate of Thy mercy." *Fatah* is the *Fatiha*, opening or gate.[52]

The sacred book of the Samaritans was the Pentateuch, which embodied the supreme revelation of the divine will, and was accordingly highly venerated. Muhammad also seems to know the Pentateuch and Psalms only, and shows no knowledge of the prophetic or historical writings.

The Samaritans held Moses in high regard, Moses being the prophet through whom the Law was revealed. For the Samaritans, Mt. Gerizim was the rightful center for the worship of Yahweh; and it was further associated with Adam, Seth, and Noah, and Abraham's sacrifice of Isaac. The expectation of a coming Messiah was also an article of faith; the name given to their Messiah was the Restorer. Here we can also notice the similarity of the Muslim notion of the *Mahdi*.

We can tabulate the close parallels between the doctrines of the SAMARITANS and the Muslims in this way:

MOSES,	EXODUS,	PENTATEUCH,	MT. SINAI/MT. GERIZIM,	SHECHEM
Muhammad,	Hijra,	Koran,	Mt. Hira,	Mecca

Under the influence of the Samaritans, the Arabs proceeded to cast Muhammad in the role of Moses as the leader of an exodus (*hijra*), as the bearer of a new revelation (Koran) received on an appropriate (Arabian) sacred mountain, Mt. Hira. It remained for them to compose a sacred book. CC point to the tradition that the Koran had been many books but of which 'Uthman (the third caliph after Muhammad) had left only one. We have the further testimony of a Christian monk who distinguishes between the Koran and the *Surat al-baqara* as sources of law. In other documents, we are told that Hajjaj (661–714), the governor of Iraq, had collected and destroyed all the writings of the early Muslims. Then, following Wansbrough, CC conclude that the Koran, "is strikingly lacking in overall structure, frequently obscure and inconsequential in both language and content, perfunctory in its linking of disparate materials and given to the repetition of whole passages in variant versions. On this basis it can be plausibly argued that the book [Koran] is the product of the belated and imperfect editing of materials from a plurality of traditions."[53]

The Samaritans had rejected the sanctity of Jerusalem, and had replaced it by the older Israelite sanctuary of Shechem. When the early Muslims disengaged from Jerusalem, Shechem provided an appropriate model for the creation of a sanctuary of their own.

> The parallelism is striking. Each presents the same binary structure of a sacred city closely associated with a nearby holy mountain, and in each case the fundamental rite is a pilgrimage from the city to the mountain. In each case the sanctuary is an Abrahamic foundation, the pillar on which Abraham sacrificed in Shechem finding its equivalent in the rukn [the Yamai corner of the Ka'ba] of the Meccan sanctuary. Finally, the urban sanctuary is in each case closely associated with the gave of the appropriate patriarch: Joseph (as opposed to Judah) in the Samaritan case, Ishmael (as opposed to Isaac) in the Meccan.[54]

CC go on to argue that the town we now know as Mecca in central Arabia (Hijaz) could not have been the theater of the momentous events so beloved of Muslim tradition. Apart from the lack of any early non-Muslim references to Mecca, we do have the startling fact that the direction in which the early Muslims prayed (the *qibla*) was northwest Arabia. The evidence comes from the alignment of certain early mosques, and the literary evidence of Christian sources. In other words, Mecca, as the Muslim sanctuary, was only chosen much later, by the Muslims, in order to relocate their early history within Arabia, to complete their break with Judaism, and finally establish their separate religious identity.

In the rest of their fascinating book, CC go on to show how Islam assimilated all the foreign influences that it came under in consequence of their rapid conquests; how Islam acquired its particular identity on encountering the older civilizations of antiquity, through its contacts with rabbinic Judaism, Christianity (Jacobite and Nestorian), Hellenism and Persian ideas (Rabbinic Law, Greek philosophy, Neoplatonism, Roman Law, and Byzantine art and architecture). But they also point out that all this was achieved at great cultural cost, "The Arab conquests rapidly destroyed one empire, and permanently detached large territories of another. This was, for the states in question, an appalling catastrophe."[55]

In *Slaves on Horses: The Evolution of the Islamic Polity* (1980), Patricia Crone dismisses the Muslim traditions concerning the early caliphate (down to the 680s) as useless fictions. In *Meccan Trade and the Rise of Islam* (1987), she argues that many so-called historical reports are "fanciful elaborations on difficult Koranic passages."[56] In the latter work, Crone convincingly shows how the Koran "generated masses of spurious information." The numerous historical events which are supposed to have been the causes of certain revelations (for example, the battle of Badr, see above), "are likely to owe at least some of their features, occasionally their very existence, to the Quran." Clearly storytellers were the first to invent historical contexts for particular verses of the Koran. But much of their information is contradictory (for example, we are told that when Muhammad arrived in Medina for the first time it was torn by feuds, and yet at the same time we are asked to believe that the people of Medina were united under their undisputed leader Ibn Ubayy), and there was a tendency "for apparently independent accounts to collapse into variations on a common theme" (for example, the large number of stories which exist around the theme of "Muhammad's encounter with the representatives of non-Islamic religions who recognize him as a future prophet"). Finally there was a tendency for the information to grow the further away one went from the events described; for example, if one storyteller should happen to mention a raid, the next one would tell you the exact date of this raid, and the third one would furnish you even more details. Waqidi (d. 823), who wrote years after Ibn Ishaq (d. 768),

> will always give precise dates, locations, names, where Ibn Ishaq has none, accounts of what triggered the expedition, miscellaneous information to lend color to the event, as well as reasons why, as was usually the case, no fighting took place. No wonder that scholars are fond of Waqidi: where

else does one find such wonderfully precise information about every-thing one wishes to know? But given that this information was all unknown to Ibn Ishaq, its value is doubtful in the extreme. And if spurious information accumulated at this rate in the two generations between Ibn Ishaq and Waqidi, it is hard to avoid the conclusion that even more must have accumulated in the three generations between the Prophet and Ibn Ishaq.

It is obvious that these early Muslim historians drew on a common pool of material fabricated by the storytellers.

Crone takes to task certain conservative modern historians, such as Watt, for being unjustifiably optimistic about the historical worth of the Muslim sources on the rise of Islam. And we shall end this chapter on the sources with Crone's conclusions regarding all these Muslim sources:

> [Watt's methodology rests] on a misjudgment of these sources. The problem is the very mode of origin of the tradition, not some minor distortions subsequently introduced. Allowing for distortions arising from various allegiances within Islam such as those to a particular area, tribe, sect, or school does nothing to correct the tendentiousness arising from allegiance to Islam itself. The entire tradition is tendentious, its aim being the elaboration of an Arabian Heilgeschichte, and this tendentiousness has shaped the facts as we have them, not merely added some partisan statements we can deduct.[57]

EDITORIAL NOTE

Most of the articles in this collection were originally published more than fifty years ago (and a couple date to the nineteenth century), when there was little consistency in the way Arabic terms were transliterated into English. Thus, the name of Islam's holy book was variously written as Kor'án, Kur'ān, Qurân, Qur'ān, Coran, etc., and the name of Islam's Prophet was transliterated as Mahomet, Mohammed, Muhammad, etc. To leave the diverse forms of these names, and many other Arabic terms, would confuse the reader; in some cases it might even obscure the fact that two authors are discussing the same person or text. Therefore, the original spellings have been changed where necessary to make them conform to modern usage and to ensure that a consistent spelling is used in every article.

Accordingly, Islam's sacred book is always referred to by its most recognizable form—Koran (even though *Qur'ān* is preferred by scholars and is closer to the actual Arabic pronunciation). The name of Islam's founder is consistently spelled Muhammad. Arabic names that used to be transliterated with an *o* will be spelled with a *'u*, e.g., 'Uthman, 'Umar (not Othman, Omar). The symbol ' is used to express Arabic *ain*; the symbol ' expresses Arabic *hamza*. Other diacritical marks have been eliminated since they mean little or nothing to nonspecialists and specialists already know the original Arabic to which the transliteration refers. The term "Prophet" with a capital "P," when used by itself, refers to Muhammad, in contrast to the same word with a lowercase "p," which refers to prophets from other religions.

The endnotes to chapters 4, 6, and 11 have been edited because the original publications contained passages in the Arabic and Hebrew scripts, which were not practical to reproduce.

Finally, English punctuation and capitalization have generally been made to conform to modern usage based on the fourteenth edition of the *Chicago Manual of Style*.

2.

The Koran

Theodor Nöldeke

THE KORAN (QUR'ĀN) IS THE foundation of Islam. It is the sacred book of more than a hundred millions of men, some of them nations of immemorial civilization, by all whom it is regarded as the immediate word of God. And since the use of the Koran in public worship, in schools, and otherwise is much more extensive than, for example, the reading of the Bible in most Christian countries, it has been truly described as the most widely read book in existence. This circumstance alone is sufficient to give it an urgent claim on our attention, whether it suit our taste and fall in with our religious and philosophical views or not. Besides, it is the work of Muhammad, and as such is fitted to afford a clue to the spiritual development of that most successful of all prophets and religious personalities. It must be owned that the first perusal leaves on a European an impression of chaotic confusion—not that the book is so very extensive, for it is not quite so large as the New Testament. This impression can in some degree be modified only by the application of a critical analysis with the assistance of Arabian tradition.

To the faith of the Muslims, as has been said, the Koran is the word of God, and such also is the claim which the book itself advances. For except in sura i.—which is a prayer for men—and some few passages where

---

Originally published in the *Encyclopaedia Britannica*, 9th ed., vol. 16 (1891), pp. 597ff.

Muhammad (vi. 104, 114, xxvii. 93, xlii. 8), or the angels (xix. 65, xxxvii. 164 sqq.), speak in the first person without the intervention of the usual imperative "say" (sing. or pl.), the speaker throughout is God, either in the first person singular, or more commonly the plural of majesty "we." The same mode of address is familiar to us from the prophets of the Old Testament; the human personality disappears, in the moment of inspiration, behind the God by whom it is filled. But all the greatest of the Hebrew prophets fall back speedily upon the unassuming human "I"; while in the Koran the divine "I" is the stereotyped form of address. Muhammad, however, really felt himself to be the instrument of God; this consciousness was no doubt brighter at his first appearance than it afterward became, but it never entirely forsook him. We might therefore readily pardon him for giving out, not only the results of imaginative and emotional excitement, but also many expositions or decrees which were the outcome of cool calculation, as the word of God, if he had only attained the pure moral altitude which in an Isaiah or a Jeremiah fills us with admiration after the lapse of ages.

The rationale of revelation is explained in the Koran itself as follows:—In heaven is the original text ("the mother of the book," xliii. 3; "a concealed book," lv. 77; "a well-guarded tablet," lxxxv. 22). By a process of "sending down" (*tanzil*), one piece after another was communicated to the Prophet. The mediator was an angel, who is called sometimes the "Spirit" (xxvi. 193), sometimes the "holy Spirit" (xvi. 104), and at a later time "Gabriel" (ii. 91). This angel dictates the revelation to the Prophet, who repeats it after him, and afterward proclaims it to the world (lxxxvii. 6, etc.). It is plain that we have here a somewhat crude attempt of the Prophet to represent to himself the more or less unconscious process by which his ideas arose and gradually took shape in his mind. It is no wonder if in such confused imagery the details are not always self-consistent. When, for example, this heavenly archetype is said to be in the hands of an exalted "scribe" (lxxx. 13 sqq.), this seems a transition to a quite different set of ideas, namely, the books of fate, or the record of all human actions—conceptions which are actually found in the Koran. It is to be observed, at all events, that Muhammad's transcendental idea of God, as a being exalted altogether above the world, excludes the thought of direct intercourse between the Prophet and God.

It is an explicit statement of the Koran that the sacred book was revealed ("sent down") by God, not all at once, but piecemeal and gradually (xxv. 34). This is evident from the actual composition of the book, and is confirmed by Muslim tradition. That is to say, Muhammad issued his revelations in flyleaves of greater or less extent. A single piece of this kind was called either, like the entire collection, *qur'ān*, i.e., "reading," or rather "recitation;" or *kitāb*, "writing;" or *sūra*, which is the late-Hebrew *shūrā*, and means literally "series." The last became, in the lifetime of Muhammad, the regular designation of the individual sections as distinguished from the whole collection; and accordingly it is the name given to the separate chapters of the existing Koran. These chapters are of very unequal length. Since many of the shorter ones are undoubtedly complete in themselves, it is natural to assume that the longer, which are sometimes very comprehensive, have arisen from the amalgamation of various originally distinct revelations. This supposition is favored by the numerous traditions which give us the circumstances under which this or that short piece, now incorporated in a larger section, was revealed; and also by the feet that the connection of thought in the present suras often seems to be interrupted. And in reality many pieces of the long suras have to be severed out as originally independent; even in the short ones parts are often found which cannot have been there at first. At the same time we must beware of carrying this sifting operation too far—as I now believe myself to have done in my earlier works, and as Sprenger in his great book on Muhammad also sometimes seems to do. That some suras were of considerable length from the first is seen, for example, from xii., which contains a short introduction, then the history of Joseph, and then a few concluding observations, and is therefore perfectly homogeneous. In like manner, xx., which is mainly occupied with the history of Moses, forms a complete whole. The same is true of xviii., which at first sight seems to fall into several pieces; the history of the seven sleepers, the grotesque narrative about Moses, and that about Alexander "the Horned," are all connected together, and the same rhyme runs through the whole sura. Even in the separate narrations we may observe how readily the Koran passes from one subject to another, how little care is taken to express all the transitions of thought, and how frequently clauses are omitted, which are almost indispensable. We are not at liberty, therefore, in every case where the connection in the Koran is obscure, to say that it is really broken, and set it down as the clumsy patchwork of a later hand. Even in the old Arabic poetry such abrupt transitions are of very frequent occurrence. It is not uncommon for the Koran, after a new subject has been entered on, to return gradually or suddenly to the former theme—a proof that there at least separation is not to be thought of. In short, however imperfectly the Koran may have been redacted, in the majority of cases the present suras are identical with the originals.

How these revelations actually arose in Muhammad's mind is a question which it is almost as idle to discuss as it would be to analyze the workings of the mind of a poet. In his early career, sometimes perhaps in its later stages also, many revelations must have burst from him in uncontrollable excitement, so that he could not possibly regard them otherwise than as divine inspirations. We must bear in mind that he was no cold systematic thinker, but an Oriental visionary, brought up in crass superstition, and without intellectual discipline; a man whose nervous temperament had been powerfully worked on by ascetic austerities, and who was all the more irritated by the opposition he encountered, because he had little of the heroic in his nature. Filled with his religious ideas and visions, he might well fancy he heard the angel bidding him recite what was said to him. There may have been many a revelation of this kind which no one ever heard but himself, as he repeated it to himself in the silence of the night (lxxiii. 4). Indeed the Koran itself admits that he forgot some revelations (lxxxvii. 7). But by far the greatest part of the book is undoubtedly the result of deliberation, touched more or less with emotion, and animated by a certain rhetorical rather than poetical glow. Many passages are based upon purely intellectual reflection. It is said that Muhammad occasionally uttered such a passage immediately after one of those epileptic fits which not only his followers, but (for a time at least) he himself also regarded as tokens of intercourse with the higher powers. If that is the case, it is impossible to say whether the trick was in the utterance of the revelation or in the fit itself.

How the various pieces of the Koran took literary form is uncertain. Muhammad himself, so far as we can discover, never wrote down anything. The question whether he could read and write has been much debated among Muslims, unfortunately more with dogmatic arguments and spurious traditions than authentic proofs. At present, one is inclined to say that he was not altogether ignorant of these arts, but that from want of practice he found it convenient to employ someone else whenever he had anything to write. After the emigration to Medina (622 C.E.) we are told that short pieces—chiefly legal decisions—were taken down immediately after they were revealed, by an adherent whom he summoned for the purpose; so that nothing stood in the way of their publication. Hence it is probable that in Mecca, where, as in a mercantile town, the art of writing was commoner than in Medina, a place of agriculture, he had already begun to have his oracles committed to writing. That even long portions of the Koran existed in written form from an early date may be pretty safely inferred from various indications; especially from the fact that in Mecca the Prophet had caused insertions to be made, and pieces to be erased, in his previous revelations. For we cannot suppose that he knew the longer suras by heart so perfectly that he was able after a time to lay his finger upon any particular passage. In some instances, indeed, he may have relied too much on his memory. For example, he seems to have occasionally dictated the same sura to different persons in slightly different terms. In such cases, no doubt, he may have partly intended to introduce improvements; and so long as the difference was merely in expression, without affecting the sense, it could occasion no perplexity to his followers. None of them had literary pedantry enough to question the consistency of the divine revelation on that ground. In particular instances, however, the difference of reading was too important to be overlooked. Thus the Koran itself confesses that the unbelievers cast it up as a reproach to the Prophet that God sometimes substituted one verse for another (xvi. 103). On one occasion, when a dispute arose between two of his own followers as to the true reading of a passage which both had received from the Prophet himself, Muhammad is said to have explained that the Koran was revealed in seven forms. In this dictum, which perhaps is genuine, seven stands, of course, as in many other cases, for an indefinite but limited number. But one may imagine what a world of trouble it has cost the Muslim theologians to explain the saying in accordance with their dogmatic beliefs. A great number of explanations are current, some of which claim the authority of the Prophet himself; as, indeed, fictitious utterances of Muhammad play throughout a conspicuous part in the exegesis of the Koran. One very favorite, but utterly untenable interpretation is that the "seven forms" are seven different Arabic dialects.

When such discrepancies came to the cognizance of Muhammad it was doubtless his desire that only one of the conflicting texts should be considered authentic; only he never gave himself much trouble to have his wish carried into effect. Although in theory he was an upholder of verbal inspiration, he did not push the doctrine to its extreme consequences; his practical good sense did not take these things so strictly as the theologians of later centuries. Sometimes, however, he did suppress whole sections or verses, enjoining his followers to efface or forget them, and declaring them to be "abrogated." A very remarkable case is that of the two verses in liii., when he had recognized three heathen goddesses as exalted beings, possessing influence with God. This he had done in a moment of weakness, to win his countrymen by a compromise which still left Allah in the highest rank. He attained his purpose indeed, but was soon visited by remorse, and declared the words in question to have been inspirations of the Evil One.

So much for abrogated readings; the case is somewhat different when we come to the abrogation of laws and directions to the Muslims, which often occurs in the Koran. There is nothing in this at variance with Muhammad's idea of God. God is to him an absolute despot, who declares a thing right or wrong from no inherent necessity, but by His arbitrary fiat. This God varies His commands at pleasure, prescribes one law for the Christians, another for the Jews, and a third for the Muslims; nay, He even changes His instructions to the Muslims when it pleases Him. Thus, for example, the Koran contains very different directions, suited to varying circumstances, as to the treatment which idolaters are to receive at the hands of believers. But Muhammad showed no anxiety to have these superseded enactments destroyed. Believers could be in no uncertainty as to which of two contradictory passages remained in force; and they might still find edification in that which had become obsolete. That later generations might not so easily distinguish the "abrogated" from the "abrogating" did not occur to Muhammad, whose vision, naturally enough, seldom extended to the future of his religious community. Current events were invariably kept in view in the revelations. In Medina it called forth the admiration of the Faithful to observe how often God gave them the answer to a question whose settlement was urgently required at the moment. The same naïveté appears in a remark of the Caliph 'Uthman about a doubtful case: "If the Apostle of God were still alive, methinks there had been a Koran passage revealed on this point." Not unfrequently the divine word was found to coincide with the advice which Muhammad had received from his most intimate disciples. "'Umar was many a time of a certain opinion," says one tradition, "and the Koran was then revealed accordingly."

The contents of the different parts of the Koran are extremely varied. Many passages consist of theological or moral reflections. We are reminded of the greatness, the goodness, the righteousness of God as manifested in Nature, in history, and in revelation through the prophets, especially through Muhammad. God is magnified as the One, the All-powerful. Idolatry and all deification of created beings, such as the worship of Christ as the Son of God, are unsparingly condemned. The joys of heaven and the pains of hell are depicted in vivid sensuous imagery, as is also the terror of the whole creation at the advent of the last day and the judgment of the world. Believers receive general moral instruction, as well as directions for special circumstances. The lukewarm are rebuked, the enemies threatened with terrible punishment, both temporal and eternal. To the skeptical the truth of Islam is held forth; and a certain, not very cogent, method of demonstration predominates. In many passages the sacred book falls into a diffuse preaching style, others seem more like proclamations or general orders. A great number contain ceremonial or civil laws, or even special commands to individuals down to such matters as the regulation of Muhammad's harem. In not a few, definite questions are answered which had actually been propounded to the Prophet by believers or infidels. Muhammad himself, too, repeatedly receives direct injunctions, and does not escape an occasional rebuke. One sura (i.) is a prayer, two (cxiii, cxiv.) are magical formulas. Many suras treat of a single topic, others embrace several.

From the mass of material comprised in the Koran—and the account we have given is far from exhaustive—we should select the histories of the ancient prophets and saints as possessing a peculiar interest. The purpose of Muhammad is to show from these histories how God in former times had rewarded the righteous and punished their enemies. For the most part the old prophets only serve to introduce a little variety in point of form, for they are almost in every case facsimiles of Muhammad himself. They preach exactly like him; they have to bring the very same charges against their opponents, who on their part behave exactly as the unbelieving inhabitants of Mecca. The Koran even goes so far as to make Noah contend against the worship of certain false gods, mentioned by name, who were worshiped by the Arabs of Muhammad's time. In an address which is put in the mouth of Abraham (xxvi. 75 sqq.) the reader quite forgets that it is Abraham, and not Muhammad (or God Himself), who is speaking. Other narratives are intended rather for amusement, although they are always well seasoned with edifying phrases. It is no wonder that the godless Quraishites thought these stories of the Koran not nearly so entertaining as those of Rostam and Ispandiar related by Nadr the son of Harith, who, when traveling as a merchant, had learned on the Euphrates the heroic mythology of the Persians. But the Prophet was so exasperated by this rivalry that when Nadr fell into his power after the battle of Badr, he caused him to be executed, although in all other cases he readily pardoned his fellow countrymen.

These histories are chiefly about Scripture characters, especially those of the Old Testament. But the deviations from the biblical narratives are very marked. Many of the alterations are found in the legendary anecdotes of the Jewish Haggada and the New Testament Apocrypha; but many more are due to misconceptions such as only a listener (not the reader of a book) could fall into. The most ignorant Jew could never have mistaken Haman (the minister of Ahasuerus) for the minister of Pharaoh, or identified Miriam the sister of Moses with Mary (=Miriam) the mother of Christ. In addition to such misconceptions there are sundry capricious alterations, some of them very grotesque, due to Muhammad himself. For instance, in his ignorance of everything out of Arabia, he makes the fertility of Egypt —where rain is almost never seen and never missed— depend on rain instead of the inundations of the Nile (xii. 49). The strange tale of "the Horned" (i.e., Alexander the Great, xviii. 82 sqq.) reflects, as has been lately discovered, a rather absurd story, written by a Syrian in the beginning of the sixth century; we may believe that the substance of it was related to the Prophet by some Christian. Besides Jewish and Christian histories, there are a few about old Arabian prophets. In these he seems to have handled his materials even more freely than in the others.

The opinion has already been expressed that Muhammad did not make use of written sources. Coincidences and divergences alike can always be accounted for by oral communications from Jews who knew a little and Christians who knew next to nothing. Even in the rare passages where we can trace direct resemblances to the text of the Old Testament (comp. xxi. 105 with Ps. xxxvii. 29; i. 5 with Ps. xxvii. 11) or the New (comp. vii. 48 with Luke xvi. 24; xlvi. 19 with Luke xvi. 25), there is nothing more than might readily have been picked up in conversation with any Jew or Christian. In Medina, where he had the opportunity of becoming acquainted with Jews of some culture, he learned some things out of the Mishna; e.g., v. 35 corresponds almost word for word with Mishna *Sanh.* iv. 5; compare also ii. 183 with Mishna *Ber.* i. 2. That these are only cases of oral communication will be admitted by anyone with the slightest knowledge of the circumstances. Otherwise we might even conclude that Muhammad had studied the Talmud; e.g., the regulation as to ablution by rubbing with sand, where water cannot be obtained (iv. 46) corresponds to a Talmudic ordinance (*Ber.* 15a). Of Christianity he can have been able to learn very little even in Medina, as may be seen from the absurd travesty of the institution of the Eucharist in v. 112 sqq. For the rest, it is highly improbable that before the Koran any real literary production—anything that could be strictly called a book—existed in the Arabic language.

In point of style, and artistic effect, the different parts of the Koran are of very unequal value. An unprejudiced and critical reader will certainly find very few passages where his aesthetic susceptibilities are thoroughly satisfied. But he will often be struck, especially in the older pieces, by a wild force of passion, and a vigorous, if not rich, imagination. Descriptions of heaven and hell, and allusions to God's working in Nature, not unfrequently show a certain amount of poetic power. In other places also the style is sometimes lively and impressive; though it is rarely indeed that we come across such strains of touching simplicity as in the middle of xciii. The greater part of the Koran is decidedly prosaic; much of it indeed is stiff in style. Of course, with such a variety of material, we cannot expect every part to be equally vivacious, or imaginative, or poetic. A decree about the right of inheritance, or a point of ritual, must necessarily be expressed in prose, if it is to be intelligible. No one complains of the civil laws in Exodus or the sacrificial ritual in Leviticus, because they want the fire of Isaiah or the tenderness of Deuteronomy. But Muhammad's mistake consists in persistent and slavish adherence to the semipoetic form which he had at first adopted in accordance with his own taste and that of his hearers. For instance, he employs rhyme in dealing with the most prosaic subjects, and thus produces the disagreeable effect of incongruity between style and matter. It has to be considered, however, that many of those sermonizing pieces which are so tedious to us, especially when we read two or three in succession (perhaps in a very inadequate translation), must have had a quite different effect when recited under the burning sky and on the barren soil of Mecca. There, thoughts about God's greatness and man's duty, which are familiar to us from childhood, were all new to the hearers —it is hearers we have to think of in the first instance, not readers—to whom, at the same time, every allusion had a meaning which often escapes our notice. When Muhammad spoke of the goodness of the Lord in creating the clouds, and bringing them across the cheerless desert, and pouring them out on the earth to restore its rich vegetation, that must have been a picture of thrilling interest to the Arabs, who are accustomed to see from three to five years elapse before a copious shower comes to clothe the wilderness once more with luxuriant pastures. It requires an effort for us, under our clouded skies, to realize in some degree the intensity of that impression.

The fact that scraps of poetical phraseology are specially numerous in the earlier suras enables us to understand why the prosaic mercantile community of Mecca regarded their eccentric townsman as a "poet," or even a "possessed poet." Muhammad himself had to disclaim such titles, because he felt himself to be a divinely inspired prophet; but we too, from our standpoint, shall fully acquit him of poetic genius. Like many other predominantly religious characters, he had no appreciation of poetic beauty; and if we may believe one anecdote related of him, at a time when every one made verses, he affected ignorance of the most elementary rules of prosody. Hence the style of the Koran is not poetical but rhetorical; and the powerful effect which some portions produce on us is gained by rhetorical means. Accordingly the sacred book has not even the artistic form of poetry; which, among the Arabs, includes a stringent meter, as well as rhyme. The Koran is never metrical, and only a few exceptionally eloquent portions fall into a sort of spontaneous rhythm. On the other hand, the rhyme is regularly maintained, although, especially in the later pieces, after a very slovenly fashion. Rhymed prose was a favorite form of composition among the Arabs of that day, and Muhammad adopted it; but if it imparts a certain sprightliness to some passages, it proves on the whole a burdensome yoke. The Muslims themselves have observed that the tyranny of the rhyme often makes itself apparent in derangement of the order of words, and in the choice of verbal forms which would not otherwise have been employed, e.g., an imperfect instead of a perfect. In one place, to save the rhyme, he calls Mount Sinai *Sinin* (xcv. 2) instead of *Sina* (xxiii. 20); in another Elijah is called *Ilyasin* (xxxvii. 130) instead of *Ilyas* (vi. 85, xxxvii. 123). The substance even is modified to suit exigencies of rhyme. Thus the Prophet would scarcely have fixed on the unusual number of *eight* angels round the throne of God (lxix. 17) if the word *thamaniyah*, "eight," had not happened to fall in so well with the rhyme. And when lv. speaks of two heavenly gardens, each with *two* fountains and *two* kinds of fruit, and again of *two* similar gardens, all this is simply because the dual termination (*an*) corresponds to the syllable that controls the rhyme in that whole sura. In the later pieces, Muhammad often inserts edifying remarks, entirely out of keeping with the context, merely to complete his rhyme. In Arabic it is such an easy thing to accumulate masses of words with the same termination, that the gross negligence of the rhyme in the Koran is doubly remarkable. One may say that this is another mark of the Prophet's want of mental training, and incapacity for introspective criticism.

On the whole, while many parts of the Koran undoubtedly have considerable rhetorical power, even over an unbelieving reader, the book, aesthetically considered, is by no means a first-rate performance. To begin with what we are most competent to criticize, let us look at some of the more extended narratives. It has already been noticed how vehement and abrupt they are where they ought to be characterized by epic repose. Indispensable links, both in expression and in the sequence of events, are often omitted, so that to understand these histories is sometimes far easier for us than for those who heard them first, because we know most of them from better sources. Along with this, there is a great deal of superfluous verbiage; and nowhere do we find a steady advance in the narration. Contrast, in these respects, "the most beautiful tale," the history of Joseph (xii.), and its glaring improprieties, with the story in Genesis, so admirably conceived and so admirably executed in spite of some slight discrepancies. Similar faults are found in the nonnarrative portions of the Koran. The connection of ideas is extremely loose, and even the syntax betrays great awkwardness. Anacolutha are of frequent occurrence, and cannot be explained as conscious literary devices. Many sentences begin with a "when" or "on the day when," which seems to hover in the air, so that the commentators are driven to supply a "think of this" or some such ellipsis. Again, there is no great literary skill evinced in the frequent and needless harping on the same words and phrases; in xviii., for example, "till that" (*hatta idha*) occurs no fewer than eight times. Muhammad, in short, is not in any sense a master of style. This opinion will be endorsed by any European who reads through the book with an impartial spirit and some knowledge of the language, without taking into account the tiresome effect of its endless iterations. But in the ears of every pious Muslim such a judgment will sound almost as shocking as downright atheism or polytheism. Among the Muslims, the Koran has always been looked on as the most perfect model of style and language. This feature of it is in their dogmatic the greatest of all miracles, the incontestable proof of its divine origin. Such a view on the part of men who knew Arabic infinitely better than the most accomplished European Arabist will ever do, may well startle us. In fact, the Koran boldly challenged its opponents to produce ten suras, or even a single one, like those of the sacred book, and they never did so. That, to be sure, on calm reflection, is not so very surprising. Revelations of the kind which Muhammad uttered, no unbeliever could produce without making himself a laughingstock. However little real originality there is in Muhammad's doctrines, as against his own countrymen he was thoroughly original, even in the form of his oracles. To compose such revelations at will was beyond the power of the most expert literary artist; it would have required either a prophet or a shameless impostor. And if such a character appeared after Muhammad, still he could never be anything but an imitator, like the false prophets who arose about the time of his death and afterward. That the adversaries should produce any sample whatsoever of poetry or rhetoric equal to the Koran is not at all what the Prophet demands. In that case he would have been put to shame, even in the eyes of many of his own followers, by the first poem that came to hand. Nevertheless, it is on such a false interpretation of this challenge that the dogma of the incomparable excellence of the style and diction of the Koran is based. The rest has been accomplished by dogmatic prejudice, which is quite capable of working other miracles besides turning a defective literary production into an unrivaled masterpiece in the eyes of believers. This view once accepted, the next step was to find everywhere evidence of the perfection of the style and language. And if here and there, as one can scarcely doubt, there was among the old Muslims a lover of poetry who had his difficulties about this dogma, he had to beware of uttering an opinion which might have cost him his head. We know of at least one rationalistic theologian who defined the dogma in such a way that we can see he did not believe it (Shahrastani, p. 39). The truth is, it would have been a miracle indeed if the style of the Koran had been perfect. For although there was at that time a recognized poetical style, already degenerating to mannerism, a prose style did not exist. All beginnings are difficult; and it can never be esteemed a serious charge against Muhammad that his book, the first prose work of a high order in the language, testifies to the awkwardness of the beginner. And further, we must always remember that entertainment and aesthetic effect were at most subsidiary objects. The great aim was persuasion and conversion; and, say what we will, that aim has been realized on the most imposing scale.

Muhammad repeatedly calls attention to the fact that the Koran is not written, like other sacred books, in a strange language, but in Arabic, and therefore is intelligible to all. At that time, along with foreign ideas, many foreign words had crept into the language, especially Aramaic terms for religious conceptions of Jewish or Christian origin. Some of these had already passed into general use, while others were confined to a more limited circle. Muhammad, who could not fully express his new ideas in the common language of his countrymen, but had frequently to find out new terms for himself, made free use of such Jewish and Christian words, as was done, though perhaps to a smaller extent, by certain thinkers and poets of that age who had more or less risen above the level of heathenism. In Muhammad's case this is the less wonderful, because he was indebted to the instruction of Jews and Christians whose Arabic—as the Koran pretty clearly intimates with regard to one of them—was very defective. Nor is it very surprising to find that his use of these words is sometimes as much at fault as his comprehension of the histories which he learned from the same people—that he applies Aramaic expressions as incorrectly as many uneducated persons now employ words derived from the French. Thus, *furqan* means really "redemption," but Muhammad (misled by the Arabic meaning of the root *frq,* "sever," "decide") uses it for "revelation." *Milla* is properly "Word," but in the Koran "religion." *Illiyun* (lxxxiii. 18, 19) is apparently the Hebrew name of God, *Elyon,* "the Most High"; Muhammad uses it of a heavenly book (see S. Fraenkel, *De vocabulis in antiquis Arabum carminibus et in Corano peregrinis,* Leyden 1880, p. 23). So again the word *mathani,* is, as Geiger has conjectured, the regular Arabic plural of the Aramaic *mathnitha,* which is the same as the Hebrew *Mishna,* and denotes, in Jewish usage, a legal decision of some of the ancient Rabbins. But in the Koran "the seven *Mathani*" (xv. 87) are probably the seven verses of sura i., so that Muhammad appears to have understood it in the sense of "saying" or "sentence" (comp. xxxix. 24). Words of Christian origin are less frequent in the Koran. It is an interesting fact that of these a few have come over from the Abyssinian, such as *hawariyun,* "apostles," *maida,* " table," and two or three others; these all make their first appearance in suras of the Medina period. The word *shaitan,* "Satan," which was likewise borrowed, at least in the first instance, from the Abyssinian, had probably been already introduced into the language. Sprenger has rightly observed that Muhammad makes a certain parade of these foreign terms, as of other peculiarly constructed expressions; in this he followed a favorite practice of contemporary poets. It is the tendency of the imperfectly educated to delight in out-of-the-way expressions, and on such minds they readily produce a remarkably solemn and mysterious impression. This was exactly the kind of effect that Muhammad desired, and to secure it he seems even to have invented a few odd vocables, as *ghislin* (lxix. 36), *sijjin* (lxxxiii. 7, 8), *tasnim* (lxxxiii. 27), and *salsabil* (lxxvi. 18). But, of course, the necessity of enabling his hearers to understand ideas which they must have found sufficiently novel in themselves, imposed tolerably narrow limits on such eccentricities.

The constituents of our present Koran belong partly to the Mecca period (before 622 C.E.), partly to the period commencing with the emigration to Medina (from the autumn of 622 to 8th June 632). Muhammad's position in Medina was entirely different from that which he had occupied in his native town. In the former he was from the first the leader of a powerful party, and gradually became the autocratic ruler of Arabia; in the latter he was only the despised preacher of a small congregation. This difference, as was to be expected, appears in the Koran. The Medina pieces, whether entire suras or isolated passages interpolated in Meccan suras, are accordingly pretty broadly distinct, as to their contents, from those issued in Mecca. In the great majority of cases there can be no doubt whatever whether a piece first saw the light in Mecca or in Medina; and, for the most part, the internal evidence is borne out by Muslim tradition. And since the revelations given in Medina frequently take notice of events about which we have pretty accurate information, and whose dates are at least approximately known, we are often in a position to fix their date with, at any rate, considerable certainty; here, again, tradition renders valuable assistance. Even with regard to the Medina passages, however, a great deal remains uncertain, partly because the allusions to historical events and circumstances are generally rather obscure, partly because traditions about the occasion of the revelation of the various pieces are often fluctuating, and often rest on misunderstanding or arbitrary conjecture. But, at all events, it is far easier to arrange in some sort of chronological order the Medina suras than those composed in Mecca. There is, indeed, one tradition which professes to furnish a chronological list of all the suras. But not to mention that it occurs in several divergent forms, and that it takes no account of the fact that our present suras are partly composed of pieces of different dates, it contains so many suspicious or undoubtedly false statements, that it is impossible to attach any great importance to it. Besides, it is a priori unlikely that a contemporary of Muhammad should have drawn up such a list; and if anyone had made the attempt, he would have found it almost impossible to obtain reliable information as to the order of the earlier Meccan suras. We have in this list no genuine tradition; but rather the lucubrations of an undoubtedly conscientious Muslim critic, who may have lived about a century after the emigration.

Among the revelations put forth in Mecca there is a considerable number of (for the most part) short suras, which strike every attentive reader as being the oldest. They are in all altogether different strain from many others, and in their whole composition they show least resemblance to the Medina pieces. It is no doubt conceivable—as Sprenger supposes— that Muhammad might have returned at intervals to his earlier manner; but since this group possesses a remarkable similarity of style, and since the gradual formation of a different style is on the whole an unmistakable fact, the assumption has little probability; and we shall therefore abide by the opinion that these form a distinct group. At the opposite extreme from them stands another cluster, showing quite obvious affinities with the style of the Medina suras, which must therefore be assigned to the later part of the Prophet's work in Mecca. Between these two groups stand a number of other Meccan suras, which in every respect mark the transition from the first period to the third. It need hardly be said that the three periods— which were first distinguished by Professor Weil—are not separated by sharp lines of division. With regard to some suras, it may be doubtful whether they ought to be reckoned among the middle group, or with one or other of the extremes. And it is altogether impossible, within these groups, to establish even a probable chronological arrangement of the individual revelations. In default of clear allusions to well-known events, or events whose date can be determined, we might indeed endeavor to trace the psychological development of the Prophet by means of the Koran, and arrange its parts accordingly. But in such an undertaking one is always apt to take subjective assumptions or mere fancies for established data. Good traditions about the origin of the Meccan revelations are not very numerous. In fact, the whole history of Muhammad previous to his emigration is so imperfectly related that we are not even sure in what year he appeared as a prophet. Probably it was in 610 C.E.; it may have been somewhat earlier, but scarcely later. If, as one tradition says, xxx. 1 sq. ("The Romans are overcome in the nearest neighboring land") refers to the defeat of the Byzantines by the Persians, not far from Damascus, about the spring of 614, it would follow that the third group, to which this passage belongs, covers the greater part of the Meccan period. And it is not in itself unlikely that the passionate vehemence which characterizes the first group was of short duration. Nor is the assumption contradicted by the tolerably well-attested, though far from incontestable statement, that when 'Umar was converted (615 or 616 C.E.), xx., which belongs to the second group, already existed in writing. But the reference of xxx. 1 sq. to this particular battle is by no means so certain that positive conclusions can be drawn from it. It is the same with other allusions in the Meccan suras to occurrences whose chronology can be partially ascertained. It is better, therefore, to rest satisfied with a merely relative determination of the order of even the three great clusters of Meccan revelations.

In the pieces of the first period the convulsive excitement of the Prophet often expresses itself with the utmost vehemence. He is so carried away by his emotion that he cannot choose his words; they seem rather to burst from him. Many of these pieces remind us of the oracles of the old heathen soothsayers, whose style is known to us from imitations, although we have perhaps not a single genuine specimen. Like those other oracles, the suras of this period, which are never very long, are composed of short sentences with tolerably pure but rapidly changing rhymes. The oaths, too, with which many of them begin, were largely used by the soothsayers. Some of these oaths are very uncouth and hard to understand, some of them perhaps were not meant to be understood, for indeed all sorts of strange things are met with in these chapters. Here and there Muhammad speaks of visions, and appears even to see angels before him in bodily form. There are some intensely vivid descriptions of the resurrection and the last day, which must have exercised a demonic power over men who were quite unfamiliar with such pictures. Other pieces paint in glowing colors the joys of heaven and the pains of hell. However, the suras of this period are not all so wild as these; and those which are conceived in a calmer mood appear to be the oldest. Yet, one must repeat, it is exceedingly difficult to make out any strict chronological sequence. For instance, it is by no means certain whether the beginning of xcvi. is really what a widely circulated tradition calls it, the oldest part of the whole Koran. That tradition goes back to the Prophet's favorite wife Aïsha; but as she was not born at the time when the revelation is said to have been made, it can only contain at the best what Muhammad told her years afterward, from his own not very clear recollection, with or without fictitious additions. Aïsha, moreover, is by no means very trustworthy. And, besides, there are other pieces mentioned by others as the oldest. In any case xcvi. 1 sqq. is certainly very early. According to the traditional view, which appears to be correct, it treats of a vision in which the Prophet receives an injunction to recite a revelation conveyed to him by the angel. It is interesting to observe that here already two things are brought forward as proofs of the omnipotence and care of God: one is the creation of man out of a seminal drop—an idea to which Muhammad often recurs; the other is the then recently introduced art of writing, which the Prophet instinctively seizes on as a means of propagating his doctrines. It was only after Muhammad encountered obstinate resistance that the tone of the revelations became thoroughly passionate. In such cases he was not slow to utter terrible threats against those who ridiculed the preaching of the unity of God, of the resurrection, and of the judgment. His own uncle, Abu Lahab, had somewhat brusquely repelled him, and in a brief special sura (cxi.) he and his wife are consigned to hell. The suras of this period form almost exclusively the concluding portions of the present text. One is disposed to assume, however, that they were at one time more numerous, and that many of them were lost at an early period.

Since Muhammad's strength lay in his enthusiastic and fiery imagination rather than in the wealth of ideas and clearness of abstract thought on which exact reasoning depends, it follows that the older suras, in which the former qualities have free scope, must be more attractive to us than the later. In the suras of the second period the imaginative glow perceptibly diminishes; there is still fire and animation, but the tone becomes gradually more prosaic. As the feverish restlessness subsides, the periods are drawn out, and the revelations as a whole become longer. The truth of the new doctrine is proved by accumulated instances of God's working in nature and in history; the objections of opponents, whether advanced in good faith or in jest, are controverted by arguments; but the demonstration is often confused or even weak. The histories of the earlier prophets, which had occasionally been briefly touched on in the first period, are now related, sometimes at great length. On the whole, the charm of the style is passing away.

There is one piece of the Koran, belonging to the beginning of this period, if not to the close of the former, which claims particular notice. This is i., the Lord's Prayer of the Muslims, and beyond dispute the gem of the Koran. The words of this sura, which is known as *al-fatiha* ("the opening one"), are as follows:—

"(1) In the name of God, the compassionate Compassioner. (2) Praise be [literally 'is'] to God, the Lord of the worlds, (3) the compassionate Compassioner, (4) the Sovereign of the day of judgment. (5) Thee do we worship, and of Thee do we beg assistance. (6) Direct us in the right way; (7) in the way of those to whom Thou hast been gracious, on whom there is no wrath, and who go not astray."

The thoughts are so simple as to need no explanation; and yet the prayer is full of meaning. It is true that there is not a single original idea of Muhammad's in it. Several words and turns of expression are borrowed directly from the Jews, in particular the designation of God as the "Compassioner," *Rahman.* This is simply the Jewish *Rahmana,* which was a favorite name for God in the Talmudic period. Muhammad seems for a while to have entertained the thought of adopting *al-Rahman* as a proper name of God, in place of *Allah,* which was already used by the heathens.[1] This purpose he ultimately relinquished, but it is just in the suras of the second period that the use of *Rahman* is specially frequent. It was probably in the first sura also that Muhammad first introduced the formula, "In the name of God," etc. It is to be regretted that this prayer must lose its effect through too frequent use, for every Muslim who says his five prayers regularly—as the most of them do—repeats it not less than twenty times a day.

The suras of the third Meccan period, which form a pretty large part of our present Koran, are almost entirely prosaic. Some of the revelations are of considerable extent, and the single verses also are much longer than in the older suras. Only now and then a gleam of poetic power flashes out. A sermonizing tone predominates. The suras are very edifying for one who is already reconciled to their import, but to us, at least, they do not seem very well fitted to carry conviction to the minds of unbelievers. That impression, however, is not correct, for in reality the demonstrations of these longer Meccan suras appear to have been peculiarly influential for the propagation of Islam. Muhammad's mission was not to Europeans, but to a people who, though quick-witted and receptive, were not accustomed to logical thinking, while they had outgrown their ancient religion.

When we reach the Medina period it becomes, as has been indicated, much easier to understand the revelations in their historical relations, since our knowledge of the history of Muhammad in Medina is tolerably complete. In many cases the historical occasion is perfectly clear, in others we can at least recognize the general situation from which they arose, and thus approximately fix their time. There still remains, however, a remnant, of which we can only say that it belongs to Medina.

The style of this period bears a pretty close resemblance to that of the latest Meccan period. It is for the most part pure prose, enriched by occasional rhetorical embellishments. Yet even here there are many bright and impressive passages, especially in those sections which may be regarded as proclamations to the army of the faithful. For the Muslims, Muhammad has many different messages. At one time it is a summons to do battle for the faith; at another, a series of reflections on recently experienced success or misfortune, or a rebuke for their weak faith; or an exhortation to virtue, and so on. He often addresses himself to the "doubters," some of whom vacillate between faith and unbelief; others make a pretense of faith, while others scarcely take the trouble even to do that. They are no consolidated party, but to Muhammad they are all equally vexatious, because, as soon as danger has to be encountered, or a contribution is levied, they all alike fall away. There are frequent outbursts, ever increasing in bitterness, against the Jews, who were very numerous in Medina and its neighborhood when Muhammad arrived. He has much less to say against the Christians, with whom he never came closely in contact; and as for the idolaters, there was little occasion in Medina to have many words with them. A part of the Medina pieces consists of formal laws belonging to the ceremonial, civil, and criminal codes, or directions about certain temporary complications. The most objectionable parts of the whole Koran are those which treat of Muhammad's relations with women. The laws and regulations were generally very concise revelations, but most of them have been amalgamated with other pieces of similar or dissimilar import, and are now found in very long suras.

Such is an imperfect sketch of the composition and the internal history of the Koran, but it is probably sufficient to show that the book is a very heterogeneous collection. If only those passages had been preserved which had a permanent value for the theology, the ethics, or the jurisprudence of the Muslims, a few fragments would have been amply sufficient. Fortunately for knowledge, respect for sacredness of the letter has led to the collection of all revelations that could possibly be collected,—the "abrogating" along with the "abrogated," passages referring to passing circumstances as well as those of lasting importance. Everyone who takes up the book in the proper religious frame of mind, like most of the Muslims, reads pieces directed against long-obsolete absurd customs of Mecca just as devoutly as the weightiest moral precepts,—perhaps even more devoutly, because he does not understand them so well.

At the head of twenty-nine of the suras stand certain initial letters, from which no clear sense can be obtained. Thus, before ii., iii., xxxi., xxxii. we find *ALM* (*Alif Lam Mim*), before xl.-xlvi. *HM* (*Ha Mim*). At one time I suggested that these initials did not belong to Muhammad's text, but might be the monograms of possessors of codices, which, through negligence on the part of the editors, were incorporated in the final form of the Koran;

but I now deem it more probable that they are to be traced to the Prophet himself, as Sprenger and Loth suppose. One cannot indeed admit the truth of Loth's statement, that in the proper opening words of these suras we may generally find an allusion to the accompanying initials; but it can scarcely be accidental that the first verse of the great majority of them (in iii. it is the second verse) contains the word "book," "revelation," or some equivalent. They usually begin with: "This is the book," or "Revelation ('down sending') of the book," or something similar. Of suras which commence in this way only a few (xviii., xxiv., xxv., xxxix.) want the initials, while only xxix. and xxx. have the initials, and begin differently. These few exceptions may easily have proceeded from ancient corruptions; at all events, they cannot neutralize the evidence of the greater number.

Muhammad seems to have meant these letters for a mystic reference to the archetypal text in heaven. To a man who regarded the art of writing, of which at the best he had but a slight knowledge, as something supernatural, and who lived amongst illiterate people, an A B C may well have seemed more significant than to us who have been initiated into the mysteries of this art from our childhood. The Prophet himself can hardly have attached any particular meaning to these symbols: they served their purpose if they conveyed an impression of solemnity and enigmatical obscurity. In fact, the Koran admits that it contains many things which neither can be, nor were intended to be, understood (iii. 5). To regard these letters as ciphers is a precarious hypothesis, for the simple reason that cryptography is not to be looked for in the very infancy of Arabic writing. If they are actually ciphers, the multiplicity of possible explanations at once precludes the hope of a plausible interpretation. None of the efforts in this direction, whether by Muslim scholars or by Europeans, have led to convincing results. This remark applies even to the ingenious conjecture of Sprenger, that the letters *KHY'S* (*Kaf He Ye 'Ain Sad*) before xix. (which treats of John and Jesus, and, according to tradition, was sent to the Christian king of Abyssinia) stand for *Jesus Nazarenus Rex Judaeorum*. Sprenger arrives at this explanation by a very artificial method; and besides, Muhammad was not so simple as the Muslim traditionalists, who imagined that the Abyssinians could read a piece of the Arabic Koran. It need hardly be said that the Muslims have from of old applied themselves with great assiduity to the decipherment of these initials, and have sometimes found the deepest mysteries in them. Generally, however, they are content with the prudent conclusion, that God alone knows the meaning of these letters.

When Muhammad died, the separate pieces of the Koran, notwithstanding their theoretical sacredness, existed only in scattered copies; they were consequently in great danger of being partially or entirely destroyed. Many Muslims knew large portions by heart, but certainly no one knew the whole; and a merely oral propagation would have left the door open to all kinds of deliberate and inadvertent alterations. Muhammad himself had never thought of an authentic collection of his revelations; he was usually concerned only with the object of the moment, and the idea that the revelations would be destroyed unless he made provision for their safe preservation, did not enter his mind. A man destitute of literary culture has some difficulty in anticipating the fate of intellectual products. But now, after the death of the Prophet, most of the Arabs revolted against his successor, and had to be reduced to submission by force. Especially sanguinary was the contest against the prophet Maslama, an imitator of Muhammad, commonly known by the derisive diminutive Musailima (i.e. "Little Maslama"). At that time (633 C.E.) many of the most devoted Muslims fell, the very men who knew most Koran pieces by heart. 'Umar then began to fear that the Koran might be entirely forgotten, and he induced the Caliph Abu Bakr to undertake the collection of all its parts. The caliph laid the duty on Zaid, the son of Thabit, a native of Medina, then about twenty-two years of age, who had often acted as amanuensis to the Prophet, in whose service he is even said to have learned the Jewish letters. The account of this collection of the Koran has reached us in several substantially identical forms, and goes back to Zaid himself. According to it, he collected the revelations from copies written on flat stones, pieces of leather, ribs of palm-leaves (not palm-leaves themselves), and such-like material, but chiefly "from the breasts of men," i.e., from their memory. From these he wrote a fair copy, which he gave to Abu Bakr, from whom it came to his successor 'Umar, who again bequeathed it to his daughter Hafsa, one of the widows of the Prophet. This redaction, commonly called *al-suhuf* ("the leaves"), had from the first no canonical authority; and its internal arrangement can only be conjectured.

The Muslims were as far as ever from possessing a uniform text of the Koran. The bravest of their warriors sometimes knew deplorably little about it; distinction on *that* field they cheerfully accorded to pious men like Ibn Mas'ud. It was inevitable, however, that discrepancies should emerge between the texts of professed scholars, and as these men in their several localities were authorities on the reading of the Koran, quarrels began to break out between the levies from different districts about the true form of the sacred book. During a campaign in A.H. 30 (650–1 C.E.), Hodhaifa, the victor in the great and decisive battle of Nehawand—which was to the empire of the Sassanians what Gaugamela was to that of the Achaemenidae —perceived that such disputes might become dangerous, and therefore urged on the caliph 'Uthman the necessity for a universally binding text. The matter was entrusted to Zaid, who had made the former collection, with three leading Quraishites. These brought together as many copies as they could lay their hands on, and prepared an edition which was to be canonical for all Muslims. To prevent any further disputes, they burned all the other codices except that of Hafsa, which, however, was soon afterward destroyed by Marwan, the governor of Medina. The destruction of the earlier codices was an irreparable loss to criticism; but, for the essentially political object of putting an end to controversies by admitting only one form of the common book of religion and of law, this measure was necessary.

The result of these labors is in our hands; as to how they were conducted we have no trustworthy information, tradition being here too much under the influence of dogmatic presuppositions. The critical methods of a modern scientific commission will not be expected of an age when the highest literary education for an Arab consisted in ability to read and write. It now seems to me highly probable that this second redaction took this simple form: Zaid read off from the codex which he had previously written, and his associates, simultaneously or successively, wrote one copy each to his dictation. These, I suppose, were the three copies which, we are informed, were sent to the capitals Damascus, Basra, and Kufa, to be in the first instance standards for the soldiers of the respective provinces. A fourth copy would doubtless be retained at Medina. Be that as it may, it is impossible now to distinguish in the present form of the book what belongs to the first redaction from what is due to the second.

In the arrangement of the separate sections, a clarification according to contents was impracticable because of the variety of subjects often dealt with in one sura. A chronological arrangement was out of the question, because the chronology of the older pieces must have been imperfectly known, and because in some cases passages of different dates had been joined together. Indeed, systematic principles of this kind were altogether disregarded at that period. The pieces were accordingly arranged in indiscriminate order, the only rule observed being to place the long suras first and the shorter toward the end, and even that was far from strictly adhered to. The short opening sura is so placed on account of its superiority to the rest, and two magical formulae are kept for a sort of protection at the end; these are the only special traces of design. The combination of pieces of different origin may proceed partly from the possessors of the codices from which Zaid compiled his first complete copy, partly from Zaid himself. The individual suras are separated simply by the superscription, "In the name of God, the compassionate Compassioner," which is wanting only in the ninth. The additional headings found in our texts (the name of the sura, the number of verses, etc.) were not in the original codices, and form no integral part of the Koran.

It is said that 'Uthman directed Zaid and his associates, in case of disagreement, to follow the Quraish dialect; but, though well attested, this account can scarcely be correct. The extremely primitive writing of those days was quite incapable of rendering such minute differences as can have existed between the pronunciation of Mecca and that of Medina.

'Uthman's Koran was not complete. Some passages are evidently fragmentary; and a few detached pieces are still extant which were originally parts of the Koran, although they have been omitted by Zaid. Amongst these are some which there is no reason to suppose Muhammad desired to suppress. Zaid may easily have overlooked a few stray fragments, but that he purposely omitted anything which he believed to belong to the Koran is very unlikely. It has been conjectured that in deference to his superiors he kept out of the book the names of Muhammad's enemies, if they or their families came afterward to be respected. But it must be remembered that it was never Muhammad's practice to refer explicitly to contemporary persons and affairs in the Koran. Only a single friend, his adopted son Zaid (xxxiii. 37), and a single enemy, his uncle Abu Lahab (cxi.)—and these for very special reasons—are mentioned by name; and the name of the latter has been left in the Koran with a fearful curse annexed to it, although his son had embraced Islam before the death of Muhammad, and although his descendants belonged to the high nobility. So, on the other hand, there is no single verse or clause which can be plausibly made out to be an interpolation by Zaid at the instance of Abu Bakr, 'Umar, or 'Uthman. Slight clerical errors there may have been, but the Koran of 'Uthman contains none but genuine elements—though sometimes in very strange order.

It can still be pretty clearly shown in detail that the four codices of 'Uthman's Koran deviated from one another in points of orthography, in the insertion or omission of a *wa* ("and"), and such-like minutiae; but these variations nowhere affect the sense. All later manuscripts are derived from these four originals.

At the same time, the other forms of the Koran did not at once become extinct. In particular we have some information about the codex of Ubai ibn Ka'b. If the list which gives the order of its suras is correct, it must have contained substantially the same materials as our text; in that case Ubai ibn Ka'b must have used the original collection of Zaid. The same is true of the codex of Ibn Mas'ud, of which we have also a catalogue. It appears that the principle of putting the longer suras before the shorter was more consistently carried out by him than by Zaid. He omits i. and the magical formulae of cxiii. cxiv. Ubai ibn Ka'b, on the other hand, had embodied two additional short prayers, whose authenticity I do not now venture to question, as I formerly did. One can easily understand that differences of opinion may have existed as to whether and how far formularies of this kind belonged to the Koran. Some of the divergent readings of both these texts have been preserved, as well as a considerable number of other ancient variants. Most of them are decidedly inferior to the received readings, but some are quite as good, and a few deserve preference.

The only man who appears to have seriously opposed the general introduction of 'Uthman's text is Ibn Mas'ud. He was one of the oldest disciples of the Prophet, and had often rendered him personal service; but he was a man of contracted views, although he is one of the pillars of Muslim theology. His opposition had no effect. Now when we consider that at that time there were many Muslims who had heard the Koran from the mouth of the Prophet, that other measures of the imbecile 'Uthman met with the most vehement resistance on the part of the bigoted champions of the faith, that these were still further incited against him by some of his ambitious old comrades, until at last they murdered him, and finally that in the civil wars after his death the several parties were glad of any pretext for branding their opponents as infidels,—when we consider all this, we must regard it as a strong testimony in favor of 'Uthman's Koran that no party—that of 'Ali not excepted—repudiated the text formed by Zaid, who was one of the most devoted adherents of 'Uthman and his family, and that even among the Shiites we detect but very few marks of dissatisfaction with the caliph's conduct in this matter.

But this redaction is not the close of the textual history of the Koran. The ancient Arabic alphabet was very imperfect; it not only wanted marks for the short, and in part even for the long vowels, but it often expressed several consonants by the same sign, the forms of different letters, formerly clearly distinct, having become by degrees identical. So, for example, there was but one character to express B, T, Th, and in the beginning and in the middle of words N and Y (I) also. Though the reader who was perfectly familiar with the language felt no difficulty, as a rule, in discovering which pronunciation the writer had in view, yet as there were many words which admitted of being pronounced in very different manners, instances were not infrequent in which the pronunciation was dubious. This variety of possible readings was at first very great, and many readers seem to have actually made it their object to discover pronunciations which were new, provided they were at all appropriate to the ambiguous text. There was also a dialectic license in grammatical forms, which had not as yet been greatly restricted. An effort was made by many to establish a more refined pronunciation for the Koran than was usual in common life or in secular literature. The various schools of "readers" differed very widely from one another, although for the most part there was no important divergence as to the sense of words. A few of them gradually rose to special authority, and the rest disappeared. Seven readers are generally reckoned chief authorities, but for practical purposes this number was continually reduced in process of time, so that at present only two "reading styles" are in actual use,—the common style of Hafs and that of Nafi', which prevails in Africa to the west of Egypt. There is, however, a very comprehensive massoretic literature in which a number of other styles are indicated. The invention of vowel-signs, of diacritic points to distinguish similarly formed consonants, and of other orthographic signs, soon put a stop to arbitrary conjectures on the part of the readers. Many zealots objected to the introduction of these innovations in the sacred text, but theological consistency had to yield to practical necessity. In accurate codices, indeed, all such additions, as well as the titles of the sura, etc., are written in colored ink, while the black characters profess to represent exactly the original of 'Uthman. But there is probably no copy quite faithful in this respect.

The correct recitation of the Koran is an art difficult of acquisition to the Arabs themselves. Besides the artificial pronunciation mentioned above, a semimusical modulation has to be observed. In these things also there are great differences between the various schools.

In European libraries, besides innumerable modern manuscripts of the Koran, there are also codices or fragments of high antiquity, some of them probably dating from the first century of the Flight. For the restoration of the text, however, the works of ancient scholars on its readings and modes of writing are more important than the manuscripts, which, however elegantly they may be written and ornamented, proceed from irresponsible copyists. The original, written by 'Uthman himself, has indeed been exhibited in various parts of the Muhammadan world. The library of the India Office contains one such manuscript, bearing the subscription: "Written by 'Uthman the son of 'Affan." These, of course, are barefaced forgeries, although of very ancient date; so are those which profess to be from the hand of 'Ali, one of which is preserved in the same library. In recent times the Koran has been often printed and lithographed both in the East and the West.

Shortly after Muhammad's death certain individuals applied themselves to the exposition of the Koran. Much of it was obscure from the beginning, other sections were unintelligible apart from a knowledge of the circumstancee of their origin. Unfortunately those who took possession of this field were not very honorable. Ibn 'Abbas, a cousin of Muhammad's, and the chief source of the traditional exegesis of the Koran, has, on theological and other grounds, given currency to a number of falsehoods; and at least some of his pupils have emulated his example. These earliest expositions dealt more with the sense and connection of whole verses than with the separate words. Afterward, as the knowledge of the old language declined, and the study of philology arose, more attention began to be paid to the explanation of vocables. A good many fragments of this older theological and philological exegesis have survived from the first two centuries of the Flight, although we have no complete commentary of this period. Most of the expository material will perhaps be found in the very large commentary of the celebrated Tabari (839–923 C.E.), of which an almost complete copy is in the Viceregal library at Cairo. Another very famous commentary is that of Zamakhshari (1075–1144 C.E.), edited by Nassau-Lees, Calcutta 1859; but this scholar, with his great insight and still greater subtlety, is too apt to read his own scholastic ideas into the Koran. The favorite commentary of Baidawi (*ob.* 1286 C.E.) is little more than an abridgment of Zamakhshari's. Thousands of commentaries on the Koran, some of them of prodigious size, have been written by Muslims; and even the number of those still extant in manuscript is by no means small. Although these works all contain much that is useless or false, yet they are invaluable aids to our understanding of the sacred book. An unbiassed European can no doubt see many things at a glance more clearly than a good Muslim who is under the influence of religious prejudice, but we should still be helpless without the exegetical literature of the Muhammadans.

Even the Arab Muslim of the present day can have but a very dim and imperfect understanding of the Koran, unless he has made a special study of its exegesis. For the great advantage, boasted by the holy book itself, of being perspicuous to everyone, has in the course of thirteen centuries vanished. Moreover, the general belief is that in the ritual use of the Koran, if the correct recitation is observed, it is immaterial whether the meaning of the words be understood or not.

A great deal remains to be accomplished by European scholarship for the correct interpretation of the Koran. We want, for example, an exhaustive classification and discussion of all the Jewish elements in the Koran; a praiseworthy beginning has already been made in Geiger's youthful essay, *Was hat Mahomet aus dem Judenthum aufgenommen?* ["What Did Muhammad Borrow from Judaism?" See chapter 11 in this volume—ed.] We want especially a thorough commentary, executed with the methods and resources of modern science. No European language, it would seem, can even boast of a translation which completely satisfies modern requirements. The best are in English, where we have the extremely paraphrastic, but for its time admirable translation of Sale (repeatedly printed), that of Rodwell (1861), which seeks to give the pieces in chronological order, and that of Palmer (1880), who wisely follows the traditional arrangements. The introduction which accompanies Palmer's translation is not in all respects abreast of the most recent scholarship. Considerable extracts from the Koran are well translated in E. W. Lane's *Selections from the Kur-an.*

Besides commentaries on the whole Koran, or on special parts and topics, the Muslims possess a whole literature bearing on their sacred book. There are works on the spelling and right pronunciation of the Koran, works on the beauty of its language, on the number of its verses, words, and letters, etc.; nay, there are even works which would nowadays be called "historical and critical introductions." Moreover, the origin of Arabic philology is intimately connected with the recitation and exegesis of the Koran. To exhibit the importance of the sacred book for the whole mental life of the Muslims would be simply to write the history of that life itself; for there is no department in which its all pervading, but unfortunately not always salutary, influence has not been felt.

The unbounded reverence of the Muslims for the Koran reaches its climax in the dogma (which appeared at an early date through the influence of the Christian doctrine of the eternal Word of God) that this book, as the divine Word, i.e., thought, is immanent in God, and consequently *eternal* and *uncreated.* That dogma has been accepted by almost all Muhammadans since the beginning of the third century. Some theologians did indeed protest against it with great energy; it was, in fact, too preposterous to declare that a book composed of unstable words and letters, and full of variants, was absolutely divine. But what were the distinctions and sophisms of the theologians for, if they could not remove such contradictions, and convict their opponents of heresy?

The following works may be specially consulted: Weil, *Einleitung in den Koran* [Introduction to the Koran], 2nd ed. 1878; Th. Nöldeke, *Geschichte des Qorâns* [History of the Koran], Göttingen, 1860; and the *Lives of Muhammad* by Muir and Sprenger.

PART TWO

The Collection and the Variants of the Koran

3.

'Uthman and the Recension of the Koran
Leone Caetani

In a recent number we availed ourselves of the kind permission of Prince
Leone Caetani to publish a translation of an essay out of his "Annali dell'
Islam." The following article is another such translation taken from the
recently published seventh volume. The first part is much abridged, it being
necessary for considerations of space to omit some most illuminating sum-
maries and criticisms of the views of such scholars as Auguste Müller,
Nöldeke, and Karl Vollers. The gist of the essay is to show first that there
are sufficient reasons for believing that the Koran as we have it today, though
not necessarily falsified in any vicious sense, at any time, does not represent
the *ipsissima verba* of Muhammad; secondly, that the famous first recension
under Abu Bakr and 'Umar is a myth, at any rate as regards its official pro-
mulgation as the unique exemplar; thirdly, that the recension of 'Uthman
was undertaken more from political than religious motives; and fourthly,
incidentally to revise our opinion of 'Uthman's character. The first is supported by the contention of Vollers, that a development in the language,
apart from the subject matter, of the Koran, can be upheld on purely philological grounds. Caetani, therefore, recapitulates his arguments briefly and
accepts his main conclusion. We note that no allusion is made to the theory
of Casanova (see review, *The Muslim World,* January, 1916) that finality was
not arrived at till a still later recension in the time of al-Hajjaj, which would
seem to receive indirect support from Vollers.—R. F. McNeile.

Originally published in *The Muslim World* 5 (1915): 380–90.

*T*HE KORAN WAS NOT COLLECTED during the Prophet's lifetime; this is clearly stated by good authorities. Those who are enumerated as collectors can certainly have collected only a part, for otherwise there is no explanation of the great pains to which the three caliphs, Abu Bakr, 'Umar and 'Uthman, put themselves after Muhammad's death to produce the single official text of the Prophet's revelations.

The tradition of the first compilation in the reign of Abu Bakr is usually accepted without questioning, but an examination of the account quickly betrays certain contradictions. Thus, if the death of so many Muslims at al-Yamamah endangered the preservation of the text, why did Abu Bakr, after making his copy, practically conceal it, entrusting it to the guardianship of a woman? Hafsah's copy seems, in fact, to be an invention to justify the corrections of that subsequently compiled under 'Uthman. I allow, however, the probability that in the time of Abu Bakr and 'Umar, quite independently of the battle of al-Yamamah, a copy of the Koran was prepared at Medina, perhaps at 'Umar's suggestion, exactly as others were compiled in the provinces, those, namely, which were afterwards destroyed by order of 'Uthman. It may be that the copy in Medina had a better guarantee of authenticity; while the statement that in the text prepared by Abu Bakr and 'Umar no verse was accepted which was not authenticated by at least two witnesses, who declared that they had themselves heard it from the Prophet, leads us to suppose that already in the first Koranic compilation other verses were suppressed which had not the required support.

If this statement can be accepted as authentic, it would indicate—as is perfectly natural and possible—that even while Muhammad lived, or at least immediately after his death, there were in circulation verses either apocryphal or erroneously attributed to the Prophet. It seems to me equally likely that in the texts made in the provinces (those, that is to say, that were destroyed by 'Uthman) there should have crept in apocryphal or insufficiently authenticated verses, or others which the Prophet and his most interested friends and Companions did not want to see preserved. Muslim traditionists for obvious reasons have tried to eliminate every kind of suspicion in this direction, for that would open an enormous field for dangerous insinuations and conjectures in countries so fertile in invention as the East. They try, accordingly, to make out that the divergences were solely in minutiae of the text or in single letters, so as not to compromise the text as it stands today or admit the existence of other verses either lost or suppressed. The small number of verses which tradition will allow to be doubtful seem to me little pieces of traditionist fraud, adduced to show the scrupulous exactness of the first compiler and the absolute security of the official text.

The official canonical redaction undertaken at 'Uthman's command, was due to the uncertainty which reigned in reference to the text. It is clear that in the year 30 A.H. no official redaction existed. Tradition itself admits that there were various " schools," one in Iraq, one in Syria, one in al-Basrah, besides others in smaller places, and then, exaggerating in an orthodox sense this scandal, tries to make out that the divergences were wholly immaterial; but such affirmations accord ill with the opposition excited by the caliph's act in al-Kufah. The official version must have contained somewhat serious modifications.

These general observations, however, do not touch on the political and moral aspect of the official compilation of the Koran under 'Uthman. In point of fact; this act, though apparently of a purely religious nature, was intimately bound up with matters of the highest importance in the history of Islam. To explain how this can be, we must first examine the origin and position of a new class of the Islamic community, those known as the *Qurra*, or Koran-readers.

It is greatly to be deplored that tradition is so dumb on the subject of how this new and singular class of Muslims first sprang into existence. They were the principal agitators in the revolt against 'Uthman, and in the civil strife which dyed Islam with blood only five and twenty years after the Prophet had passed away. If we knew with greater precision what they really were, how they were constituted, and how they acquired such influence over the people, we should have in our hand the key that would at once unlock the door of many mysteries connected with the tragedy in Medina in the year 35, with the arbitration of Adhruh in 38, and with the first Kharijite revolts. Unfortunately the knowledge we have is very vague.

The origin of the Readers reaches back to the Prophet, and springs from some practical system (though passed over in silence by tradition) by which Muhammad created a category of persons specially instructed in Koranic revelation. The silence of tradition on these first steps in Koranic doctrine is due to the slight importance attached by Muslims themselves to such mental exercises so long as the Prophet lived, who, as the prime source of all divine knowledge, could easily give light to any it. In the Prophet's time there was no real work of proselytism or Koranic propaganda in the sense intended by Muslim missionaries in later times. Hence we are forced to mistrust much of what traditions have to say on this. Muhammad's agents in the various parts of Arabia had functions specially political, fiscal or economic, military and diplomatic, and only in part religious. To be assured of this we need only remember that to Eastern Arabia Muhammad sent 'Amr b. al-'As and al-'Ala b. al-Hadrami, two political Companions, in no way remarkable for religious practice or knowledge of the Koran. The traditions on the mission to the Yemen, correctly interpreted, lead to the same conclusion, though it may be that Muhammad's representatives there, owing to the special nature of the population, had more minute instructions with regard to religious matters than the others. We must never lose sight of the fact that the traditions of later times have given an intensely religious color to all the memories of primitive Islam, and so have transformed into missionaries of Islam many of those who in reality were only ambassadors, spies, or political agents, exactors of tribute on behalf of the Lord of Medina. Muhammad regarded propaganda as his own peculiar work, and did not care for others to assume in that regard any delegation of his highest functions. Hence came about the numerous embassies from the tribes to Medina. Islamic truth must be learned immediately from the mouth of the Prophet, and for the rest a formal adhesion and the payment of certain fiscal dues sufficed for the tribe to be unquestionably considered as Muslim.

On the Prophet's death all this was radically changed through the fear which the surviving Companions felt of losing the sacred Koranic text, which was the foundation of Islam as a political, as well as a religious, institution. The spectacular triumphs of Muslim arms and the astounding extension of their rule were regarded as the direct effects of the Prophet's own work and teaching, which accordingly elicited a keen interest both among nominal Muslims, converted as they were for the most part in name only, and among those who found their place in the community simply as subjects. The political, moral and financial advantages which the name of Muslim conferred, drew the attention of all the conquered, so that what during the lifetime of Muhammad and the revolt of the tribes in the Riddah had been considered a burden and a humiliation was magically elevated into an honorable estate, the coveted sign of political power. Islam was changed into a moral and religious emblem which all Arabs became proud to wear. With their public adherence to Islam, the Arabs implicitly affirmed themselves to be masters of that region of Western Asia. The moral force of this sentiment, which constituted a valuable bond of union and cohesion in the anarchic unity of Arabia, was dimly foreseen by the sagacity of the first caliphs, especially 'Umar, who aimed by his political injunction at establishing the sentiment that Muslims constituted one great and single family. To this sentiment, therefore, it was necessary to supply a more secure and lasting moral foundation, so as to prevent it from vanishing away after the first intoxication of victory; it was necessary to create a doctrine and a rite, to act as instruments for the preservation of social discipline and moral unity among the Muslims.

So long as Muhammad lived his daily example and his word supplied every need. When he was gone, the heads of the community were forced to take steps to supply the great lack. We are so accustomed to regard Islam as an institution in itself, powerfully constituted, independent of any personal control like that of a pope, that we are apt to go astray in estimating the earliest period of transition. We do not sufficiently bear in mind that the Islam of Muhammad was a creation of an absolutely personal description, concentrated in and founded almost entirely upon his own individuality, upon his continual, daily, personal support. In his Koranic revelations he made no real provision for the future of the community, or for the moment in which the founder or master would disappear. Muhammad's successors were thus called upon to undertake the immense task of transforming Islam into an autonomous, impersonal institution, based upon the consensus of all the members of the community itself. The story of the caliphates of 'Uthman, 'Umar, and 'Ali is the story of this initial and most difficult process of transformation, and of the gloomy experiences by which the gaps in the Prophet's ordinances were filled up and the mistakes of his first successors corrected. Thus it was necessary to provide a head of the community, to fix his prerogatives and the relations which were to hold between him and the other members of the community; in fact, to create out of nothing a grand state-administration. The task would have been difficult enough if the Islamic rule had remained confined to the little kingdom of Medina as Muhammad left it; the difficulty was a hundredfold increased with the conquest and foundation of an immense empire. Everything had to be improvised, from minutiae to the greatest matters. Among other things the functions of governors in distant provinces, where the Arabs had established themselves, had to be defined. It had to be determined what these governors must accomplish to keep alive the Islamic sentiment and moral unity of their dependents. Thus the Friday assembly, which had been a personal weekly function on the part of the Prophet, was transformed into a regular, public, impersonal function, at which it was the duty of the governor, in the absence of the caliph, to preside. A special ceremonial, therefore, had to be devised whereby the governor first assumed and then exercised his controlling function in the administration. As the Friday service was also a religious function formerly presided over by Muhammad, so also in the provinces the governor, taking the place of the Prophet, must preside over the collective prayers. To the political was indissolubly united the religious function of the community.

The general lines of these functions of the governorship may indeed have been indicated by the Prophet himself to his Companions when he sent them on an expedition; but the instructions were incomplete because the command of expeditions, or Muhammad's lieutenancies in Medina when he was absent on a war, were exceptional creations and lasted but for a short period. Everyone returned before long to Medina, and only in the presence of the Prophet was the true and complete Friday ceremony. The conquest, transforming as it did the expedition of a few days or weeks into a permanent occupation and emigration, brought into being new exigencies of which Muhammad had never dreamed. Not only the caliphs, but the greater part of the Muslim society, felt keenly the immediate need of an internal and moral organization of Islam as a ceremonial doctrine. Precisely from such need sprang the special class of persons who, under the name of *al-Qurra,* assumed the task of spreading the knowledge of Islamic doctrine, of the precedents established by the Prophet, and more than all, of the Koran, the one base of the new doctrine since the disappearance of the founder.

Around the person of Muhammad there had arisen in Medina a class of men who had acquired, thanks to their being continually with the Prophet, a fairly complete knowledge of the Koranic revelations and of all the customs and rules of life, culled from the reformer. On Muhammad's death, each of these naturally established himself as a teacher of whatever he knew and remembered. Wherever Arabs settled, there migrated naturally some of these reciters, who served not only to instruct the Arab masses gathered under the banner of Islam without ever having seen the Prophet, but also to educate other *Qurra,* and to form small separate schools in every important settlement of Arabs in the conquered provinces.

At first the work of propaganda and systematic instruction, given almost always by the oral method, was carried on in a sufficiently ordered manner under the sole direction of the caliph, who kept an eye on all. They were Companions who, in the interest of the community, performed this work as a sacrifice for the social welfare. Then, however, with the dazzling growth of the empire, with the astounding multiplication of Islamic centers and the increased need of these instructors, there grew up a special class of men, pupils of the first, who, while inferior to them, were inspired more or less with sincere religious sentiment, but at the same time were bent on availing themselves of their learning to assure themselves an easier sustenance than they could get from their pension alone. Among good and sincere men there crept in hypocrites, agitators, adventurers, who acted each for himself, looking to his own interest, or to what from his own particular point of view was the interest of the community. An institution good in its inception quickly became a danger for the concord and political unity of the Muslims.

Not only did local and particularist tendencies appear, not only did these propagators of Islam assume an independent and rebellious attitude toward the central authority, believing themselves authorized to criticize and to dictate laws to the caliph himself and to his governors, but also in their instructions there appeared discrepancies in ritual; variations in the sacred text, which very few knew perfectly, began to assert themselves on every side.

The Readers must not, however, be considered as a class of people wholly distinct from others, marked off by their profession; there was no closed circle of specialists. Anyone who had some knowledge, even superficial or partial, of the text, could act as Reader for such part as he knew. They did not form a political party, for they were found in every class and in every place, among the Syrians as much as the men of Iraq. Still, owing to the special condition of Muslim society at this early period, the *Qurra* acquired a social influence and importance which was not retained in succeeding generations, when Islamic culture had spread far and wide and there had arisen so many other kinds of doctors and teachers of the people. The number of those who dedicated themselves to this profession, the influence which they acquired over the masses, and the direction which they gave to the general discontent, quickly became a source of serious preoccupation in Medina. The knowledge they claimed of the sacred text gave them a prestige which in many cases may even have raised them in the estimation of the populace above the caliph's governors, who, for the most part, were uncultured men, living continually under arms and ignorant of the Koran. We need only mention the famous Khalid b. al-Walid, who made a boast of his ignorance of the Koran.

At the moment of which we speak, the leaders of the secret agitation against the government were precisely *al-Qurra*, making use of their pretended culture as a weapon for opposition and criticism against the actions of the governor, so giving the movement a general and democratic character, which rendered it peculiarly difficult to watch and keep in check. The caliph 'Uthman and his counselors were not slow to discern all the danger of the new internal situation. The number and variety of these schools of the sacred text and of their dogmas threatened the unity of doctrine, inclination, and sentiment which was indispensable for the future success of the Muslim society. In the Koran discrepancies appeared which were bound to be increased by time. Between the people and the governor there was thus interposed a class of men who arrogated to themselves rights and a moral preeminence, the effect of which was a kind of independence from political authority. In short, availing themselves of the doctrine which they claimed to possess in a greater and better measure than the representatives of the caliph, they excited the populace against the executive power, and were the first to denounce, exaggerate, and even invent the errors of 'Uthman and his agents.

It was 'Uthman's unhappy lot to be called upon not only to seek a remedy for the financial blunders of his great predecessor 'Umar, but to oppose himself to all the moral consequences of the faulty direction which Islamic society was taking under the stress of adversity and bitter disappointments. It is our duty as impartial historians to affirm that even if 'Uthman was unable to grapple with the intricate political situation, if he was unfortunate in the choice of his governors and failed in his attempt to prop up the ruined finances of the empire, yet he was entirely in the right when he tried to forestall the incipient doctrinal anarchy which threatened the Islamic community, by taking energetic steps to prevent the multiplication of versions of the sacred text. The measure adopted by 'Uthman was a radical and bold one, and stands out in contrast to the reputation for weakness which tradition attaches to him in other acts of his administration.

'Uthman ordered the compilation of a single official text of the Koran, and the violent suppression, the destruction by fire of all other copies existing in the provinces. Such an act called for considerable political courage, for it was an open challenge to the whole class of the Readers and an effectual attempt to put an end to the monopoly of the sacred text that they claimed. The central government asserted its authority in this matter as well, and implicitly branded as falsifiers all who did not recite the Koran in a form identical with the official text. 'Uthman's edict was carried out with the greatest precision, for not a single copy antecedent to this official one has survived. The action raised the bitterest resentment of the Readers, and no doubt increased the ill-feeling against the caliph; but tradition, which would dearly have liked to speak evil of 'Uthman in this regard also, has prudently abstained here from making even the slightest insinuation against him. The subject is too delicate, and 'Uthman's action was too closely conformed to the whole spirit of later times for it to venture to protest. It should be added that even if all the existing copies of the Koran could not be traced to 'Uthman's official copy, anyone who cast aspersions on 'Uthman's action would be liable to the charge of raising doubts about the foundation of all Islam, for the Islamic world from one end to the other lives in the conviction that the text existing today represents the true, eternal, immutable word of God.

Tradition stands obviously at a disadvantage with regard to this delicate point, for it is bound to recognize that the official canonizing of the sacred text is due to the caliph, about whom for other reasons it has so much evil to say in the effort to excuse the conduct of his successor 'Ali, the Benjamin of orthodox tradition. These considerations explain the anxiety of traditionists to invent a previous compilation of the sacred text during the reign of the unimpeachable Abu Bakr, the perfect and saintly caliph, for in this way 'Uthman appears only as the copier of the text left by Abu Bakr.

The steps taken by 'Uthman and his effort to strike boldly at a powerful class of his subjects in a period of political effervescence strongly tinged with religious passion show up his rule in a new light. He is not the timid man who gives way first to his relations and then to the crowd of malcontents, but the sovereign who, for reasons of his own, issues an injunction and sees that it is completely carried out in the face of a strong agitation. We come, therefore, indirectly to infer that tradition has traversed the character of the caliph, and that though he may have been weak toward his own family and in some circumstances of minor import, he was, on the other hand, a man of valor and energy in a way that has not as a rule been recognized. His administration no longer appears as though dictated by the mind of a decrepit old man; it was rather an honest and courageous attempt to face an internal revolution which was well matured and finally burst out not through the errors of the caliph and his friends and relations, but as the result of previous irretrievable blunders which 'Uthman had had no opportunity to control.

4.

Three Ancient Korans

Alphonse Mingana

*A*BOUT 611 C.E. AN ILLUSTRIOUS member of the Arabic tribe of Quraish heard, in the cave of Hira, a voice giving him the solemn message: "Cry thou in the name of thy Lord who created, created man from clots of blood." Suratul 'Alaq (xcvi. 1–2¹).

Whatever be the degree of credence that an impartial critic may bestow upon this tradition, held as an unshakable truth by more than two hundred and fifty millions of people, we must at least bear in mind that a tradition sanctioned during the long period of thirteen centuries should command a certain respect and trust.

The man who heard this secret voice was Muhammad, and the result of the recital of the message that he received is Muhammadanism, whose only foundation is the book entitled *al-Qur'ān* [Koran], which originally means "recital" *par excellence.*

It is only during the last centuries that the Koran has been studied scientifically, and the outcome of genuine researches on this subject induces us to face today the Islamic book with a mental composure somewhat in contrast to the enthusiastic and often blind fascination which characterizes

Originally published as the Introduction of *Leaves from Three Ancient Qurâns Possibly Pre-'Othmânic with a List of their Variants,* edited by Rev. Alphonse Mingana and Agnes Smith Lewis (Cambridge, UK: 1914), pp. xi–xxxii.

the Koranic compositions of the Muhammadan world. For this reason, we earnestly wish that the spirit of a higher criticism would soon be created among modern Muslim theologians, who, attracted by so many Christian theologians, commentators, and exegetes, will then give up the puerile senility in which they have lived and still live, and the low traditionalism of doctrine which famishes all the beauty of their writings.

Let us see what Muhammad himself thinks of the inspired book by means of which he tried, if possible, to overthrow the Christian and the Jewish bulwarks, by sapping at their base, the foundations of all that the old prophets and the apostles handed down to their respective admirers:

"Say verily, were men and jinns assembled to produce the like of this Koran they would not produce its like, though the one should help the other." (Surat Bani Isra'il, xvii. 90.)

"If they say, 'The Koran is his own device' say, 'Then bring ten suras like it of your own devising; call whom ye can to your aid besides Allah.'" (Surat Hud, xi. 16.)

"If ye be in doubt as to that which we have sent down to our servant, then produce a sura like it." (Suratul Baqarah, ii. 21.)

"The Muhammadan writers, in acknowledging the claims of the Koran to be the direct utterance of the divinity, have made it impossible for any Muslim to criticise the work, and it became, on the contrary, the standard by which other literary compositions had to be judged. Grammarians, lexicographers, and rhetorians, started with the presumption that the Koran could not be wrong, and that all works only approached excellence in proportion as they more or less successfully imitated its style."[2]

Before we examine the truth of these assertions, we would wish to direct the attention of every reader of the Koran to the following points: (1) The sources of the Koran. (2) If we strip from its text the historical events and the circumstances in which it was written, it becomes an inexplicable composition. (3) How were the verses of the Koran preserved from 612 to 632? (4) Who is the compiler of the standard text that we have today, and is this compilation authentic?

The first point is very easily treated, and since the Prophet could probably neither read nor write,[3] the details which deal with the unity of God, and with the various forms of the eastern conceptions of religious obligations, viz. prayer, alms, fasting, etc. must have been inspired chiefly by oral information drawn from Christians, and specially from the strong Jewish colony of Mecca and the neighboring districts. Besides the masterly

book of Nöldeke, the reader will find trustworthy information on this subject in Geiger's *Was hat Mahomet aus dem Judenthum aufgenommen?* ["What
Did Muhammad Borrow from Judaism?" See chapt. 11 in this volume—
Ed.] (1833) for the Jewish element in the Koran, and in W. St. Clair-Tisdall's *The Original Sources of the Koran* (1905). Some good ideas may be
found in Cl. Huart's *Une nouvelle source du Qoran* ["A New Source of the
Koran"] (1904). We have to draw attention to the following details:

Long before the time of the Prophet, the Quraishites were mixed with
the Christians, and about 485 C.E. a well-known Syrian writer, Narsai, the
founder of the University of Nisibis, mentions the terrible raids that the
forefathers of Muhammad were wont to make in the district of Beith
'Arabayé, in Western Assyria: "The raid of the sons of Hagar was more
cruel even than famine, and the blow that they gave was more sore than
disease; the wound of the sons of Abram is like the venom of a serpent,
and perhaps there is a remedy for the poison of reptiles, but not for
theirs.....Let us always blame the foul inclination of the sons of Hagar,
and specially the people (the tribe) of Quraish who are like animals."[4]

The distance between Arabia and the desert of Syria will not astonish
our reader if he thinks of the seminomad life of every good Arab, when
mounted on his swift mare. We read in *Synodicon Orientale*[5] that about 486
C.E. the famous Barṣauma of Nisibis was appointed with Kardagh Nak-
wergan, Roman *dux* and king of the Arabs, to settle the differences arising
out of the rudimental delimitation of the Roman and Persian frontiers, in
the East of Arabia. A letter from Barṣauma to Acacius, Catholicos of
Seleucia, informs us that the Arabs called Tu'aites would not have permitted the inhabitants of the province of Beith 'Arabayé to live in peace
through their continual raids. These Arabs, who are not to be confounded
with Tayayés, Tay, and who molested so strangely the western parts of the
old Assyrian empire, were living in the sandy plains of the southwestern
land of the Sassanids, and by their proximity to the country of the Meccan
prophet they must have shaken more than once the primitive religious
authorities of central Arabia. In the districts adjoining the country where
Mecca is situated, several small kingdoms were almost half Christian, and
a document of supreme value[6] proves that Hira was already a bishopric in
410 C.E.

In consideration of the meagre scientific attainments of the Prophet,
the question of the sources of the Koran has been keenly debated by the
old Christian communities. The outcome of some of their thoughts

brought forth the curious *History of Rabban Behira.* The second part of this legend which tells of the interview of Muhammad with this monk, and the epoch of whose composition may be the middle of the eighth century, is an irrefragable proof both of the ignorance of the Christian scholars of that time about the genuine sources of the Koran, and of their conviction that it had a foreign origin. M. R. Gottheil, who printed this history in 1899,[7] remarks that its first part, containing the encounter of Behira with Iso'iahb, and its third part, exhibiting some apocalyptic visions on Islam, may date from the eleventh century, but its second part is much earlier. It would be interesting to know whether this second part has no historical value; but as this question is a digression from our subject, we content ourselves with a reference to it.

The internal criticism of the Koran will easily shew this elementary evidence of a foreign source; but what we can by no means explain, are the wonderful anachronisms about the old Israelite history. The only possible way of accounting for these would be the distance which separated the moment of the inspiration of the verses from the moment when the Prophet received the oral communication. Who then will not be astonished to learn that in the Koran, Miriam, the sister of Aaron, is confounded with the Virgin Mary? (Surat 'Ali-'Imran, iii. 31 *et seq.*) and that Haman is given as minister of Pharaoh, instead of Ahasuerus? (Suratul-Qasas, xxviii. 38. Suratul-Mu'men, xl. 38 *et passim*). The ignorance, too, of the author of the Koran about everything outside of Arabia and some parts of Syria makes the fertility of Egypt, where rain is never missed, for the simple reason that it is very seldom seen, depend on rain instead of on the inundation of the Nile. (Surat Yusuf, xii. 49.) Moreover, the greatest honor that the Israelite tradition bestows upon Esdras is found in *Sanhedrin,* xxi. 22, where we read that " 'Ezra would have been fully worthy to give the law, if Moses had not been before him";[8] but to state, as in Suratut-Taubah, ix. 30, that the Jews believed that Esdras was the son of God, as the Christians thought of the Messiah, is a grave error hardly justifiable. All these historical mistakes receive another and not less topical support from the utter confusion which is made between Gideon and Saul in Suratul-Baqarah, ii. 250. Such mistakes are indelible stains on the pages of the sacred book which is the object of our study, and they are not wiped out by the following statement:

"We (Allah) relate unto thee a most excellent history, by revealing unto thee this Koran, whereas thou wast before one of the negligent." (Surat Yusuf, xii. 3.) And again,

"I (Muhammad) had no knowledge of the exalted princes when they disputed about the creation of man; it is revealed unto me only as a proof that I am a public preacher." (Surat Sad, xxxviii. 67–70.)

If we try to read the Koran from beginning to end in the order in which it has been circulated from the latter half of the seventh century down to this day, we shall ascertain that it is the most incoherent of books, and the flagrant contradictions that we shall meet will astonish us. So in Suratut-Taubah, we read, "Make war upon the people unto whom the book has been delivered, who . . . forbid not what Allah and His Apostle have forbidden, and who profess not the profession of the truth, until they pay tribute out of hand in an humble condition." And again in Suratul-Baqarah, ii. 189, it is said: "And fight against them till there be no more tumult, and the only worship be that of Allah."

But in this same Suratul-Baqarah, v. 257, it is said: "Let there be no compulsion in religion"; and in Suratul-Ankabut, xxix. 45: "And dispute ye not, except in kindliest sort with the people of the book." (The Christians and the Jews, by allusion to the Torah and the Gospel, are called in the Koran *the people of the book*.)

The Muhammadan commentators noticed these contradictions, and found that the best way to remove them was that of the historical method, and availing themselves of the oldest lives of the Prophet by Zuhri, Musa ibn 'Uqba, Abu Ishaq, Mada'ini, and the better-known books of Ibn Hisham, Waqidi, and Tabari, they attempted to explain every verse by the circumstances in which it has been revealed, and they distributed the suras of the Koran into two distinct groups: those which were written in Mecca from 612 C.E. to 622, and those which were revealed in Medina, from 622 to 632. The youthful and timid essay of Muhammadan theologians has been in the last few years considerably expanded by many critics; special mention must be made here of Nöldeke's *Geschichte des Qorâns* [History of the Koran] (1860), and E. Sell's *The Historical Development of the Qoran* (1905).

By this synchronal method, the Koran becomes a historical book, and the most trustworthy source of information about the Prophet. The touchstone of veracity for any given detail of the life of Muhammad told by the historians of the period of decadence would be to find if this detail has any sufficient ground in the Islamic book. But, at any rate, if by this criticism, the chronological order is saved, the versatility of mind of the Prophet can by no means be excused, since, under the pressure of necessity, he cruelly contradicted sometimes what he had stated before. Can then the following verse inspired in Mecca excuse some flagrant contradictions of the Koran?:

"And we have not sent an apostle or prophet before thee, among whose desires Satan injected not some wrong desire, but Allah shall bring to nought that which Satan has suggested." (Suratul-Hajj, xxii. 51.)

We do not wish to discuss a youthful essay on the explanation of these difficulties, put forward by some pious commentators who say that: "Allah commanded several things which were, for good reasons, afterwards revoked and abrogated." Those abrogated passages of the Koran are distinguished by many of the rigid commentators, into three kinds, "the first, where the letter and the sense are both abrogated; the second, where the letter only is abrogated, but the sense remains; and the third, where the sense is abrogated, though the letter remains." These subtleties of the theological schools do not afford a profitable subject of study for a serious critic.

The most important question in the study of the Koran is its unchallengeable authenticity. In this theme, the first step would be the following question: How could Muhammad in all the wars by which his life was so unfortunately agitated, in all the displacements that he must have undergone, keep all the verses which had heen previously revealed to him in his memory, after an interval of several years? A plausible and final answer will probably never be given to this question, and the only tenable hypothesis is that which discards the difficulty by the assumption of the prodigious memory of his followers, who are believed to have learnt the strophes by heart, and that in a period lasting from 612 till 632. This hypothesis, which seems to be that of a *dernier ressort*, can be supported by the fact that the Prophet, who was more probably an unlettered man,[9] had never thought of writing a book, or of gathering together, in a complete code, the scattered verses which he had recited to his friends, in some circumstances of his life; so much so, that after his death, the emissaries of Abu Bakr, his successor in the caliphate, could scarcely put together some separate bits of verses, despite the good memory, and the extreme care of Zaid ibn Thabit, the real compiler of the Koran of today.

This historical fact is suggested by the first refusal of Zaid to undertake the compilation of the Koran, on the ground that the Prophet himself had never done so. "What right have I," said Zaid to Abu Bakr, "to gather in the form of a book what the Prophet has never intended to transmit to posterity by this channel? And since the Prophet never designed to give his message in this way, is it a lawful work that I am commanded to do?"

As to the prodigious memory of Eastern people who imperturbably and faithfully preserve verses of songs and poems, in their daily life, during a long space of time, we must say that this fact has been a little exaggerated; and nearly always the rural ditties, used in our day among the Bedawin and the Kurdish population of the plains of Syria and Mesopotamia, are recited by different tribes in a different way, and the changes are often more or less sensible according to the remoteness of the tribes one from the other. So, for instance, how many significant various readings can we find in the well-known Arabic elegy called 'Itabah, in the divers Bedawin tribes of Albu-Hamad, Shammar, 'Aniza, Dleim? etc. and, besides the various readings, how many new couplets of the Kurdish glee called *Mamo Ziné* are used in the deadly sept of Mira, which are absolutely unknown in the tribes of Haja, Zewiki, Shakaki, etc.?

As to the faithfulness of a tradition among Eastern people, it has been, I think, accentuated too strongly, and the best comparison for this string of traditions would be, to anyone who has travelled in the arid deserts, a great caravan of big camels walking one after another, but all being guided by a small donkey. We cannot, indeed, understand why Eastern people should deviate in this matter from the natural law of a progressive evolution, and the tenacity with which some people cling to ancient religious creeds and habits of daily life has nothing to do with the change of words and the exaggeration of historical details; and for that matter, a serious man, who knows the domestic life of the nomads, will doubtless ascertain that the donkey, which conducts the imposing caravan of camels, is sometimes smaller in the East than in the West.

Besides the ordinary channel of the wonderful memory of the Arabs, many verses have been transmitted to Zaid by writing, a kind of writing which was in use at Mecca in the time of the prophet; but since we cannot explain why some verses should have been written and others not, and specially since we are not told which are the verses transmitted to Zaid by writing, and which are those that he knew only from memory, this fact cannot come, till fuller light dawns, into the sphere of a scientific and positive study. To believe that several verses of the Koran were written by friends of the Prophet during his lifetime is in accordance with some phrases of this sacred book which mention clearly the name of *Kitab*, "what is written, scriptures," but to state that the fragmentary revelations were almost entirely written and "put promiscuously into a chest"[10] is in contradiction to the kind of life that Muhammad led, and to early and authentic sources. In accepting such low and hardly disinterested traditions of Muslim authors, why should we not regard as true other and not less authoritative narratives which inform us that all the suras were completed according to the directions of the angel Gabriel, who, on the other hand, brought only to Muhammad, in parcels, a text written on a table of "vast bigness," styled the *Preserved Table* and existing from an eternity near Allah's throne? Muhammadan pious annalists know, too, that a copy made from this eternal original, has been sent to the lowest heaven, whence Gabriel was accustomed to show it once a year[11] to the Prophet, bound in silk and adorned with gold and precious stones of Paradise. The Prophet himself puts into the mouth of God the following sentences: "By the Luminous Book!—We (Allah) have made it an Arabic Koran that ye may understand; and it is a transcript of the Archetypal Book kept by us" (Suratuz-Zukhruf, xliii. 1–3), and again: "We ourselves (Allah) have sent down to thee the Koran as a missive from on high" (Suratud-Dahr, lxxvi. 23), and again:

"That this is the honorable Koran, written on the *Preserved Table;* let no one touch it but the purified" (Suratul-Waqi'ah, lvi. 77–78), and again: "Say, the Holy Spirit hath brought it down with truth, from thy Lord." Suratun-Nahl (xvi., v. 104), etc., etc.

We know that the whole text of the Koran has been drawn up twice by Zaid ibn Thabit, who, it is said, was the amanuensis of the Prophet. The first recension was made under the caliphate of Abu Bakr, and at the instigation of 'Umar, his successor, between 11 and 15 A.H. "I fear," said this true believer, to the caliph, "that slaughter may again wax hot amongst the reciters of the Koran, on other fields of battle, and that much may be lost therefrom. Now therefore my advice is, that thou shouldst give speedy orders for the collection of the Koran." Abu Bakr agreed, and addressing Zaid ibn Thabit, he said, "Thou art a young man, and wise; against whom no one amongst us can cast an imputation. Wherefore now search out the Koran, and bring it together." Yielding to the joint entreaties of Abu Bakr and 'Umar, Zaid sought out the fragments of the Koran from every quarter and gathered them together, from date-leaves, bits of parchment, tablets of white stone, and from the hearts of men.[12]

The Koran, so collected and drawn up by Zaid, was committed by 'Umar to the custody of his own daughter Hafsa, the Prophet's widow. We are not told, by any contemporary outside writer, of what kind were these tablets of white stone, or these date-leaves, and the early sources do not suggest that the Prophet had ever used such materials. It is quite possible, therefore, that the only source which Zaid had for the greater part of the text was "the hearts of men," and some scattered scraps of parchment. This hypothesis is supported by the absolute want of any chronological order in the Koran; and this want suggests to us the idea that the book is not a result of one source of information, or of one Arab reciter, and that it has not been written in deep and laborious study, but that it is simply the outcome of many different recitals that Zaid heard day by day, and gradually wrote down in the measure and proportion that he received them. One day he received some verses "from the breast" of some inhabitants of Medina dealing with the life of the Prophet in that city, and he wrote them quickly in his book; the next day, hearing some other recitals from some inhabitants of Mecca, he embodied them with the previous verses revealed in Medîna. For this reason, we can scarcely find a long sura of the Koran which is not twice or thrice at least composite, i.e., having verses dating from the time when the Prophet was still in his native town, and some others referring to the time immediately following his flight to Yathrib. It is highly probable, too, that the bits of parchment used by Zaid contained sometimes a complete narrative of a biblical incident, and that the only work of the compiler was to put such well digested material in one of the suras of the book that he edited. In this category must be counted all the verses dealing with the history of Joseph, of the birth of the Christ, and many other stories.

Finally, if we understand correctly the following verse of Suratul-Hijr (xv. 90–91): "As we sent down upon (punished) the dividers (of the Scripture?) who broke up the Koran into parts," we are tempted to state that, even when the Prophet was alive, some changes were noticed in the recital of certain verses of his sacred book There is nothing very surprising in this fact, since Muhammad could not read nor write, and was at the mercy of friends for the writing of his revelations, or, more frequently, of some mercenary amanuenses.

The book, drawn up by this method, continued to be the authoritative and standard text till about 29–30 A.H. under the caliphate of 'Uthman. At this time the wonderful faithfulness of Arab memory was defective, and according to a general weakness of human nature, the *Believers* have been heard reciting the verses of the Koran in a different way. This fact was due specially, it is said, to the hundreds of dialects used in Arabia. Zaid was again asked to put an end to these variations which had begun to scandalize the votaries of the Prophet. That indefatigable compiler, assisted by three men from the tribe of Quraish,[13] started to do what he had already done more than fifteen years before. The previous copies made from the first one written under Abu Bakr were all destroyed by special order of the caliph: the revelation sent down from heaven was one, and the book containing this revelation must be one.

The critic remarks that the only guarantee of the authenticity of the Koran is the testimony of Zaid; and for this reason, a scholar who doubts whether a given word has been really used by Muhammad, or whether it has been only employed by Zaid on his own authority, or on the meagre testimony of some Arab reciters, does not transgress the strict laws of high criticism. If the memory of the followers of the Prophet has been found defective from the year 15 to 30 A.H. when Islam was proclaimed over all Arabia, why may it not have been defective from 612 to 632 C.E. when the Prophet was often obliged to defend his own life against terrible aggressors? And if the first recension of Zaid contained always the actual words of Muhammad, why was this compiler not content with re-establishing it in its entirety, and why was the want of a new recension felt by 'Uthman? How can it be that in the short space of fifteen years, such wonderful variants could have crept into the few copies preceding the reign of the third caliph that he found himself bound to destroy all those he could find? If 'Uthman was certainly inspired only by religious purposes, why did his enemies call him "The tearer of the Books" and why did they fasten on him the following stigma: "He found the Korans many and left one; he tore up the Book"?[14] We deem, therefore, as too categorical the following verdict of Von Hammer: "We hold the Koran to be as surely Muhammad's word, as the Muhammadans hold it to be the word of God."

Though a convincing answer worthy of *twentieth* century criticism cannot be given to the preceding questions, we believe that Zaid endeavored to reproduce, faithfully, so far as he could, the very words of Muhammad. The imperfections of all kinds, and the want of historical order found in his book, are terrible witnesses against his intellectual proficiency; but, on the other hand, the fragmentary qualities of the last suras, the good control of the first caliphs, and especially the suitable time of his compilation, when many believers were able to recite several verses by heart, testify to his faithfulness. We believe too, that if the historical attainments of the first Muslims and of Zaid himself had been less restricted, they would perhaps have modified in some way the historical and topographical errors which the Koran contains.

Now, at what date has the Koran been arranged in the order that it follows in our day? Professor D. S. Margoliouth remarks very justly that "the task of arranging the sacred texts in fixed groups might very well have appalled a Muslim; we could scarcely credit a contemporary of the Prophet with having the courage to attempt it. On the other hand, the notion that the suras existed as frames, which gradually became filled as revelations descended, has little to commend it, and involves the existence of an official copy, which we have seen to be excluded by the evidence."[15] We maintain, however, that this arrangement was made at the time of the first recension, and not at the second; the scandal which would have followed it at the time when the Koran was known by many a Muhammadan, and specially by believers in foreign countries, makes the contrary hypothesis very improbable.

> The recension of 'Othman has been handed down to us unaltered. So carefully, indeed, has it been preserved, that there are no variations of importance—we might almost say no variations at all—to be found in the innumerable copies scattered throughout the vast bounds of the Empire of Islam; contending and embittered factions, taking their rise in the murder of 'Othman himself, within a quarter of a century after the death of Mahomet, have ever since rent the Moslem world; yet but *one Coran* has been current amongst them; and the consentaneous use by all of the same scripture, in every age, to the present day, is an irrefragable proof that we have now before us the very text prepared by command of the unfortunate Caliph. There is probably no other work in the world which has remained for 12 centuries with so pure a text..... It is one of the maxims of the Muslim world (supported perhaps by Sura xi. 2) that the Coran is incorruptible, and that it is preserved from error and variety of reading by the miraculous interposition of God himself.... According to the orthodox doctrine, every syllable of the Coran is of divine origin, eternal and uncreate as the Deity itself.[16]

From what we have said in the preceding pages, it is evident that if we find a manuscript of the Koran presenting various readings of consonants and of complete words, and more specially if this manuscript offers some interpolations and omissions, it would not be too rash to suppose that it goes back to a pre-'Uthmanic period. The conclusion is clear and is corroborated by the constant history of the Muhammadan world, from the seventh century down to our own day.

Viewing the linguistic wording of the text of the Koran, we desire to examine a question which concerns us more than the others. Does the Koran contain the flower of the Arabic language, and is the challenge given by the Prophet himself true? Besides the sentences quoted in the preceding pages, the Prophet repeats several times with a certain emphasis: "We gave a Koran written in Arabic; it is in Arabic that this Koran has been revealed, etc." Philologists will not be much offended, if we send our reader, for an answer to this question, to the excellent works of a man who deserves the gratitude of every Orientalist, Th. Nöldeke, and chiefly to his *Geschichte des Qorâns* (History of the Koran) already mentioned. We would wish only to draw attention to the following remarks:

> The Arabic literature preceding the epoch of the Prophet is imperfectly known; but we may be allowed to state that it was not very flourishing, since the traces that it left for future generations are scanty in comparison with the formidable swarm of useful lucubrations of the post-Muhammadan time. This being, so, the Muslim authors are not to be blamed when they call that time the epoch of *Ignorance*[17] though they mean specially, by this qualification, an ignorance about Allah and his immediate attributes. The works of the best writers have been collected at the beginning of the IXth century by Asma'i and Tarafa, Amrul-Kais, 'Antara, Zuhair, Nabigha, 'Alkama.[18]

If we add to this number Ta'abbata-Sharran and Shanfara and some others found in the book of Louis Cheikho[19] but with some restriction about the authenticity of all their poems we may have the approximate number.

Now when we compare the style, the method of elocution, the purity of vocables, the happy adjustment of words, the choice of good rhymes in these pre-Islamic writings with the Koran, we are often tempted to give them an unchallengeable superiority; and it is only the kind of life, foreign to all learning, that can explain the great uneasiness that the author of the Koran shows when he wishes to write in rhyme, and finds himself short of common lexicographical terms. So in Suratul-Jinn the author had certainly an intention to write in rhymed prose (*saj'*), but his linguistic knowledge failing him, he repeats the [same] word six times at the end of twenty-eight short sentences. Besides the repetitions, being quite short of rhymes, even through this method, he changes the letter *Dal* to a *ba'* in *vv.* 5, 8, 15, to a *qaf* in *vv.* 6, 13, 16. This example, chosen amongst hundreds of others which are found frequently in the final suras, is not weakened by some foreign and cacophonic terms of which the author of the Koran is enamoured (ex. sura lxxvi. 18; sura viii. 42; ii. 181; iii. 2 *et passim*; sura lxix. 36; lxxxiii. 7, 8; lxxvi. 70; Suratun-Nisa [iv. 78 *et passim*]; Suratul-Maidah [v. 111–112, etc.], etc.).[20] We believe, moreover, that it is by the want of good literary attainments that we can explain the vulgar disfigurement of the names John (Yohannan), Jesus (Esho') into *Iahya* and *'Isa*. Muhammad seems to have taken the vulgar form of these names given in the popular language to children by some Christians of Jewish descent just as in English the name of Margaret becomes in colloquial fashion Margie (*Scottice*, Maggie, Meg, Peggie), that of Elizabeth, Lizzie or Bessie, and Robert, Bob, or Bertie.

Another and not less wonderful instance of spelling is used in Suratut-Tin, where the name of Mount Sinai (in Arabic *Sina'* as in Suratul-Mu'minin, xxiii. 20), is written *Sinina* (!) to make it rhyme with the preceding verse and the following one. The disfigurement, too, of the name of Elijah (in Arabic *Yasa* as in Suratul-An'am, vi. 85) into *Yasina* (!) to make it rhyme with the final words of the phrase, suggests on this point a systematic habit on the part of the Prophet (cf. Suratus-Safat, xxxvii. 130).

This disfigurement of proper nouns is sometimes used in such an awkward manner that, if we wish to set aside an interminable tergiversation, we must attribute the origin of some unknown names, so strangely altered, to Muhammad's own invention. So, who will easily be convinced that the Hud of Suratul-A'raf (vii. 63 *et pas.*) is the same man as the Eber of the Bible,[21] that the Saleh of Surat Hud (xi. 64, etc.) is the same man as Peleg of Genesis (xi. 16),[22] and that the Shu'aib of Suratush-Shu'ara (xxvi. 177, etc.) is the same name as Hobab[23] (Numb. x 29)? No tradition, however corrupted it might have been, would have altered these biblical names in such a wonderfully different mold.

Other alterations of names may perhaps be sufficiently explained by a traditional Christian or Jewish channel; so in Suratul-An'am (vi. 74) Terah, Abraham's father, is called "Azar," and we know that in some Judaeo-Christian circles, Terah was called "Athar."[24] The Djalut, too, of Suratul-Beqarah (ii. 250) is unmistakably Goliath; likewise, the Karun of Suratul-Qasas (xxviii. 76) seems to be the Korah of the Bible. At any rate, philology will be, for a long time, unable to explain convincingly how the name of Saul could become Talut, as in Suratul-Baqarah (ii. 248, 250), nor how the name of Enoch could become Idris, as in Surat Mariam (xix. 57, etc.), nor, finally, how the name of Obadiah (1 Kings xviii. 4) or of Ezechiel could become Dhul-Kifl, as in Suratul-Anbia' (xxi. 85), in spite of a brilliant suggestion that Ezechiel is called by the Arabs Kefil (!).[25]

In any case, whatever view we may take of the claims of Muhammad, no one can deny that he was a great man, ranking with men of the highest genius, as a skillful administrator after the Eastern fashion, and wielding every kind of spiritual weapon to attract and captivate his hearers and his countrymen. His legislation, though perhaps too theocratic for the democratic spirit of our day, was perfection at the time when he lived; *Exitus acta probat.* A man who put an end, in less than ten years, to two formidable kingdoms, the kingdom of the old Achemenides represented by the classic Sassanids, and that of the Roman Caesars of Eastern countries, by means of some camel-drivers of Arabia, must be, at any rate, taken into consideration.[26] A controller of conscience and soul to so many millions, and in the plain light of civilization, is indeed greater than Alexander and Bonaparte known only today in historical books. The proclamations of a semi-nomad Arab of the obscure town of Mecca have been recited by the wide Islamic world thirteen centuries ago, and are recited today; even the cross of the Messiah has been for many years nearly eclipsed by the Crescent, and the name of the *Praised One* of Arabia has been on many occasions on the point of overrunning the last refuge of Christianity. What history is unable to find, even in the twentieth century, is a name more terrible than that of Muhammad.

II

For a scientific comprehension of the text of the Koran, three kinds of study may be found useful: (1) The commentators of the Koran; (2) the grammarians who applied to it the Arabic vowels and diacritical points; (3) the divers forms of script formerly used in the Arabic language.

When the seminomad Arabs started to conquer the world, they did not carry with them, on their camels, any productions of a progressive and latent literature, for they were not brought up in high schools of science and philology. The most picturesque figure amongst these first Arabs is that of the caliph 'Umar entering the holy city of Jerusalem (637), mounted on his camel, a bag of dates and a skin of water by his side; this provision being judged sufficient for his simple wants. It is worth observing how exactly the Aramaeo-Syrian population of that period of conquests called these Arabs by derision: *Hagarians, Ishmaelites,* with the purpose of indicating precisely the semibarbarous literary education that they had received.[27] But an end was soon made to this awkward situation; and the intelligent Arabs, attracted by the example of their neighbors, began to spread everywhere the language of the Koran, and to devote themselves to the sciences which had long given to their new fellow-countrymen an unchallenged superiority. A well-known Syriac writer, Bar Hebraeus, tells us a significant fact, that the Umayyad caliph Walid ordered that the official acts of Damascus should henceforth be drawn up in Arabic, and no longer in Greek.[28] The sanguinary battles of Yarmuk (636) and Kadesia (637), in imposing a new rule over the remains of the once classic empires, gave them a new sacred language.

With regard to the commentaries on the Koran, the only question in Arabic literature which concerns our subject, they are very important for the criticism of the text, since the commentators, when quoting and explaining a given verse in their books, quote it faithfully, and they often try to discuss it with all the resources of their science, literally and spiritually. The first commentator of the early epoch of Islam, was Ibn 'Abbas, cousin of Muhammad, who seems to have been the main source of the traditional exegesis of the Koran. On theological grounds, a great number of his opinions have been considered heretical. He and his disciples deal with the sense and connection of a complete verse, and neglect the literal meaning of a separate word. His commentaries are therefore what Christian writers would call more spiritual than literal. No complete commentary either by the relatives of the Prophet or by extraneous writers has come down to us from this period.

The greatest commentator of a later generation is the well-known Tabari[29] (839–923 C.E.). He is a mine for the knowledge of the wide Islamic legislation, and has sometimes excellent views about the occasion of the revelation of several verses. He is first of all a historian, availing himself of the method of *isnad*, and by this channel he preserves several interesting traditions of the early age of Muhammadanism.

Another good commentator is az-Zamakhshari[30] (1075–1144). He is, according to the judgment of Nöldeke, too subtle a man, trying to apply his rhetorical and philosophical theories to the most practical of men: Muhammad.

In our own days, the commentary most used by Muslim theologians is that of al-Baidhawi ([†]1286) who employed the same method as that of az-Zamakhshari in a more methodical manner.

The end of the thirteenth century, which marks the decadence and the close of the 'Abbassid Caliphate, marks, too, the apogee of the Arabic investigations in the Koran. The numerous commentators of a later date content themselves with quoting, abridging the old authors, and writing books more popular than original.

A good commentary needs good reading, and good reading, in the Semitic languages, involves an accurate knowledge of the right position of the vowels, with all the orthoepical signs of punctuation. We ought to say at once that according to the measure of scientific investigations of today, the Arabs, apart from seven or ten marks of intonation, never used the *rhetorical signs* employed sometimes so fantastically and so awkwardly by the Aramaeans. The Arabic language possessing a kind of inflection like the Greek and the Latin, did not experience any great necessity for reaching even the fortieth part of the frightful number forty that the Aramaeans have invented for an intelligent reading of their Bible, and which are called by the curious and general name of *Puhames*, "similarities, comparisons."[31] A practical reason must have deterred the Arabs from adopting such a complicated system, and this reason is found in the script of their language which distinguishes several consonants by means of one, two or three dots placed either under or over a letter. The adoption of the *Puhames* of the Aramaeans would have created an insurmountable mental difficulty in distinguishing a diacritical point from an orthoepical one dealing specially with a proper accent of voice in the reading of a sentence.

While the Aramaeans and the Hebrews admitted several vowels and invented a special sign for every vowel pronounced open or closed, short or long, the prudent Arabs adopted only three vowels, but these three vowels, represented by a stroke of the pen under or over the letter, respond quite sufficiently to all philological exigencies, since each one of them, when followed by a weak letter, is considered as long, ex. gr. *zārūnī*, "they have visited me," and it is considered short, when followed by a letter which is not quiescent, ex. gr. *qutila*, "he has been killed," and it is shortly closed when followed by a quiescent or reduplicated letter, ex. gr. *ijtartum*, "you have chosen." By this method, every vowel becomes quantitatively three, and so the system is more ingenious than that of the Hebrews, and of the Aramaeans, who by a long use and borrowing very often neglected the short vowel, so important in poetry and in euphonic sounds.

The history of the vowels is somewhat obscure. It is certain that their invention cannot go back to the period preceding the Umayyad caliphate of Damascus. The period of conquest and of intestine war caused by the crucial question of the divine caliphate, which covered the Muhammadan world with blood, at the time of 'Uthman and onwards, was not very suitable for scientific researches. The Umayyad Empire, though distinguished by some great productions of poetry and historical science, is unknown (except for some mere names such as that of Abul-Aswad Ad-Do'ali, or 'Abdur-Rahman ibn Ormiz, a Persian scholar, etc.) as a starting point for grammatical and morphological studies. The first period of conquest lasted from the death of the Prophet, 632 to 661 C.E., when Mu'awiah entered Kufa and became the sole representative of Muhammad; the second period from 661 till January 25, 750 C.E., when the battle of Shaharzur gave the sceptre to the 'Abbassids. Therefore, till the accession of Saffah, no center of grammatical learning has left a trace to posterity. But at this time, the two other branches of the Semitic stock, the Israelites and the Aramaeans, had already passed the time of the careful elaboration of their Massorah, and their vowel-system had acquired a firm foundation, being, in fact, almost at the end of its final evolution.

From the middle of the sixth century, the Monophysite, Ahud-Emmeh, Metropolitan of Tagrit, had opened a path for the Syriac grammar. Some years before him, the famous Joseph of Ahwaz, had established, in the University of Nisibis, a solid foundation for orthoepical studies and for the right pronounciation of the vowels. In the middle of the seventh century, a school founded by Abba Sabrowy, at Beth Shehak, near Nisibis, made the Nestorian system of vowels known even among the Monophysites, their enemies. Before 700 C.E. Jacob of Edessa, by his well-known sentence *Edessa, our mother, thou shalt live in quietness,* which represents all the vowels of the Aramaic language used today, marks the end of a systematic evolution of phonetic studies in the Syriac grammar. The school of Edessa, the University of Nisibis, the monasteries of Tel'eda, Kennesrin, and Karkaphta, had then made complete, in the period lasting from 450 to 700 C.E., the phonetic essays which the writers of a later period were content to abridge or to modify in some insignificant details.[32]

On the other hand, the strong Israelite colony which had remained behind from the old Babylonian captivity vied in a laudable zeal with the Aramaeans. By means of some prudently distributed bribes, they could always secure a satisfactory political condition under the Sassanid Sapor I and his successors. Their prestige was so widely felt that, in the fourth century, they contrived to be favored by the harem of the Queen Ephra

Hormizd, to whom Christian writers of that time attribute the frightful ordeal that Sapor II, the enemy of the Roman legions, inflicted, in 341, on the Christians of the Persian Empire.[33] According to the Talmud, the Jews of Babylonia are from a purer race even than those of Palestine; we read, in fact, in the *Talm. Bab.* under the treatise *Kiddusin* the following sentences:[34] "Tous les pays sont comme de la pate relativement à la Palestine, mais ce pays l'est relativement à la Babylonie."* By the works of Christian writers in Mesoptamia, we know how great was the influence that they exercised in that country and in the neighboring districts. Of the twenty-three homilies of Jacob Aphrahat (fourth century) nine are devoted to the anti-Judaic controversy. Narsai ([†]502) has also some striking discourses against them.

The Torah was always the subject of a special study among the Jews of the Captivity either under the Arsacido-Parthians or under the Sassanido-Persians, but we know that from the third century and onwards the study has been considerably extended. The great *Sidra* of Sora, founded in this epoch, acquired a worldwide renown, and could not be eclipsed by other celebrated schools established at Nehardea, Perozsabur, Mahôzé (Seleucia), and Pumbaditha.[35] The Rabbinic Massorah flourished in these centers, if not more than in the highest schools of Galilee, at least in an equal degree with them, and the scientific investigations of Babylonian Jews contributed more to the final fixing and delimitation of the complicated Massoretic system as we have it today than the researches of any other writers. In several MSS. of the Old Testament, the work of these Israelite centers of learning is designated by the gloss *the East,* and we know that in the sacred books of the Jews, the "Babylonian punctuation" is in many cases better even than the "Tiberian punctuation."

When the 'Abbassid dynasty appeared in the East, and new caliphs settled in Baghdad, the grammatical studies of their neighbors were then at their apogee. The intestine dissensions about the caliphate having been at last cut short by the two-edged sword of Abu Muslim, a new and deeper direction of studies was given to Arabic phonetics and morphology. Two celebrated centers of Arabic studies soon flourished in southern Mesopotamia: the school of Basra and that of Kufa. We do not wish our readers to understand that we positively deny that these two schools may have existed

---

*"All countries are like a medley compared to Palestine, but the latter is a medley compared to Babylonia."

before the accession of the 'Abbassid dynasty, but it is quite certain that to assign their foundation to the time immediately following Muhammad's death, as some scholars state, and to believe that they exercised an influence as strong as that which they had, at a later time, under the eastern caliphate, would perhaps overstep the limits of safe criticism.

The first grammarian specially known for Arabic meter is Khalil ibn Ahmad (718–791 C.E.) of the school of Basra. Besides having the glory of being considered the first Arabic grammarian, he is believed to have been the inventor, in the latter half of the eighth century, of the *hamza*, a semiguttural consonant, in comparison with the weak aliph. So far as I know, no complete grammatical treatise of his is extant today. Some grammatical sketches are attributed to him by authors of a late date, but their authenticity seems to be more than doubtful.[36] The earliest Arabic grammarian whose works have come down to us is Sibawaihi[37] (753–793 C.E.), a disciple of Khalil.

The grammarians of the school of Kufa seem to have paid more attention to the spoken dialect of the Bedawin, and for this reason their attempts could not influence, at the beginning, the right reading of the Koran and could still less reach, in a later generation, a celebrity like that of the school of Basra, in spite of the illustrious Kisa'i, Ibn as-Sekkit, and Farra'.... To some extent, their task was very difficult, and to Arabize all the Semitic and Aryan dialects, spoken in the old Chaldaean lands, such as the Mandaitic[38] and the Katrian, was a harder task than many suppose.[39]

The. foundation of the Arabic vowels is based on the vowels of the Aramaeans. The names given to these vowels is an irrefragable proof of the veracity of this assertion. So the *Phath* corresponds in appellation and in sound to the Aramaic *Phátha*; the *Khaphedh* is exactly the Aramaic *Hbaṣa*. But though the Arabs imitated the Syrians in the verbal designation of the vowels, they recoiled, and very justly, from the absurd servility to Hellenism of the masters, who, after the time of Christological controversies and onwards, could not shrink from the Greek method; and placing their morphology and syntax on fresh bases, they laid the first foundation of a high philology which excites our admiration in the present day. Viewing the intimate formation of words, they divided them into biliteral, triliteral, and quadriliteral with essential letters, in such a steady method, that even the strongest philologists of the twentieth century are obliged to walk in their steps and to accept their impeccable terminology. Our thanks are due to the sagacity of scholars who in a short period of time perfected the delicate science of the deep constitution of their language.

The sagacity of the professors in the two schools of Basra and of Kufa was for a number for years challenged by a high seat of learning which the 'Abbassids established in Baghdad and which flourished greatly from the beginning of the ninth century and onwards under the control of Christian physicians. This new school acquired a decided superiority over the others, because it taught several sciences derived from Greek and Syriac books translated into Arabic by the group of Nestorian doctors of the family of Bokhtisho', Hunain and Maswai.[40] Physicians have always had a preponderating authority at the courts of Eastern monarchs, and going back into past history, we shall find one man, Gabriel the Drustbed, eclipsing the prestige of all the formidable Dyophysite community, in the palace of the Sassanid Chosroes II Parwez.[41]

The first discoverer of the Arabic vowels is unknown to history. The opinions of Arab authors, on this point, are too worthless to be quoted; the critics of our day, too, have not clearly established their position on this subject. To find a way of unravelling this tangled question, and to discern the truth among so many positively expressed opinions, is by no means an easy task. If we may advance an opinion of our own, we think that a complete and systematic treatise on these vowels was not elaborated till the latter half of the eighth century, and we believe that such an attempt could have been successfully made only under the influence of the school of Baghdad, at its very beginning. On the one hand, besides the insufficiency of the grounds for assuming an earlier date, we have not a manuscript which can be shown to be before that time, adorned with vowels; on the other hand, the dependence of these vowels on those of the Aramaeans obliges us to find a center where the culture of the Aramaic language was flourishing, and this center is the school of Baghdad, which was, as we have already stated, under the direction of Nestorian scholars, and where a treatise on Syriac grammar was written by the celebrated Hunain.

As to the forms of the Arabic script (we do not speak of the script used in the pre-Koranic inscriptions), we can reduce them to three principal divisions: the Kufi, the Naskhi, and the Kufo-Naskhi. The Kufi type is characterized by more square and more compact and united letters, and generally by thicker and bigger strokes of the pen. The Naskhi has smaller, thinner and less compact strokes, and resembles more than other types the writing used, in our days, in printed books. The Kufo-Naskhi is intermediate between these two scripts.[42] It is often very difficult to know, with certitude, the age of a manuscript only by its being written in one of these three types, since we find many documents written in one of them and belonging to the same period. For instance in the *The Palaeographical Society*,[43] we meet with manuscripts written in these three scripts and dating from the eighth century. Therefore, it is very often by the specific characters used in each of these three types, and especially by a more or less use of diacritical points, that we are guided when we ascribe a manuscript to a given epoch.[44]

For the diacritical points which distinguish the sound of many Arabic letters one from another, it is very puzzling to find a general and infallible criterion. Since many consonants, like the صـ and the سـ which are distinguished today only by the dot on the letter, were generally distinguished in the early time by a somewhat different stroke of the pen, it may be supposed that the diacritical point has been invented at a late date; but can we assert the same for the case of the ـنـ and the ـثـ ? The question thus becomes quite different, especially when these letters are followed or preceded, in the middle of the word, by a ىـ and a ں which have almost the same form even in the most ancient MSS. that we possess; ex. gr. in how many different ways can the following word be read without diacritical points: اسـب ?

After this elementary dissertation, it becomes clear that a manuscript, and especially a manuscript of the Koran, is sometimes to be considered more or less ancient according to the want or the existence of vowels, and according to the greater or less employment of diacritical points in its text, except perhaps in the case of letters which have exactly the same form, such as ـنـ and ـثـ .

5.

The Transmission of the Koran

Alphonse Mingana

*n*OT MANY SACRED BOOKS are better known than the Koran, and only a few of them have more obscure origins. The outcome of early Koranic researches was summarized in Hammer's well-known verdict: "We hold the Kur'an to be as truly Muhammad's word as the Muhammadans hold it to be the word of God." This, however, has not been found in the last few years to be irrefragable. Scholars who like Nöldeke had believed that the Koran was wholly authentic, without any interpolation —"Keine Fälschung; der Korân enthält nur echte Stücke"[1]—were obliged to revise their opinion and admit without restriction the possibility of interpolations ("Ich stimme aber mit Fischer darin Überein, dass die Möglichkeit von Interpolationen in Qoran unbedingt zugegeben werden muss").[2]

In England, where the views of Nöldeke had gathered considerable weight, no serious attempt was made for some years to study the subject afresh. It is, therefore, with warm welcome that one receives original and well considered opinions such as those found in Hirschfeld's "New Researches," in St. Clair-Tisdall's *Original Sources,* and in D. S. Margoliouth's masterly publications.[3] The first writer has suggested that the four verses

Originally published in *The Journal of the Manchester Egyptian and Oriental Society* (1916) and subsequently reprinted in *The Muslim World* 7 (1917): 223–32; 402–14.

in which the name "Muhammad" occurs were spurious.[4] In the same sense many good works have lately appeared in France, the gist of which is embodied in Lammens's studies in the series *Scripta Pontificii Instituti Biblici*, and in the interesting book of Casanova who has demonstrated convincingly the existence of many interpolated passages.[5]

We do not intend to offer in the present essay an exhaustive investigation of the sacred book of Islam, nor to dilate on minutiae regarding a given verse in particular; we propose to write on something more essential and more general, on the all-important question of how the book called the Koran, which most of us read in a more scientific and comparative way than a Zamakhshari or a Baidawi ever knew, has come to be fixed in the form in which we read it in our days.

ACCORDING TO MUSLIM WRITERS

The first historical data about the collection of the Koran have come down to us by the way of oral Hadith, and not of history. This is very unfortunate; because a critic is thrown into that medley and compact body of legends, true or false, genuine or spurious, which began to receive unchallenged credit at the time of the recrudescence of Islamic orthodoxy which gave birth to the intolerant Caliph Mutawakkil (847–861 C.E.). The reader is thus astonished to find that the earliest record about the compilation of the Koran is transmitted by Ibn Sa'd (844 C.E.) and by the traditionists Bukhari (870 C.E.) and Muslim (874 C.E.). Before their time nothing is known with certainty, not even with tolerable probability, and the imposing enumeration of early commentators dwindles in face of the fact that two-thirds of their authority and at least one-third of their historicity are thrust back into the mist of the prehistoric; at the most they could have been some of those oral *Qurra's* of whom L. Caetani has spoken in his "Annali dell' Islam."[6]

The most ancient writer, Ibn Sa'ad, has devoted in his *tabakat*[7] a long chapter to an account of those of the "Companions" who had "collected" the Koran in the time of the Prophet. He has preserved *ten* somewhat contradictory traditions, in which he enumerates ten different persons, each with a list more or less numerous of traditions in his favor;[8] these persons are: Ubai ibn Ka'b (with eleven traditions); Mu'adh (with ten traditions); Zaid ibn

Thabit (with eight traditions); Abu Zaid (with seven traditions); Abud-Darda (with six traditions); Tamimud-Dari (with three traditions); Sa'ad ibn 'Ubaid (with two traditions); 'Ubadah ibnus Samit (with two traditions); Abu Ayyub (with two traditions); 'Uthman ibn 'Affan (with two traditions).

On page 113 another curious tradition informs us that it was 'Uthman ibn 'Affan who collected the Koran *under the caliphate of 'Umar*, and, therefore, not in the time of the Prophet. Another tradition reported by the same author, already noticed by Nöldeke,[9] attributes the collection of the Koran in *suhufs* to the caliph 'Umar himself.

The second in date, but the most important, Muslim traditionist, Bukhari, has a very different account in connection with the collectors of the Koran in the time of the Prophet.[10] According to one tradition which he reports, these collectors were *four Helpers*: Ubai ibn Ka'b, Mu'adh ibn Jabal, Zaid ibn Thabit, Abu Zaid.[11] According to another tradition they were: Abud-Darda, Mu'adh ibn Jabal, Zaid ibn Thabit, Abu Zaid.

On page 392 is found the famous tradition endorsed by many historians, and recently by the present writer also,[12] on the authority of Nöldeke; it states that the Koran was collected in the time of Abu Bakr, and not in the time of the Prophet:

> We have been told by Musa b. Isma'il, who heard it from Ibrahim b. Sa'd, who heard it from ibn Shihab, who in his turn heard it from 'Ubaid b. Sabbak, who related that Zaid b. Thabit said: "At the massacre of Yamamah, Abu Bakr summoned me,[13] while 'Umar ibnul-Khattab was with him; and Abu Bakr said: 'Slaughter has waxed hot among the readers of the Koran, in the day of Yamamah, and I fear that it may again wax hot among the readers in other countries as well; and that much may be lost from the Koran. Now, therefore, I deem that thou shouldest give orders for the collection of the Koran.' I said to 'Umar, 'How doest thou something that the Apostle of God—may God pray on him and give him peace—has not done?' And 'Umar said: 'By Allah, this is good.' And 'Umar did not cease to renew it repeatedly to me, until God set my breast at ease towards it, and I considered it as 'Umar had considered it." Zaid added and said: "Abu Bakr then said 'Thou art a young man and wise, against whom no man can cast an imputation, and thou wast writing down the Revelation for the Apostle of God—may God pray on him and give him peace—search out then the Koran and collect it.' By Allah, if I were ordered to transfer a mountain it would not have been more difficult for me than this order to collect the Koran; and I said: 'How canst

thou do something that the Apostle of God—may God pray on him and give him peace—has not done'; and (Abu Bakr) said: 'By Allah, this is good'; and he did not cease to renew it repeatedly to me, until God set my heart at ease towards it, as He has done for 'Umar and Abu Bakr—may God be pleased with both of them—and I sought out the Koran, collecting it from palm-branches, white-stones, and breasts of men.... And the *suhufs* (rolls) were with Abu Bakr until God took him to Himself, then with 'Umar, in all his life-time, then with Hafsah, the daughter of 'Umar—may God be pleased with him."[14]

This tradition proves that the Koran was all collected (*a*) under the caliphate of Abu Bakr, and (*b*) exclusively by Zaid ibn Thabit.

The tradition is immediately followed by another which runs thus:

We have been told by Musa b. Isma'il, who took it from Ibrahim, who said that he had been told by Ibn Shihab, who said that Anas b. Malik told him as follows: "Hudaifah b. Yaman went to 'Uthman, and he had fought with the inhabitants of Syria for the conquest of Armenia and had fought in Adhurbaijan with the inhabitants of Iraq; and because their divergencies in the recital of the Koran had terrified him, Hudaifah said to 'Uthman, 'O, Commander of the Faithful, overtake this nation before they have discrepancies about the Book as the Jews and the Christians have.' 'Uthman, therefore, sent to Hafsah saying: 'Send us the *suhufs* in order that we may transcribe them in the *masahifs*, and then we will send them back to thee.' And Hafsah sent them to 'Uthman, who ordered Zaid ibn Thabit, and 'Abdallah b. Zubair, and Sa'id b. 'As, and 'Abdur-Rahman b. Harith b. Hisham, to transcribe them in the *masahifs*. And 'Uthman said to the company of the three Quraishites: 'If there is divergence between you and Zaid b. Thabit about anything from the Koran, write it down in the dialect of the Quraishs, because it has been revealed in their dialect';[15] and they did it, and when they transcribed the *suhufs* in the *masahifs*, 'Uthman gave back the *suhufs* to Hafsah, and sent to every country a *mishaf* of what they had transcribed, and ordered that everything else from the Koran (found) in (the form of) *Sahifah* or *mishaf* should be burnt."[16]

This is the oral record which, appearing 238 years after the Prophet's death, was accepted as true and authentic, to the exclusion of any other, by the most eminent Orientalists of the last century, led by Nöldeke. Why we should prefer these two traditions to the great number of the above traditions sanctioned by Ibn Sa'd, an author anterior by twenty-six years to Bukhari, and by Bukhari himself, I do not know. Professor Casanova remarks: "Quant à admettre une seule des traditions comme vraie au détriment de l'autre, c'est ce qui me paraît impossible sans tomber dans l'arbitraire."[17] Nöldeke, however, believes that Bukhari is right and Ibn Sa'd wrong, because if the Koran was collected in the time of the Prophet, why should people have taken such trouble to collect it after his death? ("Wenn sie aber den ganzen Qorân gesammelt hatten, warum bedurfte es denn später so grosser Mühe, denselben zusammenzubringen?").[18] But the question is, Why should we prefer at all the story of Bukhari to that of Ibn Sa'd who is at least credited with priority of time? What should we do then with the other two traditions of Bukhari which are in harmony with Ibn Sa'd in assigning the collection of the Koran to the lifetime of the Prophet? What, too, should we make of the tradition reported by Ibn Sa'd to the effect that the Koran was collected by 'Uthman b. 'Affan alone, under the caliphate of 'Umar? What, finally, should we say about the numerous persons who in the traditions reported above alternate so confusedly in this "collection"? Which of them has effectively collected and which of them has not?

In examining carefully all these oral traditions coming into play more than 230 years after the events, at the time of those numerous polemics in which the Muslim writers were obliged to use the same weapons as those handled by the *People of the Book*, we are tempted to say that the same credence ought to be attributed to them as that which has long ago been attributed to the other *isnadic* lucubrations of which only those who read the detailed oral compilations of Bukhari and his imitators have a true idea. "La (critique) a mis en pleine lumière la faible valeur documentaire, sinon de la primitive littérature islamique, du moins du riche développement ultérieur, représenté notamment par le recueil de Bokhari."[19] Another authorized writer[20] has justly pointed out: "Les détails qui entourent cette figure principale (de Muhammad) sont vraiment bien estompés et finissent même par s'effacer dans la brume de l'incertitude." Not many years ago similar honours of genuineness were conferred upon the imposing list of the so-called "early Arabian poems," but the last nail for the coffin of the majority of them has lately been provided by Professor D. S. Margoliouth;[21] and it is to be hoped that, until fuller light dawns, they will never rise again.

We quote, with some reserve, the ironical phrases of an able French scholar: "Nous l' avons noté précédemment: à côté des poètes, nous possédons la *Sira*, les *Maghazi*, les *Sahih*, les *Mosnad*, les *Sonan*, bibliothèque historique unique en son genre, comme étendue et variété. A leur témoignage concordant qui oserait dénier toute valeur?"[22]

We can dispense with traditional compilers of a later date who throw more confusion than light on the theme, and who for the most part only quote their masters Bukhari, Muslim, and Tirmidhi; Nöldeke has already referred to the majority of them,[23] and the critic who has time to spare, can easily examine them in his book. We must mention, however, the account of the author of the *Fihrist* who, although writing several years after the above traditionists, is nevertheless credited with a considerable amount of encyclopaedic learning which many a writer could not possess in his time. After giving the tradition of Bukhari which we have translated, he devotes a special paragraph to the "Collectors of the Koran in the time of the Prophet,"[24] and then proceeds to name them without any *isnad*. They are according to him:—'Ali b. Abi Talib, Sa'd b. 'Ubaid, Abud-Darda, Mu'adh b. Jabal, Abu Zaid, Ubai ibn Ka'b, 'Ubaid b. Mu'awiah. These names occur in the list of Ibn Sa'd and that of Bukhari combined; but the *Fihrist* adds two new factors: 'Ali b. Abi Talib, and 'Ubaid b. Mu'awiah.

The historian Tabari has another account:[25] " 'Ali b. Abi Talib, and 'Uthman b. 'Affan wrote the *Revelation* to the Prophet; but in their absence it was Ubai b. Ka'b and Zaid b. Thabit who wrote it. "He informs us, too, that people said to 'Uthman: "The Koran was in many books, and thou discreditedst them all but one";[26] and after the Prophet's death, "People gave him as successor Abu Bakr, who in his turn was succeeded by 'Umar; and both of them acted according to the Book and the Sunnah of the Apostle of God—and praise be to God the Lord of the worlds; then people elected 'Uthman b. 'Affan who ... tore up the Book."[27]

A more ancient historian, Wakidi,[28] has the following sentence in which it is suggested that 'Abdallah b. Sa'd, b. Abi Sarh, and a Christian slave, ibn Qumta, had something to do with the Koran. And ibn Abi Sarh came back and said to Quraish: "It was only a Christian slave who was teaching him (Muhammad); I used to write to him and change whatever I wanted." And the pseudo-Wakidi (printed by Nassau Lees[29]) brings forward a certain Sharahbil b. Hasanah as the amanuensis of the Prophet.

A second series of traditions attributes a kind of collection (*Jam'*) of the Koran to the Umayyad caliph 'Abdul-Malik b. Marwan (684–704 C.E.) and to his famous lieutenant Hajjaj b. Yūsuf. Barhebraeus,[30] has preserved the interesting and important tradition: " 'Abdul-Malik b. Marwan used to say, 'I fear death in the month of Ramadan—in it I was born, in it I was weaned, in it *I have collected the Koran* (*Jama'tul-Qur'ana*), and in it I was elected Caliph.'" This is also reported by Jalalud-Din as-Suyuti,[31] as derived from Tha'alibi.

Ibn Dukmak, in his *Description of Egypt*,[32] and Makrizi in his *Khitat*[33] say about the Koran of Asma: "The reason why this Koran was written is that Hajjaj b. Yusuf Thakafi wrote Korans and sent them to the head-provinces. One of them was sent to Egypt. 'Abdul-'Aziz b. Marwan, who was then governor of Egypt in the name of his brother 'Abdul-Malik, was irritated and said: 'How could he send a Koran to a district of which I am the chief?'" Ibnul-Athir[34] relates that al-Hajjaj proscribed the Koran according to the reading of Ibn Mas'ud. Ibn Khallikan[35] reports that owing to some orthographical difficulties such various readings had crept into the recitation of the Koran in the time of al-Hajjaj that he was obliged to ask some writers to put an end to them, but without success, because the only way to recite rightly the Koran was to learn it orally from teachers, each word in its right place.

At the end of this first part of our inquiry, it is well to state that not a single trace of the work of the above collectors has come down to posterity, except in the case of Ubai ibn Ka'b and Ibn Mas'ud. The *Kashshaf* of Zamakhshari and in a lesser degree the *Anwarut-Tanzil* of Baidawi record many Koranic variants derived from the scraps of the Koran edited by the above named companions of the Prophet. The fact is known to all Arabists and does not need explanation.[36] We need only translate a typical passage from the newly published *Dictionary of Learned Men* of Yakut:[37]

Isma'il b. 'Ali al-Khatbi has recorded in the "Book of History" and said: "The story of a man called b. Shanbudh became famous in Baghdad; he used to read and to teach the reading (of the Koran) with letters in which he contradicted the *mishaf*; he read according to 'Abdallah b. Mas'ud and Ubai b. Ka'b and others; and used the readings employed before the *mishaf* was collected by 'Uthman b. 'Affan, and followed anomalies; he read and proved them in discussions, until his affair became important and ominous; people did not tolerate him anymore, and the Sultan sent emissaries to seize him, in the year 828; he was brought to the house of the vizier Muhammad b. Muklah who summoned judges, lawyers, and Readers of the Koran. The vizier charged him in his presence with what he had done, and he did not desist from it, but corroborated it; the vizier then tried to make him discredit it, and cease to read with these disgraceful anomalies, which were an addition to the *mishaf* of 'Uthman, but

he refused. Those who were present disapproved of this and hinted that
he should be punished in such a way as to compel him to desist. (The
vizier) then ordered that he should be stripped of his clothes and struck
with a staff on his back. He received about ten hard strokes, and could
not endure any more; he cried out for mercy, and agreed to yield and
repent. He was then released and given his clothes…and Sheikh Abu
Muhammad Yusuf b. Sairafi told me that he (b. Shanbudh) had recorded
many readings."

A study of Shi'ah books reveals also some variants derived from the
recension of 'Ali's disciples. They will be discussed in a subsequent article.

TRANSMISSION OF THE KORAN ACCORDING TO CHRISTIAN WRITERS

In considering the question of the transmission of the Koran according to
Christian writers, the reader will feel that he is more in the domain of historical facts than in that of the precarious Hadith; unfortunately, any information found in books written at the very beginning of Islam is naturally
scanty. In face of the conflagration which in a few years shook the political
foundations of the near East, Christian writers were more anxious to save
their skin from the onslaughts of the *Ishmaelites* and *Hagarians*—as they
used to call the early Arabs—than to study the kind of religion they professed. Syriac books, however, contain important data which throw great
light upon our subject, and overshadow by their antiquity the tardy
Muslim Hadith of the ninth century.

The first account is, in order of date, the colloquy or the discussion
which took place in Syria between 'Amr b. al-'As and the Monophysite
patriarch of Antioch, John I, in the eighteenth year of the Hijra (Sunday,
9 May, 639 C.E.). It has been published from a MS. in the British Museum
dated 874 C.E. by F. Nau, in the *Journal Asiatique*.[38] The patriarch was summoned before 'Amr along with five bishops and a great number of notable
Christians, and some days after the discussion, the patriarch and the
bishops wrote a careful report of what had happened, and sent it to the
Christians of Mesopotamia, asking them to "pray for the illustrious Amir,
that God might grant him wisdom and enlighten him in what is the will of
the Lord." The questions that 'Amr asked and the introductory words of
the colloquy are as follows:

...We inform your love that on the ninth of this month of May, on the holy Sunday, we went in before the glorious General Amir. The blessed Father of all was asked by the Amir whether the Gospel, which is in the hands of all who are called Christians in all the world, was one and without any difference whatever. The blessed Patriarch answered.... Then the Amir asked why if the Gospel was one, faith was different; and the Patriarch answered...

The Amir then asked, "What do you think of the Christ? Is He God or not? Our Father then answered..." And the glorious Amir asked him this question, "When the Christ, whom you call God, was in the womb of Mary, who was holding and governing heaven and earth?" Our blessed Father answered.... And the glorious Amir said, "What were the views and the belief of Abraham and Moses?" Our blessed Father answered... And the Amir said, "Why did they not write clearly and show their belief about the Christ?" and our blessed Father answered.... When the Amir heard these things, he only asked whether the Christ born of Mary was God, and whether God had a son, and whether this could be proved from the Torah and by reason. And our blessed Father said, "Not only Moses, but all the holy prophets have previously related these points of the Christ...." And the glorious Amir said that he would not accept the proof of these points by quotations from the prophets; but only required that it should be proved to him by quotations from Moses that the Christ was God. And the blessed Father among other quotations, brought forth the following from Moses, "Then the Lord from before the Lord brought down fire and brimstone upon Sodom and Gomorrah;"[39] and the glorious Amir required that this quotation should be shown to him in the Book. And our Father showed it to him without delay,[40] in the complete Greek and Syriac Books. In that assembly, some Hagarians (Muslims) were pre-sent with us, and they saw the text[41] with their own eyes, and the exis-tence of the glorious name of the Lord twice. And the Amir called a cer-tain Jew, who was believed by the Jews to be a Knower of Books, and asked him if this was literally true in the Torah; and the Jew answered, "I do not know with certainty."

Then the Amir digressed from this point and asked about the laws of the Christians, how and what they were, and if they were written in the Gospel; and asked, too, if a man dies and leaves sons or daughters, with a wife, a mother, a sister and a cousin, how would his heritage be divided between them?... A long discussion ensued; and not only the best-known men among the Hagarians (Muslims) were present there, but also the heads and the rulers of the town, and of the faithful and Christ-loving tribes: Tannukhians, Tu'ians, and 'Akulians.[42] And the glorious Amir said,

"I want you to do one of these three things: either to show me that your
laws are written in the Gospel, and that you are following them, or to
follow the laws of the Hagarians (Muslims)." And our Father answered,
"Our laws, the laws of us Christians, are just, equitable, and in harmony
with the teaching and the Commandment of the Gospel, the prescriptions
of the Apostles and the laws of the Church." It is with this that the first
gathering of that day ended, and up to now we have not been again before
the Amir.

From this important document written in the fifth year of 'Umar's
caliphate and possibly[43] some months after the terrible *year of ashes,* and of
plague,[44] we can safely infer (1) that no Bible was translated into Arabic at
that early period;[45] (2) that the teaching of the Koran on the matter of her-
itages, the denial of the divinity and the death of Christ, and on the subject of the Torah, which is given a marked predilection in Muhammad's
oracles, was familiar to the Muslims present in the discussion; (3) that no
Islamic book was mentioned when the colloquy took place; (4) that some
of the early Arab conquerors knew how to read and to write.[46]

About 647 C.E., in the first years of 'Uthman's caliphate, the famous
patriarch of Seleucia, Isho'yahb III, said in one of his letters which he
wrote when still bishop of Nineveh, "In excusing yourselves falsely, you
might perhaps say, or the Heretics might make you say, 'What has happened was due to the order given by the Arabs' (Tayyayé); but this would
not be true at all, because the Arab Hagarians (Muslims) do not help those
who attribute sufferings and death to God, the Lord of everything."[47] From
what we know of Isho'yahb, he would have surely mentioned or quoted the
Islamic book, had he known it, or even heard of it (cf., ibid., p. 251).

The anonymous writer printed by Guidi[48] knows nothing about a
sacred book of Islam in 680 C.E., at the time of the Umayyad caliphate of
Yazid, son of Mu'awiah. He believed the Arabs to be simply the descen-
dents of Ishmael, who professed the old Abrahamic faith, and gives
Muhammad as a mere general, without any religious character.

Then God raised against (the Persians) the sons of Ishmael like the sand
of the sea-shores, with their leader Muhammad.... As to the Ka'bah we
cannot know what it was, except in supposing that the blessed Abraham
having become very rich in possessions, and wanting to avoid the envy of
the Canaanites, chose to dwell in the distant and large localities of the
desert; and as he was living under tents, built that place for the worship

of God and the offering of sacrifices; for this reason, this place received its title of our days, and the memory of the place was transmitted from generation to generation with the evolution of the Arab race. It was not, therefore, new for the Arabs to worship in that place, but their worship therein was from the beginning of their days; in this, they were rendering honour to the father of the head of their race ... and Madinah was called after Madian, the fourth son of Abraham from Keturah; the town is also called Yathrib.

John Bar Penkayé[49] has some interesting records in his chronicle about the early Arab conquests and the famous *Shurat* of whose exploits he was an eyewitness, but he does not know that these Arabs had any sacred book in 690 C.E., when he was writing, under the caliphate of 'Abdul-Malik.

The Arabs, as I have said above, had a certain order from the one who was their leader, in favour of the Christian people and the monks; they held also, under his leadership, the worship of one God, according to the customs of the Old Covenant; at the outset they were so attached to the tradition of Muhammad who was their teacher, that they inflicted the pain of death upon any one who seemed to contradict his tradition.[50] ... Among them there were many Christians, some from the Heretics,[51] and some from us.[52]

From these quotations and from many passages of some contemporary writers, it is evident that the Christian historians of the whole of the seventh century had no idea that the "Hagarian" conquerors had any sacred book; similar is the case among historians and theologians of the beginning of the eighth century. It is only towards the end of the first quarter of this century that the Koran became the theme of conversation in Nestorian, Jacobite, and Melchite ecclesiastical circles. The Christians, in spite of the intolerant attitude of Muslim caliphs and governors, continued to write, frequently under pain of death, many polemical lucubrations in refutation of the sacred book of Islam, which met with a swarm of answers from the Muslim side. For the end of the century the reader will find good information in Steinschneider's well-known work.[53] Some years before this date two important publications, not yet edited, saw the light, *viz.*, the "Refutation of the Koran" by Abu Noh, secretary to the governor of Mosul,[54] and the "Apology of Christianity" by Timothy, Nestorian patriarch of Seleucia, recently made known by Braun in *Oriens Christianus*.[55]

So far as the transmission of the Koran is concerned, by far the most important work is the apology of al-Kindi, critically studied in 1887 by W. Muir.[56]

Casanova writes: "Il faut, je crois, dans l'histoire critique du Coran, faire une place de premier ordre au Chrétien Kindite."[57] According to this Kindite, who wrote some forty years before Bukhari, the history of the Koran is, briefly, as follows:[58]

Sergius,[59] a Nestorian monk, was excommunicated for a certain offense; to expiate it he set out on a mission to Arabia; in Mecca he met Muhammad with whom he had intimate converse. At the death of the monk, two Jewish doctors, 'Abdallah and Ka'b, ingratiated themselves with Muhammad and had great influence over him. Upon the Prophet's death, and at the instigation of the Jews, 'Ali refused to swear allegiance to Abu Bakr, but when he despaired of succeeding to the caliphate, he presented himself before him, forty days (some say six months) after the Prophet's death. As he was swearing allegiance to him, he was asked, "O Father of Hasan, what hath delayed thee so long?" He answered, "I was busy collecting the Book of the Lord, for that the Prophet committed to my care." The men present about Abu Bakr represented that there were scraps and pieces of the Koran with them as well as with 'Ali; and then it was agreed to collect the whole from every quarter together. So they collected various parts from the memory of individuals (as Suratul-Bara'ah, which they wrote out at the dictation of a certain Arab from the desert), and other portions from different people; besides that which was copied out from tablets of stone, and palm-leaves, and shoulder-bones, and such like. It was not at first collected in a volume, but remained in separate leaves. Then the people fell to variance in their reading; some read according to the version of 'Ali, which they follow to the present day; some read according to the collection of which we have made mention; one party read according to the text of ibn Mas'ud, and another according to that of Ubai ibn Ka'b.

When 'Uthman came to power, and people everywhere differed in their reading, 'Ali sought grounds of accusation against him, compassing his death. One man would read a verse one way, and another man another way; and there was change and interpolation, some copies having more and some less. When this was represented to 'Uthman, and the danger urged of division, strife, and apostasy, he thereupon caused to be collected together all the leaves and scraps that he could, together with the copy that was written out at the first. But they did not interfere with that which was in the hands of 'Ali, or of those who followed his reading. Ubai was dead by this time; as for ibn Mas'ud, they demanded his exemplar, but he refused to give it up. Then they commanded Zaid ibn Thabit, and with him 'Abdallah ibn 'Abbas, to revise and correct the text, eliminating all that was corrupt; they were instructed, when they differed on any reading, word, or name, to follow the dialect of the Quraish.

When the recension was completed, four exemplars were written out in large text; one was sent to Mecca, and another to Medina; the third was despatched to Syria, and is to this day at Malatya; the fourth was deposited in Kufa. People say that this last copy is still extant at Kufa, but this is not the case, for it was lost in the insurrection of Mukhtar (A.H. 67). The copy at Mecca remained there till the city was stormed by Abu Sarayah (A.H. 200); he did not carry it away; but it is supposed to have been burned in the conflagration. The Medina exemplar was lost in the reign of terror, that is, in the days of Yazid b. Mu'awiah (A.H. 60–64).

After what we have related above, 'Uthman called in all the former leaves and copies, and destroyed them, threatening those who held any portion back; and so only some scattered remains, concealed here and there, survived. Ibn Mas'ud, however, retained his exemplar in his own hands, and it was inherited by his posterity, as it is this day; and likewise the collection of 'Ali has descended in his family.[60]

Then followed the business of Hajjaj b. Yusuf, who gathered together every single copy he could lay hold of, and caused to be omitted from the text a great many passages. Among these, they say, were verses revealed concerning the House of Umayyah with names of certain persons, and concerning the House of 'Abbas also with names.[61] Six copies of the text thus revised were distributed to Egypt, Syria, Medina, Mecca, Kufa, and Basra.[62] After that he called in and destroyed all the preceding copies, even as 'Uthman had done before him. The enmity subsisting between 'Ali and Abu Bakr, 'Umar and 'Uthman is well known; now each of these entered in the text whatever favored his own claims, and left out what was otherwise. How, then, can we distinguish between the genuine and the counterfeit? And what about the losses caused by Hajjaj? The kind of faith that this tyrant held in other matters is well-known; how can we make an arbiter as to the Book of God a man who never ceased to play into the hands of the Umayyads whenever he found opportunity?

Then al-Kindi, addressing his Muslim friend, says: "All that I have said is drawn from your own authorities, and no single argument has been advanced but what is based on evidence accepted by yourselves; in proof thereof, we have the Kur'an itself, which is a confused heap, with neither system nor order."

It should be noticed here that something which might be termed an answer to al-Kindi from the Muslim side has been discovered among the Arabic manuscripts of the John Rylands Library, Manchester. In a MS., dated 616 of the Hijrah, I found the *Kitabud-Dini wad-Daulah*, "Book of Religion and Empire," written in 855 C.E., by the physician 'Ali b. Rab-banat-Tabari, at the request of the caliph Mutawakkil. It is an official apology of Islam, appearing at an interval of some twenty years after the apology of Christianity by al-Kindi. On the important point of the transmission of the Kur'an, the author is content to appeal to the piety, asceticism, and devotion of the early caliphs and disciples of the Prophet, and says, "If such people may be accused of forgery and falsehood, the disciples of the Christ might also be accused of the same." This is a meagre answer to the historical indictments of al-Kindi.

We trust that the Arabists will rightly value the outstanding importance of this new work, written before all the traditional compilations of the second half of the ninth century. So far as the religious system of Islam is concerned, it is of an unparalleled significance, containing, as it does, many traditions dealing with the Prophet, his religion and his disciples, which are not found elsewhere. I have prepared the text for the press and translated it with some critical annotations required by its antiquity and its extrinsic and intrinsic importance.[63] After a long introduction in which the author praises Islam, gives good advice to be followed in discussions, and shows the laudable zeal of the caliph Mutawakkil in the propagation and vindication of his faith, he sets forth the reasons why people of the tolerated cults do not embrace Islam and why they should embrace it, and because the greater number of the non-Muslim population were Christian, he addresses the Christians more frequently; in the second rank come Jews, Magians, Hindus, and Dualists, who, however, are attacked more sharply. The order of the chapters is as follows:

(*a*) Different forms of historical facts and common agreement. (*b*) Criteria for the verification of historical facts. (*c*) The Prophet called to the unity of God and to what all the prophets have believed. (*d*) Merits of the ways of acting and the prescriptions of the Prophet. (*e*) Miracles of the Prophet which the "People of the Book" have rejected. (*f*) The Prophet foretold events hidden from him, which were realized in his lifetime. (*g*) Prophecies of the Prophet, which were realized after his death. (*h*) The

Prophet was an unlettered man, and the book which God revealed to him is, therefore, a sign of prophetic office. (*i*) The victory won by the Prophet is a sign of prophetic office. (*j*) The disciples of the Prophet and the eye-witnesses of his career were most honest and pious: (1) asceticism of Abu Bakr; (2) asceticism of 'Umar; (3) asceticism of 'Ali; (4) asceticism of 'Umar b. 'Abdul-Aziz, of 'Abdallah b. 'Umar b. Khattab, and of some other pious Muslims. (*k*) If the Prophet had not appeared the prophecies of the prophets about him and about Ishmael would have been without object. (*l*) Prophecies of the prophets about him: Moses, David, Isaiah, Hosea, Micah, Habakkuk, Zephaniah, Zechariah, Jeremiah, Ezekiel, Daniel, Christ and His disciples. (*m*) Answer to those who have blamed the pre-scriptions of Islam. (*n*) Answer to those who are shocked that the Prophet should have innovated and changed some prescriptions of the Torah and the Gospel. (*o*) Answer to those who pretend that no one but the Christ has mentioned the Resurrection. (*p*) Conclusion.

In his biblical quotations, the author refers to the version of a certain "Marcus the Interpreter," of which we are still unable to find any trace in any other book, either Syriac or Arabic.

Apart from the question of an official edition of the Koran being unknown to Christian writers till the second half of the eighth century, the idea gathered from the ancient Christian compositions is in complete agreement with "the theory that Islam is primarily a political adventure;"[64] and as in the Semitic mind political adventures cannot succeed without some "persuasions" to heaven, and "dissuasions" from hell, it is the merit of the first caliphs to have so skilfully handled, after their master and in imitation of "the people of the Book," the spiritual instrument which was easy and handy and which brought them such wonderful results. (Ist der Islam) "Keineswegs als ein Religionssystem ins Leben getreten, sondern als ein Versuch sozialistischer Art, gewissen überhandnehmenden irdischen Miss-ständen entgegenzutreten."[65]

CONCLUSION

From all the above facts and documents, any impartial critic, interested in the Koranic literature of the Muslim world, can draw his own conclusions. If we may express our opinion, we would be tempted to say:

(1) If all signs do not mislead us, very few oracular sentences, if any,

were written in the time of the Prophet. The kind of life that he led, and
the rudimentary character of reading and writing in that part of the world
in which he appeared, are sufficient witnesses in favor of this view. Our
ignorance of the Arabic language in that early period of its evolution is
such that we cannot even know with certainty whether it had any writing
of its own in Mecca and Medina. If a kind of writing existed in these two
localities, it must have been something very similar to the Estrangelo or the
Hebraic characters. Ibn Khaldun[66] informs us that the people of Taif and
Quraish learnt the "art of writing" from the Christians of the town of
Hirah, and the first Quraishite who learned it was Sufyan b. Umayyah.[67]
Further, Hirschfeld[68] has already noted that "The Qoran, the text-book of
Islam, is in reality nothing but a counterfeit of the Bible"; this verdict
applies in a more accentuated manner to the compilation of the Koran. No
disciple of Moses or of Christ wrote the respective oracles of these two
religious leaders in their lifetime, and probably no such disciple did so in
the case of the Prophet. A man did not become an acknowledged prophet
in a short time; years elapsed before his teaching was considered worth
preserving on parchment. Lammens[69] has observed, "Le Prophète s'était
fait intimer par Allah (Qoran, lxxv. 16–17) l'ordre de ne pas se presser pour
éditer le Qoran, comme recueil séparé. La précaution était prudente, étant
donné le caractère inconsistant de certaines révélations."

   (2) Some years after the Prophet's death many of his companions,
seeing that his cause was really flourishing and gathering considerable
momentum by means of able generals, vied in writing down, each one in
his own sphere, the oracles of their master. This work gave them prestige,
and sometimes high posts which they could scarcely have obtained otherwise; in this series is to be included the compilation of Ubai b. Ka'b, Ibn
Mas'ud, 'Uthman b. 'Affan, and probably 'Ali b. Abi Talib. When 'Uthman
obtained the caliphate, his version was naturally given a royal sanction, to
the detriment of the three other recensions. The story of the Quraishite
scribes who were told by 'Uthman to write down the Revelation in the
dialect of Quraish, ought to be discarded as half legendary. We all know
how ill adapted was the Arabic writing even of the eighth century to
express all the phonetic niceties of the new philological schools; it is
highly improbable, therefore, that it could express them in the first years
of the Hijrah. Moreover, a very legitimate doubt can be entertained about
the literary proficiency of all the collectors mentioned in the tardy Hadith
of the ninth century. Most of them were more tribal chieftains than men

of literature, and probably very few of them could even read or write; for this reason the greater part of their work must have been accomplished by some skilled Christian or Jewish amanuensis, converted to Islam.

(3) This last work of Companions and Helpers does not seem to have been put into book form by 'Uthman, but was written on rolls of parchment, on *suhufs,* and it remained in that state till the time of 'Abdul-Malik and Hajjaj ibn Yusuf. At this time, being more familiar with writing by their intercourse with the Jews and Christians of the enlightened capital of Syria, and feeling more acutely the necessity of competing on even terms with them, the caliph and his powerful lieutenant gave to those rolls the character and the continuity of a book, and very possibly, added new material from some oral reciters of the Prophet's oracular sentences. At any rate, the incident of both Hajjaj and 'Uthman writing copies of the Koran and sending them to the head-provinces is very curious. We will conclude the first chapter of this enquiry with the following sentences by Professor Casanova[70] to which we fully adhere:

Mais les fragments d'os, de palmier, etc., sur lesquels étaient écrits, de la main des secrétaires, les versets dictés par le Prophète, et qui avaient servi à la première recension, sous Aboû Bakr, que sont-ils devenus? Je me refuse à croire qu'ils auraient été détruits. Quel extraordinaire sacrilège! Comment aurait-on pu traiter ainsi ces témoins les plus directs de la révélation. Enfin s'ils avaient existé, comment expliquer la crainte que 'Oumar et Aboû Bakr témoignèrent de voir le Coran disparaître par la mort des récitateurs? S'ils n'avaient pas existé, tous les passages si nombreux où le Coran est désigné (par le mot *Kitab*) auraient été introduits après coup! Voilà bien des contradictions inhérentes au récit traditionnel, et toutes se résolvent par la conclusion que j'adopte: Le Coran a été mis, par écrit, pour la première fois par les soins d'al Hajjaj qui probablement s'appuyait sur la légende d'un prototype dû à 'Outhmân. Il est possible qu'il y ait eu des transcriptions antérieures, mais sans caractère officiel, et par conséquent sans unité. [See note 70 for translation]

6.

Materials for the History
of the Text of the Koran

Arthur Jeffery

CRITICAL INVESTIGATION OF THE TEXT of the Koran is a study which is still in its infancy. Within the fold of Islam it seems never to have attracted much attention. The growth of the *Qurra'* is evidence that there was some interest in the question in the early days of Islam[1] but with the fixing of the text *ne varietur* by the Wazirs Ibn Muqla and Ibn 'Isa in 322 A.H. at the insistence and with the help of the savant Ibn Mujahid (d. 324)[2], and the examples made of Ibn Miqsam (d. 362) and the unfortunate Ibn Shanabudh (d. 328) who persisted in making use of the old readings after this fixing of the text[3], such interest as there was seems to have come to an end. Variant readings within the limits of the seven systems[4] that were admitted as canonical by the decision of Ibn Mujahid naturally continued to be studied by a limited group of scholars, and the readings of the other uncanonical Readers occasionally received attention, more particularly the systems of the Ten[5] and the Fourteen[6], who were nearest to canonical position, though at times others also were included[7]. No definite attempt, however, was made to construct any type of critical text of the Koran[8], and for the most part textual studies were confined to questions of orthography

Originally published as the Introduction (pp. 1–18) and pp. 20–24, 114–16, 182–84 of *Materials for the History of the Text of the Qur'ān: The Old Codices,* edited by Arthur Jeffery (Leiden: E. J. Brill, 1937).

(*rasm*) and pause (*waqf*). Thus the older variants, even though they were known to be represented in some of the older codices, for the most part survived only in the works of two classes of savants, firstly certain exegetes who were interested in the theological implications of such variants, and secondly the philologers who quoted them as grammatical or lexical examples. It is thus that in the Koran commentaries of az-Zamakhshari (d. 538),[9] of Abu Hayyan of Andalus (d. 745),[10] and the more recent Yemenite writer ash-Shawkani (d. 1250)[11] who seems to have used some good old sources no longer available to Western scholars, we find recorded a goodly number of old variants representing a different type of consonantal text from that officially known as the 'Uthmanic text, and in the philological works of such writers as al-'Ukbari (d. 616)—the blind philologer of Baghdad[12], Ibn Khalawaih (d. 370)[13]—the savant of the Hamdanid Court of Saif ad-Dawla at Aleppo, and the even more famous Ibn Jinni (d. 392),[14] a not inconsiderable amount of such material has been preserved, which in some cases, indeed, proves to be one source from which it came to the exegetes.

To apply this material to a critical investigation of the text of the Koran seems never to have occupied the attention of any Muslim writer. In the *Itqan*[15], as-Suyuti's great compendium of Muslim Koranic science, we have recorded a great deal that concerns matters of the Muslim Massora, matters of considerable interest for the history of the exegesis of the Koran, but very little that bears on the investigation of the text.

Nor has the subject attracted much attention in the West. Nöldeke opened it up in 1860 in the first edition of his *Geschichte des Qorans*, and Goldziher drew attention to its importance in the first lecture of his *Richtungen*,[16] but it received no systematic treatment until Bergsträsser undertook his *Geschichte des Qorantexts*[17] as the third part of the revised edition of Nöldeke's work, and with characteristic thoroughness began to work down to bedrock on the subject. It is an extraordinary thing that we still have no critical text of the Koran for common use. Flügel's edition which has been so widely used and so often reprinted, is really a very poor text, for it neither represents any one pure type of Oriental text tradition, nor is the eclectic text he prints formed on any ascertainable scientific basis. Some of the Kazan lithographs[18] make an attempt at giving the seven canonical systems on the margin, but only very incompletely. The same is true of the curious Teheran lithograph of 1323, which prints parts of the text in Kufic script (with interlinear naskhi) and parts in ordinary script, with a selection of the seven on the margins. The best text so far available is the

Egyptian standard edition of 1342 (1923)[19] of which there are several later prints. This edition attempts to present a pure type of text according to one tradition of the Kufan school as represented by Hafs 'an 'Asim, though unfortunately some corruptions have crept in owing to the use by its editors of younger authorities on the Kufan tradition instead of going back to older and better sources.[20]

The orthodox Muslim theory of the text is well known. According to this theory the Prophet arranged to have the revelations written down immediately they were revealed and used to collate once every year with the Angel Gabriel the material that had thus far been revealed. In the last year of his life they so collated it twice[21]. When the Prophet died the text of the Koran was thus already fixed, and all the material gathered in an orderly fashion though it had not yet been written out, at least not in book form. Under the caliphate of Abu Bakr took place the writing of it out in a first official recension. Later, in the caliphate of 'Uthman it was discovered that all sorts of dialectal peculiarities had crept into the recitation of the text, so 'Uthman formed a committee, borrowed from Hafsa the copy made by Abu Bakr, and on its basis had a standard codex written out in the pure dialect of Quraish. Copies of this were made and sent to the chief centers of the Muslim empire where they became metropolitan codices, and all other codices that had been formed were ordered to be burned. This was the second recension and all modern editions produced in the East are supposed to be exact reproductions of the text (though not of the form) of this 'Uthmanic recension.[22]

Very little examination is needed to reveal the fact that this account is largely fictitious. Nothing is more certain than that when the Prophet died there was no collected, arranged, collated body of revelations. Recent research by Dr. Bell of Edinburgh and Prof. Torrey of Yale has suggested that there is internal evidence in the Koran itself that the Prophet kept in his own care a considerable mass of revelation material belonging to various periods of his activity, some of it in revised and some of it in unrevised form, and that this material was to form the basis of the *Kitab* he wished to give his community before he died. Death, however, overtook him before anything was done about the matter. If this is so we are at a loss to know what became of this material, which obviously would have been the community's most precious legacy.[23] The earliest strata of tradition available to us make it quite certain that there was no Koran left ready as a heritage for the community. The Prophet had proclaimed his messages orally, and, except in the latter period of his ministry, whether they were recorded or not was often a matter of chance. Some pieces of revelation material seem to have been used liturgically and so probably would have been written. Some pieces he himself caused to be written down in permanent form as they were of a definite legislative character.[24] Besides these there were numerous portions, generally small pieces, though sometimes pieces of considerable extent, that were in the possession of different members of the community, either memorized or written down on scraps of writing material that happened to be handy. Certain individuals among the early Muslims, perhaps even a little before the Prophet's death, had specialized in collecting or memorizing this revelation material. They and their successors became known as the *Qurra'*—the Reciters, later the Readers, who constituted as it were the depository of revelation. Tradition says that it was the slaughter of a great number of these at the Battle of Yamama in 12 A.H. that caused interest to be aroused in getting all the revelation material set down in permanent written form, lest with the passing away of the *Qurra'* much of it should be lost.[25]

That Abu Bakr was one of those who collected revelation material was doubtless true. He may possibly have inherited material that the Prophet had stored away in preparation for the *Kitab*. That he ever made an official recension as the orthodox theory demands is exceedingly doubtful. His collection would have been a purely private affair, just as quite a number of other Companions of the Prophet had made personal collections as private affairs. It was after the death of the Prophet that these collections became important. We have well-known stories of how 'Ali, Salim, Abu Musa and others had collections, and there are traditions which give lists of those who had commenced making collections or memorizing during the lifetime of the Prophet. As no two of these lists agree with one another to any great extent one is driven to conclude that while it was known that such collections were made there was no accurate information, save with regard to a few names, as to who made them.[26] Orthodox theory, even to the present day, has insisted that the word *jama'a* "to collect" used in these traditions means nothing more than "to memorize" and so does not imply that the collection was made in written form. As, however, 'Ali brought along what he had collected on the back of his camel, as some of the collections had come to have independent names, and as 'Uthman, after sending out his official copies to the metropolitan cities, had to order all other copies to be burned, there cannot be the slightest doubt that there were written collections.

What we find in early Islam, as a matter of fact, is only what we might have expected to find. Different members of the community who were interested began to collect in written form so much as they could gather of the revelation material that had been proclaimed by the Prophet. Later, with the gradual expansion of the Muslim empire, some of these collections began to acquire notoriety as they came to be in some sort authoritative in different centers. Naturally it would be those collections that could claim some completeness that would attain to this position of eminence. Thus we read that the people of Homs and Damascus followed the codex of Miqdad b. al-Aswad[27], the Kufans that of Ibn Mas'ud, the Basrans that of Abu Musa al-Ash'ari, and the Syrians in general that of Ubai' b. Ka'b (Ibn al-Athir, *Kamil*, III, 86). Here we have the beginning of metropolitan codices, each great center following that collection, or perhaps we may say that type of text, which had local fame.

Now when we come to the accounts of 'Uthman's recension, it quickly becomes clear that his work was no mere matter of removing dialectal peculiarities in reading, but was a necessary stroke of policy to establish a standard text for the whole empire. Apparently there were wide divergences between the collections that had been digested into codices in the great metropolitan centers of Medina, Mecca, Basra, Kufa and Damascus, and for political reasons if for no other it was imperative to have one standard codex accepted all over the empire. 'Uthman's solution was to canonize the Medinan codex[28] and order all others to be destroyed. It is very significant that the *Qurra'* were violently opposed to 'Uthman because of this act,[29] and there is evidence that for quite a while the Muslims in Kufa were divided into two factions, those who accepted the 'Uthmanic text, and those who stood by Ibn Mas'ud, who had refused to give up his codex to be burned.[30]

There can be little doubt that the text canonized by 'Uthman was only one among several types of text in existence at the time.[31] To canonize the Medinan text was doubtless the natural thing to do, since in spite of the fact that Kufa early came to have the reputation of being par excellence the center of Koranic studies, the prestige of Medina, the Prophet's own city, must at that time have been enormous, and the living tradition would doubtless have been most abundant there. We may even say that a priori the Medinan text had all the chances in its favor of being the best text available. Nevertheless it is a question of the utmost importance for any study of the history of the Koranic text, whether we can glean any information as to the rival types of text that were suppressed in the interests of 'Uthman's standard edition.

In the works of the exegetes and the philologers we not infrequently come across variant readings that have been preserved from one or other of these displaced codices. Sometimes the reference is merely to a "codex of the Sahaba" or "a certain old codex" or "in certain of the codices" or "in the former text." At times it is to one of the cities—"a codex of Basra," "a codex of Homs," "a codex of Ahl al-Aliya" (Baghawi II, 52). Sometimes it is to a codex in the possession of some particular person, as "a codex belonging to al-Hajjaj" (Khal. 122; Gin. 60), or "a codex belonging to the grandfather of Malik b. Anas" (*Muqni'* 120), or a codex used by Abu Hanifa (see Massignon's *al-Hallaj*, I, 243 n. 5), or one of Hammad b. az-Zibriqan (Khal. 55; *Muzhir* II, 187). Mostly, however, the references are to the well-known old codices of Ibn Mas'ud, Ubai' b. Ka'b, etc., which were known to go back to the time before the canonization by 'Uthman of one standard type of text.

The amount of material preserved in this way is, of course, relatively small, but it is remarkable that any at all has been preserved. With the general acceptance of a standard text other types of text, even when they escaped the flames, would gradually cease being transmitted from sheer lack of interest in them. Such readings from them as would be remembered and quoted among the learned would be only the relatively few readings that had some theological or philological interest, so that the great mass of variants would early disappear. Moreover, even with regard to such variants as did survive there were definite efforts at suppression in the interests of orthodoxy. One may refer, for instance, to the case of the great Baghdad scholar Ibn Shanabudh (245–328), who was admitted to be an eminent Koranic authority, but who was forced to make public recantation of his use of readings from the old codices.

Ibn Shanabudh's was not the only case, and such treatment of famous scholars[32] was not encouraging to the study of the variants from the pre-'Uthmanic period. That orthodoxy continued to exert this same pressure against uncanonical variants is revealed to us from many hints from the period subsequent to Ibn Shanabudh. For example, Abu Hayyan, *Bahr* VII, 268, referring to a notorious textual variant, expressly says that in his work, though it is perhaps the richest in uncanonical variants that we have, he does not mention those variants where there is too wide a divergence from the standard text of 'Uthman. In other words, when we have assembled all the variants from these earlier codices that can be gleaned from the works of the exegetes and philologers, we have only such readings as were useful for purposes of *Tafsir* and were considered to be sufficiently near orthodoxy to be allowed to survive.[33]

Modern Muslim savants almost invariably set aside the variants recorded from the old codices on the ground that they are *Tafsir*, or as we should say, explanatory glosses on the 'Uthmanic text, and they roundly condemn such ancient scholars as Ibn Khalawaih and Ibn Jinni for not knowing the difference between *Qira'at* and *Tafsir*. It is clear, however, that only such *qira'at* as were of the kind that could be used for *tafsir* had any likelihood of being preserved.

THE MASAHIF BOOKS

In the fourth Islamic century there were three books written on this question of the old codices which had some influence on later studies. These were the works already mentioned of Ibn al-Anbari, Ibn Ashta, and Ibn Abi Dawud. In each case the book was entitled *Kitab al-Masahif,* and in each case the work, while dealing with the 'Uthmanic text, its collection, orthography, and the general Massoretic details with regard to it, dealt also with what was known of the old codices which it had replaced. The most famous of the three was that of Ibn al-Anbari (d. 328), a work which was doubtless composed before the canonization by Ibn Mujahid of the Seven Readers. The work is lost but from the use made of it by later writers such as-Suyuti,[34] one gathers that it contained a certain amount of *Tafsir* as well as information as to the readings from the old codices. The work of Ibn Ashta (d. 360) seems to have been of somewhat similar scope. He was a pupil of Ibn Mujahid and wrote a special work *al-Mufid* on the subject of the uncanonical variants,[35] besides this work on the codices which was also used by as-Suyuti.[36] The only work of this kind that has survived, however, is that of Ibn Abi Dawud (d. 316) which, unfortunately, seems to have been the narrowest in scope of them all.

'Abdallah b. Sulaiman b. al-Ash'ath Abu Bakr b. Abi Dawud[37] as-Sijistani was born in 230 A.H. the son of the Imam Abu Dawud whose collection ranks third among the canonical collections of Hadith. He was born in Sijistan but his father took him early on his travels and he is said to have visited Khorasan, Isfahan, Fars, Basra, Baghdad, Kufa, Medina, Mecca, Damascus, Egypt, al-Jazira and ath-Thughur. In every place where there were scholars his father set him to learn from them, so that he may be said to have been the pupil of most of the great savants of his day.[38] There is a story that when he came to Kufa he had only one dirham which he spent on thirty bushels of broad beans. Each day he ate a bushel of the beans and by the time they were finished he had mastered a thousand traditions (or some say 30,000) from the Kufan teacher Abu Saʻid al-Ashajj.

His chief fame all his lifetime was as a tradionist. There is a story that he returned to Sijistan in the days of ʻAmr b. al-Laith and some of his fellow townsmen gathered together to request him to recite to them Hadith that he had learned on his journeyings. He refused on the ground that he had no book, but they retorted, "What need has the son of Abu Dawud of books?" So he submitted with good grace and dictated a great number of traditions from memory. When he got back to Baghdad he found that the story had preceded him and the Baghdadis were saying that he had fooled the innocents of Sijistan. But when they hired scribes to go to Sijistan and bring back copies of what Ibn Abu Dawud had dictated there, they found that on comparing them with the authorities in Baghdad they could find only six mistakes in all that he had dictated from memory.

In Koranic studies he was a pupil of Abu Khallad Sulaiman b. Khallad (d. 262), Abu Zaid ʻUmar b. Shabba (d.262),Yunus b. Habib (d.267), Musa b. Hizam at-Tirmidhi (c. 260), and Yaʻqub b. Sufyan (d. 277), and was one of the teachers of Ibn Mujahid (d. 324) and an-Naqqash (d. 351). He wrote a number of works on Koranic subjects. In the *Fihrist*, pp. 232, 233 we find mentioned:

A book of *Tafsir* (see also *Fihrist* 34 [11]; Dhahabi, II, 80; al-Khatib, IX, 464).
Kitab an-Nasikh waʼl-Mansukh (see *Fihrist* 37 [25]; Dhahabi, II, 80).
Kitab Nazm al-Koran.
Kitab Fadaʼil al-Koran.
Kitab Shariʻat at-Tafsir.
Kitab Shariʻat al-Maqariʼ.

Dhahabi also mentions a book called *al-Quran*, which probably means his *Kitab al-Masahif*,[39] which is also sometimes called, though with less justice, *Kitab Ikhtilaf al-Masahif*. Al-Khatib mentions a book on *qiraʼat* which may refer to the *Masahif*-book or may be another work, for Abu ʼl-Mahasin in *an-nujum az-Zahira* (Eg. ed. III, 222) mentions him as a writer on *qiraʼat*.

There are a number of traditions going back to him that are not pleasing to orthodoxy and so there was put into circulation the legend that his father had branded him as a liar, and therefore no attention is to be paid to material that is dependent on his authority. This, of course, is tendential, and the biographers usually regard him as trustworthy, the *Mughni* even noting that his father's branding him as a liar was over something other than Hadith.[40] To the last he seems to have held the respect of his townspeople for there is a pleasing story of how when he was old and blind he used to come and sit on the mimbar while his son Abu Ma'mar would sit on the step below him with the book. From his book the son would mention the particular Hadith and then from memory the old man would go on reciting to the people.

Of his *Kitab al-Masahif* there are three manuscripts known, one in the Zahiriya Library at Damascus (*Hadith*, No. 407), one in the Egyptian State Library (*Qira'at*, No. 504), and one in my own possession. Both these latter, however, are copies of the Zahiriya MS, so that we are really dependent on the one manuscript for establishing the text.

The number of actual variants given in this text is very small and obviously represents only those that happened to be found in his particular collection of traditions; Most of the variants he notes are also to be found in other Koranic works. His chief importance is that he brings before us so many codices of which we have no mention as such in any other source at present available. The codices of Ibn Mas'ud, Ubai b. Ka'b, Hafsa, Anas and others are mentioned in numerous other sources, but though we find numerous references to *shadhdh* readings of such early authorities as 'Ubaid b. 'Umair, 'Ikrima, al-A'mash, Sa'id b. Jubair and others, we did not know of actual codices of theirs, though in some cases we strongly suspected their existence. An interpolation in the text might seem at the first glance to be seeking to avoid the implications of this fact by making Ibn Abi Dawud say that he uses the word *mushaf* (codex) in the sense of *harf* or *qira'a* (reading) so that the variants he quotes need not be regarded as coming from actual written codices. There can be little doubt, however, that when he speaks of the *mushaf* of So and So he really means a written codex. In the case of some of the codices he mentions we have, of course, ample evidence from other sources of their independent existence, and in the case of some others the nature of the variants quoted strongly suggests that they must have been derived from written codices.

There are a few other old codices mentioned in other works which are not given by Ibn Abu Dawud. Adding them to his lists in the interests of completeness we can draw up the following scheme of the old codices.

(a) Primary Codices:

Salim (d. 12)	Zaid b. Thabit (d. 48)
'Umar (d. 23)	'A'isha (d. 58)
Ubai' b. Ka'b (d. 29)	Umm Salama (d. 59)
Ibn Mas'ud (d. 33)	'Abdallah b. 'Amr (d. 65)
'Ali (d. 40)	Ibn 'Abbas (d. 68)
Abu Musa al-Ash'ari (d. 44)	Ibn az-Zubair (d. 73)
Hafsa (d. 45)	Ubaid b. 'Umair (d. 74)
	Anas b. Malik (d. 91)

(b) Secondary Codices:

'Alqama b. Qais (d. 62)
Ar-Rabi' b. Khuthaim (d. 64)
Al-Harith (b. Suwaid c. 70)
Al-Aswad (d. 74)   } All of which are based on the
Hittan (d. 73)   codex of Mas'ud.
Talha (b. Musarrif d. 17)
Al-A'mash (d. 148)
Sa'id b. Jubair (d. 94)
Mujahid (d. 10l.
'Ikrima (d. 105
'Ata' (b. Abi Rabah, d. 115)
Salih (b. Kaisan, d. 144)
Ja'far as-Sadiq (d. 148)

It is of course obvious that all the information we can gather regarding the text of these early codices is of the utmost importance for the textual criticism of the Koran. This in the absence of any direct manuscript evidence[41] gives us our sole witness to the types of text which 'Uthman's standard text superseded. It is possible, as we have already seen, that in choosing the Medinan text tradition for canonization 'Uthman chose the best of the texts available. We can never know this for certain the one way or the other unless the unexpected happens and we recover some considerable portion of one of the rival texts. A collection of the variants still surviving from the old codices is our sole means of forming any judgment as to the type of text they presented.

The question arises, of course, as to the authenticity of the readings ascribed to these old codices. In some cases it must be confessed there is a suspicion of readings later invented by the grammarians and theologians being fathered on these early authorities in order to gain the prestige of their name. This suspicion is perhaps strongest in the case of distinctively Shi'a readings that are attributed to Ibn Mas'ud, and in readings attributed to the wives of the Prophet. It is also felt in regard to some of the readings attributed to Ibn 'Abbas, who as the "Übermensch des *tafsir*" (Goldziher, *Richtungen*, 65) tended to get his authority quoted for any and every matter connected with Koranic studies. On the whole, however, one may feel confident that the majority of readings quoted from any Reader really go back to early authority.

The more difficult question is that of defective transmission. Occasionally in reading the Commentaries one finds a reading that is commonly known as coming from a certain early Reader attributed to quite another source. Where authorities can be weighed it is generally possible to decide which attribution is correct, but in cases where a variant is quoted by only one source which is otherwise known for the carelessness of its citation of authorities, one can never be sure that that particular variant is correctly attributed to the Reader given. A similar problem of accurate transmission naturally attaches to the variants themselves. Being uncanonical variants there was none of the meticulous care taken over their transmission such as we find for the canonical readings, and we not infrequently have various forms of the variant attributed to the same Reader in different sources. In such cases nothing can be done but to give them all in the hope that further information may enable us to decide between them. Some of the variants in the form in which they have survived to us seem linguistically impossible, and in certain cases this has been noted in the source which quotes the variant. The defect is doubtless due to faulty transmission, and it is possible that some scholar may even now spot where the corruption lies and restore us the original reading.

Bergsträsser in his preliminary collection of the uncanonical readings of lbn Mas'ud and Ubai'[42] made an attempt to estimate the value of these two texts as compared with the 'Uthmanic text. With the increase of material one feels less inclined to venture on such a judgment of value. It is true that in some cases the uncanonical variants from these old codices may be interpreted as improvements on the 'Uthmanic text, as e.g., *bīma* [regarding] instead of *bimithli mā* [like, as] in II, 137/131 may have been suggested by motives of piety: or expansions thereof as in II, 275/276 where the added *yaumu'l-Qiyama* [the day of resurrection] may be regarded as an explanatory inflation. In such cases the 'Uthmanic text would seem to be the more primitive text which the other types assume as their basis. But on the other hand there are equally many cases where the facts point the other way. For instance in II, 9/8 the 'Uthmanic *yakhadi'ūna* [endeavor to deceive] may be regarded as an attempt to soften the idea of deceiving Allah which is suggested by the alternative reading *yakhda'ūna* [deceive]; or *allāhi* [to God] in II, 196/192 may have been set for theological reasons instead of *lilbayti* [to the house of God] or the present form of II, 240/241 may be taken as an expansion of the simpler form given in the other codices. Bergsträsser drew attention to the number of cases where the variant in the old codices was merely a synonym for the word in the text but the cases are about evenly balanced for the simpler word being in the 'Uthmanic text or in the variant.

Remembering that we have in our hands only a very small portion of the variants from these codices, and that what we have consists in the main only of such variants as were not too unorthodox, we may take the following collections as the base for our further investigation into the earliest stage in the formation of the text of the Koran.

The material which follows is taken from the writer's collections made with a view to a critical text of the Koran. They will of course appear in their place in the apparatus criticus to that text when it appears, but the assembling of them here under the individual names was essential that scholars might be able to deal critically with the evidence of each codex as a whole. The main sources from which the variants have been drawn are:

Abu Hayyan, *Al-Bahr al-Muhitt,* 8 vols., Cairo 1328.
Alusi, *Ruh al-Ma'ani fi Tafsir al-Koran wa Sab' al-Mathani,* 30 vols., Cairo, n. d.
Baghawi, *Ma'alim at-Tanzil,* 7 vols., Cairo 1332 (On margin of the *Tafsir al-Khazin*).
Baidawi, *Anwar at-Tanzil wa Asrar at-Ta'wil,* 5 pts., Cairo 1330.
Balawi, *Kitab Alif Ba',* 2 vols., Cairo 1287.
Banna', *Ithaf Fudala' al-Bashar fi'l-Qira'at al-Arba'ata 'ashar,* Cairo 1317.
Fakhr ad Din ar-Razi, *Mafatih al-Ghaib,* 8 vols, Cairo 1327.

Farra', *Kitab Ma'ani al-Koran.* Ms. Stambul, Nuru Osmaniya 459.

Ibn al-Anbari, *Kitab al-Insaf,* ed. Gotthold Weil, Leiden 1913.

Ibn Hisham, *Mughni al-Labib,* 2 pts., Cairo 1347.

——, *Tahdhib at-Tawadih,* 2 pts., Cairo 1329.

Ibn Jinni, *Nichtkanonische Koranlesarten im Muhtasab des Ibn Ginni,* von G. Bergsträsser, Munchen 1933.

Ibn Khalawaih, *Ibn Halawaihs Sammlung nichtkanonischer Koranlesarten,* herausgegeben von G. Bergsträsser, Stambul 1934.

Ibn Manzur, *Lisan al-'Arab,* 20 vols., Cairo 1307.

Ibn Ya'ish, *Commentary to the Mufassal,* ed. Jahn, 2 vols., Leipzig 1882.

Khafaji, *'Inayat al-Qadi wa Kifayat ar-Radi,* 8 vols., Cairo 1283.

Marandi, *Qurrat 'Ain al-Qurra',* Ms. Escorial 1337.

Muttaqi al-Hindi, *Kanz al-'Ummal,* 4 vols., Hyderabad 1312.

Nasafi, *Madarik at-Tanzil wa Haqa'iq at-Ta'wil,* 4 vols., Cairo 1333.

Nisaburi, *Ghara'ib al-Koran* (on the margin of *Tafsir at-Tabari*).

Qunawi, *Hashia 'ala l-Baidawi,* 7 vols., Stambul 1285.

Qurtubi, *Al-Jami' li Ahkam al-Koran,* 2 vols. (all so far published), Cairo 1935.

Shawkani, *Fath al-Qadir,* 5 vols., Cairo 1349.

Sibawaih, *Le Livre de Sibawaih,* ed. Derenbourg, 2 vols., Paris 1889.

Suyuti, *Al-Itqan fi 'Ulum al-Koran,* ed. Sprenger, Calcutta 1857

Suyuti, *Ad-Durr al-Manthur fi 't-Tafsir al-Ma'thur,* 6 vols., Cairo 1314.

Suyuti, *Al-Muzhir,* 2 vols., Cairo 1282.

Tabari, *Jami' al-Bayan fi Tafsir al-Koran,* 30 vols., Cairo 1330.

Tabarsi, *Majma' al-Bayan fi 'Ulum al-Koran,* 2 vols., Teheran, 1304.

'Ukbari, *Imla' fi 'l-I'rab wa 'l-Qira'at fi Jami' al-Koran,* 2 pts., Cairo 1321.

'Ukbari, *I'rab al-Qira'at ash-Shadhdha,* MS Mingana Islamic Arabic 1649.

Zamakhshari, *Al-Kashshaf,* ed. Nassau Lees, Calcutta 1861.

CODEX OF IBN MAS'UD (D. 33)

'Abdallah b. Mas'ud (sometimes quoted in the sources as 'Abd Allah and sometimes as Ibn Umm 'Abd)[43] was a Companion and one of the early Muslims who could boast that he had joined the faith earlier than 'Umar. As a youth he had herded cattle for 'Uqba b. Abi Mu'ait and so was sometimes referred to contemptuously as the Hudhali slave (Tabari, *Annales,* 1, 2812). When he became a Muslim he attached himself to the Prophet and became his personal servant. He went on the Hijra to Abyssinia and also to Medina and was present at both Badr and Uhud. It was his boast that he had learned some seventy suras directly from the mouth of the Prophet, and tradition has it that he was one of the first to teach Koran reading (Ibn Saʻd, III, i, 107). He seems not to have been a great success when tried in an official capacity, but at Kufa, to which the caliph sent him, he became famous as a traditionist and as an authority on the Koran. Tradition tells that he was one of the four to whom Muhammad advised his community to turn for instruction in the Koran.[44] It was doubtless his close personal contact with the Prophet over so many years that gave such prestige to his opinions on Sunna and Koran.

We have no information as to when he began to make his codex. Apparently he began to collect material during the lifetime of the Prophet and worked it up into codex form when he was established at Kufa and was looked to as the authority on Koranic matters. At any rate we find his codex in use there and followed by the Kufans before the official recension was made by ʻUthman. When ʻUthman sent to Kufa the official copy of his standard text with orders that all other texts should be burned, Ibn Masʻud refused to give up his copy, being indignant that the text established by a young upstart like Zaid b. Thabit should be given preference to his, since he had been a Muslim while Zaid was still in the loins of an unbeliever.[45] There seems to have been considerable difference of opinion in Kufa over this question of the codex, some accepting the new text sent by ʻUthman, but a great many continuing to hold by the codex of Ibn Masʻud,[46] which by that time had come to be regarded as the Kufan text. The strength of the position of his codex in Kufa is well illustrated by the number of secondary codices of which some information has come down to us and which followed the text of Ibn Masʻud. It was from its vogue in Kufa that his codex came to be favored by Shiʻa circles, though one is not disposed to accept as genuine all the Shiʻa readings that are attributed to his codex, nor indeed those found in Sunni sources in favor of Ahl al-Bait.

It was well known in the early days of Islam that one peculiarity of Ibn Masʻud's codex was that it did not contain suras I, CXIII and CXIV, i.e. the *Fatiha*, which is an opening prayer to the book, and the *Muʻawwidhatani* with which it ends.[47] Modern scholarship on quite other grounds holds that these were not origianlly part of the Koran but are of the nature of liturgical additions. That Ibn Masʻud knew of these passages as used liturgically is evident from the fact that we have preserved to us notes of words in which he differed from the customary way of reading them.

A second peculiarity equally well known was that the order of suras in his recension differed considerably from that of ʻUthman's recension. Two lists giving this sura order have been preserved to us, which do not, however, entirely agree with one another. The earlier is that given by Ibn an-Nadim (377)[48] in the *Fihrist* p. 26 (ed. Flügel) on the authority of al-Fadl b. Shadhan (d. before 280), which runs as follows:

2, 4, 3, 7, 6, 5, 10,[49] 9, 16, 11, 12, 17, 21, 23, 26, 37, 33, 28, 24, 8, 19, 29, 30, 36, 25, 22, 13, 34, 35, 14, 47, 31, 39, (40 bis 46), 40, 43, 41, 46, 45, 44, 48, 57, 59, 32, 50, 65, 49, 67, 64, 63, 62, 61, 72, 71, 58, 60, 66, 55, 53, 51, 52,[50] 54, 69, 56, 68, 79, 70, 74, 73, 83, 80, 76, 75, 77, 78, 81, 82, 88, 87, 92, 89, 85, 84, 96, 90, 93, 94, 86, 100, 107, 101, 98, 91, 95, 104, l05, 106, 102, 97, 103, 110, 108, 109, 11l, 112.

The suras missing here are 1, 15, 18, 20, 27, 42, 99, 113, 114. That suras 1, 113, 114 were omitted in his codex we have already seen, but as variants from all the others omitted here are found quoted from him, the material of which they are composed must have been in his codex. Indeed they are all to be found in the list of his suras given in the *Itqan*. When we examine these missing suras we discover that 15 is the last in the *ALR* [*Alif, Lam, Ra*] series; 18 comes immediately before the *KHY'S* [*Kaf, Ha, Ya, Ain, Sad*] sura (19) and is suspected to have had some connection therewith (Goossens in *Der Islam* XIII, 211); 20 is the sole *ṬH* [*Ṭa, Ha*] sura; 27 is the *ṬS* [*Ṭa, Sin*] sura which breaks in between two *ṬSM* [*Ṭa, Sin, Mim*] suras; 42 is the *HM 'SK* [*Ha, Mim Ain, Sin, Kaf*] sura which breaks into the *ḤM* [*Ḥa, Mim*] suras, so that one may suspect that there is something behind their omission in the *Fihrist*. Yet in view of the fact that the missing suras are in the list in the *Itqan*, and the *Fihrist* itself expressly says that it reckoned 110 suras whereas there are only 105 in the list, the probability is that the list as we have it has been defectively written.

The second list is in the *Itqan* of as-Suyuti (ed. Calcutta, p. 151), quoting from Ibn Ashta a statement going back to Jarir b. 'Abd al-Hamid (d. 188), who related traditions from al-A'mash and others of Ibn Mas'ud's school.[51] This list runs:

2, 4, 3, 7, 6, 5, 10, 9, 16, 11, 12, 18, 17, 21, 20, 23, 26, 37, 33, 22, 28, 27, 24, 8, 19, 29, 30, 36, 25, 15, 13, 34, 35, 14, 38, 47, 31, 39, 40, 43, 41, 42, 46, 45, 44, 48, 59, 32, 65, 68, 49, 67, 64, 63, 62, 61, 72, 71, 58, 60, 66, 55, 53, 52, 51, 54, 56, 79, 70, 74, 73, 83, 80, 76, 77, 75, 78, 81, 82, 88, 87, 92, 89, 85, 84, 96, 90, 93, 86, 100, 107, 101, 98, 91, 95, 104, 105, 106, 102, 97, 99, 103, 110, 108, 109, 111, 112, 94.

Here we find missing besides the expected 1, 113, 114, the suras 50, 57, 69, for whose omission no reason can be suggested save that they may have dropped out by scribal error. Well known variants are quoted from each of them and they are all in the list in the *Fihrist*. The two lists correspond sufficiently closely for us to supply the missing members of the one from the other, and we may treat them as variants of a common tradition as to the sura order in Ibn Mas'ud's codex.

The value of this tradition is another matter.[52] It is not a priori likely that the arrangement of material in any of the rival codices would have followed the same combination into suras as in the text established for 'Uthman by Zaid b. Thabit. In the accounts of that official recension we find bits of material coming in and the committee considering the most appropriate place to put them, and it is against all probability that the composite suras made up of bits of Meccan and bits of Medinan material, of very different date and provenance, would have been fitted in exactly the same way by different collectors. Neither is it likely that the different collectors would have chosen the same titles for the suras. The traditions as to the sura order, in the case of this and of other of the old codices, come from persons who were familiar with the 'Uthmanic sura order, but knew that the material was differently disposed in the other codices, and so constructed a sura list to express the difference.[53]

The variant readings which follow are necessarily arranged according to the order of the present official text. Sometimes in the sources the variant is expressly said to come from the codex of Ibn Mas'ud. More often it is merely given as a reading (*harf* or *qira'a*) of Ibn Mas'ud. Occasionally also readings are given as coming from the Companions of Ibn Mas'ud, but as these obviously represent the tradition as to his text they are included here. In view of the great importance of the readings of Ibn Mas'ud and Ubai, all readings from them that survive are included in the lists even where they do not depend on a different consonantal text from that of 'Uthman. It has also seemed worth while to note the places where they are specially recorded as supporting the textus receptus.

CODEX OF UBAI B. KA'B (D. 29 OR 34)

Ubai b. Ka'b was one of the *Ansar* who after the Prophet's coming to Medina served as his secretary.[54] He is said to have been the one who wrote out the treaty with the people of Jerusalem (Ibn 'Asakir II, 329). He was one of those who specialized in the collection of revelation material and figures among the four to whom Muhammad is said to have advised his community to turn for Koran instruction. In some respects his authority on Koranic matters was even greater than that of Ibn Mas'ud. He was known as *Sayyid al-Qurra'* ["the Chief of the Readers of the Koran"], the Prophet is said to have referred to him as *aqra'a ummati* ["he who made the Muslim community recite"] and to have been commanded by Allah to hear Ubai recite to him portions of revelation, which probably means that Ubai was the repository of certain material of a legislative character which the Prophet would have him read over to him from time to time.

We have no knowledge of when his codex was made, but we do know that before the appearance of the 'Uthmanic standard text his codex had already come into vogue in Syria. Ibn Abi Dawud...has a story of how some Syrians made a codex and came to Medina to check it over with Ubai, and though at that time the standard text was in use, no one dared to dispute the peculiar readings that were derived from Ubai. He seems to have had an important part in the actual work of producing the canonical text for 'Uthman at Medina. His name appears in these stories in various connections but the whole account is too confused to enable us to understand precisely what his relation to the standard text was.[55]

His codex is definitely stated to have been among those destroyed by 'Uthman. Its sura order was reported to have differed from that of 'Uthman's, and as in the case of Ibn Mas'ud's codex, we have two lists of his sura order. According to the *Fihrist*, p. 27, his order was—

1, 2, 4, 3, 6, 7, 5, 10, 8, 9, 11, 19, 26, 22, 12, 18, 16, 33, 17, 39, 45, 20, 21, 24, 23, 40, 13, 28, 27, 37, 34, 38, 36, 15, 42, 30, 43, 41, 14, 35, 48, 47, 57, 58, 25, 32, 71, 46, 50, 55, 56, 72, 53, 68, 69, 59, 60, 77, 78, 76, 75, 81, 79, 80, 83, 84, 95, 96, 49, 63, 62, 65, 89, 67, 92, 82, 91, 85, 86, 87, 88, 64, 98, 61, 93, 94, 101, 102, al-Khal', al-Hafd, 104, 99, 100, 105, 107, 108, 97, 109, 110, 111, 106, 112, 113, 114.

In this list are missing suras 29, 31, 44, 51, 66, 70, 73, 74, 90, 103, but we have two extra suras, al-Khal' and al-Hafd. As, however, we actually know of variants from him in all of these save 103, the probability is that the material of them formed part of his codex.

The other list is in the *Itqan* 150, l51, which gives the order—

1, 2, 4, 3, 6, 7, 5, 10, 8, 9, 11, 19 26, 22, 12, 15, 16, 33, 17, 39, 20, 21, 24, 23, 34, 29, 40, 13, 28, 27, 37, 38, 36, 15, 42, 30, 57, 48, 47, 41, 46, 50, 55, 56, 72, 53, 70, 73, 74, 44, 31, 45, 52, 51, 68, 69, 59, 60, 77, 78, 75, 81, 65, 79, 64, 80, 83, 84, 95, 96, 49, 63, 62, 66, 89, 90, 92, 82, 91, 86, 87, 88, 61, 98, 93, 94, 101, 102, 103, 104, 99, l00, 105, 106, 107, 108, 97, 109, 110, 111, 112, 113, 114.

From this are missing suras 18, 25, 32, 35, 43, 54, 58, 67, 71, 76, 85, but all these save 54 are to be found in the list of the *Fihrist*, and we know of variants from 54. It is evident that we cannot place any reliance on the lists, which as in the case of the lists for Ibn Mas'ud's codex, must be regarded as later formations not based on the original codex.

His codex seems not to have been the source of any secondary codices, though it would seem to have been copied, and if we are to believe the *Fihrist*, a copy of it was still extant in the time of Ibn Shadhan, i.e., in the middle of the third Islamic century. There is also a story of how Ibn 'Abbas presented a man with a codex written according to the *qira'a* of Ubai (*Durr* IV, 170).

There are some tales about the survival of Ubai's codex, but it is clear that it perished early, for there is the account in Ibn Abi Dawud, p. 25 of how some people from 'Iraq came to Ubai's son Muhammad and asked to consult his father's codex, but Muhammad had to tell them that was impossible as the codex had been seized by 'Uthman. Bergsträsser was inclined to think the readings from Ubai's codex less significant than those of Ibn Mas'ud, but the truth seems to be that his codex, not having the support of a great metropolitan center like Kufa, left permanent record of less of its peculiar readings than is the case of the codex of Ibn Mas'ud.

It is remarkable how often his variants agree with those of Ibn Mas'ud against the 'Uthmanic codex. One suspects that sometimes there has been a confusion in the tradition, and that readings of the one have been attributed to the other. This is certainly so when we find a single source attributing to Ubai a reading that is known as a peculiarity of Ibn Mas'ud, and it is curious that al-Marandi's *Qurat 'Ain al-Qurra'*, which is our richest source for Ubai's readings, attributes to him a great many readings, which are found elsewhere recorded only for Ibn Mas'ud.

In the MS of Ibn Abi Dawud only four readings from Ubai's codex are listed, but as he is quoted in the Commentaries for so large a number one suspects that some leaves were missing in this place in the original from which the Zahiriya MS was copied.

CODEX OF 'ALI (D. 40)

There is persistent tradition among the Shi'as that 'Ali b. Abi Talib was the first after the death of the Prophet to make a collection of the material of the Koran, and even Sunni sources know that he prepared a codex of his own. The most widely accepted form of the story is that after the Prophet's death, while the Companions were busy about electing a successor, 'Ali shut himself up in his house and made a vow that he would not put on this outdoor cloak until he had made an assemblage of the Koranic material into a codex. This caused some little comment as he did not come out to pay homage to Abu Bakr the newly elected caliph, but 'Ali explained his oath, and when the work was finished he packed it up on the back of his camel and brought it to the Companions saying "here is the Koran that I have assembled."[56]

There are many variations of the story. Some said that it was only six months after the Prophet's death that 'Ali set about making a recension.[57] Others say that he sat down and in three days wrote it all out from memory and arranged it in the order in which it was revealed.[58] A more interesting embellishment is that when the Prophet was about to die he summoned 'Ali and told him where the material for the Koran was hidden in a secret place behind his couch, and bade him take it from thence and edit it.[59]

Although the common story is that 'Ali's codex had the suras arranged in some sort of chronological oder (*Itqan*, 145), quite different arrangement is given by al-Ya'qubi (*Historiae* II, 152ff.) according to whom 'Ali arranged the suras in seven groups,[60] each group beginning with one of the seven long suras and called by its name. The schema is:

I. 2, 12, 29, 30, 31, 41, 51, 76, 32, 79, 81, 82, 84, 81, 98
    Al-Baqara. 886 verses, sixteen suras.

II. 3, 11, 12, 15, 33, 44, 55, 69, 70, 80, 91, 97, 99, 104, 105, 106.
    Al-'Imran. 886 verses, fifteen suras.

III. 4, 16, 23, 36, 42, 56, 67, 74, 107, 111, 112, 103, 101, 85, 95, 27.
     An-Nisa'. 886 verses, seventeen suras.

IV. 5, 10, 19, 26, 43, 49, 50, 54, 60, 86, 90, 94, 100, 108, 109.
    Al-Ma'ida. 886 verses, fifteen suras.

V. 6, 17, 21, 25, 28, 40, 58, 59, 62, 63, 68, 71, 72, 77, 93, 102
Al-An'am. 886 verses, sixteen suras.

VI. 7, 14, 18, 24, 38, 39, 45, 47, 57, 73, 75, 78, 88, 92, 110.
Al-A'raf. 886 verses, sixteen suras.

VII. 8, 9, 20, 35, 37, 46, 48, 52, 53, 61, 64, 65, 83, 113, 114.
Al-Anfal. 886 verses, sixteen suras.

This makes only 109 suras actually recorded, those missing being 1, 13, 34, 66, and 96. Unfortunately, no reliance can be placed on it for it is obviously dependent on the sura divisions of the 'Uthmanic text, which 'Ali's codex was hardly likely to follow, and of course it contradicts the other tradition that he arranged the material chronologically. This tradition of chronological arrangement is incidentally supported by the fact that there lingered for long the knowledge that in 'Ali's codex the first suras were 96, 74, 68, 73, 111, 81 (*Itqan*, 145). In any case the above list is not accurate, for division I which is said to contain 16 suras contains only 15, division II which is said to have 15 actually has 16, division III said to contain 17 has only 16, and division III said to contnin 16 has only 15.

When 'Uthman made his official recension 'Ali seems to have warmly supported it, saying that had he been in 'Uthman's position he would have done the same thing. It would appear that he gave up his own codex in favour of the new edition and it was probably burned at that time. Had it survived it is quite certain that the Shi'as would have adopted it as their standard codex, whereas in Shi'a hands we find only copies of the 'Uthmanic text even when they are said to have been written by 'Ali or one of this sons,[61] and the one pre-'Uthmanic codex whose readings seem to have been favored by the Shi'as is that of Ibn Mas'ud.[62]

Even when in later literature we have references to the codex of 'Ali, as when Ibn Sirin (d. 110) is said to have written to Medina for some information regarding it, or when ath-Tha'labi in his *Tafsir* (Sprenger, *Leben* III, xliv) notes that in 'Ali's codex sura II had 286 verses, or when Ibn an-Nadim, *Fihrist* 28, tells us that a copy lacking a few leaves was preserved in the 'Alid family for generations, the probability is that the reference is to a copy of the 'Uthmanic text made by or for 'Ali rather than to his own pre-'Uthmanic text.

Consequently, we have to bear in mind that all uncanonical variants quoted from 'Ali, while they may go back to variant readings that he remembered were in his own recension of the Koran, may on the other hand be merely his interpretation of the 'Uthmanic text.

Ibn Abi Dawud lists 'Ali's codex, apparently meaning his noncanonical codex, but quotes only one reading from it.

7.

Progress in the Study of the Koran Text

Arthur Jeffery

ERHAPS IT WOULD BE AS well to begin with a word about the origins of the Plan. It grew out of a suggestion made to the writer in Madras many years ago by the late Canon Sell, that one of the most pressing needs of Islamic studies was a reliable critical commentary on the Koran. Orthodox Muslim commentaries we have in great abundance, and both rival schools of the Ahmadiyya movement have been busy providing us with apologetic commentaries intended to make the Koran more palatable to people with a Christian background. What we needed, however, was a critical commentary which should embody the work done by modern Orientalists as well as apply the methods of modern critical research to the elucidation of the Koran.

No great advance had been made, however, in the collection of material for such a commentary, when it became evident that a necessary preliminary was a volume on the theology of the Koran, which would provide us with some account of the development of the teaching of the Koran, and make possible a reliable scheme according to which would be arranged the masses of material that were available to be digested into the commentary. Now no such volume existed, for Grimme's "System der Koranischen Theologie" in the second part of his *Mohammed* (Münster, 1895) was

Originally published in *The Muslim World* 25 (1935): 4–16. Reprinted with permission.

quite unsatisfactory, and Sacco's work *Le Credenze religiose di Maometto,* when it appeared (Rome, 1922), proved to be the work of a writer inadequately prepared for the task. It was necessary, therefore, to make an attempt to fill this need.

Here also it did not take long to discover that such a work could not be written until we had a satisfactory lexicon to the Koran, such a lexicon as the older Grimm-Thayer, or the more recent Milligan-Moulton lexicon to the New Testament. In other words, no adequate examination had ever been made of the Koranic vocabulary. Very little work at the native commentaries is sufficient to demonstrate how much at sea they were with regard to much of the technical religious vocabulary of the Koran, and how much more inclined they were to interpret the Koranic verses in the light of the theological and juristic controversies of their own day, than to work back to discover the original meaning of the passages.[1] The native lexicons are also as a rule far from helpful when it comes to Koranic vocabulary, so that without an independent investigation it is almost impossible to know what exactly Muhammad meant by the terms he used. Before we can discuss the development of the theological ideas of the Koran, therefore, we must make an exhaustive investigation of the vocabulary of the Koran.

A preliminary study along this line was made by the writer in 1925–26 in a thesis on the foreign vocabulary of the Koran, which unfortunately, owing to the printing costs, it has not yet been possible to publish. This study took up all the technical and cultural terms in the Koran of Hebrew, Aramaic, Syriac, Ethiopic, Iranian, and other origins, i. e., the non-Arabic element in the Koranic vocabulary. It made clear, however, that before we can tackle the study of the Arabic element in any scientific manner, we must have a critical text of the Koran. There is little use in making a lexicon to the standard text of the Koran when it is known that it is but one form of tradition as to the text, and that there are thousands and thousands of textual variants, many of them representing a much older type of text than the one we have in our hands.

It is an amazing fact that up to the present we have no critical text of the Koran. What type of text it was that was published in 1530 or thereabouts at Venice by Paganini Brixensis we cannot tell, as this first European edition of the text of the Koran was entirely destroyed at the command of the pope.[2] The editions of Abraham Hinckelmann in 1694[3] and Ludovico Marraccio in 1698[4] were monuments of industry at that date, but naturally not constructed on any critical basis. Flügel's edition of 1834,[5] which has been frequently reprinted, is still the text used by practically all Western scholars, but while it is a beautiful and carefully printed text, it is useless for critical purposes. It has no critical apparatus, but, worse than that, the text represents no consistent Oriental tradition either in orthography or reading, and if Flügel used some critical principle in constructing his text, no one to this day has been able to discover what it is.

Oriental lithographs of the Koran are legion. The vast majority of them give with more or less accuracy the text-tradition of Hafs from 'Asim, i.e., the best known of the three traditions from the Kufan School which may be said to represent the *textus receptus* in Islam. In North Africa the lithographs usually follow the text tradition of Warsh from Nafi', i.e., the tradition of the Medinan School. I have heard of Korans written according to the text tradition of ad-Duri from Abu 'Amr, i.e., the tradition of the Basran School. This tradition used to be followed in the Sudan up to a generation ago,[6] but apparently no texts were ever lithographed according to this tradition. With the passage of time the lithographs of the Hafs text had become progressively normalized to the customary orthography of the day, and thus could not be said to represent that tradition accurately. In 1923, however, the Egyptian government issued a standard edition under the editorship of a board of Muslim savants, and in this edition an attempt is made to reproduce as faithfully as possible the original Hafs tradition. Owing to the use of modern *qira'at* works instead of going back to the oldest sources of the tradition, the editors did not quite succeed in their endeavor, but their edition is nevertheless the nearest approach to a critical edition ever produced in the Orient.[7] It, however, contains no *apparatus criticus*. In some of the Kazan lithographs published in the middle of the last century there are given on the margin the variant readings of the Seven, and these appear also in certain Indian lithographs which are derived from the Kazan text. These readings, however, are given very imperfectly and frequently inaccurately. There appeared at Teheran in 1323 A.H. a lithograph giving a reproduction of a considerable portion of an old Kufic text, along with the Hafs text, and on the margin a not always accurate attempt at reproducing the variants of the Seven.[8]

In brief outline, the history of the Koran text is this. When Muhammad died there was no collection of his revelations in any official form. It is possible that he meant to make such a collection to clear up finally what had been abrogated and what not, but he died before this was done. Portions of revelations had been written down during his lifetime by various persons in his community, portions had been memorized and indeed some portions had apparently been used liturgically in the community. After his death several of his followers made the attempt to collect all the known revelations and write them down in codex form. Codices of Ibn Mas'ud, Ubai b. Ka'b, 'Ali, Abu Bakr, Abu Musa al-Ash'ari, Miqdad b. al-Aswad, etc., were known and referred to. With the spread of Islam and the founding of metropolitan centers, the necessity of having the Koran in written form was urgent, and we find growing up what we may call metropolitan codices in the centers of Mecca, Medina, Damascus, Kufa, and Basra.

As the differences between these various codices threatened to become a scandal and a disrupting force within Islam, the third caliph, 'Uthman, made an attempt to canonize the Medinan codex. He had copies of this written out and sent to each of the metropolitan centers, and ordered all other codices to be burned. 'Uthman seems to have been very successful in his destruction of the codices, for all the old Kufic manuscripts that have survived to us[9] apparently represent the same type of text with insignificant variants, which can usually be put down to the vagaries of the scribes. 'Uthman's work was intended to standardize the consonantal text, yet for long after 'Uthman's time there is evidence that variant traditions as to the consonantal text survived among the learned, and we can gather a great mass of material as to the readings in the text of Ubai or Ibn Mas'ud.[10] As only one type of text continued to be copied, however, it is clear that only such readings from the older codices as had some philological or theological interest would be likely to survive.[11]

This consonantal text, however, was unpointed. That is, there was nothing to distinguish a *b* from a *t*, a *th*, an *n* or a *y* at the beginning or middle of a word. Similarly *f* and *q*; *j*, *h* and *kh*; *s* and *d*; *r* and *z*; *s* and *sh*; *d* and *dh*; *t* and *z* were indistinguishable. Thus even in the 'Uthmanic standard text there was possible a great variety of variant readings according to the way in which the skeleton text was pointed. Besides this there was the vowelling, for even when the consonants (*huruf*) were settled, they might be vowelled very differently. Thus there grew up in the different metropolitan centers what one might call schools of readers who developed variant traditions as to how the pointing and vowelling of the text should be done. It was generally the work of some great teacher, whose system was followed by generation after generation of pupils. Pupils were required to memorize two things—first a tradition as to the *huruf* and then a tradition as to the vowelling. Of many authorities of the second and third Islamic centuries we read that so and so had an *ikhtiyar fi'l huruf*, i.e., a tradition of his own as to what the *huruf* should be.

The curious thing is that in many cases we find that this *ikhtiyar* does not confine itself to a choice among possible pointings of a standard consonantal text, but frequently represents a different consonantal text altogether. Sometimes this represents a correction of some mistake or inelegancy of the 'Uthmanic text,[12] but in the majority of cases suggests that in the different metropolitan centers some of the readings of the older codices were strong enough to survive in the schools alongside the 'Uthmanic readings. The authority of the standard text, however, naturally grew as standard texts always do,[13] and these variants from it came to be recorded merely as curiosities. Before the end of the third century it was to all intents and purposes fixed, and the main differences between the schools were in the matter of vowelling the consonantal texts.

Gradually these variations crystallized themselves into the traditions of the great schools of Koranic learning at Medina, Mecca, Damascus, Basra, and Kufa. Homs for a time seemed about to develop a school of its own, but it soon coalesced with that of Damascus. Later still, these traditions attached themselves to the names of certain famous teachers. In the year 322 A.H. the great Koranic authority Ibn Mujahid at Baghdad succeeded through his influence with the *wazirs* [viziers], Ibn 'Isa and Ibn Muqlah, in having an official fixing *ne varietur* of the permissible readings of the text. Not only was there a definite canonization of one system of *huruf* (supposedly the 'Uthmanic) with a prohibition of the use of any other *ikhtiyar*, but also a limiting of the variations in vowelling the text to the systems of the seven.[14]

The seven chosen by Ibn Mujahid were Nafi' of Medina († 169), Ibn Kathir of Mecca († 120), Ibn 'Amir of Damascus († 118), Abu 'Amr of Basra († 154), 'Asim of Kufa († 128), Hamza of Kufa († 158) and al-Kisa'i of Kufa († 182). The curiosity in this list is in the choice of three readers from Kufa. The choice of al-Kisa'i seems to have been due to some personal predilection of Ibn Mujahid. Al-Kisa'i had a great, though hardly deserved, reputation as a grammarian, but his Koran readings in general follow those of Hamza, and where he differs from Hamza his variation is rarely of any importance. There was a considerable body of opinion that Ya'qub of Basra († 205) ought to have been chosen in his place, while some were in favor of Khalaf of Kufa († 229), or of Abu Ja'far of Medina († 130).

Thus in spite of Ibn Mujahid there continued to be memorized and handed on the tradition as to the ten. Besides these there survived, with varying degrees of authority, the traditions of Ibn Muhaisin of Mecca († 123), al-Yazidi of Basra († 202), al-Hasan of Basra († 110), and al-A'mash of Kufa († 148), making the fourteen.

We now have, then, two classes of variants to the Koran text, the canonical, consisting of the variants of the seven canonized by Ibn Mujahid, and with lesser degree of authority those of the ten, and uncanonical (technically known as *shawadhdh*) consisting of all other variants—those of the four who make up the fourteen coming nearest to recognition as canonical. As was natural, we soon had differences of tradition within the schools as to the readings of each of the seven, but by the next century two lines from each of the seven had been chosen as the orthodox tradition, and when the traditions came to be digested into book form only these two lines were given. Thus we have the system[15]—

> Nafi' of Medina according to Warsh († 197) and Qalun († 220).
> Ibn Kathir of Mecca according to al-Bazzi († 270) and Qunbul († 280).
> Ibn 'Amir of Damascus according to Hisham († 245) and Ibn Dhakwan († 242).
> Abu 'Amr of Basra according to ad-Duri († 250) and as-Susi † 261).
> 'Asim of Kufa according to Hafs († 190) and Abu Bakr († 194).
> Hamza of Kufa according to Khalaf († 229) and Khallad († 220).
> Al-Kisa'i of Kufa according to ad-Duri († 250) and Abu'l-Harith († 261).

Of these, as we have already indicated, only the systems of Warsh from Nafi', of Hafs from 'Asim, and of ad-Duri from Abu 'Amr seem to have gained any wide acceptance, and for some reason which has not yet been fully elucidated, the system of Hafs quickly gained such an ascendancy over all the others as to have become the *textus receptus* of Islam, being used today everywhere except in the stretch of North Africa from Tripoli to Morocco.

Early in the fifth Islamic century the systems of the seven were digested into book form. The outstanding work of this kind was the *Taisir* of the Andalus scholar ad-Dani († 444) who himself followed the system of Warsh. The *Taisir* was versified by *ash-Shatibi*, († 590) in a work called *Hirz al-Amani* (also commonly known as *Ash-Shatibiya*, which has been the subject of innumerable commentaries and is still the chief source used by Muslim savants in their studies of the Koran text.

The task of preparing a critical edition of the Koran, therefore, is two-fold—first that of presenting some form of tradition as to the text itself, and secondly that of collecting and arranging all the information scattered over the whole domain of Arabic literature, concerning the variant readings both canonical and uncanonical. The writer had begun to collect variant readings years ago, when he first became interested in the Koran, but in 1926 began the task of consistently working through all the Arabic commentaries, lexicons, and philological works to collect the various readings recorded. That same year Professor Bergsträsser published the first fascicle of his *Geschichte des Qorantexts* and it was evident that our studies were interlocking. We met at Munich in 1927, and agreed to collaborate on a much bigger plan of assembling all the material that would assist in some day making it possible to elucidate fully the history of the Koran text. I was to go on with my task of collecting the variants and preparing an edition of the text, while Bergsträsser was to commence gathering material for an archive of photographs of all the oldest Kufic manuscripts of the Koran, a collation of which he hoped would throw light on the history of the text. Then we were to pool our resources with a view to a large volume dealing with the variants.[16]

Meanwhile there remained much supplementary work to do. A large number of source books that we needed were still in manuscript, and some indeed had yet to be discovered. A pupil of Bergsträsser's, Dr. Otto Pretzl, was at work already on a critical edition of the famous *Taisir* of ad-Dani, of which we possessed as yet only a very poor lithograph from Hyderabad. This *Taisir* was published in the *Bibliotheca Islamica* in 1930,[17] followed in 1932 by an edition in the same series of the *Muqni'* of ad-Dani,[18] both edited by Dr. Pretzl. Meanwhile at Damascus in 1927 had appeared the two large volumes of Ibn al-Jazari's *Kitab an-Nashr fi'l-Qira'at al-'Ashr,* so that for the first time in our hands a sound basis for the study of the seven and the ten. That is, with regard to the canonical readings, we were now in a position to go back as near as we are ever likely to get to the original sources. In the winter of 1928 Professor Bergsträsser spent some months in Cairo and commenced the photographing of the Kufic codices preserved here. Also he was able to make considerable progress with the task of editing the text of Ibn Khalawaih's work on the uncanonical readings,[19] which we have reason to think represents Ibn Mujahid's own teaching on this subject, as the *Taisir* of ad-Dani represents his teaching on the canonical variants. Also he was able to extract from the manuscripts of the *Muhtasab* of Ibn Jinni, that important philologist's references to uncanonical variants.[20] Before returning to Germany he also made arrangements for a Cairo edition of the *Tabaqat al-Qurra'* of Ibn al-Jazari, a large work giving biographies of all the early Koranic authorities, and what is more important, the *isnads* showing through what lines of tradition their readings reached them.

Another pupil of his, Dr. Eisen, was set to work on an edition of the *Kitab Fada'il al-Koran* of Abu 'Ubaid, which will be published shortly. Meanwhile the search for older sources went on. Following on Bergsträsser's discovery of the work of Ibn Khalawaih, the present writer has discovered two manuscripts of the lost *Kitab al-Masahif* of Ibn Abi Dawud, and more recently has unearthed a beautiful complete manuscript of the *I'rab al-Qira'at ash-Shadhdha* of al-'Ukbari. In the autumn of 1930, Dr. Pretzl visited Stambul [Istanbul] and carefully examined the many libraries there, unearthing many manuscripts of great interest for the text history of the Koran, and providing material for many years of work.[21] Other source material has also appeared in the Orient. In 1932 the firm of al-Halabi in Cairo completed tbe printing of the commentary of the Yemenite scholar ash-Shawkani, which is very rich in uncanonical variants, and particularly useful because the author apparently had access to sources which are no longer available to us. Also the same firm published an edition of the famous old commentary of Abu Sham on the *Shatibiya*, viz., *Ibraz al-Ma'ani min Hirz al-Amani,* on the margin of which are two works by a living Koranic scholar ad-Dabba,[22] one a supercommentary to the *Shatibiya* and the other an explication of the readings of the three extra who make up the ten. Bergsträsser, indeed, was very hopeful of enlisting the interest of modern Muslim savants to publish a whole corpus of *qira'at* works, at least of those which from their point of view would be considered orthodox. Cf. the *Jami' al-Bayan,* which is ad-Dani's biggest work, the *Lata'if al-Isharat* of al-Qastallani, the *Kitab al-Hujja* of Abu 'Ali al-Farisi, the *Kitab at-Tajrid* of Ibn Fahham, the *Ma'ani al-Qur'an* of al-Farra', the *Suq al-'Arus* of Abu Ma'shar at-Tabari, etc., etc.

In the summer of 1933 while I was in Oxford, working in the Bodleian Library on one little item of our plan, Bergsträsser was lost in a mountaineering accident in the Bavarian Alps during his summer vacation. His death is a tremendous loss to Islamic studies in general, and to Koranic studies the loss is irreparable. On my way back to Cairo in the winter I stopped at Munich to spend some time with Dr. Pretzl, who is at present carrying on Bergsträsser's work, and we have made the best arrangements we can for carrying out the plan. Dr. Pretzl is finishing the third fascicule of the *Geschichte des Qoran-texts.* The edition of Ibn Khalawaih is finished, and my annotations thereto, which were originally to have been a *Nachtrag* [appendix] to the volume, will now appear separately in one of the journals, possibly in *Islamica*. Dr. Pretzl will continue to gather the material for the archive of Kufic codices and other material for the history of the text.[23] I shall produce the text with *apparatus criticus* and also attempt the volume of notes on the variant readings, though how this latter can ever be adequately done without the assistance of the massive learning and critical acumen of Professor Bergsträsser is more than I can see.

This, then, is how the plan stands. For the text it had been my original intention to commence with Flügel's text as a basis, and endeavor to reconstruct the earliest possible type of text. There were two strong objections, however, to this: in the first place, by reason of the condition of the sources it would be largely a subjective piece of work, and thus perhaps not any better than Flügel's, and secondly, it would be entirely unacceptable to Muslims. The only reasonable plan with regard to the text is to print consistently one type of Oriental tradition, and the obvious one among them is that of Hafs, which is so generally acclaimed as the *textus receptus*. This text will be constructed according to the oldest sources we have concerning the tradition of Hafs, but will be printed according to *saj'* and the Kufan verse numbering, with Flügel's numbering, however, also given for convenience of reference. Pausal signs and the *ajza'* will be noted, and on the margin a selection of marginal references such as those in a reference Bible, which will facilitate reference to parallel passages.

At the foot of each page will be the *apparatus criticus.* All the thousands of variants gleaned from the commentaries, lexicons, works of traditionists, theologians, and philologers, and even from some of the Adab books, will be given with symbols indicating the Reader or Readers who are quoted for each variant. It is hoped by means of different types to indicate in these symbols whether the authority concerned is earlier than the canonical seven, of the circle of the canonical readers, or more recent. It may also be possible to arrange some symbolical way of indicating from which school or schools the reading in question comes. It cannot be hoped that this *apparatus criticus* will be complete, for one finds variant readings noted in the most unexpected places, and a complete collection would involve the superhuman task of combing through the whole of Arabic literature printed and unprinted. All the more important sources that are available, however, will be utilized.

To the text it is hoped that some day there will be a volume of introduction, to provide for English readers what German readers already have in the second edition of Nöldeke's *Geschichte des Qorans*. It will certainly be accompanied by a volume of annotations, which will be in the nature of a commentary to the *apparatus criticus*. The bare citation of the reading with the symbol for the Reader in the *apparatus* will be sufficient for the Koranic expert in most cases, but the vast majority of students who use the *apparatus* will want more. It is for the purpose of explaining these readings, discussing the origins, provenance and signification, that the annotations are provided, and also in cases where there is dispute over a reading to give scholars the necessary additional information that will enable them to reach their own conclusions as to the value of the various lines of tradition. A fourth volume is planned to contain a Koranic lexicon.

Apart from these four volumes it is planned, if time and money are available, to issue another series of volumes. Prof. Bergsträsser had thought of editing a series of *Studien zur Geschichte des Korantexts*, in which would appear material such as his already mentioned work on Ibn Jinni and Ibn Khalawaih. The necessity for such a series still exists. The manuscripts of Ibn Abi Dawud and Al-'Ukbari recently brought to light by the present writer, the relevant section of the Berlin manuscript of the *Mabani*, Ibn al-Anbari's *Waqf wa Ibtida'*, and similar works, must be published, and the intensive search now being made for some of these lost *qira'at* books will certainly have some success in recovering to us texts that will demand publication. It is also possible that the archive of Kufic codices may hold surprises that will call for early publication. The plan is, therefore, to look toward the issue of a series of *Studies in the Text of the Koran*, where such material, as it becomes available, can be placed in the hands of students.

This then is where the Koran plan stands at present. Whether it will be possible to carry it through in whole, or even in part, is of course another question.

8.

A Variant Text of the Fatiha

Arthur Jeffery

*S*URA I OF THE KORAN bears on its face evidence that it was not originally part of the text, but was a prayer composed to be placed at the head of the assembled volume, to be recited before reading the book, a custom not unfamiliar to us from other sacred books of the Near East. The Koranic style, as is well known, is that in it, from beginning to end, Allah is addressing man. In the *Fatiha*, however, it is man addressing Allah, and the common explanation that the word "Say!" is to be understood at its beginning, is obviously due to the desire to bring this first sura into harmony with the style of the rest of the book. The sura, moreover, when we examine it, proves to be more or less a *cento* of ideas and expressions taken from other parts of the Koran. It is possible, of course, that as a prayer it was constructed by the Prophet himself, but its use and its position in our present Koran are due to the compilers, who placed it there, perhaps on the fly-leaf of the standard codex. Its division into seven members in orthodox Muslim tradition has suggested the idea that it was put together as an Islamic counterpart to the Lord's Prayer.

The peculiar nature of the *Fatiha* has been recognized by Western scholars[1] from Nöldeke downward, but it is not merely a hostile Western opinion, for Fakhr ad-Din ar-Razi[2] quotes Abu Bakr al-Asamm († 313)[3] as

Originally published in *The Muslim World* 29 (1939): 158–62. Reprinted with permission.

saying that he considered it not to be part of the Koran and apparently the oldest commentaries began with *Surat al-Baqara*. It is also well-known that the *Fatiha* was not included in the codex of Ibn Mas'ud.[4] It is said that some early Kūfic manuscripts of the Koran are to be found which commence with the second sura, and if they have the *Fatiha*, have it only at the end; but the present writer has never seen such an exemplar.

It should not surprise us then if the *Fatiha* should have been handed down in somewhat different forms. One such variant form has for long circulated in Shī'a circles. In the *Tadhkirat al-A'imma* of Muhammad Bāqir Majlisī (edition of Teheran, 1331, p. 18) it is given:

Nuḥammidu'llāha, Rabba'l-'ālamī na,
'r-raḥmāna'r-raḥī ma,
Mallāka yaumi'd-dī ni,
Hayyāka na'budu wa wiyyaka nastaʾī nu,
Turshidu sabī la'l-mustaqī mi,
Sabī la'lladhī na na' 'amta 'alaihim,
Siwā'l-maghḍū bi 'alaihim, wa la'ḍ-ḍallī na,

which we may translate:

We greatly praise Allah, Lord of the worlds,
he Merciful, the Compassionate,
He who has possession of the Day of Judgement.
Thee do we worship, and on Thee do we call for help.
Thou dost direct to the path of the Upright One,
The path of those to whom Thou hast shown favor,
Not that of those with whom Thou are angered, or those who
     go astray,

Last summer in Cairo I came across a similar variant version. It is given in a little manual of Fiqh, whose beginning, unfortunately, is missing, so that we do not know the name of the author. It is a quite unimportant summary of Shāfi'ī Fiqh, written, if one may venture a judgment from the writing, about one hundred and fifty years ago, perhaps a little earlier, in a clerkly hand, and the variant version is written on the inside cover under the rubric-*qirā'a shadhdha li'l-Fatiha*. The manuscript is in private possession, and though the owner was willing to let me copy the passage, and use it if I saw fit, he was not willing that his name be revealed, lest he come into disrepute among his orthodox neighbors for allowing an unbeliever to see such an uncanonical version of the opening sura of their Holy Book.

The text of this variant has certain similarities to that already given, and runs:

> *Bismi'llāhi'r-raḥmāni'r-raḥimi.*
> *Al-ḥamdu li'llāhi, Sayyidi'l-ʿālamīna,*
> *'r-razzāqi'r-raḥimi,*
> *Mallāki yaumi'd-dīni,*
> *Innā laka na'budu wa innā laka nastaʿīnu,*
> *Arshidnā sabīla'l-mustaqīmi,*
> *Sabīla'lladhīna mananta ʿalaihim,*
> *Siwā'l-maghḍūbi ʿalaihim, wa ghaira'ḍ-ḍāllina.*

which, being interpreted, means:

> In the Name of Allah, the Merciful, the Compassionate.
> Praise be to Allah, Lord of the worlds,
> The Bountiful, the Compassionate,
> He who has possession of the Day of Judgment,
> As for us, to Thee do we worship, and to Thee we turn for help,
> Direct us to the path of the Upright One,
> The path of those on whom Thou hast bestowed favors,
> Not that of those with whom Thou art angered,
> Nor that of those who go astray.

Under the text follows the statement: *Riwāyat Abī'l-Fatḥi'l-Jubbāʿī ʿan shaikhihi's-Susī ʿan an-Nahrawānī ʿan Abī's-Saʿādāti'l-Maidānī ʿan al-Marzubānī ʿan al-Khalīl b. Aḥmad.*

On the readings in the two texts we may note: *Sayyid* for *Rabb* is merely a case of replacement by synonym. *Sayyid* is used in sura xii: 25 for Joseph's master down in Egypt, and in iii: 34 of John Baptist, who is announced as a *sayyid*, a chaste one, and a prophet, and the plural form is used in xxxiii:67 for the chiefs whom the infidels followed and were led astray. It is not, however, used of Allah.

Ar-razzāq occurs as a title of Allah in li: 58—*inna'llāha huwa'r-razzāq.*

Mallak is a reading attributed to the third Kūfan Reader among the

Seven, al-Kisa'i († 189), cf. al-Alusi, *Ruhu'l-Ma'ani*, I, 78 and Abu Hayyan, *Bahr*, I, 20. It is curious that both the variant texts agree in this reading. *Mallāk* is perhaps more precise and emphatic than the alternative forms *malik, mālik* and *malīk*, the first of which is perhaps the best attested reading, and the second is the TR [*textus receptus,* "accepted text"—Ed.].

Innā laka. This, and *hiyyāka, wiyyāka, ayyāka, iyāka* and the *iyyāka* of the TR, seem all to be independent attempts to interpret the unvoweled, unpointed skeleton form that stood in the original codex. *Hiyyāka* or *hayyāka* was the reading of Abu's-Sawwar al-Ghanawi (c. 180) and Abu'l-Mutawakkil († 102); *wiyyāka* or *wayyāka* was read by Abu Raja' († 105).

Arshidnā means much the same as the *ihdinā* of the TR and was the reading in Ibn Mas'ud's codex (az-Zamakhshari *in loc.*, and Ibn Khalawaih, p. 1). This imperative does not occur elsewhere in the Koran, but other forms from the root are commonly used, and the Shi'a variant uses the imperfect of Form IV.

Sabīl is a commoner word than the *ṣirāṭ* of the TR, and is much more commonly used in the Koran, though both are foreign words, borrowed through the Aramaic. *Ṣirāṭa'l-mustaqīm,* taking it as in *iḍāfa,* where *al-Mustaqīm* is a title of Allah, i.e., "the Upright One", was the reading of Ubai, Ja'far as-Sadiq and 'Abdallah b. 'Umar, so that it has very early and good attestation. It is a possible and appropriate reading, even though *al-Mustaqīm* is not one of the Ninety-nine Names. That *sabīla'l-mustaqīm* should occur in both these texts is curious.

Mananta and *na''amta* are simple replacements by synonym for they do not affect the meaning. Form IV of *n'm* is more common in the Koran than Form II, which is used only once in lxxxix: 14, but *manna,* with much the same meaning, is used still more often.

Siwā for *ghair* is a similar replacement by synonym, though *siwa* is not used elsewhere in the Koran.

Ghair for *lā* was the reading of 'Umar, 'Ali, Ubai, Ibn az-Zubair, 'Ikrima and al-Aswad among the early codices, and was supported by Ja'far as-Sadiq and Zaid b. 'Ali, so that it has respectable authority for a claim to be the original reading. It makes no change in the sense.

It will have been noticed that the sense of the *Fatiha* is precisely the same whether we read the TR or either of these variants. There is no ascertainable reason for the variant readings. They are not alterations in the interests of smoother grammatical construction or of clarity, nor do they seem to have any doctrinal significance. They are just such variants as one might expect in the transmission of a prayer at first preserved in an oral form, and then fixed later when the Koran was assembled.

The second variant form comes from Khalil b. Aḥmad, who as a Reader belonged to the Basran School, though he is said to have taken *huruf* from both 'Aṣim of Kufa and Ibn Kathir of Mecca, among the seven, and is even noted as the one who transmitted the variant *ghaira* from Ibn Kathir (Abu Hayyan, *Bahr*, I, 29; Ibn al-Jazari, *Tabaqat*, I, 177, 275; Ibn Khalawaih, p. 1). But he was also known to have transmitted from 'Isa b. 'Umar († 149) (Ibn Khallikan, II, 420) and was a pupil of Ayyub as-Sakhtiyani († 131), both of whom were Basrans and famous for the transmission of uncanonical readings. It is thus quite possible that Khalil had access to good old tradition as to the primitive reading of the *Fatiha*. I can make nothing of the rest of the *isnad* from Khalil to al-Jubba'i, and possibly it is much later than the *matn* from Khalil.

9.

Abu 'Ubaid on the Verses Missing from the Koran

Arthur Jeffery

*T*HAT OUR PRESENT TEXT OF the Koran represents an honest effort to assemble all that was still extant of genuine proclamations of Muhammad during the years of his prophetic activity need not be questioned. It is possible but not very probable that a few passages have crept in which are not genuine proclamations of the Prophet. That a great many quite genuine proclamations, however, could no longer be found, and are thus not included in the volume, is certain.

Occasionally in Arabic works one comes across references to some of these missing verses, and in Nöldeke-Schwally, *Geschichte des Qorâns*, I, 234–59 these references are gathered together and commented upon. In the sources from which Schwally drew his list one finds very frequent reference to the authority of Abu 'Ubaid, and in Munich this summer, through the kindness of Prof. Otto Pretzl, I was able to consult the photographs of the Berlin manuscript of Abu 'Ubaid's *Kitab Faḍa'il-al-Qur'an*, folios 43 and 44 of which contain a chapter on the verses which have fallen out of the Koran.

Abu 'Ubaid al-Qasim b. Sallam (154–244 A.H), who studied under the famous masters of both the Kufan and the Basran schools, was the son of a Greek slave, and though born on the outskirts of the Muslim empire,

Originally published in *The Muslim World* 28 (1938): 61–65. Reprinted with permission.

became a famous teacher at Baghdad, renowned equally as a philologist, a jurist, and an authority on the Koranic sciences.[1] By reason of his early date and the reputation he had in the eyes of later writers, his chapter on the missing verses of the Koran merits translation here.[2]

Said Abu 'Ubaid:

Isma'il b. Ibrahim related to us from Ayyub from Nafi' from Ibn 'Umar who said—Let none of you say, "I have learned the whole of the Koran," for how does he know what the whole of it is, when much of it has disappeared? Let him rather say, "I have learned what is extant thereof."

Ibn Abi Maryam related to us from Ibn Luhai'a from Abu'l-Aswad from 'Urwa b. az-Zubair from 'A'isha who said, "Surat al-Ahzab (xxxiii) used to be recited in the time of the Prophet with two hundred verses, but when 'Uthman wrote out the codices he was unable to procure more of it than there is in it today."

Isma'il b. Ibrahim and Isma'i b. Ja'far related to us from al-Mubarak b. Fadala from 'Asim b. Abi'n-Nujud from Zirr b. Hubaish who said—Ubai b. Ka'b said to me, "O Zirr, how many verses did you count (or how many verses did you read) in Surat al-Ahzab?" "Seventy-two or seventy-three," I answered. Said he, "Yet it used to be equal to Surat al-Baqara (ii), and we used to read in it the Verse of Stoning." Said I, "And what is the Verse of Stoning?" He said, "If a grown man and woman commit adultery, stone them without hesitation, as a warning from Allah, for Allah is mighty, wise."

'Abdallah b. Salih related to us from al-Laith from Khalid b. Yazid from Sa'id b. Abi Hilal from Marwan from Abu Umama 'Uthman b. Sahl that Khaliya said—The Apostle used to recite to us the Verse of Stoning, "If a grown man and woman commit adultery, stone them unhesitatingly as a reward for their (illicit) enjoyment."

Hashim related to us—I heard az-Zuhri say, 'Ubaidallah b. 'Abdallah b. 'Utba related to us from Ibn 'Abbas who said—'Umar was preaching and said, "Some people say 'What is this about the stoning? there is nothing in Allah's book except a scourging', whereas the Apostle stoned and we stoned with him. By Allah, were it not that people might say that 'Umar had added something to Allah's book, I would have written it in just as it was revealed."

Hashim related to us saying—'Ali b. Zaid b. Hidh'an informed us from Yusuf b. Mihran from Ibn 'Abbas from 'Umar who said—"I indeed wanted to write on the margin of the codex, 'Umar b. al-Khattab and

'Abd ar-Rahman b. 'Auf bear witness that the Apostle of Allah stoned and we also stoned.' "

'Abd al-Ghaffar b. Dawud related to us from Abu Luhai'a from 'Ali b. Dinar from Khalid that 'Umar b. al-Khattab passed by a man who was reading aloud from a codex, "The Prophet is nearer akin to the believers than they are themselves, his wives are their mothers and he is their father" (xxxlii:6). Said 'Umar, "Separate not from me till we find Ubai b. Ka'b." When they came to Ubai b. Ka'b he said, "O Ubai, may we not hear how you recite this verse?" Said Ubai, "It was among the things that dropped out." Said 'Umar, "And why were you away from it then?" Said he, "There kept me away from it what did not keep you."

'Abdallah b. Salih related to us from al-Laith from Hashim b. Sa'd from Zaid b. Aslam from 'Ata' b. Yasar from Abu Waqid al-Laithi who said, "When the Apostle of Allah had a revelation we would come to him and he would repeat to us what had been revealed to him. One day I came to him and he said, 'Allah, blessed and exalted be He, says, "We have sent down wealth for the performance of prayer and the giving of alms, but if the son of Adam had a valley (full of wealth) he would want a second, and if he had a second he would want to add a third to them. Nothing indeed will really fill man's belly save the dust, and Allah turns to whom He wills." ' "

Hajjaj related to us from Hamid b. Salama from 'Ali b. Zaid b. Jid'an from Abu Harb b. Abi'l-Aswad from Abu Musa al-Ash'ari, who said— There was revealed a sura about the size of al-Bara'a (ix), which was later withdrawn, of which I remember (the words) "Allah will help along this religion by means of a people for whom is no portion. Had the son of Adam two valleys full of gold he would yearn for a third. Nothing will really fill man's belly but the dust, and Allah turns to whom He will."

Abu Nu'aim related to me from Yusuf b. Shu'aib from Habib b. Yasar from Zaid b. Arqam who said—We used to recite in the time of the Prophet, "Had the son of Adam two valleys of gold he would desire a third. Nothing will really fill man's belly but the dust, and Allah turns to whom He wills."

Hajjaj related to us from Ibn Juraij who said—Abu'z-Zubair informed me that he heard Jabir b. 'Abdallah say—We used to recite, "Had the son of Adam a valley full of treasure he would want another like it. Nothing will really fill man's belly save the dust, and Allah turns to whom He wills."

Hajjaj related to us from Ibn Juraij who said—'Ata' informed me saying,—I heard Ibn 'Abbas say—"I heard the Apostle of Allah say the like of this, but I do not know whether it is Koran or not."

Hajjaj related to us from Ibn Juraij who said—Ibn Abi Humaid informed me from Jahra bint Abi Ayyub b. Yunus saying—I read to my father when he was eighty years of age from 'A'isha's codex—"Verily Allah and His angels pray for the Prophet. O ye who believe, pray for him and speak peace upon him and upon those who pray in the first ranks" (xxxiii:56). She said, "It is said that 'Uthman altered the codices." Said he, "Ibn Juraij and Ibn Abi Jamil have related to me from 'Abd ar-Rahman b. Hurmuz and others the like of this about 'A'isha's codex."

Hajjaj related to us from Shu'ba from al-Hakam b. 'Ubaid from 'Adi b. 'Adi who said—We used to read, "Turn not away from your fathers for that is godlessness on your part." Then he said to Zaid b. Thabit,—"Is that so, Zaid b. Thabit?", and he answered, "Yes."

Ibn Abi Fahm related to us from Nafi' b. 'Umar al-Jumahi, who said,—Ibn Abi Mulaika related to me from Musawwar b. Makhrama who said,—'Umar said to 'Abd ar-Rahman b. 'Auf,—"Did you not find in what was revealed, 'Strive as ye strove the first time,' for we cannot find it." He answered, "It dropped out among what dropped from the Koran."

Said Abu 'Ubaid,—These *huruf* that we have mentioned in these passages are among the extras, which the savants did not hand down, saying that they are similar to what is between the covers (of the Koran), because they used to recite them during prayers. Thus they did not consider as an unbeliever anyone who rejected them, even though they were recited in prayer, for they only passed judgment of unbelief against any one who rejected what was between the covers, for that is what was in the *Imam* which 'Uthman caused to be written out with the approval of the *Muhajirs* and the *Ansar*.

10.

Textual Variations of the Koran

David Margoliouth

*I*F UNIFORMITY OF TEXT BE required in a sacred book, the Hebrew Bible would seem to fulfill the demand better than either the Greek New Testament or the Arabic Koran. The varieties which have been collected from manuscripts of the first are almost negligible; important differences are found either in alternate copies of the same documents which are incorporated in the Old Testament, or in ancient versions, the use of which for textual criticism is hazardous. In the criticism of the New Testament the ancient versions play an important part; but the manuscripts also are far from uniform, and in some parts exhibit widely differing recensions. Until January of this year no ancient version of the Koran had been introduced into the criticism of that book; Dr. Mingana, who has discovered a Syriac version of high antiquity, and described it in the *Bulletin of the John Rylands Library,* is the pioneer in this matter. The same scholar in his *Leaves from Three Ancient Korans* (Cambridge, 1914) called attention to noteworthy variants in old manuscripts. But orthodox Islam does not assume uniformity of text for its sacred book; it admits seven or even ten canonical recensions, differing ordinarily, but not always, in minutiae; and in addition to these there are a great number of uncanonical readings, attested by distinguished personages. Ahmad b. Musa b. Mujahid (ob. 324

Originally published in *The Muslim World* 15 (1925): 334–44.

A.H.) composed nine works embodying the readings of different authorities, one of them the Prophet himself! These by no means exhausted his activities in the collection of various readings. We may endeavor to classify these varieties and account for their existence.

The Koran (ii. 100) assumes that it is perpetuated partly in the memory and partly in writing; and asserts that Allah at times commits texts to oblivion or causes them to be erased, to substitute something better or not inferior. This process was regarded by some of the Prophet's contemporaries as clear evidence of imposture (xvi. 103); leaving this matter alone, we may at least notice that *nescit vox missa reverti*; a text might be officially removed, yet survive, owing to those in possession of it being ignorant of the abrogation or neglecting it. Hence among the various readings which are quoted some may actually represent an earlier or a later form of the same revelation. Thus in v. 91 the ordinary text prescribes a fast of three days for impecunious persons who wish to compensate for perjury: Tabari (ob. 310 A.H.) quotes authorities for the assertion that Ubayy b. Ka'b and 'Abdallah b. Mas'ud added the word *successive*, making the penance much more severe. He adds that as the word is "not found in our copies," we cannot build anything upon it; the analogy of compensation for failure to fast in Ramadan (ii. 181) indicates that the days need not be successive; still it would be safer to make them so. Shafi'i (ob. 204 A.H.) seems to leave it to the individual Moslem to choose the reading which he prefers.[1] It is a conceivable view that the word *successive* might have been added or omitted by the Prophet himself.

The fact that the revelations might be abrogated is likely to have seriously affected the importance attached to the Koran in the Prophet's time; he had the reputation of being at the mercy of each speaker (ix. 61). The story told by Bokhari about iv. 97[2] illustrates the effect of this quality on the Koran. A text had been revealed asserting that the believers who stayed at home were not the equals of those who went out to fight. A blind man complained that the latter course was impossible for him. A revelation came adding the words *except those who suffer from some infirmity.*

When with the Prophet's death revelation ceased, such texts as had been preserved acquired vast importance; they were all that could be known of the will of God. Since, if the tradition is to be believed, there was no official copy in existence, those who claimed the monopoly of portions might aspire to be dictators of the community: a far safer plan than that tried by those who claimed to be prophets. We may well believe that the measure taken by the third caliph, of issuing an official edition and ordering all unofficial copies to be burned, was a political necessity. That this act brought about an insurrection wherein he was murdered is the most probable explanation of the first civil war of Islam. Dr. Mingana[3] has called attention to a tradition that another official edition was produced by the famous (or notorious) Hajjaj b.Yusuf (ob. 95 A.H.) near the end of the first century; and to this there may be a reference in an Abbasid manifesto of the year 284 A.H. wherein the Umayyads are charged with "altering the Book of Allah,"[4] though no attempt is there made to substantiate the charge. According to another authority (as will be seen) what this personage did was to introduce punctuation. What both supposed recensions imply is that there was variety—or at any rate something to be altered—before they were made. Some variants might remain in oral transmission after they had been officially condemned.

If the collectors of the Koran had to trust for portions of it to oral tradition, it is unlikely that the standard of accuracy was sufficiently high to ensure uniformity. In the article "Parallel Passages in the Koran" (*Moslem World,* July 1925) Mr. E. E. Elder shows that there are noteworthy variations in the different versions of the same narrative which the Koran contains. Even when it quotes itself, the quotations are not always what we should call accurate. An example may be taken from v. 139, "He has sent down unto you in the Book that when ye hear the signs of Allah discredited and ridiculed, ye shall not sit with them until they plunge into another topic." The reference would seem to be to vi. 67, "When thou seest those who plunge into our signs, turn aside from them until they plunge into another topic." Clearly the former is a loose paraphrase rather than a quotation, since the differences are many and serious. We need not credit the earliest transmitters of the Koran with greater accuracy. For a long time there was uncertainty as to what was Koran and what was not. Verses of poets were at times cited in the pulpit as the Word of Allah.[5] There are occasions when the inaccuracy of those who cite it is astounding. The caliph Mansur, when in his controversy with an 'Alid pretender he wished to prove that an uncle could be called a father, cited xii. 38: "I (Joseph) followed the sect of my fathers, Abraham and Ishmael and Isaac and Jacob";[6] the argument depends on the name Ishmael, which is not found in the text! The proof-passage intended by Mansur is ii. 127, where Jacob's sons say to him, "We shall worship the God of thy fathers, Abraham and Ishmael and Isaac"; where, as Mansur observes, "he began with him (the uncle) in preference to the immediate parent." Neither Mubarrad nor Ibn Khaldun, who produce the letter with the quotation from xii. 38, notices the mistake; Tabari[7] omits the wrong quotation, but apparently cannot find the right one. An even more extraordinary case is that of Bokhari, who in the first section of his *Kitab al-Manaqib* mentions an occasion in consequence of which "there was revealed *Unless ye contract relationship between me and you*." No such revelation is found in the Koran. In justice to the commentators it must be mentioned that they are puzzled by this statement of the foremost traditionalist. Their expedients, however, are rather desperate: one is the suggestion that such a text had been revealed, but was afterward abrogated; another that Bokhari is giving the sense of some passage in lieu of citing it verbally, procedure for which the example of the Prophet's encomiast Hassan b. Thabit is cited, who however had the excuse of verse.[8]

It is unlikely that those from whose memories portions of the Koran were collected were more accurate than Mansur and Bokhari, and the elimination of oral tradition by the reduction of the whole to writing was a great step toward uniformity. Only the script chosen for the Koran left much to be desired. The script in use in pre-Islamic Arabia is clear, efficient, and beautiful; the signs for the twenty-nine consonants are distinct, and a vertical line separates word from word. The script chosen for the Koran is a modification of the North Semitic alphabet of twenty-two consonants, not however in the direction of increase but in that of decrease; whence the same sign stands for sounds which bear no resemblance to each other. In a work on textual corruption by an author whose death-date is 382 A.H.[9] the necessity of learning the Koran from teachers is illustrated by the case of one Hamzah who afterward became the author of a canonical recension; he started reading without such aid and read the opening words of surah II, "That Book *la zaita fihi* (no oil in it)," where he should have read *la raiba* ("no doubt"). He got, in consequence, the title *al-Zayyat*, "the dealer in oil." There was no difference in the signs representing these two words. According to this author the word used for *corruption of the text* means properly *employment of manuscript* in lieu of oral instruction, which was a necessity. He quotes verses which prove that the reading of such a text unaided was a difficult performance. One is by the poet Tammam (ob. 228 A.H.)[10]: "When they are fettered they march along, but when they are unfettered they cannot get away"; i.e., when the words are given diacritic points they can be read, but not otherwise. Another is by an earlier author, Ru'bah (ob. 145 A.H.), who however refers not to any Muslim writing but to the Christian Gospel[11]:

As though it were some doctor's Gospel, whose punctuator makes clear
that which his pen has written thereon with ink; when some reader spells
it out under his breath, the diacritic points bring out the words intended,
and the distinguishing circles or tattooing reveal the contents to the
intelligence of one who takes them in, unless indeed he has to have it
translated.

This reference to the two systems of Syriac punctuation is of great
interest; moreover the poem can be dated with fair accuracy, since the
caliph to whom it is dedicated reigned 132–36 A.H. (750–754 C.E.). In
another passage this poet alludes to the Arabic alphabet[12]: "'Tis as though
they were lines of a pointed text, uttering the *qāf* or the *lām*."

It is possible or even probable that this script was chosen in order to
maintain the esoteric character of the book; the Koran is a work of this
sort, and indeed in its opening sentences declares itself "guidance to the
pious, i.e., to those who observe the ordinances of Islam." Unbelievers are
not to handle it, or indeed know anything about it. There may then have
been an oral tradition of the way wherein it should be read. But it is clear
from the various readings that this tradition was to a great extent lost. In
order to facilitate reading diacritic points, distinguishing the letters (as in
the case cited, *r* from *z,* and *b* from *t*), were invented, according to the
author of the work on textual corruption at the instance of Hajjaj b. Yusuf
by one Nasr b. 'Asim. Somewhat later vowel-signs were introduced. The
caliph Ma'mun (198–218 A.H.) is said to have forbidden the use of both.[13]
The use of both came in very gradually as students of Arabic papyri know.
The caliph Walid b. Yazid (125 A.H.) notices that an epistle is "dotted," if
the line be genuine.[14] Abu Tammam a century later compliments a corre-
spondent for so marking his script that it leaves no doubt to the reader; it
not only has dots, but signs which indicate the cases, etc.[15]

It is surprising that the introduction of these signs into the text of the
Koran should have taken place without a civil war or the like. We may
define the business of the readers whose work became canonical as the
proper assignation of these points and vowel-signs. On the one hand they
had to build up a system of grammar from the Koran; on the other to apply
that system to its interpretation. In numerous cases the ambiguity of the
script which led to various readings was of little consequence; when, e. g.,
Allah was the subject, the verb might be read, "He shall," or "We shall,"
without affecting the sense. Yet there are places wherein this ambiguity is

by no means unimportant; in the account of the miracle of Badr (iii. 11) the nature of the miracle varies seriously according as we read "ye saw them" or "they saw them."

We should have expected the various readings to be based on tradition; the commentators rather assume that they are based on consideration of the evidence. In sura vi. 91 it depends on the location of a couple of dots whether we read "ye make it" or "they make it." "Ibn Kathir and Abu 'Amr," (two of the canonical readers) says Baidawi, "only read the third person to suit the preceding 'they did not esteem' " (where the form is unambiguous). They were not, then, reproducing what they had learned from teachers, but doing their best to decipher a text. It is surprising to find a various reading in the short "Opening" sura, which enters largely into the ritual. Some read *maliki yaumi 'l-dīn,* others *māliki,* meaning respectively "king of" and "possessor of" the Day of Judgment. Parallels are cited from the Koran in defense of the one and the other reading.

Where the readings are traced to contemporary authorities, there is at times a suspicion that this evidence is fictitious. In iv. 117 the text before the Readers ended in an obscure word: "They do not invoke in lieu of Allah other than...."; the last word was ordinarily read *ināthan* ("females"). It was not clear that this statement was accurate; certainly many of the deities worshiped in pagan Arabia were male. In xxix. 16, however, the Koran says, "Ye only worship in lieu of Allah *authānan* ('idols')." The emendation *idols* for *females* was clearly plausible; only the form *authānan* involved the insertion of a letter, whereas the form *uthunan* was doubtful Arabic. Tabari[16] tells us that someone had found the former in 'A'isha's copy,[17] while others averred that Ibn 'Abbas, the interpreter of the Koran par excellence, read the latter, which might be an alternative form of plural.

Ordinarily the readers did not venture to tamper with the consonants. Thus Mubarrad (ob. 285 A.H.)[18] dealing with the difficult verse lxxii. 4, wherein *ja(d)du ra(b)bina* is ordinarily read, ascribes a variant *jada* to Sa'id b. Jubair (ob. 95 A.H.), but says it cannot be accepted because it disagrees with the writing; and the same objection, he states, would apply to a reading *jiddan.* Any reading which did not involve such alteration would be permissible. On the whole this is the view maintained in the great grammatical work of Sibawaihi (ob. 180 A.H.). The vocalization was settled by critical and grammatical considerations. In xxxi. 26 he quotes the reading *wal-bahra,* but, he adds, some people read *wal-bahru* in accordance with certain usage.[19] The principle whereon the "people of Medina" prefer the reading *in kullan* to *inna kullan* in xi. 113 is elaborately explained. "I am informed," he writes, "that one of them read in cxi. 4 *hāmmalata* for *hammālatu*, treating the word not as a predicate, but as though he had said *I mean etc.*, by way of vituperation."[20] Yet he occasionally records variants which imply a difference in the consonantal text. The ordinary reading of lxviii. 9 *fayudhinūna* seems certified by the rhyme, while the grammar requires the subjunctive; Sibawaihi says, "Harun asserted that *fayudhinu* was to be found in certain copies."[21] "They aver," he says, "that in the text of Ibn Mas'ud of xi. 75 there was *shaykhan*" (i.e., with a final *a*) in lieu of *shaykhun*. Sibawaihi's formulae imply that he accepts no responsibility for the statements which he records.

Did these Readers ever go outside the Koran and the grammatical rules which they had formulated in order to determine the correct reading and vocalization of the text? The tradition that one of them read *Ibraham* in lieu of *Ibrahīm* suggests such research; it was a bold alteration, for the form *Ibrahīm* seems certified by the rhyme in xxi. 61, 63. It would appear that some historical study was bestowed on the opening words of sura xxx. 1, containing a famous oracle. The natural way to vocalize the words would appear to give the sense, "The Romans have been victorious in the nearest part of the earth (the Near East!) and they after their victory shall be victorious." This was rejected by the Readers, who read either, "The Romans have been conquered in the nearest part of the earth and they after their conquest (defeat) shall conquer"; or "The Romans have conquered in the nearest part of the earth and they after their conquest shall be conquered." The former, which is the ordinary, view made the first reference to the defeat of the Byzantines by the Persians, and the second to their later defeat of the Persians, which is foretold; the second view made the first reference to the defeat of the Persians by the Byzantines, and the second to the defeat of the Byzantines by the Muslims. Since the text proceeds to say, "and that day shall the Believers rejoice," probably the second view is really right.

The introduction of diacritic points and vowel-signs stabilized the text of the Koran so far as it was possible to stabilize it; gradually out of the large number of recensions made by the processes that have been sketched a certain number became authoritative, and such various readings as were presented outside this number were quoted chiefly in support of one or other of the interpretations which the canonical recensions were supposed to admit. The process whereby this came about bears a resemblance to what happened in the case of the schools of law; among many rival schools ultimately four came to be regarded as orthodox, and the others, even when attached to illustrious names, fell into oblivion.

One who deciphered the Koran afresh in these days—i.e., based a new edition on an unpointed text—would be likely to adopt many uncanonical readings, and might even introduce some that were new. He might, e.g., substitute *Yuhanan* for *Yahya* as the name of the Baptist. He might be able to obelize certain texts as later than the Prophet's time. But in the endeavor to produce a Koran such as the Prophet might have approved he would be confronted with the difficulty which was too great for the original collectors—the theory of *substitution*, the limits of which he would be unable to fix. Where the same narrative is repeated, should one version only be retained? The exercise of this theory would reduce the Koran to a fraction of its present bulk; yet repetition of narratives has no place in a single book, equally with or without discrepancies. The case of the four Gospels offers no parallel, since here we have not one book, but four books ascribed to different authors.

In normal cases a collection of various readings furnishes the history of the corruption of a text through carelessness or interpolation. Occasionally it may include a record of alterations made by the author himself. The case of the Koran differs from these in some important respects. The greater number of variants are different attempts at deciphering the same text; often there is agreement about the consonants intended, but disagreement about the vowels to be supplied; the oracle about the Romans shows that such disagreement may affect the meaning seriously. Owing to the ambiguity of the signs used for consonants there is often disagreement about the interpretation of these signs; the variation that has been quoted between *females* and *idols* shows that the difference of sense which results may be considerable. Less frequently the difference of reading extends to the number of signs in the text; the addition of one letter in vii. 142 changes "I shall show to you" into "I shall cause you to inherit." "The latter," says Zamakhshari, "is a good reading, because it agrees with vii. 133." At times, however, it extends to the omission or addition of whole words or phrases. We have good reason for believing that parts of the Koran were obtained by the collectors from oral tradition and not from manuscript; and here we have the possibilities that the same passage was variously reported by those who remembered it, that one form was substituted for another by the Prophet himself, and that the alterations were due to copyists, and made intentionally or unintentionally. And thus we ascend by easy stages from lower to higher criticism.

It is worthy of note that in spite of the reputation of the Umayyads for impiety the stabilization of the Koran, so far as it was accomplished, was achieved during their dynasty. In this context it should be remembered that the founder of that dynasty appealed to the arbitrament of the Koran when his rival 'Ali would have preferred that of the sword, and the Koran appeared to favor the former's claim. And we have seen that the founder of the 'Abbasid capital was by no means *Bibelfest*, if that phrase may be applied to the Koran.

PART THREE

The Sources
of the Koran

11.

What Did Muhammad Borrow from Judaism?

Abraham Geiger

*I*N THE CASE OF ANY SINGLE INSTANCE of borrowing, the proof that the passage is really of Jewish origin must rest on two grounds. First, it must be shown to exist in Judaism, and to prove this we have every facility. Secondly, in order to attain to certainty we must prove that it is really borrowed, i.e., that it is not founded on anything in old Arabian tradition, which Muhammad used largely as a foundation though he disputed some points. Then again we must show that it had its origin in Judaism and not in Christianity. For the complete discussion of the last two points it would be necessary to write two treatises similar to the one on which I am now engaged, of which the respective subjects would be—(1) the points of contact between Islam and the ancient tradition of the Arabs, and (2) the points of contact between Islam and Christianity; and only in this way could certainty on these points be attained. But these investigations would, on the one hand, lead us too far away from our particular subject, and, on the other, they would require a much more exact treatment than could be given while handling our main subject. Then, too, they are made unnecessary by the means which we use in each individual case, and which will be shown in the different divisions of the work; so that on most points we can without them attain to a high degree of probability, practically sufficient for all scientific purposes. For the sake of clearness, it may be well to divide the

---

Originally published as part of *Judaism and Islam* (Madras, 1898).

material borrowed from Judaism into thoughts belonging to it, and narratives taken from it, and later we shall have to subdivide again.

THOUGHTS BELONGING TO JUDAISM
WHICH HAVE PASSED OVER INTO THE KORAN?

The new thoughts borrowed by one religion from another are of a twofold nature. Either they are radically new, there being hitherto in the borrowing religion not even a foreshadowing of them, so that the very conceptions are new, and require accordingly new words for their expression; or else the component parts of these thoughts have long been in existence but not in this combination, the form in which these conceptions are blended being a novel one, and the view, therefore, which arises from this unusual presentation being new. We must therefore divide this chapter according to these distinctions.

CONCEPTIONS BORROWED FROM JUDAISM?

As the ushering in of hitherto unknown religious conceptions is always marked by the introduction of new words for their expression, and as the Jews in Arabia, even when able to speak Arabic, kept to the rabbinical Hebrew names for their religious conceptions, so words which from their derivation are shown to be not Arabic but Hebrew, or better still Rabbinic, must be held to prove the Jewish origin of the conceptions expressed. The passage already quoted about the foreign language spoken by those who were accused of helping Muhammad in writing the Koran seems to point to the use among the Jews of a language other than Arabic. The object of this chapter is to enumerate the words which have passed from rabbinical Hebrew into the Koran, and so into the Arabic language.

Tabut, Ark. The termination *ut* is a fairly certain evidence that the word is not of Arabic but of rabbinical Hebrew origin; for this dialect of Hebrew has adopted in the place of other endings this termination, which is very common also in Chaldaic and Syriac; and I venture to assert that no pure Arabic word ends in this way. Our word appears in two different passages with two different meanings: first, where the mother of Moses is told to put her son into an ark,[1] the signification being here purely Hebrew; but from this it arose that the ark of the covenant was also called by this name. It is used thus especially[2] in the sense of coming before the ark in prayer. In the second sura[3] we kind it mentioned as a sign of the rightful ruler that through him the ark of the covenant[4] should return.

Taurat, the Law.[5] This word like the Greek equivalent in the New Testament is used only for the Jewish revelation; and although Muhammad, having only oral tradition, was not able to distinguish so exactly, yet it is obvious that he comprehended the Pentateuch alone under this name;[6] for among the Jewish prophets after the patriarchs he counts Moses alone as a lawgiver. For the most part the Law is mentioned in connection with the Gospel.[7]

Jannatu 'Adn, Paradise. The word "'Adn" is not known in the Arabia language in the sense of pleasure or happiness, but this is the meaning which suits the word in this connection.[8] In Hebrew this is the radical meaning; still this expression, viz., Garden of Eden, which occurs often in the Bible, is never to be explained out and out as Paradise; but rather Eden is there the proper name of a region which was inhabited by our first parents in their innocence, and the part in which they actually lived was a garden of trees. It is only natural that this earthly region of the golden age should by degrees have come to be regarded as Paradise, in that the word itself no longer stands for the name of a place but is applied to a state of bliss,[9] though the Jews still held to Eden as a locality also. It is clear from the translation "gardens of pleasure" that the Jews of that time not merely transferred the name Eden into Arabic, but carried over its supposed etymology as well. The more distinctively Christian name[10] occurs seldom in the Koran, though it also is not quite strange to later Judaism, as is shown by the story of the four who went alive to Paradise.[11]

Jahannam, Hell. This word also, like its opposite Paradise, is of Jewish origin. According to its primary meaning and biblical usage it too is the name of a place, though of a locality far less important than that which gave its name to Paradise. The vale of Hinnom was nothing more than a spot dedicated to idol worship; and it is remarkable that the horror of idolatry led to the use of its name to designate hell. That this is the ordinary name for it in the Talmud needs no proof, and from it is derived the New Testament name Gehenna. Now, it might be asserted that Muhammad got this word from the Christians; but, even setting aside the argument that, as the name for Paradise is Jewish the probabilities are in favor of a Jewish origin for the word for hell also, the form of the word itself speaks for its derivation from Judaism. We lay no stress on the fact that the aspirate *he,* which is not expressed in the Greek, reappears in the Arabic, because this aspirate though not always indicated by grammarians in writing, appears to have been always sounded in speech. This holds good of other Greek words which have passed into Syriac.[12] The letter *mim,* which stands at the end of the Arabic (*Jahannam*), not being found in the Syriac word, proves the derivation from the Hebrew word (*Gehinnom*). The word is found in many places in the Koran.[13]

Aḥbar.[14] This word is found in several places in the Koran in the sense of teacher. Now the real Hebrew word *ḥabber,* companion, has acquired in the Mishna a meaning similar to that of *parush;* only that the latter was the name of a sect, and the former the name of a party within a sect. The word *parush* means, properly speaking, one separated, i.e., one who withdraws himself out of motives of piety, a Pharisee, as distinguished from one who grasps without scruple all the pleasures of this life, a Sadducee. Among those who were thus separated there grew up a difference from others not only in social customs, but especially in that they adopted a different doctrinal view, viz., a belief in oral tradition. They had also some very strict principles for the guidance of their lives. But the matter was no longer merely one of great carefulness in life and conduct; it became one of special learning and knowledge, which naturally could not be imparted in equal measure to all members of this sect. Hence these learned men, each of whom possessed some special knowledge, became greatly reverenced; and in this way again a community was formed in contradistinction to which the remaining people of the country were called the laity.[15] The individual members of this community however were called *ḥabberim,* "fellows;" and thus, though the meaning "teacher" is not, properly speaking, in the word itself, yet the peculiar development of this community is the cause of the new meaning of the word.

The excessive veneration paid to these "fellows" by the Jews gives rise to Muhammad's reproof in the two passages last alluded to. He reproaches the Christians too in both places[16] on account of the esteem in which they held the *ruhban.* This word *ruhban* is probably not derived from *rahiba,* to fear (thus god-fearing); but, like *qissisun* the word which accompanies it in sura V. 85, is to be derived from the Syriac, which language maintained its preeminence among the Christians in those regions; thus *ruhban* is derived from the Syriac word *rabhoye,* and *qissisun* from the Syriac *qashishoye.*

So then *ruhban* does not really mean the ordinary monks, who are called *daire,* but the clergy; whereas *qissis* stands for the *presbyter,* the elder, who is called *qashisho* in Syriac.

Darasa, to reach the deep meaning of the Scripture by exact and careful research. Such a diligent enquiry is mentioned in several passages.[17] But this kind of interpretation, which is not content to accept the obvious and generally accepted meaning of a passage, but which seeks out remote allusions—this (though it may bring much of importance and value to light, if used with tact and knowledge of the limits of the profitable in such study) is very apt to degenerate and to become a mere laying of stress on the unimportant, a searching for meanings where there are none, and for allusions which are purely accidental. And so the word acquired a secondary meaning, viz., to trifle, to invent a meaning and force it into a passage. Compare the standing expression current among many who seek the simple primary meaning. The word in this usage occurs in the Koran, particularly in the mouth of Muhammad's opponents; though until now this fact has not been recognized. The obviously misunderstood passage in sura VI. 105 is thus explained, also that in VI. 157. The former may be thus translated: "And when we variously explain our signs, they may say if they like: Thy explanations are far fetched, we will expound it to people of understanding"; and the latter as follows: "Lest ye should say: the Scriptures were only sent down unto two peoples before us, but we turn away from their system of forced explanation"; i.e., they have left the Scriptures to us so overlaid and distorted that we cannot follow them. It is remarkable that this word, which is not a usual one in the Koran, appears in this sense only in the sixth sura where it occurs twice; and this is evidence that just at the time of the composition of this sura the word in its secondary meaning was used by some persons as a reproach to Muhammad. This observation furthermore might well serve to indicate the unity of this sura.

Rabbani, teacher. This rabbinical word is probably formed by the addition of the suffix *an* (like *nu*) to the word *rab,* thus, our lord or teacher. For though the termination *an* is common in later Hebrew, yet the weaker word *rabbi* shows that people did not hesitate to append a suffix to the word *rab,* and then to treat the whole as a new word. However that may be, *rabban* is a word of itself now, and is only conferred as a title on the most distinguished teachers. The rabbinical rule runs thus "Greater than *rabbi* is *rabban.*" It appears as a title of honor in suras III. 73, V. 48, 68. *Rabbani* is evidently a word of narrower meaning than the word *aḥbar* explained above; and this explains why *rabbani* is put before *aḥbar* in the two passages last mentioned, where they both appear, and also the striking omission of our word in the other two places where *aḥbar* occurs, and where Muhammad finds fault with the divine reverence paid to teachers,

describing them with the more general word. The case is the same with
qissis and *ruhban*. Both classes are mentioned with praise in sura V. 85, and
with blame in sura IX. 31, 34, the latter class however only in connection
with *ahbar*, in that *ruhban* (like *ahbar*) is of wider meaning: and further, on
account of the combination in one passage of two different classes among
the Jews and Christians, viz., the *ahbar* and the *ruhban* (cf. other similar
combinations) no special differentiation was to be attempted.

Sabt,[18] day of rest, Saturday. This name continued to be applied to Saturday throughout the East by Christians as well as Muslims, though it had
ceased to be a day of rest.[19] In one place[20] Muhammad seems rather to
protest against its being kept holy. The well-known Ben Ezra remarks on
this in his commentary on Exodus xvi. 1, where he says: "In Arabic five
days are named according to number, first day, second day, etc. But the
sixth day is called the day of assembly, for it is the holy day of the week;
the Sabbath however is called by the Arabs *sabt*, because the Shin and the
Samech, (i.e., the Arabic *sin* which is pronounced like the Hebrew Samech)
interchange in their writings. They have taken the word from Israel."

Sakinat,[21] the presence of God. In the development of Judaism in order
to guard against forming too human an idea of the Godhead, it was customary to attribute the speaking of God, when it is mentioned in the
Scripture, to a personified word of God,[22] as it were embodying that emanation from the Deity which came in Christianity to a veritable Incarna-
tion. In like manner also when in the Scriptures the remaining stationary,
or the resting of God is mentioned, something sensible proceeding from
Him is to be thought of. This is especially so in the case of God's dwelling
in the Temple;[23] and this "emanation of the Godhead," to adopt the speech
of the Gnostics, was called on this account the *Shekinah*, the resting. From
this derivation *Shekinah* came to be the word for that side of divine providence which, as it were, dwells among men and exerts an unseen influence
among them. In the original meaning, viz. that of the presence in the
temple over the Ark of the Covenant between the cherubim,[24] the word is
found in sura II. 249. In the sense of active interposition and visible effectual rendering of aid it occurs in sura IX. 26, 40;[25] in the sense of supplying
peace of mind and at the same time giving spiritual aid it is found in sura
XLVIII. 4, 18, 26. It is remarkable that the word appears in three suras only
(but several times in the two last mentioned) and with a somewhat different meaning in each; and it seems here again, as we remarked above on
the word *darasa*, as though outside influence had been at work, i.e., that the

use of this word by other people seems to have influenced Muhammad at the time of the composition of these suras.

Taghut, error. Though this mild word for idolatry is not found in the rabbinical writings,[26] still the Jews in Arabia seem to have used it to denote the worship of false gods, for it appears in the Koran[27] in this sense.

Furqan, deliverance,[28] redemption. This is a very important word, and it is one which in my opinion has till now been quite misunderstood. In the primary meaning it occurs in the 8th sura: "O true believers; if ye fear God, He will grant you a deliverance[29] and will expiate your sins, etc." Elpherar gives five different explanations to this verse, each as unsuitable as Wahl's translation, and the passage seems to me truly classical for the primary meaning of the word. This meaning appears also in sura VIII. 42, where the day of the victory of Badr is called the day of deliverance, and in sura II. 181 where this name is given to the month Ramadhan as the month of redemption and deliverance from sin. Muhammad, entirely diverging from Jewish ideas, intended to establish his religion as that of the world in general; further he condemned the earlier times altogether calling them times of ignorance.[30] He declared his creed to have been revealed through God's apostles from the earliest times, and to have been only renewed and put into a clearer and more convincing form by himself. Hence the condition of anyone outside his belief must have seemed to him a sinful one, and the divine revelation granted to himself and his predecessors appeared to him in the light of deliverance from that sinful life which could only lead to punishment; and therefore he calls revelation itself in many places *furqan*, as in many he calls it *rahmat*, mercy. In some passages he applies the term to the Koran,[31] and in others to the Mosaic revelation.[32]

In this way all the passages fit in under the primary signification of the word, and there is no need to guess at a different meaning for each.

Ma'un, refuge. This word bears a very foreign impress, and is explained by the Arabic commentators in a variety of ways. Golius, following them, forces the most diverse meanings into it. It appears in sura CVII. 7, and seems to me to mean a refuge—"they refuse refuge," i.e., they give no shelter to those asking for help. Later on the word seems to have been regarded as derived from *'ana* (certainly not from *ma'ana* to which Golius refers it), and thence it acquired the meaning of support, alms.

Masani, repetition. There has been much perplexity about this word, mainly because it has been considered as an Arabic word and has not been traced back to its source. As by degrees other teaching, viz., tradition,[33] grew up by the side of that contained in Holy Writ, the whole law was divided into two parts, the written teaching, that is the Bible, and the teaching by word of mouth or tradition. To occupy oneself with the former was called "to read;" to occupy oneself with the latter was called "to say." In the Chaldaic Gemara the latter word means to speak after, to repeat the teacher's words after him. In like manner the word *tinnah* was used almost exclusively of choral music, in which the choir repeated verses after the preceptor. Thus teaching by word of month was called *mishnah*, and so also the collection of oral teaching—the whole tradition; and afterwards when this was all written down the book received the same name. Now, however, an etymological error crept in and derived this word from *shanah* in its true Hebrew meaning "to repeat," and then applied it to the repetition of the written teaching. The error of this explanation is shown both in the use of the word and in its inflection. Still it seems to have been accepted by the Roman Jews, and thus it came about that in Justinian's *Novels* the *mishna* is called *secunda editio*. The same thing happened in the case of the Arabian Jews, and so we get our word *masani*. Muhammad putting his book in the place of the whole Jewish teaching calls it not only *Qur'ān (miqra)* but also *masani*.[34]

Malakut, government. This word is used only of God's rule, in which connection it invariably appears also in rabbinical writings.[35] It occurs in several passages in the Koran.[36] From this narrow use of the word, and from a false derivation from *mala'k* or *malak* (a word which comes from quite a different root, and which in Arabic has only the meaning of a messenger of God) it came to be used for the realm of spirits.

These fourteen words, which are clearly derived from the later, or rabbinical Hebrew, show what very important religious conceptions passed from Judaism into Islam,—namely, the idea of the divine guidance, *sakinat, malakut*; of revelation, *furqan, masani*; of judgment after death, *jannatu 'adn* and *jahannam*, besides others which will be brought forward as peculiar to Judaism.

VIEWS BORROWED FROM JUDAISM

While in the foregoing section we were content to consider it certain that a conception was derived from Judaism, if the word expressing that conception could be shown to be of Jewish origin, we must now pass on from this method of judging and adopt a new test. We must prove first in detail that the idea in question springs from a Jewish root; then to attain to greater certainty we must further show that the idea is in harmony with the spirit of Judaism, that apart from Judaism the conception would lose in importance and value, that it is in fact only an offshoot of a great tree. To this argument may be added the opposition, alluded to in the Koran itself, which this foreign graft met with from both Arabs and Christians. For the better arrangement of these views we must divide them into three groups: A. Matters of Creed or Doctrinal views, B. Moral and Legal Rules, and C. Views of Life.

A. Doctrinal Views. We must here set a distinct limit for ourselves, in order on the one hand that we may not drift away into an endless undertaking and attempt to expound the whole Koran; and on the other that we may not go off into another subject altogether and try to set forth the theology of the Koran, an undertaking which was began with considerable success in the *Tübingen Zeitschrift für Evang. Theol. (1881), 3tes Heft.* Furthermore, certain general points of belief are so common to all mankind that the existence of any one of them in one religion must not be considered as proving a borrowing from another. Other views again are so well-known and so fully worked out that we need not discuss them in detail, but shall find a mere mention of them sufficient. Of this kind is that of the idea of the unity of God, the fundamental doctrine of Israel and Islam. At the time of the rise of the latter, this view was to be found in Judaism alone, and therefore Muhammad must have borrowed it from that religion. This may be considered as proved without any unnecessary display of learning on the point. The idea of future reward and punishment is common to all religions, but it is held in so many different ways that we shall be obliged to consider it in our argument. Cardinal points of faith have also passed from Judaism into Christianity. To decide whether these points as adopted in the Koran have come from the Jews or from the Christians, we must direct our special attention to a comparison between the forms in which the beliefs are held in both those religions, and the form in which they are presented to us by Muhammad. This is to answer the objection, that in the following discussion so little is to be found about the cardinal dogmas, for even the enumeration of them is foreign to our purpose.

Every religion which conceives God as an active working providence must have some distinct teaching on the creation, and this Muhammad gives in accordance with the Bible, viz., that God created heaven and earth and all that therein is in six days;[37] although in another place he diverges somewhat and says that the earth was created in two days, the mountains and the green herbs in four days, and the heavens with all their divisions in two days more.[38] Though this passage is nothing but a flight of poetic fancy, still it shows how little Muhammad knew of the Bible, inasmuch as he is aware of nothing but the general fact that the creation took place in six days, and that he has not any knowledge of each day's separate work. We have already remarked that he calls the seventh day *sabt*, but does not recognize its sanctity. It remains here to be added that Muhammad appears to allude to and reject the Jewish belief that God rested on the seventh day.[39] He evidently thought that a necessity for rest after hard labor was implied, for after mentioning the creation as having taken place in six days, he adds "and no weariness affected us." On this Jalalu'd-din comments as follows: "This was revealed as an answer to the Jews who said that God had rested thoroughly on the sabbath and therefore weariness left Him." The same thing is to be found in Elpherar's commentary but not so clearly expressed.

The idea of several heavens, which is indicated by the biblical expression "heaven of heavens," came to Muhammad probably from the Jews, also the notion that they were seven in number, a notion due to the different names applied to heaven. In Chagiga[40] we find the assertion that there are seven heavens, and then the names are given. All these names occur in the Scripture except the first, viz. *vilon*, from the Latin *velum*. This name in which heaven is compared to a curtain, which veils the glory of[41] God, is a very important one in the Talmud. Muhammad speaks often of the seven heavens,[42] and in one passage he calls the heavens the seven strongholds[43] and in another the seven paths.[44] This last expression occurs also in the Talmud. During the creation, however, His throne was upon the waters.[45] This idea also is borrowed from the Jews, who say:[46] "The throne of glory then stood in the air, and hovered over the waters by the command of God." This is somewhat more clearly expressed by Elpherar who says: "And this water was in the middle of the air."

A second pivot of every revealed religion is the belief in a judgment after death; for while the fact of the creation sets forth the omnipotence of the Creator, the doctrine of a final account teaches that it is God's will that His revealed laws shall be obeyed. This, then, in Judaism developed into a local paradise and hell, and both conceptions have passed, as we have already shown, into Islam. These localities, although at first mere symbols, mere embodiments of the spiritual idea of a state, afterwards became crystallized, and suffered the fate of every symbol, i.e., they were taken for the thing symbolized, and the places were more definitely indicated. Thus the Jews have a saying: "The world is the sixtieth part of the garden, the garden is the sixtieth part of Eden;"[47] and in the Koran we find a similar expression, viz., "paradise whose breadth equalleth the heavens and the earth"[48] Generally speaking, fear is stronger than hope, and the dread of a terrible condemnation appeals far more powerfully than the hope of eternal happiness to a nature which pure religious feeling does not impel to piety of life. This is probably the reason for describing hell in a more detailed and particular manner than paradise.

Seven hells are pictured as forming different grades of punishment, and these have been developed out of the seven different names mentioned in the Talmud.[49] These names with one exception (*Erets tahtith,* subterranean realm, which is clearly adopted from the Roman ideas at the time of their ascendancy) are biblical. Later on these names came to be construed as seven hells, e.g., in the Midrash on the Psalms at the end of the eleventh Psalm where it is said, "There are seven abodes of the wicked in hell," after which the above mentioned names are cited with a few variations. It is also said that David by a sevenfold reiterated cry of "my son" (*beni*) rescued Absalom from the seven habitations of hell;[50] furthermore hell is said to have seven portals.[51] Muhammad is not behind hand, for we read in one passage that[52] "it (hell) hath seven gates, unto every gate a distinct company of them shall be assigned." According to the Jews, a tree stands at the entrance to hell:[53] "Two date palms grow in the valley of Ben Hinnom, smoke issues from between them and this is the entrance to hell"; but Muhammad knows a tree of hell called *al-Zaqqum*[54] which serves sinners for food, about which he has much to relate. The step from such a definite idea of hell to the notion of a personality connected with it is an easy one, and we find such an individual mentioned by the rabbis as the "prince of *Gehinnom*," he is called however in the Koran simply *Jahannam.* In one rabbinical book[55] we find the following: "That the prince of hell says daily, 'Give me food to satisfy me,' comes from Isaiah, v. 14." Muhammad says similarly: "On that day We will say unto hell, 'Art thou full?' and it shall say 'Are there more'?"

When the conceptions of paradise and hell became so definite, and their names were no longer general terms for reward and punishment, a third destination had to be provided for those whose conduct had not been such as to entitle them to the former nor condemn them to the latter place. Thus while the righteous found their place in paradise, and the sinners had their portion in hell, those who belonged to neither class were placed in a space between paradise and hell, of which it is said in the Midrash on Ecclesiastes, vii. 14: "How much room is there between them? Rabbi Jochanan says a wall; R. Acha says a span; other teachers however hold that they are so close together that people can see from one into the other."[56] The idea just touched upon in this passage is most poetically worked out in sura VII. 44,[57] "And between the blessed and the damned there shall be a veil; and men shall stand on Al-Araf who shall know them by their marks; and shall call unto the inhabitants of paradise saying, 'Peace be upon you'; yet they shall not enter therein, though they earnestly desire it. And when they[58] shall turn their eyes towards the companions of hell fire, they rejoice that they are not among them, and show them the folly of their earthly walk and hopes."

It is interesting to compare this view of a threefold dealing with the dead with the very similar Platonic idea.[59]

The idea of the bliss of eternal life, as well as the metaphor which expresses the difficulty of attaining it, is common to the Koran and Judaism. There is a rabbinical saying[60] to the effect that "one hour of rapture in that world is better than a whole life-time in this." With this we may compare the Koran:[61] "And what is this life in comparison with the life to come except a passing amusement?" Then for the difficulty of attaining paradise we may compare the rabbinical picture of the elephant entering the needle's with the words in sura VII. 38 "Neither shall they enter into paradise until a camel pass through the eye of a needle." This last metaphor seems to be borrowed from Christianity (partly because of the similarity of the figure, in that "camel" is the metaphor used in the Gospels, and partly because of the frequent mention of the same by the Evangelists),[62] and is only deserving of mention here, because the fact that in the Talmud elephant is used seems to confirm the ordinary translation of the Greek word in the Gospels, and the Arabic word in the Koran, and to remove the doubt as to whether they might not be better rendered "cable."

Given the pure conception of immortality, viz., that the life of the soul never ceases, it becomes unnecessary to fix a time at which the judgment shall take place; and so in most Talmudic passages a future world is pictured in which everything earthly is stripped away and pious souls enjoy the brightness of God's presence. Echoes of this teaching are to be found in the Koran. In one passage[63] we read of a soul gazing on its Lord, and in another[64] the condition of a perfectly peaceful soul is beautifully described. But this entirely spiritual idea was not thoroughly carried out. Rather by the side of the pure conception of a continued life of the soul after the death of the body,[65] there existed that of the quickening of the dead.[66] Thus because the man cannot receive the requital of his deeds while he is still in a state of death, the time of resurrection must be the time for the judgment.[67]

These two views of the resurrection and the judgment day, though different in themselves, are both closely connected in Judaism and more especially in Islam.[68] In Judaism there is a third period, the advent of a Messiah, which it is not easy to separate from the other two. Naturally this time, which is to bring forth two such important events as judgment and resurrection, will be ushered in by terrible signs. In Judaism statements to this effect are to be found only about the third period, which is generally connected with the other two, viz., the earthly period of the Messiah; in Islam on the contrary everything is attributed to the last day. The utterance most in accord with the Talmud is that in Sunnas 41 and 141, which says that learning shall vanish, ignorance shall take root, drunkenness and immorality shall increase. With this we must compare the passage in Sanhedrin 97: "At the time when David's son comes the learned diminish, and the place of learned meetings serves for immorality." The descriptions in the Koran refer more to the last day itself, and remind us of many passages in Holy Scripture, where it is also said of those days that the world will bow itself before God, the heavens will be rolled together[69] and vanish in smoke,[70] all cities will be destroyed,[71] and men will be drunken and yet not drunken.[72]

Another very distinct sign of the advent of a Messiah, which is remotely alluded to in the Bible but which attained to an extraordinary development in the Talmud and especially in later writings, is the battle of Gog, Prince of Magog.[73] Gog and Magog are, however, named by the rabbis as two princes, and this view has taken root in the Koran in the rabbinical form,[74] since two persons, Gog and Magog, are mentioned as dwellers in the uttermost parts of the earth.[75]

In the details of the idea of future retribution many resemblances are to be found, which, by virtue of the unity of the Jewish view and its derivation from the Scriptures, show themselves as borrowings from Judaism. Thus according to the Talmud, a man's limbs themselves shall give testimony against him;[76] in one passage we find these words: "The very members of [77] a man bear witness against him, for it is said: 'Ye yourselves are my witnesses saith the Lord.'" With this we may compare sura XXIV 24: "Their own tongues, and hands, and feet, shall one day be witness against them of their own doings.[78] The judgment day gains also a greater importance from the fact that not only individuals and nations appear at it, but also those beings who have been honored as gods by the nations, and they too receive punishment with their worshippers. In Sukkah XXIX we find this statement: "As often as a nation (on account of idolatry) receives its punishment, those beings honored by it as gods shall also be punished; for, it is written:[79] 'Against all the gods of Egypt I will execute judgment.'" That this general sentence admits of a reference to the punishment of the last day is not expressly stated, but it is worthy of acceptation. Muhammad expresses himself still more clearly about it:[80] "Verily both ye and the idols which ye worship besides God shall be cast as fuel into hell fire."

A view closely interwoven with Judaism and Islam is that retributive punishment is entirely confined to the state after death, and that any single merit which a sinner has gained will be rewarded in this world, to the end that nothing may impede the course of judgment in the next. The same view, only reversed, holds good in the case of the righteous. It is a view which was thought to explain the course of destiny upon earth, which so often seems to run contrary to the merits and demerits of men.

The rabbinical view is expressed in the following passage: "Whereunto are the pious in this world to be compared? To a tree which stands entirely in a clean place; and when a branch bends to an unclean place, it is cut off and the tree itself stands there quite clean. Thus God sends afflictions in this world to the righteous, that they may possess that which is to come, as it is written: 'Though thy beginning was small, yet thy latter end should greatly increase.'[81] Sinners are like a tree which stands in an altogether unclean place; if a branch bends over to a clean place, it is cut off and the tree itself stands there quite unclean. Thus God allows the ungodly to prosper, in order to plunge them into the lowest depth of hell, as it is written: 'There is a way which seemeth right unto a man, but the end thereof are the ways of death.' "[82] Muhammad expresses this same view in several passages, but restricts himself to the latter part which refers to the prosperity of sinners, partly because his own ideas were too unspiritual for him to be able to imagine the righteous as truly happy without earthly goods, partly because in so doing his teaching would have lost in acceptability to his very degraded contemporaries. Thus in one passage[83] we read: "We grant them long and prosperous lives only that their iniquity may be increased,"[84] still the second view is to be found among the Arabians also, e.g., Elpherar in his comments on Koran XII. 42 says: "It is said that the righteous are punished and tried, in order that the day of resurrection may be perfect in light and power, as the contumacy of the righteous has been already expiated." Muhammad naturally avoided specifying any time at which the judgment should take place, though he was much pressed to do so. He excused himself with the Jewish saying that with God a thousand years are as one day,[85] which was divested of its poetic adornment and taken by the rabbis in a purely literal sense.[86] Muhammad says[87]: "Verily one day with thy Lord is as a thousand years of those which ye compute"; and again[88]: "On the day whose length shall be a thousand years of those which ye compute."

As has been already shown, with the establishment of the doctrine of the day of judgment, the view of the resurrection and of the quickening of the dead was also formed; and this the more readily, because it found support in expressions in the Scripture, as, e.g., those in Ezekiel, xxxvii.[89] "I have opened your graves, and caused you to come up out of your graves, ... ye shall live," etc.; and those in other passages referring partly to the metaphorical quickening of the dead land of Israel. Of this doctrine it is said that it is such a fundamental teaching of the Jewish faith that the declaration that it did not belong to the law entailed the exclusion of him who thus spoke from eternal life.[90] The Koran is, so to speak, founded upon this doctrine along with that of the unity of God, and there is scarcely a page in it where this doctrine is not mentioned. To adduce proofs here would be as easy as it would be useless; and indeed it is not required by our purpose, since Christianity also has inherited this view from Judaism, as is shown in the argument of Jesus in refutation of the Sadducees. Only one point deserves particular mention, because on the one hand it contains a detail adopted from Judaism, and on the other it shows the low level of thought at that time.

As soon as it becomes a question not merely of the immortality of the soul, but also of the resurrection of the body, then the soul without its body is no longer regarded as the same person, and the question naturally presents itself to the ordinary understanding: "How can this body which we have seen decay rise again, so that the same personality shall reappear?" Neither the soul alone nor the body alone is the person, but the union of the two. Now one part of this union is dissolved; another body can indeed be given to this soul, but by this means he who died does not reappear, but a new man, another personality, another consciousness comes into being. This question dimly anticipated obtrudes itself, and can only be set at rest by proving that the very same personality can appear again. Instead of showing this Muhammad contents himself with the parable, used also occasionally in the Talmud, of the renewal of the dried up earth by fertilizing rain. He found however that he could not silence the common convictions of men thereby,[91] and so he was compelled to come back to it again and again. The Jews also sought to give prominence to this resemblance, and they put the eulogium "Who sendeth down the rain" into the second benediction which treats of the resurrection.[92] The fact that the righteous rise actually in their clothes[93] (which after all is not more wonderful than in their bodies) is explained by the parable of the grain of wheat, which is laid in the earth without covering, but springs up again with many coverings. The passage in Koran VI. 96 contains a similar statement. This view is not strange to Islam, for a saying which is attributed to Muhammad runs thus: "The dead man shall be raised in the clothes in which he died."

That from the standpoint of revealed religion the belief in the possibility of revelation is fundamental needs of course no proof, and in this the views of all revealed religions are alike; yet differences can be found in the manner of conceiving of the revelation, and here we recognize again that Muhammad derived his view of it from Judaism, of course with some modification.

The Jews have a saying that "all the prophets saw through a dark glass, but Moses through a clear one,"[94] and Muhammad says:[95] It was not granted to a man that God should speak unto him otherwise than in a vision or from behind a veil;[96] and then he adds: "or by the sending of a messenger to reveal by His permission that which He pleaseth." This messenger is the Holy Spirit,[97] or simply the spirit,[98] like the spirit in the story of Micaiah's vision.[99] The Arabic commentators take this holy spirit to mean Gabriel, a view which is not unknown to the Jews, for the Jewish commentators understand the words[100] "the definitely speaking Spirit" to refer to Gabriel. One of Muhammad's own utterances, one which is fully explained only by the 52nd Sunna, is much more striking:[101] "And they will ask thee of the spirit, say: the spirit (proceedeth) at my Lord's command."

With this the teaching about angels is closely connected, and it also had its beginning in Scripture, but appears to have been developed in later days especially through Parseeism. Muhammad is unwearied in his descriptions of angels; so too are the later Jews in their many prayers on the day of atonement, but these are of rather late origin.[102] The angel of death[103] is especially mentioned in sura XXXII. 11.

While angels were regarded as purely spiritual beings who execute God's commands, a class of beings was imagined who stood between man and the purest spirits; these were mixed spirits, who were made out of fire,[104] who possessed superior mental powers, but who were mostly inclined to evil; they were called demons, but there are numerous other names for them in Arabic. The Talmud has the following statement about them: "Demons are declared to possess six qualities, three of which are angelic and three human. The three which pertain to angels are that they have wings, that they can fly from one end of the earth to the other (i.e., they are bound by no space), and that they know the future beforehand. They know the future beforehand? No! but they listen behind the curtain. The three human qualities are that they eat and drink, increase and multiply,[105] and die."[106] Muslim tradition cannot do enough in their description, but there is but little about them in the Koran. The fact that they listened at the canopy of heaven gained for them in the Koran the nickname of the stoned,[107] for, say the commentators, the angels threw stones to drive them away when they found them listening.[108] Thus it is said expressly:[109] "We have appointed them (the lamps of heaven) to be darted at the devils." The seventy-second sura treats of them in detail, and seeks especially to set forth their assent to the new doctrine. The Talmud also states that they are present at the giving of instruction. The following passage from the Berachoth shows this: "The press in the school is caused by them, the demons." With this we may compare the Koran: "When the servant of God stood up to invoke Him, it wanted little but that the genii had pressed on him in crowds."[110] It cannot be maintained that the greater part of the teaching about genii was adopted from Judaism, it must rather be said to have come from the same dark source whence the Jews of those times drew these conceptions, viz., Parseeism.

Still here, as in the case of any point which is of inaccessible origin, a reference to a mere similarity is not without use.

Under these four heads then, viz., (1) Creation, (2) Retribution including the Last Judgment and the Resurrection, (3) Mode of Revelation, and (4) Doctrine of Spirits, details are found, the adoption of which from Judaism we may regard as sufficiently proved. The precaution against representing, out of love for our theme, that which is common either to the general religious feelings of mankind, or to all revealed religions, or at least that which belonged to other known religious parties in Muhammad's time as peculiar only to Judaism, compels us to fix these limits. We have found much of interest especially under the second head, so that the demands of our theme might seem to be fairly well satisfied.

B. Moral and Legal Rules. It is obvious that in a revealed religion all individual commands form part of the religion, and therefore one cannot draw any sharp line of distinction between the "religious" and the "moral." We have accordingly considered nothing which has to do with conduct under the heading A, even though it might be immediately connected with the points of belief under discussion and so we are able to bring together here all commands as to conduct. From the fact that every individual command is divine, a conflict of duties may easily arise, which cannot be readily decided by private judgment, seeing that all the commandments are equal,[111] so far as their Author is concerned. Rules for such cases must therefore be laid down. For instance, we find the following statement in the rabbinical writings:[112] "If a father saith (to his son if he is a priest), 'Defile thyself' or if he saith, 'Make not restitution (of the thing found to the owner)', shall he obey him? Therefore, it is written:[113] 'Let every man reverence his father and mother, but keep my Sabbaths all of you, ye are all bound to honor me.'" And Muhammad says:[114] "We have commanded man to show kindness towards his parents, but if they endeavor to prevail with thee to associate with me that concerning which thou hast no knowledge, obey them not."

Judaism is known to be very rich in single precepts, and Muhammad has borrowed from it much that seemed to him suitable.

1. Prayer: Muhammad like the rabbis prescribes the standing position for prayer. Thus: "Stand obedient to the Lord; but if ye fear any danger, then pray while walking or riding";[115] and also: "Who standing, and sitting, and reclining, bear God in mind."[116]

These three positions are mentioned again in sura X. 13: "When evil befalleth a man he prayeth unto us, lying on his side or sitting or standing," where with a true perception of the right order, the least worthy position is the first spoken of.[117]

Baidhawi comments thus on sura III. 188, the passage alluded to above: "The meaning is that the man may take any of the three positions according to his strength, as Muhammad said to Amran Ibn Husain: 'Pray standing if thou art able; if not, sitting; and if thou canst not sit up, then leaning on the side." The Jews were not so strict in this matter, yet they too have the rule that prayer should be offered standing;[118] and in rabbinical writings it is also said that he who rides on an ass is to dismount, but the addition is made that, if he cannot dismount he is to turn his face (towards Jerusalem).[119] As the bodily position may be altered in urgent cases, so the prayer itself may be shortened on similar occasions.[120] So we find the permission to shorten prayer in time of war: "When ye march to war in the earth, it shall be no crime in you if ye shorten your prayers." The Jews also were permitted to pray a short prayer when in a dangerous place.[121] Muhammad is quite opposed to senseless chattering, for he counts it a merit in believers to "eschew all vain discourse."[122] Therefore because attention and pious concentration of thought are to be aimed at, he enjoins[123] on believers not to draw near to prayer when they are drunk. This is in accordance with the Talmudic rule: "Prayer is forbidden to the drunken."[124] It is also forbidden to those who have touched women.[125] These persons may not engage in prayer before washing with water, which cleansing is recommended as a general rule before prayer both in the Koran[126] and in the Talmud. Instead of water, purification with sand may take place.[127] So in the Talmud: "He cleanses himself with sand and has then done enough." As concentrated thought is urged as a duty, it follows that prayer though audible must not be noisy,[128] and so Muhammad says: "Pronounce not thy prayer aloud, neither pronounce it with too low a voice, but follow a middle way between these;" and in the Talmud we find:[129] "From the behavior of Hannah who in prayer moved her lips we learn that he who prays must pronounce the words, and also as her voice was not heard we learn that he must not raise his voice loudly." But because our mood does not at all times move us to fervency of prayer, outward ceremony is necessary, and indeed prayer in a great congregation, whose devotion will stir up our own.[130] "The prayer in the congregation" is greatly praised also by the Jews. Daybreak, which is mentioned in the Talmud in connection with the Shema prayer, as the time when "one can distinguish between a blue and a white thread,"[131] is not mentioned in this connection in the Koran it is true, for the Koran knows nothing of a Shema prayer, but it appears in connection with the beginning of the Fast Day:"[132] Until ye can discern a white thread from a black thread by the daybreak."

2. Some rulings in respect of women tally with Judaism; e.g., the waiting of divorced woman for three months before they may marry again.[133] The time of suckling is given in both as two years:[134] "Mothers shall give suck unto their children two full years." Similarly in sura XLVI. 14 we find: "His bearing and his weaning is thirty months," which is explained by Elpherar as follows: "He takes the shortest duration of pregnancy, viz., six months, and the shortest of suckling, viz., twenty-four months." Compare the Talmudic saying :[135] "A woman is to suckle her

child two years, after that it is as though a worm sucked." That those relatives to whom intermarriage is forbidden in the Scripture are precisely those whom Muhammad permits[136] to see their near relations unveiled has been already noticed by Michaelis in the Mosaic system, and he has shown the connection between these two laws.

As Muhammad had very little intention of imposing a new code of individual laws, since his aim was much more the spread of new purified religious opinions, and as in the matter of practice he was far too much of an Arab to deviate from inherited usages, unless they came directly into opposition to these higher religious views, it is easily to be explained how so few borrowings are to be found in this part and much even of what is adduced might perhaps be claimed to be general Oriental custom. We shall find moreover in the Appendix that Muhammad mentions many Jewish laws which were known to him; he alludes to these sometimes as binding on the Jews, sometimes merely for the sake of disputing them, and hence we see that it was not want of knowledge of them that kept him back from using them, but his totally different purpose. This remark must apply also to our third heading, under which isolated instances of adaptation only will be found, except in cases where the view is directly connected with the higher articles of faith adopted from Judaism, which have been already mentioned.

C. Views of Life. In putting together these single fragmentary utterances, it is scarcely worth while to arrange them according to any new system, and we will therefore follow the order of the Koran.

Death with the righteous is to be prized, hence the request in the Koran: "Make us to die with the righteous,"[137] which corresponds with that of Balaam, "Let me die the death of the righteous."

"Say not of any matter, 'I will surely do this tomorrow,' unless thou add, 'If God please.' "[138] Full understanding is first imputed to a man when he is forty years old,[139] and it is said in the Mishna: "At forty years of age a man comes to intelligence." So the hunting for some particular persons, to whom this sentence of the Koran shall apply, as the Arabic commentators do, appears altogether unnecessary; it is also rendered very dubious by the wide differences between the various opinions.

In the Koran a comparison is found between those who bear a burden without understanding the nature of it and who thus carry without profit, and an ass carrying books.[140]

"He who intercedeth (between men) with a good intercession shall have a portion thereof."[141] This saying is very similar to the Hebrew one:

"He who asks for mercy for another while he needs the same thing himself obtains help first." In Sunna 689 it is said: "Three things follow the dead, but two of them turn back; his family, his goods, and his works follow him; his family and his goods forsake him again, and only his works remain with him." This is also found in great detail in rabbinical Hebrew:[142]

> Man has three friends in his lifetime—his family, his property, and his good works. At the time of his departure from earth he collects the members of his family, and says to them, "I beg you, come and free me from this evil death." They answer: "Hast thou not heard[143] that no one has power over the day of death?" It is also written:[144] "None of them can by any means redeem his brother, even his wealth which he loves avails not; he cannot give to God a ransom for him, for the redemption of their soul is costly and must be let alone for ever; but enter thou into peace, rest in thy lot till the end of days.[145] May thy part be with the righteous." When the man sees this, he collects his treasures and says to them: "I have labored for you day and night, and I pray you redeem and deliver me from this death"; but they answer: "Hast thou not heard that riches profit not in the day of wrath?"[146] So then he collects his good works and says to them: "Then you come and deliver me from this death, support me, let me not go out of this world, for you still have hope in me if I am delivered." They answer: "Enter into peace! but before thou departest we will hasten before thee; as it is written, Thy righteousness shall go before thee, the glory of the Lord shall be thy reward."[147]

STORIES BORROWED FROM JUDAISM

This division will prove to be the largest, partly, because these narratives, draped in the most marvelous garb of fiction, lived mostly in the mouth of the people; partly, because this fairy-tale form appealed to the poetic fancy of Muhammad, and suited the childish level of his contemporaries. In the case of the Old Testament narratives, which are seldom related soberly, but are for the most part embellished, it needs scarcely a question, or the most cursory enquiry, as to whether or no they have passed from the Jews to Muhammad; for the Christians, the only other possible source to which they could be attributed, bestowed very little attention in those days on the Old Testament, but in their narratives kept to what is strictly Christian, viz., the events of the life of Jesus, of his disciples and his followers, and of the multitude of subsequent saints and wonder-workers, which afforded them abundant material for manifold embellishments. The Christians, for all that they accepted the Old Testament as a sacred writing, and although in those days no doubt had arisen as to whether or no they were to put the Old Testament on a level with the New in respect of holiness and divine inspiration, a doubt which has been brought forward for example by Schleiermacher in later times—the Christians of that period, I say, had nevertheless a more lively interest in the New Testament, since it was the expression of their separation and independence. The Old Testament was common to them and the Jews, and indeed they could not deny to the latter a greater right of possession in it, for the Jews possessed it entirely, and were versed in it even to the minutest details, an intimate knowledge with which we cannot credit the Christians. Further, just those points in the Old Testament which were specially suited to the Christian teaching are found to be scarcely touched upon in the Koran; thus, for instance, the narrative of the transgression of the first human pair is not at all represented as a fall into sin, involving the entire corruption of human nature which must afterwards be redeemed, but rather Muhammad contents himself with the plain, simple narration of the fact. This may be taken as an instance to prove that the narratives about persons mentioned in the Old Testament are almost all of Jewish origin, and this will be more clearly shown when we come to details.

As we proceed to the enumeration of the individual borrowed stories, the necessity is forced upon us of arranging them in some order. We have no reason for arranging them according to their sources (Bible, Mishna, Gemara, Midrash, etc.) as Muhammad did not gain his knowledge of these narratives from any of these sources, but was taught them all verbally by those round him, and so they were all of the same value for him, and were all called biblical; furthermore we must pay no attention to their contents, for the narratives are not given as supporting any doctrines of Islam, but are merely quoted as records of historical facts; and even in those cases where they are intended to set forth a doctrine, it is almost always either that of the unity of God, or that of the resurrection of the dead. It appears therefore advisable to arrange then chronologically, by which means it will be most easy to recognize the numerous anachronisms among them. Either Muhammad did not know the history of the Jewish nation, which is very probable, or the narration of it did not suit his object, for only once is the whole history summed up in brief,[148] and only the events in the lives of a few persons are mentioned. In this chronological arrangement we shall have to pay more attention to the personal importance of individuals than to any changes in the condition and circumstances of the nation, and thus in this arrangement we shall have the following divisions: (1) patriarchs; (2) Moses; (3) the three kings who reigned over the undivided kingdom, viz., Saul, David, and Solomon; and (4) holy men who lived after them.

PATRIARCHS

A. From Adam to Noah. The great event of the creation of the first man gave occasion for much poetical embellishment. Before the appearance of Adam, the jealousy of the angels, who had counseled against his creation, was roused, and God shamed them by endowing Adam more richly with knowledge than any of them. In the Koran we have the following description:[149]

> When thy Lord said unto the angels, "I am going to place a substitute on earth"; they said, "Wilt thou place there one who will do evil therein and shed blood? but we celebrate thy praise and sanctify thee." God answered: "Verily I know that which ye know not"; and He taught Adam the names of all things, and then proposed them to the angels, and said: "Declare unto me the names of these things, if ye say truth." They answered: "Praise be unto thee, we have no knowledge but what thou teachest us, for thou art knowing and wise." God said: "O Adam, tell them their names"; and when he had told them their names, God said: "Did I not tell you that I know the secrets of heaven and earth, and know that which ye discover, and that which ye conceal?"

The corresponding Hebrew passage may be thus translated:[150]

> When the Holy One, blessed be He! would create man, he took counsel with the angels, and said to them: "We will make man in our image";[151] then they said: "What is man that thou art mindful of him?[152] What will be his peculiarity?" He said: "His wisdom is greater than yours." Then He brought beasts, cattle, and birds before them, and asked for their names, but they knew them not. But when He had created man He caused the animals to pass before him and asked him for their names, and he replied: "This is an ox, that an ass, this a horse and that a camel." "But what art thou called?" "It is fitting that I should be called earthy, for I am formed of the earth." "And I?" "Thou art called LORD, for thou rulest all Thy creatures."

From this arose the other legend[153] that God, after the creation of man, commanded the angels to fall down before him, which they all did except Iblis,[154] the devil. The legend bears unmistakable marks of Christian development, in that Adam is represented in the beginning as the God-man, worthy of adoration, which the Jews are far from asserting.[155] It is true that in Jewish writings great honor is spoken of as shown by the angels to Adam, but this never went so far as adoration; indeed when this was once about to take place in error, God frustrated the action. We find in Sanhedrin 29, "Adam sat in the Garden of Eden, and the angels roasted flesh for him, and prepared cooling wine"; and in another passage it is said,[156] "After God had created man, the angels went astray in regard to him, and wanted to say before him, 'O Holy one!' Then God permitted sleep to fall on him, and all knew that he was of earth." In favor of the Christian origin of this narrative we must count the fact that the name used by Christians for the devil is the one used in all the passages referred to instead of the general Hebrew name.[157] From this event according to Muhammad arises the hatred of the devil against the human race, because on their account he became accursed of God; and so his first work was to counsel man in the Garden of Eden[158] to eat of the tree of knowledge.[159] In this narrative the devil is again given his Hebrew name,[160] and yet the first explanation of the temptation through the snake as coming from the Devil seems to be entirely Christian, as no such reference is to be found in the older Jewish writings; the passage quoted below can only be regarded as a slight allusion:[161] "From the beginning of the book up to this point[162] no Samech is to be found; as soon however as woman is created, Satan (with the initial letter Sin like Samech) is created also."

Still we find in a book which, though forged, is undoubtedly old,[163] the following statement: "Samael, the great prince in heaven, took his companions and went down and inspected all God's creatures; he found none more maliciously wise than the serpent, so he mounted it, and all that it said or did was at the instigation of Samael."[164] Thus this legend, even if not entirely Jewish, appears to have been derived by Muhammad from the Jews. In the details of this narrative some confusion is found between the tree of knowledge and the tree of life. The former only is mentioned in Scripture as prohibited by God,[165] and to the eating of that alone the serpent incites Eve. After the transgression has taken place, we find the fear mentioned lest men should eat of the tree of life and live for ever.[166] Muhammad confuses the two. In one passage he puts into the devil's mouth the statement that men through eating of this tree would become "angels," or "immortal,"[167] but in another passage he mentions only the tree of eternity.[168]

All the rest of the history of the first human pair is omitted, and only one event in the life of Cain and Abel is depicted. This is depicted for us quite in its Jewish colors. In this passage, and indeed throughout the Koran, they are called sons of Adam, but in later Arabic writings their names are given as Qabil and Habil, which are clearly chosen out of love for the rhyming sounds. The one event mentioned is their sacrifice and the murder which it led to.[169] Muhammad makes them hold a conversation before the murder, and one is likewise given in the Jerusalem Targum[170] on the strength of the words in Genesis, "Cain said unto Abel his brother." Still, the matter of the conversation is given so differently in each case that we do not consider it worthwhile to compare the two passages more closely. After the murder, according to the Koran, God sent a raven which scratched the earth to show Cain how to bury Abel. What is here attributed to Cain is ascribed by the Jews to his parents, and in a rabbinical writing we find the following passage:[171] "Adam and his companion sat weeping and mourning for him (Abel) and did not know what to do with him, as burial was unknown to them. Then came a raven, whose companion was dead, took its body, scratched in the earth and hid it before their eyes; then said Adam, I shall do as this raven has done, and at once he took Abel's corpse, dug in the earth and hid it." In the Koran a verse follows[172] which, without knowledge of the source from which it has come, seems to stand in no connection with what has gone before, but which will be made clear by the following explanation. The verse according to my translation runs thus: "Wherefore we commanded the children of Israel, that he who slayeth a soul, without having slain a soul, or committed wickedness in the earth, shall be as if he had slain all mankind; but he who saveth a soul alive, shall be as if he had saved the lives of all mankind." One perceives here no connection at all, if one does not consider the following Hebrew passage:[173] "We find it said in the case of Cain who murdered his brother: 'The voice of thy brother's bloods crieth.'[174] It is not said here *blood* in the singular, but bloods in the plural, i.e., his own blood and the blood of his seed. Man was created single in order to show that to him who kills a single individual, it shall be reckoned that he has slain the whole race; but to him who preserves the life of a single individual it is counted that he hath preserved the whole race." By this comparison it is made clear what led Muhammad to this general digression; he had evidently received this rule from his informants when they related to him this particular event. Another allusion to Cain is found in the Koran in a passage where he is called the man "who has seduced among men."[175]

No one else is mentioned in this period excepting Idris[176] who, according to the commentators, is Enoch. This seems probable from the words,[177] "And we uplifted him to a place on high," and also from a Jewish writing in which he is counted among the nine who went to paradise alive. Jalalu'ddin brings this point even more prominently forward:[178] "He lived in paradise where he had been brought after he had tasted death; he was quickened, however, and departed not thence again." He appears to have gained his name[179] on account of the knowledge of the divine law attributed to him. Elpherar remarks: " He was called Idris (searcher) on account of his earnest search in the revealed Scriptures." It is remarkable that in both these passages of the Koran[180] he is mentioned after Ishmael.

B. From Noah to Abraham. The corruption which spread in the time of Noah is not described with any details in the Koran, and one event which is stated by the rabbis to have taken place at this period is transferred by Muhammad to Solomon's time, to which he considered it better suited, as it treats of angels and genii. The rabbinical passage runs thus:[181]

Rabbi Joseph was asked by his scholars: "What is Azael?" and he answered: "When men at the time of the Flood practiced idolatry, God was grieved at it, and two angels, Shamhazai and Azael, said to him: 'Lord of the world, did we not ask unto Thee at the creation: "What is man that Thou art mindful of him?" ' [182] But He said: 'What shall become of the world?' They answered: 'We would have made use of it.' 'But it is well-known to Me that, if you lived on the earth, lust would overcome you, and you would become even worse than man.' 'Then give us permission to live with men, and Thou wilt see how we shall sanctify Thy name.' 'Go and live with them.' Then Shamhazai saw a maiden by name Istahar. He cast his eyes on her and said: 'Listen to me;' to which she replied: 'I will not listen to thee until thou teachest me the explicit name of God, through the mention of which thou risest to heaven.' He taught her this name which she then uttered and rose unspotted to heaven. Then God said: 'Because she turned herself from sin, well! fasten her between the seven stars, that ye may enjoy her for ever'; and so she was fastened into the Pleiades. But they lived in immorality with the daughters of men, for these were beautiful, and they could not tame their lusts. Then they took wives and begat sons, Hiwwa and Hiyya. Azael was master of the meretricious arts and trinkets of women which beguile men to immoral thoughts."

It is evident that this story is alluded to in the passage in the Koran,[183] where the two angels Harut and Marut are said to have taught men a charm by which they might cause division between a man and his wife.[184]

During this state of corruption of morals Noah appears, teaching men and seeking by exhortation to turn them from their evil ways. He builds himself the ark and is saved, while the rest of the people perish.[185] His whole appearance as an admonisher and seer is not biblical but rabbinical, and serves Muhammad's ends perfectly, as Noah in this way is a type of himself. According to rabbinical writings,[186] Job, xii. 5 refers to Noah, "who rebuked them and spake to them words as severe as flames, but they scorned him and said: 'Old man, for what purpose is this ark?' He, however, said: 'God is going to bring a flood upon you.'" Other particulars also accord with rabbinical tradition, e.g., "The people laughed at the ark"[187] accords with "They mocked and laughed at him in their words." "The waters of the Flood were hot"[188] with "The generation of the deluge was punished with hot water."

Still many inaccuracies and perversions are to be found; for instance, Muhammad makes Noah to have lived 950 years before the Flood,[189] whereas this is really the whole term of his life; and he represents one of Noah's sons as disobedient to him, and states that this same son did not follow him into the ark, but believed himself safe on a mountain peak.[190] This idea probably arose from a misunderstanding of Ham's evil conduct after the Deluge.[191] Muhammad also makes out Noah's wife to have been nonbelieving,[192] although he is silent as to wherein her unbelief consisted; and I can find no reason for this statement, which is not mentioned either in the Bible or in the rabbinical writings.

Perhaps Muhammad was misled by the analogy of the wife of Lot, who is mentioned in the same context. While these variations are due to errors and to the confusion of different times and events, others are to be ascribed to deliberate[193] alteration and elaboration. And of this kind are those details not mentioned in Jewish history, which represent Noah as one occupying the same position as Muhammad and speaking in his spirit. This applies particularly to that which is put into his mouth as admonisher. This is the case not only with Noah, but with all who appear in the character of the righteous in any evil age. Thus he puts into the mouth of Luqman, as a wise man known to the Arabs,[194] words suitable to his own circumstances and opinions, and the same thing happens in the case of Noah and the other preachers of Jewish history to whom he alludes. Noah, although he worked no miracle, was saved in a miraculous way, and so Muhammad cannot put into his mouth the same words which he uses of himself, as well as ascribes to other forerunners of himself after Noah's time, viz., that he is a mere preacher; yet he makes him say everything which is not clearly contrary to the historical facts related about him. He was only an unimportant man,[195] and did not pretend to be anyone wonderful or supernatural.[196] But he was divinely commissioned to warn the people, and for this he asked no reward.[197] *O sancta simplicitas!* one would exclaim in considering this last point, if Muhammad had written it down with full consideration of Noah's position as one threatening the world with punishment, and if it had not been rather that he saw everything from his own distorted point of view and was determined to make everything accord with his ideas. In another place he goes so far as to interpolate a verse into Noah's discourse, which is entirely characteristic of his own, and in which the little word (translated "speak")[198] actually occurs, which is always regarded as a word of address to Muhammad from God (or Gabriel). The same thing will be noted further on in the case of Abraham.

After Noah the next mentioned is Hud who is evidently the biblical Eber. This seems a striking example of the ignorance of Muhammad, or, as it appears to me more probable here, of the Jews round about him. According to the rabbinical opinion[199] the name Hebrew is derived from Eber, but in later times this name was almost entirely forgotten and the name Jew[200] was commonly used. The Jews, to whom it was known that their name was derived from an ancestor, believed that the name in question was that in use at the time, and that the ancestor therefore was this patriarch Hud. His time is that in which a second punitive judgment from God on account of bold, insolent behavior is mentioned in the Scripture, and this is treated of in several chapters of the Koran.[201] In order to have the right to refer what is said about Hud to the time of the confusion of tongues, or, as the rabbis call it, the Dispersion, we must adduce some particulars which point to this reference, for the statements are very general in their tenor and might be referred to other occurrences. The following verse[202] possibly refers to the building of the Tower: "And ye erect magnificent works, hoping that ye may continue for ever." The Arabic commentators take it that the buildings would afford them a perpetual dwelling-place, but the verse might also mean, "make by building it an everlasting name for yourselves." The neighborhood is called in the Koran the "Possessor of Pillars."[203] In one passage[204] there appears to be a reference to Nimrod, who lived at this time and in this region, since the children of Ad are here reproached for obeying the command of every contumacious hero.[205] The idea that they were idolators, which is brought up against them in all the passages in the Koran, agrees perfectly with the rabbinical view expressed as follows:[206] "And it came to pass when they journeyed from the beginning (East), that is to say, when they withdrew themselves from Him Who is the beginning of the world." Muhammad says of these people[207] that they built an (idolatrous) symbol on every high place in order to play there (i.e., to practice idolatry). And the rabbis tell us that the race of the dispersion contemplated building a tower and putting an idol on its summit.

Resemblances are also to be found with reference to the punishment which overtook them. Muhammad tells us[208] they were followed in this world by a curse, and that they shall be followed by the same on the day of resurrection, and the rabbis say[209] that the race of the dispersion had no part in the next world, for the twice-mentioned dispersion applies to this world and the other. In Muhammad's treatment the essential point of the punishment is lost sight of, for instead of describing it as a simple dispersion and confusion of tongues, he speaks of an absolute annihilation of the sinners by a poisonous wind.[210] One sees at once the mistaken source from which this change is derived. We recognize partly from our knowledge of Muhammad's motives in making the alteration, and partly from the minuteness with which the new punishment is described, which would not have been accorded to a fiction. It appears therefore that the history reached this development in the mouth of the people, who delight in minute descriptions of punishment.

The remaining deviations and additions, particularly the latter, are caused, as we have already remarked in the case of Noah, by confusion with Muhammad's own time and person. This is the case when he transfers unbelief in the resurrection to the time of Hud and counts it among the sins of that time which were worthy of punishment.[211] This is seen too especially in the great importance assigned to Eber and to his desire to turn the people from their evil ways. Decided traces of this are certainly to be found in Jewish writings,[212] where we are told that Eber was a great prophet, who by the Holy Spirit called his son Pelag, because in his days the earth was divided[213] (which Eber had known beforehand). Much also is said of the school of Eber, and Rebekah is said to have gone there; for it is written: "She went to enquire of the Lord,"[214] and Jacob is supposed to have stayed there for fourteen years. But of the fact that Eber preached to the people, he being their brother (on which Muhammad places great stress, because he himself was sent as an Arab to the Arabs), not a trace is to be found, still less of the fact that he took no reward from them.[215]

One point still remains to be cleared up, why the race under discussion is called in the Koran the people of Ad. The commentators state that Ad was the son of Uz, the son of Aram, the son of Shem, the son of Noah; and Muhammad seems also to have been of this opinion, whence it comes that he transfers the events to the land of Aram or Iram.[216] Nevertheless it seems to have come about chiefly from the fact that all these occurrences are described with an Arabian coloring, and so they were attributed to Arab tribes, amongst which an ancient extinct one had the name of Ad;[217] perhaps in it there is also an etymological reference to a "return" to the early evil conduct of the generation of the Deluge. In another passage there is an allusion to this occurrence,[218] where the fact itself is brought forward much more in accordance with the biblical account, but quite without specification of time or persons: "Their predecessors devised plots heretofore, but God came into their building to overthrow it from the foundation, and the roof fell on them from above and a punishment came upon them which they did not expect." On this Elpherar remarks: "These are Nimrod, the son of Canaan, who built a tower in Babel in order that he might mount to heaven"; and further: "And when the tower fell the language of men became confused, and so they could not finish it; then they spoke seventy-three languages; on this account the city was called Babel (confusion); before this the language of men was Syriac." The rabbis, too, assert that before this men spoke in Hebrew, but afterwards in seventy languages. Jalalu'd-din says the same thing,[219] and adds that Nimrod built the Tower "in order that he might mount out of it into heaven to wage war with the inhabitants thereof." But the identity of this narrative with that of Hud and Ad is no more accepted by Abulfeda[220] than it is by Elpherar and Jalalu'd-din, even on the view that Hud is the same as Eber. Although the coloring of this narrative as given in the Koran differs much from that of the biblical account, yet the identity of the two can be shown by putting this and that together, and by explaining the way in which the individual differences arose.

But in the case of another narrative which follows this one in almost all the passages of the Koran,[221] it is very difficult to find out the subject of which it treats and the Bible characters to which it refers. This narrative is about Samud, which like Ad is an ancient extinct Arab tribe,[222] to whom their brother Salih was sent when they fell into sin.[223] Salih is said to have exhorted the

Samudites to righteousness and to have commended to them a certain she-camel as especially under divine protection; he even bade them share water with her.[224] But the unbelievers of his time (according to one passage[225] only nine in number) hamstrung her, and so divine punishment overtook them. I find no similar occurrence in Jewish writings, but the likeness of the name points to Shelah,[226] who, however, as the father of Eber, would have deserved mention before him.[227] On the whole, the word is so general in its meaning of "a pious man" that we cannot treat it here with certainty as having been originally a proper name. Perhaps the story of the houghing is founded on the words in Jacob's blessing of his sons,[228] and the sharing of the water on the etymology of the name Samud. Moreover Samud was, according to the commentators, the son of Gether, the son of Aram, the son of Shem, the son of Noah, which fits in fairly well with the date already assigned to Shelah. It is however impossible for me to give any more exact explanation from Jewish writings.

C. Abraham to Moses. Though the saints mentioned earlier bore some likeness to Muhammad, and though their condition, so similar to his own, encouraged him as well as verified his statements, yet Abraham was his great prototype, the man of whom he thought most highly, and the one with whom he liked best to compare himself and to make out as one with himself in opinion. Abraham's faith is that which is preached in the Koran.[229] He was a believer in the unity of God.[230] He was neither Jew nor Christian for it is written:[231] "Abraham was not a Jew, nor a Christian, but he was a believer in the unity of God, given up to God (a Muslim)."[232] He is represented as the friend of God, and this is his name throughout the East.[233] Abraham's importance and the rich legendary material concerning him, which Judaism offered, lead as to expect much about him in the Koran, and our expectation is not disappointed. It is to him that the founding of the Ka'bah is traced back.[234] He is supposed to have lived in the temple,[235] and to have composed books.[236] This opinion is also held by the rabbis, many of whom attribute to Abraham the well-known cabalistic and undoubtedly very ancient Sepher Jazirah.

Passing to the events of his life, we first come across the beautiful legend of his attaining to the true knowledge of God. We are told also how he tried to persuade his father and his people thereto. A special instance of this was when he destroyed the idols, and, putting the staff into the hand of the largest, attributed the action to him. He sought thus to convince the people, who quite perceived the impossibility of the idols having done it, since they could not move, but they were not thereby persuaded.[237]

Abraham is represented as praying in vain that his father might be released from the punishment of hell.[238] We are told too that the people, embittered by Abraham's conduct towards the idols, wanted to have him burnt alive, but that he was rescued from that fate by divine intervention.[239] The whole story is taken from the rabbinical writings, where we read as follows.[240]

> Terah was an idolator: once he went away and left Abraham to sell his idols. Whenever a buyer came, Abraham asked him his age. If he replied, I am fifty, or sixty years old, Abraham said: "Woe to the man of sixty who desires to worship the work of a day," so that the buyer went away ashamed.[241] Once a woman came, with a dish of wheat and said, "Here, put this before them"; but Abraham took a stick and beat down all the idols, and put the stick into the hands of the largest idol. When his father returned, he said, "Who has done this!" On which Abraham replied, "Why should I deny it? A woman came with a dish of wheat and bade me set it in front of them. I had scarcely done so when each wanted to eat before the other, and the greatest beat them all down with the stick which he had in his hand." Terah said: "What art thou inventing for me? Have they then understanding?" Abraham replied. "Do thine ears not hear what thy mouth says?" Then Terah took him and gave him over to Nimrod, who said: "We will worship fire." Abraham said: "Rather water, which extinguishes fire." Nimrod replied: "Water then." "Rather the cloud which carries water." "The cloud then." "Rather the wind which scatters the cloud." "The wind then." "Rather men, who endure the wind." Nimrod at this became angry and said: "Thou art only making a speech. I worship fire and will throw thee into it. The God whom thou dost worship may come and save thee out of it." Abraham was then thrown into a glowing furnace, but was saved from it.

The intercession for his father is not mentioned in Jewish writings; and that this was fruitless, yea that Abraham, arriving at a clearer understanding, desisted from his attempt,[242] seems to directly contradict the Jewish view as expressed in the following passage.[243] "By the words, 'Thou shalt go to thy fathers in peace,' it was shown to Abraham that his father was a partaker in eternal life." Further, a rabbinical saying[244] declares as a general rule that "the son makes the father clean, but not the father the son." But Muhammad very often combats this view and the similar one that the merits of ancestors count for good to their posterity. For example he says: "That people (the Patriarchs) are now passed away; they have what they gained and ye shall have what ye gain, and ye shall not be questioned concerning that which they have done."[245] That Muhammad brings forward a dialogue between Abraham and the people, where the Midrash has one with his father only, is explained by the fact that Abraham is intended to be a type of Muhammad, and so it is necessary that he should be represented as a public preacher.

Another circumstance which is mentioned in the Koran, viz., that Lot became a believer with and through Abraham,[246] may possibly have arisen from a passage in the Midrash immediately following that quoted above, which says that Haran, the father of Lot, was at first irresolute, but turned to Abraham's opinion after the deliverance of the latter. Haran, however, failed in the ordeal of fire to which he was then subjected. The idea of Lot's conversion, however, is chiefly derived from the account given of his subsequent life, in which he shows himself to be a pious man; and it is probably for this reason that Muhammad connects him with the event just related. Muhammad appears sometimes to have so confounded himself with Abraham that, in the middle of speeches ascribed to the latter, he indulges in digressions unsuitable to any but himself, and thus falls from the part of narrator into that of admonisher. In one passage[247] a long description of hell and paradise is found, and in another,[248] the declaration that those who came before had also been charged with imposture. No doubt Abraham might have said this with reference to Noah, Hud, and Salih; still the words here seem rather forced into his speech, and indeed in one verse we find the word "say" which is to be regarded in the Koran as the standing address of God (or Gabriel) to Muhammad.[249] This view renders it unnecessary to adopt the desperate expedient of Wahl, who supposes a transposition of verses, or an interpolation. The true explanation is rather Muhammad's entire identification of Abraham with himself. Further, he is not content with making Abraham preach against idolatry; he represents him also as teaching the doctrine of the resurrection of the dead.[250] The lack, however, of full certainty about this doctrine[251] caused Abraham, according to the Muhammadan view, to pray for a tangible proof of it, and then was vouchsafed to him what the rabbis call the "covenant between the divided pieces."[252]

He was convinced through the fact that the divided birds came together again and became living,[253] a view which is foreign to Judaism. How Muhammad came to call Abraham's father (whose name is given in the Bible as Terah) Azar[254] is at first sight not clear, but is completely explained when we consider the source[255] of his information, namely Eusebius. In his *Church History*, Eusebius calls him Athar which is an easy transition from Thara, and then the Greek Athar was easily converted into the Arabic Azar.[256] The reason which is given by some Arabic commentators[257] is ridiculous. They maintain that Azar is like Yazzar, and that this means: "O, perverted one, O, erring one;" and Abraham is supposed to have thus addressed his idolatrous father.

We now pass on to the more mature married life of Abraham and come to his meeting with the angels,[258] whom he receives as guests.[259] Abraham took them for Arabs, was much surprised that they did not eat and stepped back in fear, whereupon they announced to him that he would have a son and told him also of the coming destruction of Sodom. In one passage of the Talmud[260] we read: "They appeared to him nothing else but Arabs;" and in another passage[261] it is said, "The angels descended and ate. They ate? No, but it appeared as though they ate and drank." There is only one error to be found in the account as given in the Koran. The doubt as to whether in the advanced age of the pair a son could come into the world (which in other passages and in the Bible is put into the mouth of Sarah) is here uttered by Abraham, but in very mild words.[262] It is true that in the other biblical account of the promise to Abraham, he himself is represented as doubting God's word.[263] In other passages the position of words and clauses might give rise to many errors, if we did not know the story better beforehand from the Bible. Thus in one passage[264] the laughter of Abraham's wife is given before the announcement is made, which leads the Arabic commentators to manifold absurd guesses. Elpherar by the side of these explanations (many of them quite wanting in truth) gives the right one in the following words: "Bin 'Abbas and Wahib say: 'She laughed from astonishment that she should have a child, for both she and her husband were of a great age.' Then the verse was transposed, but it ought to run thus: 'And his wife stood while We promised him Isaac, and after Isaac, Jacob, and then she laughed.'" It might seem that this son who was promised to Abraham was with deliberate forgery identified with Ishmael, because he is regarded as the ancestor of the Arabs; and so too the ensuing temptation[265] connected with the sacrifice of his son is made to refer to Ishmael.

Ground for this acceptation is given in another passage,[266] when after the dispute about the idols has been related, we read from v. 99 as follows: "Wherefore We acquainted him that he should have a son who should be a meek youth, and when he had attained to years of discretion.... Abraham said unto him: 'O, my son! I saw in a dream that I should offer thee in sacrifice.'" He declared himself ready, on which Abraham heard a voice telling him that he had already verified the vision; and a noble victim ransomed him. And then the passage continues:[267] "And We rejoiced him with the promise of Isaac, a righteous prophet; and We blessed him and Isaac; and of their offspring were some righteous doers, and others who manifestly injured their own souls." That the announcement of Isaac first appears here is proof that the preceding context refers to Ishmael. It is therefore evident that according to Muhammad's representation the sacrificial action was performed on Ishmael, and further on this will be shown more in detail. But it is not clear that the announcement of the angels refer to him, seeing that in one of the three places where the same word[268] is used of this angelic announcement, it is explicitly applied to Isaac. That the angels had a twofold mission—(1) to Abraham, in order to show him his fatherhood and the destruction of Sodom, and (2) to Lot, in order to remove him from Sodom before the destruction was accomplished—is biblical and Muhammad follows the Bible narrative. We have already mentioned that Lot is supposed to have become a believer through Abraham. The visitation of the angels, which is related in Genesis, xix. 1–27, is mentioned in several passages in the Koran.[269] On the whole the narrative is fairly true, but the details are not entirely free from embellishment. For example, in some passages[270] the warning addressed to the people of Sodom on account of their unchaste use of men is treated quite separately from the narrative of the angels, and Muhammad makes out that the angels told Lot and even Abraham[271] beforehand that Lot's wife should not be saved. The unbelief of Lot's wife receives particular notice in one passage,[272] while the destruction of the cities is mentioned in many passages.[273] Muhammad especially attributes to Lot the distinguishing mark common to all preachers, viz., that they ask for no reward.[274]

It has already been remarked that, according to Muhammad's showing, Ishmael[275] was the son whom Abraham was commanded to sacrifice; and the reasons have been given which persuaded Muhammad to represent Ishmael as a very righteous man,[276] to include him in the ranks of the patriarchs and prophets,[277] to mention him as the righteous son of Abraham,[278] and to make out that he laid the foundation stone of the Ka'bah in connection with his father.[279]

This view is certainly not Jewish, but at the same time it is not contrary to Judaism, for the rabbis tell us[280] that by the utterance: "Thou shalt be buried in a good old age (Genesis, xv. 15.) God showed Abraham that Ishmael would repent." And in the Talmud it is said[281] that Ishmael repented during his father's lifetime. From his habit of reckoning Ishmael among the patriarchs, Muhammad fell into the error of counting him as an ancestor of Jacob. Thus in one passage[282] he says: "The God of thy fathers, Abraham and Ishmael and Isaac," which Baidhawi attempts to explain in the following manner; "He counts Ishmael among his ancestors, connecting him with the father—the grandfather also is the same as the father—and as Muhammad says, 'The uncle is a part of the father.' Then pointing to 'Abbas, his uncle, he said, 'This is the survivor of my forefathers.'"

As he hereby transfers to Ishmael the action, which as the most worthy, is attributed by the Jews to Isaac, viz., readiness to be sacrificed, the latter remains simply a pious man, about whom there is little to relate and who is quite destitute of all legendary adornment. In consequence of this, Isaac appears only in the lists of the patriarchs, and almost always in those passages where Abraham's deliverance from the fire is mentioned and also his reward for his piety. In these passages Muhammad following more the popular tradition mentions Isaac and Jacob but not Ishmael.

We are now struck by the strange confusion which seems to have existed in Muhammad's mind about Jacob. He seems to have been uncertain whether he was Abraham's son, or his grandson, the son of Isaac. While there is no passage which says explicitly that he was Abraham's son, yet this idea is conveyed to all who have not learned differently from the biblical history. In the angel's announcement[283] it is said, "after Isaac, Jacob;"[284] and in other passages[285] we read: "We gave to him (i.e., to Abraham) Isaac and Jacob." In the Sunna, however, Joseph is called clearly the grandson and Jacob the son of Abraham.[286] Although these passages do not prove the point absolutely, yet those passages which can be brought forward in support of the opposite view are much less powerful. For if it must be allowed that in two passages[287] Abraham and Isaac, and in one of these Jacob also, are mentioned as the forefathers of Joseph, we can also show another passage[288] where Ishmael is mentioned as a forefather of Jacob without any continuous genealogy having been given. And further, since in the passage last cited Abraham, Ishmael, and Isaac are counted as the fathers of Jacob, it is clear from the mention of Ishmael among the others how great was the confusion which reigned in Muhammad's mind about Jacob's parentage.

We by no means assert that Muhammad took Jacob for the son of

Abraham, but it is evident that the relationship between the two was not clear to him. This error did not spread; on the contrary, the later Arabs were better acquainted with these relationships. Thus, e.g., Zamakhshari says:[289] "It is related of the prophet that he said, 'If you are asked, who is the noble one?' answer: 'The noble one, the son of the noble one, the son of the noble one, the son of the noble one is Joseph, the son of Jacob, the son of Isaac, the son of Abraham.'"[290] But this is no testimony to the full certainty of Muhammad himself, for often the traditions spread among the later Arabs are more correct than those given in the Koran, as we said before in the case of the sacrifice of Isaac. Only a little is given of Jacob's life. There is an allusion to his wrestling with the angel in the following words:[291] "All food was allowed to the children of Israel before the revelation of the Law, except what Israel (as he is here called)[292] forbade himself." This is evidently an allusion to the biblical passage where the prohibition against eating the sinew of the thigh is mentioned,[293] which Baidhawi also gives, but assigns a wrong reason for it. Beyond this allusion and the history of Joseph, in which he is also involved and which we will give later on, the only other thing told about Jacob is his admonition before his death. This is given in accordance with rabbinical sources as follows:[294] "And Abraham commanded this to his sons,[295] even to Jacob: 'My children, verily God hath chosen this religion for you, therefore die not unless ye also be resigned.' Were ye present when Jacob was at the point of death? When he said to his sons, 'Whom will ye worship after me?' they answered: 'We will worship thy God and the God of thy fathers Abraham and Ishmael and Isaac, one God, and to him will we be resigned.'" We find something similar in the rabbinical writings:[296] "At the time when Jacob was leaving the world, he called his twelve sons and said to them: 'Hear your father Israel.[297] Is there any doubt in your hearts about God?' They said: 'Hear Israel our father. As in thy heart there is no doubt about God, so also there is in ours; but the Lord is our God, the Lord is one.'[298] Then he spoke out and said: 'Praised be the name of his glorious kingdom, for ever.'" The sons of Jacob are not individually mentioned, but they appear in the list of the Patriarchs as "the tribes,"[299] so called because of the subsequent division into tribes, Joseph alone enjoying an honorable exception.

Besides being alluded to in one other passage,[300] Joseph forms the theme of almost the whole of the twelfth sura,[301] which is named after him. This sura contains the narrative given us in Genesis,[302] with many abbreviations it is true, but also with many additions and alterations, which must be pointed out. We must first mention the additions which are derived from Jewish legend. Among these is the statement that Joseph was inclined towards Potiphar's wife, but that a sign warned him from her.[303] The rabbinical comment on the words "He went into the house to do his work"[304] runs as follows:[305] "Both intended to commit sin"; and on the words "She caught him by his garment saying, 'Lie with me,' " Rabbi Yohanan remarks, "Both had got on to the bed, when the form of his father appeared to Joseph at the window and said: 'Joseph, Joseph, one day the names of thy brethren will be graven on the stones of the Ephod, also thine; wilt thou that it shall be effaced?' "[306] The fable that the Egyptian women mocked at Potiphar's wife, were invited in by her, and in contemplating Joseph's beauty[307] were so absorbed that they cut their own hands, is found in an old Jewish writing which, though not genuine, is certainly very ancient, and is written in very pure Hebrew. This work is sometimes referred to in the Midrash Yalkut under the name of "The Great Chronicle." In an old Jewish German translation, however, it bears another title. It is this translation which I have before me as I write, and for this reason I will not quote the actual words.[308] Also the discussion about the tearing of the clothes, whether they were torn in front or at the back,[309] is found in the same way in the Sepher Hayyashar. In the words, "and a witness bore witness,"[310] which we here do not take strictly according to the meaning of the context, but rather in the sense of an "arbitrator decided,"[311] others see an allusion to a witness who was present at what occurred between Joseph and the woman, and some of the commentators quoted in Elpherar express themselves quite in harmony with the Sepher Hayyashar as follows: "Sa'id Ben Jubair and Dhuhak say it was a child in the cradle which God permitted to speak. This is the tradition of the Uphite commentator according to 'Abbas." In the Sepher Hayyashar it is also asserted that there was present a child of eleven months who till then could not talk, but then attained to speech. But there is a difference in that the Jewish book makes the child confirm the utterance of Joseph, while the Arabic commentator puts into its mouth the decision about the rent clothing, which other Arabic writers reject as highly unsuitable. Many commentators say that this was no child, but rather a wise man full of penetration. It follows from this that Muhammad either mixed the two legends inappropriately, or else that the second one came later into Arabic tradition and was read by the Arabs into the words of the Koran. The words[312] which Wahl translates: "But the devil would not allow it that he (the cupbearer) thought of him (Joseph)," are explained by the following passage:[313] "The talk of the lips tendeth only to penury,[314] because although Joseph reminded the cup-bearer twice[315] that he should remember him, yet he had to remain two more years in prison; for it is written, 'And it was after two years.'"[316] The seeking of protection from the butler is here regarded as sinful, and therefore Muhammad says: "And Satan made him (Joseph) forget the remembrance of his Lord (God)," in that he trusted not in God but in man.[317] In the same sura[318] Jacob recommends his sons to enter by different gates; in like manner we read in the rabbinical writings[319] that Jacob said to them: "Do not enter by the same door."[320] The statement[321] that the brothers said, when they found the cup in Benjamin's sack: "If he be guilty of theft his brother hath also been guilty," is evidently an erroneous change in the words of a passage found in the Midrash quoted above,[322] according to which they said, "See a thief, son of a thief," with reference to Rachel's having stolen the Teraphim.[323] From the Koran it appears[324] that Jacob knew by divine communication that Joseph still lived, which is opposed to one Jewish view[325] but agrees with another,[326] which runs as follows: "An unbeliever asked our teacher, 'Do the dead live on? Your fathers did not accept this, and will you accept it? It is said of Jacob, that he refused to be comforted.[327] If he had believed that the dead live on, would he have refused comfort?' Then he answered him. 'Foolish one! he knew through the Holy Ghost that he still lived (in the flesh), and one does not take comfort concerning the living.'" The story that Joseph told Benjamin beforehand who he was is common to the Koran[328] and the Sepher Hayyashar.

Besides these additions from Jewish legends there is also other matter which owes its origin to error, or possibly to traditions unknown to us. Muhammad's statement[329] that the brothers asked their father to send Joseph with them contradicts the biblical account;[330] and the statement that one of the Ishmaelites who went to draw water found Joseph in the pit is against the clear word of the Scripture that the pit was dry.[331] Muhammad makes Joseph expound Pharaoh's dream, and only afterwards does he have him fetched from prison,[332] in contradiction to the Bible narrative.[333] He asserts that Jacob became blind from grief, but that he recovered his sight by the application of a shirt to his eyes. He was perhaps thinking of Jacob's loss of sight[334] later on, or possibly the idea is based on some legend unknown to me. According to the Koran Joseph's parents[335] came to him in Egypt, in spite of the fact that according to the testimony of the Scriptures[336] Rachel was long since dead. Muhammad's idea probably was to bring about a complete fulfillment of the dream, which mentions both parents.[337]

On this, however, some of the rabbis remark that this is a sign that no dream is without a mingling of some vain matter, while others say that Bilhah, Joseph's subsequent foster-mother, is alluded to. Something like this is quoted by Zamakhshari, to the effect that "this means his father and his aunt;"[338] while Elpherar has still more clearly: "Katada and Sada say that by the moon is meant his aunt, because his mother Rachel was already dead." Thus it is possible that Muhammad means this aunt here, even as Elpherar remarks on another passage,[339] to wit, that "most commentators say that by these are meant his father and his aunt Leah, his mother having died at the birth of Benjamin." It is quite in accordance with Muhammad's usual procedure to put into Joseph's mouth a long discourse on the unity of God and the doctrine of a future life. This is given before the interpretation of the dreams of his two fellow-prisoners.[340] With Joseph we finish the first period, for between Joseph and Moses Muhammad mentions no one else. It almost seems as if, with Justin, Muhammad regarded Moses as Joseph's son, although of course we cannot seriously attribute such an opinion to him.

MOSES AND HIS TIME

The history of the earlier times was preserved only in brief outlines, and was not so important either in itself, or in the influence which it exerted on the subsequent ages; therefore Muhammad adopted from it only such legends as were edifying in themselves and to which he could append pious reflections. In the period of which we are now going to treat, there is certainly still a long array of legends, but historical facts are preserved for us with greater distinctness and clearer detail, and these facts are of greater religious importance The giving of the Mosaic Law and the eventful life and noble personality of Moses himself afford Muhammad plenty of material for his narrative. Here we will first put together the whole life of Moses as represented in the various passages of the Koran, and then we will go on to consider the details to be commented upon. Among the oppressive enactments of Pharaoh against the children of Israel was an order that their children should be thrown into the water. Moses, the son of Amram, was laid by his mother in an ark; Pharaoh's wife, who saw the child there, saved it from death and had it nursed by its mother. When

Moses was grown up he tried to help his oppressed brethren, and once killed an Egyptian; the next day, however, he was reminded by an Israelite of his yesterday's deed. This made him afraid, and by the advice of a friend he fled to Midian, and married there the daughter of a Midianite.[341] When he wished to leave Midian he saw a burning bush, approached it, and received a command to go to Egypt to warn Pharaoh and to perform some miracles to make him believe; he asked for his brother Aaron as an assistant in this work.[342] He obeyed the command and accomplished his mission, but Pharaoh remained unbelieving and assembled his magicians, who indeed imitated the wonders, but were so far surpassed by Moses and Aaron that they themselves became believers in spite of the threats of Pharaoh.[343] But a mighty judgment overtook Pharaoh and his people, who remained stubborn in their unbelief; and at last the Egyptians were drowned in the sea, while the Israelites were saved.[344] Nothing is related of the journey of the children of Israel before the giving of the Law, except the striking of the rock with the staff so that water flowed out, and this comes in only incidentally in two passages;[345] in the former of which, however, other facts about the stay in the wilderness are related. Moses then received the Law,[346] and prayed to see God's glory.[347] During his absence the Israelites made the golden calf, which Moses on his return dashed into pieces and gave to the Israelites to drink;[348] and after that he appointed seventy men.[349] Later on he sent spies to Canaan, but they all except two were godless. The people let themselves be deceived by then, and in consequence were obliged to wander for forty years in the wilderness.[350] Further, Moses had a dispute with Korah, whom the earth swallowed up,[351] and he was wrongly accused. This last statement may be either a reference to the matter of Korah, or to the dispute with Aaron and Miriam.

These are the main events of Moses's life as they are given in the Koran, and we have arranged them partly according to the order of their mention in that book, but more with reference to our better source. Besides all this, a wonderful journey which Moses is said to have taken with his servant[352] is given, about which we shall speak further on. To pass on now to details.

Haman[353] and Korah[354] are mentioned as counselors of Pharaoh and persecutors of the Israelites. The latter is alluded to in this capacity by the rabbis,[355] who say: "Korah was the chief steward over Pharaoh's house." As to the former, Muhammad must at some time have heard him mentioned as the Jews' enemy, and therefore have put him in here, although later Arabians do not thus designate the Haman[356] who lived in the time of Ahasuerus. The rabbis also say a good deal about Pharaoh's advisers, amongst whom they sometimes mention Balaam, Job, and Jethro. Of these the first agreed with Pharaoh and for this reason he was afterwards killed by the Israelites; the second remained silent, therefore he had to endure sufferings; the third fled, and so the happiness of being the father-in-law of Moses fell to his lot. The two chief magicians, who are also mentioned in a letter of the apostle Paul, are specially named as abettors. Fear on account of some dream[357] is given as the greatest cause of persecution; and this is in accord with the statement of the rabbis that it was foretold to Pharaoh by the magicians[358] that a boy would be born who would lead the Israelites out of Egypt; then he thought, if all male children were thrown into the river, this one would be thrown with them.

The finding of Moses is attributed to Pharaoh's wife,[359] and she is mentioned as a believer,[360] evidently having been confounded with Pharaoh's daughter, by whom Moses was found according to the Scriptures,[361] and in the same way the name given to Pharaoh's wife by the commentators is a corruption of the name[362] by which his daughter was known among the Jews.

The words of the Bible: "Shall I go and call thee a nurse of the Hebrew women?"[363] give rise to the following rabbinical fable:[364] "Why must the nurse be a Hebrew woman? This shows that he refused the breast of all the Egyptian women. For God said: 'Shall the mouth that is one day to speak with me suck an unclean thing?' "[365]

According to Muhammad Moses regarded his slaying of the Egyptian as sinful and repented thereof,[366] which is contrary to the Jewish view,[367] expressed as follows; "The verse in the 24th Psalm (according to the reading of the Kethibh; 'Who took not away his soul out of vanity') refers to the soul of the Egyptian, which Moses did not take away, until he had investigated his case judicially and had found that he deserved death." That the Hebrew whom he released strove again on the following day with an Egyptian,[368] and that he betrayed Moses, because he would not uphold him, but on the contrary reproved him for his quarrelsome temper is mere embellishment, as is also the very happy invention of a man who warned Moses to flee.[369]

There is a mistake to be found in the very brief account of Moses' flight to Midian and his residence there, for Muhammad speaks of two[370] instead of seven[371] daughters of the Midianite. Instead of letting the vision in the bush be the occasion of Moses' leaving Midian, as it is in the

Bible,[372] Muhammad erroneously makes out that Moses had formed the resolution to leave the country before this event, and that the vision appeared to him on the way.[373]

The appearance of Moses before Pharaoh is connected in a remarkable way with the divine commission to the former. So closely are the two circumstances bound together that in many places Pharaoh's answer follows immediately upon God's command, without its having first been mentioned that Moses and Aaron had gone in obedience to God to Egypt, had done wonders before Pharaoh, and had admonished him. But on the other hand in those passages where only the admonitions given by Moses to Pharaoh are related, without the preceding events being given, the part elsewhere omitted is of course supplied, but as we might expect with changes.

Pharaoh is said to have reproached Moses with the murder of the Egyptian.[374] This is a very simple invention, which however is contrary to the literal sense of the Scriptures,[375] unless we accept the rabbinical explanation[376] of the words, "the king of Egypt died,"[377] that is, "he became leprous and a leper is as one dead;" and also of the words, "for all are died who sought thy life"[378] which is as follows: "Were they dead? They were Dathan and Abiram, who were involved in the dispute of Korah. This only means that they had become powerless."[379] Further, Moses is supposed to have shown the sign of his leprous hand before Pharaoh,[380] which is not mentioned in Scripture,[381] but which agrees with the following statement in the rabbinical writings:[382] "He put his hand into his bosom, and drew it out as white as snow from leprosy; they also put their hands into their bosoms and drew them out as white as snow from leprosy."

The magicians who were summoned asked at first, in distinction from God's messengers, for their reward;[383] but when they had seen their serpents swallowed by that of Moses, they believed, praised God and were not intimidated by Pharaoh's threats. This is quite contrary to the Bible, in which such a confession is found only after the plague of lice,[384] and there too only in the form of a mere hint. Among Moses' own people only his own tribe is said to have believed on him,[385] and the rabbis say[386] that "the tribe of Levi was exempt from hard labor."

Pharaoh himself was also a magician, and this he claims, according to my opinion, in his address to the other magicians.[387] This is in accord with the rabbinical statement[388] that the Pharaoh who lived in the days of Moses was a great magician. In other passages of the Koran,[389] Pharaoh claims for himself divinity, which assumption no doubt is intended to be accepted by the people. This trait is also developed in Jewish legend,[390] where we read: "Pharaoh said to them: 'From the first have ye spoken an untruth, for lord of the world am I, I created myself and the Nile; as it is written:[391] my river is mine own and I have made it for myself.' " In another passage[392] Muhammad puts the following words into Pharaoh's month: "Is not the kingdom of Egypt mine and these rivers which flow beneath me?" Elpherar, with others,[393] remarks on the words "beneath me," that they mean "by my command."

A quite new but charming fiction is that of a pious Egyptian, who warned his countrymen not to despise the teaching of Moses and not to persecute him.[394] Certain features of this story sound familiar. For instance, the words in verse 29: "If he be a liar, on him will the punishment of his falsehood light; but if he speaketh the truth, some of those judgments with which he threateneth you will fall upon you," bear a resemblance to the words of Gamaliel in the New Testament. The allusion to Joseph in verse 86 is found in a very dissimilar Jewish tradition, as follows;[395] "If Joseph had not been, we should not be alive."

Muhammad is not clear about the plagues. In some passages[396] he speaks of nine plagues. In another passage[397] he enumerates five, which stand in the following order: flood, locusts, lice, frogs, and blood. Although we cannot here find fault with the want of order in the plagues and with the omission of some of them since Muhammad here is not, any more than is the Psalmist,[398] to be considered as a strict historian, yet the mistaken inclusion of a flood, which is not to be confounded with the overthrow in the sea,[399] may fairly be considered as a proof of the want of reliable information on the subject. The fear of the Israelites[400] at the approach of the Egyptians by the Red Sea is also mentioned by Muhammad.[401]

Now we come to a circumstance, which is also taken from Jewish legend, but which has been almost entirely misunderstood, from ignorance of its origin. The passage[402] may be translated as follows:

> And we caused the children of Israel to pass through the sea, and Pharaoh and his army followed them in a violent and hostile manner, until when he was drowning, he said: "I believe that there is no God but He on Whom the Children of Israel believe, and I am now one of the resigned"; on which God said [or perhaps this is to be read in the first person, so that this verse too expresses Pharaoh's penitence, and the next verse begins the expression of God's answer], "Thou hast been hitherto one of the rebel-

lious and wicked doers. This day, however, will we save thee with thy body, that thou mayest be a sign to those who shall be after thee."[403]

This is the quite simple meaning of the words, which has been turned and twisted about by others, because they were ignorant of the following Jewish legend:[404] "Recognize the power of repentance! Pharaoh, King of Egypt, rebelled excessively against the Most High saying: 'Who is God that I should hearken to His voice?'[405] but with the same tongue he repented saying: 'Who is like Thee, O Lord, among the Gods?'[406] God delivered him from the dead, for it is written: 'For now I had put forth my hand and smitten thee,'[407] but God let him live to proclaim His power and might, even as it is written in Exodus, ix. 16."

On the occasion of the striking of the rock Muhammad makes twelve streams gush out, so that each individual tribe had its own particular stream. Apparently this is a confusion of the events at Raphidim, where the rock was struck,[408] with those at Elim where the Israelites found twelve wells.[409] On these wells the commentator Rashi, probably following earlier expositors says: "They found them ready for them, in number as the twelve Tribes."

When it came at last to the giving of the Law, the Israelites are said to have rebelled; but God threatened them that He would overturn the mountain[410] upon them if they would not accept the Law. The Jews also say that God threatened to cover them with the mountain as with a basin turned upside down.[411] But now the Israelites demanded that they themselves should see God; they died at the sight of Him, but were afterwards raised again.[412] The corresponding rabbinical statement may be translated as follows:

> The Israelites desired two things of God, that they might see His glory and hear His voice; and both were granted them, as it is written:[413] "Behold the Lord our God hath showed us His glory and His greatness, and we have heard His voice out of the midst of the fire." Then they had no power to bear it, for when they came to Sinai and He appeared to them, their soul departed at His speech, as it is written:[414] "My soul went forth when he spake." The Law (the Torah) however interceded with God for them saying: "Would a king marry his daughter and slay all is household?" The whole world rejoices (on account of my appearance), and shall thy children (the Israelites) die? At once their souls returned to them, therefore it is written:[415] "The Law of the Lord is perfect, restoring the soul."

The story of the calf is also one of those which Muhammad, following the rabbis, has found it easy to embellish. He says that the people would have killed Aaron, if he had not made them a calf;[416] and the rabbis say:[417] "Aaron saw Hur (who had wished to oppose them) killed; then he thought: if I do not listen to them they will do with me as with Hur." According to another statement of the Koran[418] one of the Israelites, named Samiri, led them astray and also made the calf. This arose perhaps from Samael, the name of one who is supposed by the Jews to have been helpful at the making of the calf; but at any rate the tale has been differently developed by Muhammad. According to him this was one of the Israelites who was present, and whom Moses condemned to everlasting wandering,[419] so that he was compelled to say perpetually, "Touch not." One recognizes that this legend is composed of different elements. It is not foreign to Jewish tradition that another Israelite, not Aaron, made the calf, and according to one legend, Micah,[420] who is mentioned in Judges, helped in the making;[421] whence it comes that many Arabians assert that Samiri and Micah are one and the same person;[422] Perhaps Muhammad formed the word Samiri from a confusion with the name Samael.

Samiri was the name for Samaritan, and according to the Arabians the Samaritans said, "Touch us not."[423] With how much reason the Arabians hold this is indeed unknown, perhaps only from confusion with a sect of the Pharisees described as bad in the Talmud, where it is named "The set-apart, touch me not;" but I have only a dim recollection of the passage. In short the Samaritans were certainly known to later Arabians by this name, and Muhammad doubtless knew them by it too; and since he gave the name of Samaritan to the maker of the calf, this man must have seemed to him to be the founder of the sect, and the "Touch me not" must have originated with him, which as a punishment was known to Muhammad from the similar story of the wandering Jew. Muhammad says that the calf lowed as it come forth.[424] With this is to be compared the rabbinical statement: "There came forth this calf[425] lowing, and the Israelites saw it. Rabbi Jehuda says that Samael entered into it and lowed in order to mislead Israel."[426] In the Koran it is said[427] that among the people of Moses there was a tribe which kept to the truth. This seems to refer to the tribe of Levi and especially to their behavior about the calf, although possibly it may refer also to their belief in Moses's mission to Pharaoh of which we have spoken before. In the biblical account a statement is made,[428] which is explained by the rabbis as follows:[429] "From Exodus, xxxii. 26, it is clear that the tribe of Levi was not implicated in the matter of the golden calf." The Arabian commentators produce the most unedifying fables about this passage.

In the events which follow abbreviations are to be found, but neither changes nor embellishments, except in the story of the dispute with Korah, which gives rise to some. Korah is said to have had such riches that a number of strong men were required to carry the keys of his treasure-chamber,[430] and the rabbis tell, "Joseph buried three treasures in Egypt, one of which became known to Korah. Riches kept by the owner to his hurt[431] may be applied to the riches of Korah. The keys of Korah's treasure chamber were a burden for three hundred white mules." It is implied in the same Talmudic passage that he became overbearing and quarrelsome from the possession of such riches, and Muhammad embellishes this idea in a fine manner. One passage in the Koran may refer to this dispute, for it says there that some persons had accused Moses, but that God cleared him from the charge which they had brought against him.[432] Some of the commentators also refer the passage to this event, while they bring forward the following story, which we give in Elpherar's words: "Abu'l-'Aliah says that it refers to the fact that Korah had hired a bad woman, who accused Moses before all the people of bad conduct with herself. God made her dumb, cleared Moses of the accusation, and destroyed Korah." This is actually supposed to have happened after Moses had made known the law about adultery, and after the enquiry as to whether it applied to him also had been answered by him in the affirmative.[433] The rabbis also allude to this in the following words:[434] "And when Moses heard it, he fell on his face. What did he hear? That he was blamed for being intimate with the wife of another"; and in another passage we read:[435] "Each man suspected his wife on account of Moses."

Other commentators understand that the accusation was that Moses had killed Aaron, because the two were alone together when Aaron died on Mount Hor; but Moses was cleared from this by the angels, who produced Aaron's corpse. This is also a rabbinical idea, for we read in the Midrash Tanchuma:

> All the congregation saw that Aaron was dead.[436] When Moses and Eleazar came down from the mountain, the whole congregation came together against them asking them: "Where is Aaron?" They said: "He is dead." They replied: "How can the death angel come to a man who has once resisted him and held him back? for it is written:[437] He (Aaron) stood

between the dead and the living and the plague was stayed. If you produce him, well; if not, we will stone you." Moses then prayed: "Lord of the world, clear me from this suspicion." Then God immediately opened the grave and showed Aaron to them, and to this refers the passage: "The whole congregation saw, etc."

Here I omit entirely a third very insipid fable which the commentators mention, and which seems to them to be the most probable occasion of the verse, but I cannot trace it to any Jewish source. The most correct view is, as Wahl has already remarked, that the verse refers to the reproaches of Aaron and Miriam.[438] In short the fifth verse of sura LXI is about the answer of Moses to the disputants. Here the commentators give only the fable not quoted by us, just because here, as in the second passage, they repeat only the most universally accepted view. But this cannot prevent us from holding to our opinion. Of the journey described by Muhammad[439] I could not find a trace in Jewish writings, although the coloring is Jewish.[440] Moses is said to have gone with his servant to see the place where two seas meet, and to have forgotten a fish, which they were taking with them for food and which sprang into the sea. When they went back to seek it, a servant of God met them and made the journey with them, telling them beforehand that his actions would rouse their impatience. He sank a ship, killed a youth and propped up a wall; and only when they parted did he give sufficient reasons for these actions. The story following this about Dhu'l-Qarnain[441] might well refer to Moses, the shining one,[442] if anything of the sort were known about him.

Of the individual laws which are mentioned historically in the Koran, only one, viz., that relating to the red heifer,[443] affords material for a narrative, and that is given[444] in very unnecessary fullness and with manifold errors. In the first place Muhammad confounds the red heifer[445] with the calf which is slain for one murdered by an unknown hand,[446] and he also makes the dead man live again[447] on being struck with a piece of the animal. In view of such great distortions we must not deal hardly with him for the following small one; he says that the cow must be of one year,[448] in contradiction to the rabbinical statement that she had to be a two-year old.[449]

As to those persons who come into the history of Moses, we have already disposed of Pharaoh, Aaron and Korah, while we have only mentioned others and therefore must add more about them. Miriam is praised in the Scripture and called a prophetess, but the rabbis value her still more highly and say of her:[450] "The angel of death had no power over Miriam, but she died from the divine afflation, and therefore worms could not touch her." According to Muhammad[451] Miriam is the mother of Jesus.[452] Although Miriam's name is not mentioned in the passage where she is alluded to in the history of Moses,[453] yet there is not the slightest doubt that Muhammad took both Marys for one and the same person; for the Talmudic utterance already cited, viz., that Miriam did not die through the angel of death, could easily be turned into a statement of a long, if not endless, life for her, especially by Muhammad, who treats chronology pretty much according to his own pleasure. The other person who appears in the history of Moses is his father-in-law Jethro. Now it is true that his name, like that of Miriam, is not mentioned in the story of Moses,[454] hence the Muhammadan tradition connects this Midianite (as the Koran simply designates the father-in-law of Moses) with Shu'aib, the Arabic name for Jethro, and so they came to be considered as one and the same, not however without more or less opposition. Thus Elpherar says:[455] "Opinions are divided as to the name of Moses' wife's father. Many say he was the prophet Shu'aib; others that he was Jethro, the nephew of Shu'aib who died before him; others again that he was a man who believed on Shu'aib." But the most widespread tradition is that it was Shu'aib himself.

Thus Elpherar always calls him by this name, when mentioning him in connection with these events and Abulfeda[456] relates just this one thing about Shu'aib, viz., that he was the father-in-law of Moses, without giving any other opinion. Though his name is not mentioned in this connection in the Koran, other events independent of Moses' life are related of him, particularly his admonition of the Midianites, which is said by the rabbis to have been the cause of the hatred of that people towards him.[457] Muhammad took up the admonition without mentioning the consequence which it entailed on Jethro, viz., the driving away of his daughters, which was just the circumstance which led to Jethro's connection with the life of Moses. According to Muhammad an immediate punishment fell on the Midianites.[458] The rabbis have the following on the subject:[459]

The priest of Midian had seven daughters.[460] God hates idolatry and did He give Moses a refuge with an idolater? Concerning this our teachers tell us: Jethro was priest of the idols, but knew their worthlessness, despised idolatry and had thought of being converted even before Moses came. Then he called his fellow-townsmen and said to them: "Till now I

have served you, but now I am old, choose you another priest: and he
gave them back the vessels of service." Then they put him under a ban,
so that no one conversed with him, no one worked for him, no one tended
his flocks; and when he asked this service from the shepherds, they would
not give it. The shepherds came and drove them away.[461] Was it possible?
Jethro was the priest of Midian and the shepherds drove away his daughters? But this shows that they had put him under a ban, and for this reason
they drove his daughters away.

In the mouth of the people, or more probably from Muhammad himself, the legend received the embellishment that Jethro wanted to convert
his fellow-countrymen to the faith, and that they were punished on
account of their unbelief. A reproach which is specially brought against
them, or rather the point of the exhortation, viz., to give just weight and
measure,[462] must be founded on some legend or other, although I have not
yet come across it in Jewish writings.[463] Jethro shows himself as a preacher
quite according to Muhammad's ideas. He preaches about the Last Day[464]
and asserts that he desires no reward;[465] on the other hand his townspeople
reproach him with working no miracles.[466] I have presented the facts and
quotations here as though there were no doubt that all these passages refer
to Jethro, but exception might be taken to this. An altogether different
name is found in the Koran, and it is not easy to explain how Jethro came
by it. However, we must first try to show that Shu'aib and Jethro are identical, and then put forward our conjectures as to how the many-named
Jethro added this name to his others. The identity is first shown by the fact
that those to whom he was sent are called "Midianites;"[467] in the second
place, the two first passages[468] give the events concerning him between the
story of Lot and that of Moses.

Now if we can find among the rabbis any intimation favorable to this
supposition, then nothing important will remain to oppose its adoption[469]
as a probable hypothesis. Very little, however, can be adduced to show how
Shu'aib and Jethro came to be one and the same person. Muhammad may
have confused the name Hobab—often used for Jethro and probably pronounced Chobab—with Shu'aib. Perhaps an etymological explanation may
be thought of here, for the rabbis assert that the staff used later by Moses
and called the divine staff grew in Jethro's garden.[470] Now Sha'ba means
staff and Shu'aib may be taken as the possessor of the staff. If Shu'aib is the
same as Jethro, there are passages[471] in which the former is mentioned,

while those to whom he is sent are not called Midianites; and so we find a new name for these people, viz., "men of the wood," which name is evidently derived from the thorn bushes which were in the vicinity.

It remains for us to justify the bringing forward of two more passages,[472] and it is all the more difficult for us to do so, because in order to prove our point we must accuse Muhammad himself of a misunderstanding. In these passages Shu'aib is not mentioned, but the people who are held up as a warning are called "men of the well," without any other particulars being given about them. But further these "men of the well"[473] are mentioned in one passage along with the "men of the wood," and so it seems certain that Muhammad regarded them as two different peoples; but nevertheless we allow ourselves to believe them to be really identical.

The real reason for bringing Jethro into the Koran is, as we have already remarked, the quarrel of the shepherds with his daughters, although the fact itself is not mentioned in that book; and it is thus easy to understand that the Jews may have sometimes called the Midianites by this name, i.e., "men of the well." No other circumstances related about these persons mentioned in the Koran would authorize this appellation. The story of Jacob at the well (setting aside the fact that not the slightest allusion to it is to be found in the Koran) has in it no trace of hostility; and so the conjecture is not too daring that, as a matter of fact, all these three, viz., the Midianites, the people of the wood, and the people of the well, are the same, but that Muhammad regarded the first two only as identical and looked on the last as different. Still this tradition seems to have been received even among the Arabs, for we find in Elpherar[474] among other explanations the following: "Wahb says that the people of the well sat beside it (the well), and the shepherds served idols. Then God sent Shu'aib, who was to exhort them to Islam, but they remained in their error, and continued their efforts to harm Shu'aib. While they sat round the well in their dwellings the spring bubbled up and gushed over them and their houses, so that they were all ruined." In like manner Jalalu'd-din says:[475] "Their prophet is called by some Shu'aib, by others differently." This admission of the Arabic commentators strengthens our opinion considerably.

Another person of some importance in the Mosaic age is said by some Arabic commentators to be alluded to in the Koran[476] but many others dispute the allusion. Elpherar quotes four different opinions on this passage. The first opinion is that it refers to Balaam, for which he quotes many authorities, and relates the history of Balaam in almost complete accord with the Bible narrative. Jalalu'd-din and Zamakhahari refer this to Balaam, and call him Balaam the son of Ba'ura. Beyond these no other persons who come into the life of Moses, or who were important in his time, are mentioned, and thus our second part comes to an end.

THE THREE KINGS WHO RULED OVER UNDIVIDED ISRAEL

The history following immediately on the time of Moses, including the time of the Judges, must either have seemed to Muhammad unedifying, which is improbable, as the story of that heroic age was quite in accord with his feelings and aims; or else it must have been wholly unknown to him, and this appears to have been the case from the fact that he speaks of the choosing of a king as an event happening after Moses,[477] in terms which can only mean immediately or very soon after Moses. Saul stands very much in the background; for on the one hand his history was known to Muhammad only in a very abbreviated form, and on the other hand the Prophet had such an undefined notion of Saul's personality that he attributes to him the actions of others. Saul's history is related in the Koran[478] in the following manner:

> After Moses the Israelites desired a king, in order that they might go out under him to the Holy War;[479] to which however only a few of them afterwards went. The prophet (Samuel) gave out that Saul was sent of God, still he seemed despicable in the eyes of the people.[480] As a sign that the rule pertained to Saul, the prophet of Israel announced the return of the Ark of the Covenant. Saul then proved his troops, and allowed only those to belong to his army who drank water lapping it with the hand; this was done by very few, and even these were afraid of Goliath and his armies. David at length overcame the Philistine hosts and gained the dominion.

The circumstance that through Saul the Ark of the Covenant came back[481] is contrary to Scripture, according to which the Ark came back earlier. The story of Saul's proving his troops is evidently a confusion with that of Gideon, concerning whom this is related in the Bible,[482] and has doubtless risen from the similar story of Saul's forbidding food to the army.[483] This confusion with Gideon accounts too for the saying that only a few mighty men followed Saul. The name of the prophet is not given, and later Arabians also are in ignorance about it. Saul is called Talut,[484] a name probably given on account of his height.[485] Muhammad notices in the Koran that Saul was of great height,[486] and Baidhawi gives this derivation for his name. Goliath is called Jalut.

The personality of David is certainly more clearly grasped in the Koran, but the actual historical events of his life are scarcely touched upon. David's victory over Goliath is mentioned incidentally in the history of Saul. Again, the story of David and Bathsheba is only distantly alluded to, in that (setting aside the passage[487] in which he is called "Penitent" probably with reference to her) the parable of the case in law devised by the Prophet Nathan[488] is narrated,[489] and to it is added[490] that David perceived that this was a sign; and after he had repented, he was received back into favor by God. According to the Koran the case in dispute is not related by the prophet, but the two disputants themselves come before David. In another passage[491] mention is made of David's and Solomon's excellent judgment on the occasion of some quarrel unknown to us about shepherds tending flocks on strange fields at night. A remarkable circumstance is given in several passages,[492] where it is stated that David compelled the mountains and the birds to praise God with him, which, as Wahl rightly remarks, owes its origin to David's poetical address to all creatures, in which address he imagines them endowed with life and reason, and calls on them to join with him in extolling the Almighty. According to the Koran[493] mankind is indebted to David for the invention of armor. This legend probably arose from David's warlike fame, although there is much said in the Bible about Goliath's armor. In another passage[494] we find a general mention of David. In one of the Sunnas[495] it is mentioned that David did with very little sleep; and Elpherar,[496] in a long chain of tradition beginning with Ibn 'Abbas and ending with 'Amru, says: "The Apostle of God said: '(David) slept half the night, rose for a third, and then slept again for a sixth.'" The rabbis also speak of this, on the strength of the[497] verse, "At midnight I will rise to give thanks unto Thee," and they assert that David used to sleep only during sixty respirations.[498] David is also known to Muhammad as the author of the Psalms.[499] The affair of the Sabbath-breakers, who were punished by being changed into apes, is also supposed to belong to the time of David, but the circumstance is mentioned[500] only in general terms, and nothing definite is given about time or details, except in verse 82, where the time is given, but not the fact. Among the Jews there is no trace of this legend.

The life of Solomon is in itself unimportant, and it is only the wisdom for which he is famed in the Bible which makes him the hero of the whole East, one might therefore expect to find much more about him in the Koran than really exists there. Muhammad speaks of his wisdom,[501] and especially brings forward the fact that Solomon understood the language of the birds. This is also asserted by the rabbis, and is founded on the Biblical statement:[502] "He spake of trees...and birds." The winds also performed his will, and the Genii were found in his following;[503] this is also related, e.g., in the second Targum on the Book of Esther,[504] thus: "To him were obedient demons of the most diverse sorts, and the evil spirits were given into his hand." This legend is derived primarily from a mistaken interpretation of a passage in Ecclesiastes.[505] Muhammad relates the following tale:[506]

> On one occasion the lapwing was not found in attendance on Solomon, and the King regarding him as a truant threatened to kill him. Then the lapwing came with the news that he had discovered a land as yet unknown to Solomon, which was not subject to him, the land of Sheba, in which the people together with the Queen worshipped the sun. Solomon sent the bird back with a letter summoning these people to adopt the belief in the Unity of God. He himself went thither at once with his troops, and had the Queen's throne brought to him by a ministering angel. The Queen had been already converted, and she came into Solomon's camp; he had her brought before him into a hall, of which the flooring was glass, and she imagining it to be water, exposed her legs.

This same story is to be found in the Targum[507] already referred to, together with some other circumstances which I shall omit here. The story runs as follows:

> Thereupon the partridge was sought and not found among the birds, and the King commanded angrily that it should be fetched, and he wanted to kill it. Then the partridge answered the King: "My lord and King, attend and hear my words, for three months I considered and flew about the whole world to find the town where thou wast not obeyed. Then I saw a town in the East called Kitor, where there are many people, but a woman rules over them; she is called the Queen of Sheba. If it please thee now, my lord King, I will go to that town and bind the Queen with chains and its nobles with iron fetters and bring them all here." And it pleased the

King, and Scribes were called who wrote letters and bound them to the wings of the partridge. When the bird came to the Queen she saw the letter tied on to its wing, she opened it, and these were the contents: "From me, Solomon the King, greeting to thee and to thy princes! Thou knowest well that God hath appointed me King over the beasts of the field and the birds of the heaven, and over the demons, spirits and spectres of the night, and that the kings of all the countries under heaven approach me in submission. If thou also wilt do this, great honor will be shown thee; if not, then I will send against thee kings and legions and horsemen. The kings are the beasts of the field; the horsemen, the birds of the air; the armies, demons and spirits; while the legions are nightmares, which will strangle you in your beds." When the Queen had read this, she rent her clothes and sent for the elders and lords and said: "Do you know what King Solomon has sent me?" They said: "We neither know him, nor heed him." But the Queen did not trust them, but called for ships and sent presents to the king, and after three years she went herself. When the king heard that she had come, he seated himself in a glass room. She thought the king was sitting in the water, and bared herself to go through it. When she saw his magnificence, she said:[508] "Blessed be the Lord thy God, which delighted in thee, to set thee on the throne . . . to do judgment and justice."

We must forgive Muhammad the two slight changes he makes in the story, viz., that he turns the matter from one of government into one of religion, and that he begins the letter[509] with the words: "In the name of the Merciful God." Solomon built the Temple also by the help of the spirits, who even went on building after his death, while he remained sitting on his throne till a worm gnawed him.[510]

Once when Solomon became arrogant he was driven from the kingdom, and a spirit reigned in his stead until he repented.[511] The Sanhedrin[512] gives the following brief account: "At first Solomon reigned even over the exalted ones, as it is written:[513] Solomon sat on the throne of the Lord; but afterwards only over his own stick, as it is written:[514] What profit hath man of all his labor? and further,[515] this was my portion from all my labor."[516] When he repented, he gave up his useless extravagances, and had his horses disabled,[517] to which the following passage alludes:[518] "It is wisely ordained that the reasons for the commandments are not given; they were given in two cases, and one of the greatest of men sinned. For it is written:[519] The king shall not multiply horses to himself, nor cause the people to return to Egypt, to the end that he should multiply horses. Then Solomon thought, I will get me many horses and not send to Egypt; but it is written:[520] And a chariot came up and went out of Egypt for six hundred shekels of silver." A story about spirits, which is said to have happened in Solomon's time,[521] has already been mentioned in connection with Noah. A story about the nets, which fled before Solomon's army, is related in the Koran,[522] and remains to be noticed. It is evidently founded on the verse,[523] "Go to the ant thou sluggard... and be wise;" and based on this same foundation we have a beautiful fable in the Talmud[524] but I could find there no trace of the story given in the Koran.

The story of the lapwing has gained a firm foothold in Arabic legend, and a pretty myth about the bird is found in Fakihat Elcholafa.[525] For Muhammad there were no very important personages between Moses and Jesus; and such as he does mention he merely alludes to. This is not to be wondered at when Solomon, the wise man of the East, who is endowed with all manner of legendary adornment comes, comparatively speaking, so little before us in the Koran.

HOLY MEN AFTER THE TIME OF SOLOMON

Many important men might be mentioned here, but Muhammad knew but few of them, and about those whom he does name he gives for the most part nothing special, but mentions them only with other pious persons. Some only are treated with a little more detail, and we will mention them here first, so as then to put the others together briefly. Of Elijah[526] his dispute with the people about the worship of Baal is related briefly. In the legends of Islam as well as in those of later Judaism Elijah plays a very important part. He is that mystical person known under the name of Khizr. He is therefore the same as Phinehas, erroneously called by some the nephew of Aaron instead of his grandson, and, like Elijah the prophet in later Jewish traditions, he is the mediator between heaven and earth. It is he who appears to the pious under the most varied forms, who visits tho schools, and imparts to famous teachers that which God communicates about this or that opinion expressed by them. The Muslims too know him in this capacity, and they recognize him in the servant of God who proposed himself as a travelling companion to Moses,[527] and in these actions they have the prototype of his ministry as one who appears in a miraculous manner, has intercourse with men in human fashion, and performs incomprehensible actions which only receive true significance through knowledge which is hidden from man.

Jonah is mentioned in several passages of the Koran.[528] His mission to Nineveh, his being swallowed by the fish, his rescue from it, and the story of the gourd which shaded him, are all given very briefly.[529] Job's sufferings and healing are mentioned in two passages,[530] and in the latter passage Muhammad adds that Job produced a cooling and refreshing fountain for himself by stamping on the earth. We know of no parallel passage to this in the rabbinical writings.

We come now to a passage[531] hitherto wrongly referred which translated runs thus: "Slain were the men of the pit of the burning fire, when they sat around the same, and were witnesses of what was done to the true believers, and they wished to punish them only because they believed in the mighty and glorious God," etc. Commentators make this refer to the punishment of a Jewish Himyarite king who persecuted the Christians, but the appellation "believers" as applied to Christians has no parallel elsewhere in the Koran, no detail bearing on this event is mentioned, and just this one form of persecution (burning) is not given by the martyrologists.

If we compare the passage with the story of the three children[532] all fits in perfectly.

The three believers would not bow themselves before an idol, and were thrown into the fiery furnace; those who threw them in were slain by the heat and the believers were saved. Evidently Muhammad here alludes to this.[533]

It is possible that there is an allusion to the story of the revival of the dry bones[534] in a passage of the Koran,[535] which tells us that many who left their habitations for fear of death were slain by God, but were afterwards restored to life.[536] The Talmud treats the narrative given in Ezekiel more in detail.[537]

Another biblical reference may perhaps be found in the words:[538] "Dost thou not see how thy Lord stretches (lengthens) out the shadow when he will, makes it quiescent, then sets the sun over it as an indicator?" This I think is perhaps an allusion to the sign given to Hezekiah.[539]

We find more in the Koran about Ezra, if not about his history, yet about the way in which the Jews regarded him. According to the assertion of Muhammad the Jews held Ezra to be the Son of God.[540] This is certainly a mere misunderstanding which arose from the great esteem in which Ezra was undoubtedly held. This esteem is expressed in the following passage:[541] "Ezra would have been worthy to have made known the law if Moses had not come before him." Truly Muhammad sought to cast suspicion on the Jews' faith in the unity of God, and thought he had here found a good opportunity of so doing.

This utterance as an expression of the Jewish opinion of that time loses much in value when we consider the personality of that Phineas the son of Azariah, to whom it is attributed.

In the traditions of Islam there is a great deal about Ezra as the compiler of the Law. In this character also he comes before us in Scripture, and the Jews believed this of him; so the probability becomes great that Muhammad, on the one hand, intentionally exaggerated, and, on the other hand, eagerly caught up the hasty and mocking utterance of some individual to prove this point against the Jews.

The Arabian commentators according to Maraccius[542] refer another passage in the Koran[543] to Ezra, namely, the one where it is related of some person that he passed by a ruined city and doubted if it could ever be restored. God let him die for one hundred years, then revived him and imparted to him the assurance that one hundred years had gone by, while he believed that but one day had passed. The proof was that his food and drink had perished and his ass was mouldering away. Then behold! God put together the bones of the animal and clothed them with flesh, so that the man acknowledged: "God is mighty over all." The fable is derived, as Maraccius rightly observes, from the ride round the ruined city of Jerusalem made by Nehemiah,[544] who is often confused with Ezra.

Two other biblical characters are merely mentioned: Elisha in two passages,[545] and each time strangely enough immediately after Ishmael; and Dhul-Kifl,[546] who according to his name which means the nourisher, and from the fact related of him that he nourished a hundred Israelites in a cave, must be Obadiah.[547] Perhaps, however, he may be Ezekiel; who according to Niebuhr[548] is called Kephil by the Arabs.[549]

Now all the historical allusions have been put together, and when we examine them we see unmistakably in them the verification of the hypothesis which we laid down at the beginning—namely, that Muhammad borrowed a great deal from Judaism, that he learned that which he did borrow from oral tradition, and that he sometimes altered it to suit his purpose.... We have attempted to show that Muhammad really did borrow from Judaism, and that conceptions, matters of creed, views of morality, and of life in general, and more especially matters of history and of traditions, have actually passed over from Judaism into the Koran.

And now our task is practically ended. If a thorough demonstration has been made of all these points, then the questions as to whether Muhammad did borrow from Judaism, and *what* and *how* he so borrowed, have been sufficiently answered. Now, as a supplementary note we add a summary of the passages in which Muhammad's attribute towards Judaism seems to be negative and even hostile. Some of these passages oppose Judaism, some abrogate laws binding on the Jews, and some allude to Jewish customs without imposing them upon the Arabs. But since we consider the question, the answer to which forms the subject of our theme, as now fully answered, without giving the results of further investigation, we therefore do not give these results as a part of this work itself, but add them as an appendix.

APPENDIX: STATEMENTS IN THE KORAN HOSTILE TO JUDAISM

Just as we tried before to show from the personality of Muhammad and from the spirit of his time that borrowing from Judaism had taken place, even so we wish here to show that statements hostile to Judaism are to be found in the Koran. Muhammad's aim was to bring about a union of all creeds, and no religious community stood more in the way of the attainment of this end than the Jews with their many cumbersome laws, unknown to other religions. Further, Muhammad's aim was to establish in and through this union such religious doctrines only as were in his opinion purified. The observance of individual laws did not seem to him of great importance, except in so far as such laws resulted immediately from those special doctrines; moreover, he loved the old Arabian customs and kept to them. The Jews on the contrary laid the greatest stress upon the punctilious fulfillment of the revealed law, and showed not the slightest desire to depart from it. While these two causes of mutual separation were founded upon the difference in the fundamental opinions of Muhammad and the Jews, another may be added which arose more from an external difference. As we have already remarked, the Jews pressed Muhammad very hard, and often annoyed him with repartee and evasions, thus rousing in him an inextinguishable hatred. Governed by this he misunderstood their religions doctrines, putting false constructions upon them, and so justifying his own deviation from them. He wished therefore to make a final separation from these hateful Jews, and to this end he established entirely different customs. Later Arabians confess that he made changes "from the necessity of abolishing resemblances to the Jews."[550] Thus, Muhammad asserts that the Jews are the enemies of the Muslims,[551] that they slew prophets,[552] a probable reference to Jesus; further, that they in common with Christians thought themselves specially favored by God,[553] that they believed that they alone should possess paradise,[554] that they held Ezra to be the son of God,[555] that they trusted in the intercession of their self-pious predecessors,[556] that they had perverted the Bible[557] because in its existing form that book contained no allusions to him, and that the Jews built temples on the graves of the prophets.[558] Such accusations and the reasons given earlier supplied Muhammad with grounds on which to justify his departure from Jewish laws.

A. *Prayer.*—Supper precedes prayer.[559] This is in direct opposition to the Talmud, which lays down exactly how long before prayer one may eat that the hour of prayer may not be let slip. Truly in this Muhammad wished to live so as to please his Arabs.

B. *Laws about women.*—Muhammad says:[560] "It is lawful for you on the night of the fast to go in unto your wives." This is clearly prescribed in opposition to the directly contrary ruling in the Talmudic law prohibiting cohabitation on the night before the fast day in Abh, that being counted as part of the fast day itself.

The laws of divorce[561] are probably identical with those of the ancient Arabs. There is a remarkable passage in the Koran,[562] which says that the man after he has put away his wife for the second time cannot marry her again until she has married another man, and been divorced by him too. This is directly contrary to the teaching of the Bible.[563]

The Muslims assert[564] that the Jews of that period laid down that cohabitation was to take place in the usual way. On this Muhammad to please himself and his Arabs says:[565] "Your wives are your tillage; go in therefore unto your tillage in what manner soever ye will," etc.

C. The most important and prominent change to be considered in this connection is the removal of the prohibition about food, concerning which Muhammad asserts that it was imposed upon the Jews only on account of their iniquity.[566] (It is interesting that Jesus states just the converse when he speaks of the abolition of divorce.[567]) Muhammad abolishes the law about meat in several passages,[568] but holds to part of it in others;[569] following it would seem the precedent of the apostles, to whom almost the same utterance is attributed in the New Testament.[570] Thus he forbids carrion, blood, swine's flesh, and that which has been slain for an idol; to which he adds in the first passage, that which is not properly killed, viz., that slain by strangling, or by a blow from an axe, that killed by a fall from a mountain, that which is gored, and that torn by wild beasts. These last rules, considering the total silence about them in other later passages, may be regarded as "abolished." In another passage[571] Muhammad mentions particular meats which were forbidden to the Jews.[572]

D. Lastly, the following utterance[573] of Muhammad is decidedly combative: "We have therein commanded them that they should give life for life, and eye for eye, and nose for nose, and ear for ear, and tooth for tooth; and that wounds should also be punished by retaliation; but whoever should remit it as alms it should be accepted as an atonement for him. And whoso judgeth not according to what God hath revealed they are unjust." The passage of Scripture which Muhammad here has in mind is in Exodus;[574] and those who do not observe it are the Jews, in that they extend to all cases the permission to make atonement with money, which is given only when the injured party agrees to it. The Mishna[575] runs as follows: "If a man has blinded another, or cut off his hand, or broken his foot, one must regard the injured person as though he were a slave sold in the market, and put a price upon him and reckon how much he was worth before the injury and how much now, etc."

These are about all the chief points showing a consideration of Judaism, and the collecting of them gives us another proof that Muhammad had a personal knowledge of Judaism through acquaintance with the Jewish manner of life and through intercourse with the Jews.

If we now once more consider this treatise as a whole, we shall find that by the establishment of the fact which was to be demonstrated, viz., that Muhammad borrowed from Judaism, we come to a clear understanding of the Koran in general as well as of individual passages in it. Furthermore, the state of culture of the Arabians of that day, and especially of the Arabian Jews, is to some extent made clear, and light is thrown upon the plan of Muhammad and upon his intellectual power and knowledge by many authentic documents. Then in collecting the passages which serve as proofs we are compelled to dismiss at once the ill-considered confidence with which people are apt to speak of each legend as a dream of the rabbinical Talmudists; for although the author neither can nor will maintain that no passage bearing on his thesis has escaped him in the rabbinical literature, still this must be accepted as a fact until it can be proved that this or that has been omitted, and thus for the present we must attribute to some other source everything of which the Jewish origin has not been proved. By this, however, I do not intend to say that everything which, according to our ideas, is mythical and for which a Jewish source appears to be forthcoming, may be laid upon Judaism; for, on the one hand, the opinion or legend may originally have had a different signification and it may have reached its present extravagant development in the mouth of the people, and, on the other hand, the source itself may have had no obligatory importance, and therefore does not hold the same place with regard to Judaism as the Koran holds with regard to Islam. We must distinguish between Judaism and views derived from the Jews; this distinction, however, is unfortunately, either from ill-will or ignorance often not made.

And now I submit this treatise to you, honored readers, and your judgment will convince me of the correctness or falsity of my opinions, and as to whether my work fulfills its end or has failed in its purpose.

12.

The Sources of Islam

W. St. Clair-Tisdall

Foreword

*T*HIS REMARKABLE BOOK HAS BEEN written by the Rev. W. T. St. Clair-Tisdall, Missionary, C.M.S., Julfa, Persia. It takes up a subject never as yet brought properly under discussion either by Muslims or Christians—namely, the origin of the Koran, and the sources from which both it and tradition have been derived. By the teaching of Muhammad the Koran is of divine origin, and was brought down, as tradition tells us, word by word by Gabriel to the Prophet's ear. The original is "written on a Tablet, kept in Heaven,"[1] sent down on the night of al-Qadr"[2] by the Almighty. Thus the Koran comes from God alone, heavenly, divine, and uncreate from all eternity. Now if it can be shown that much of this grand book can be traced to human sources existing daily around the Prophet, then Islam falls to the ground. And this is what the author proves with marvellous power and erudition.

Such sources as were derived from the Arabs themselves are treated first (chap. II). The shadow of divine unity still subsisted among them. There were a multitude of gods and idols, of which each tribe had its special ones, as Lat and 'Uzza for the Quraish. The intercession of these was

Originally published c. 1901 in London by S.P.C.K.

sought; but above and beyond them all was the ancient memory of one great God, Allah—the *Al* ("the") a proof of sovereign unity. Curious that the word occurs in the Prophet's family, his father and uncle being called Abdallah and Ubaidallah. There was thus a local source to build upon. Then we have the multitude of national habits and practices, as the Hajj, the Ka'aba, etc., maintained in the new faith, though all of earthly origin. It was indeed the Prophet's endeavor to pull down all purely idolatrous worship;[3] and so he did, except the kissing of the Black Stone, too popular a practice to be abandoned. A curious example of a purely local source may be found in a number of verses of the Koran which are shown to be taken from the *Mu'allaqat,* a plagiarism rather difficult for the Muslim to conjoin with the heavenly origin of his revelation.

Chapter III explains the influence of Judaism. And first we are told that the five times of prayer were borrowed from the Sabeans. The Jews were numerous and powerful throughout Arabia, and Muhammad, having sought their conversion in vain, at last fought against them and banished them from the country. But in the meantime he had taken much of his teaching from their books, the Talmud, their commentaries, etc. The first *qibla* was Jerusalem, and the marvellous tales thus derived cannot be read without astonishment. Thus there is the story of Cain and Abel, and of their parents weeping while the raven showed how to bury the dead; Abraham cast by Nimrod into the fire unhurt;[4] the Queen of Sheba uncovering her legs as she walked before Solomon over the glass floor, which she takes for a sheet of water; the descent of Harut and Marut and other spirits from above to tempt mankind; Sammael, the Angel of Death, speaking out of the golden calf—and other fictitious tales too numerous to mention. It is strange that though the Jewish and Christian Scriptures are spoken of throughout the Koran with the utmost devotion, only one passage is quoted from them, namely, "The meek shall inherit the earth." In respect also of the Tables of the Testimony put by Moses into the ark, the Muslims, following the extravagant notions of the Jews who fancied that all their sacred books with the Talmud were also in the ark, place on the "Preserved Table" their own Koran! A vast emerald mountain has also arisen out of the word *Cau* in the Talmudic explanation of *Thohu,* Genesis i. 2; of which it takes 2000 years to make the circuit, and 500 the assent. Such are the wild vagaries of Muslim tradition and the sources whence they come.

Chapter IV next shows the apocryphal Christian sources from which Islam has so largely borrowed. There were many Christian tribes in Arabia belonging to heretical sects who had sought refuge there from persecution in Roman lands. Little versed in their own Scriptures, they spent the time in imaginary and childish fables. The Prophet, longing for a universal faith, listened gladly to such stories, which thus became the source of much we find in the Koran.

First we have the fairy tale of the cave wherein the seven sleepers slumbered for ages, fearing persecution.[5] Next we have endless stories of the Virgin Mary, both in the Koran and with vast detail also in tradition; her mother Hannah, her childhood as fed by angels in the temple, Joseph chosen by a miraculous rod, etc., much as in the Proto-Evangelium and other Egyptian and Coptic writings.[6] Then there are the tales of Jesus, as of his speaking in the cradle, breathing life into birds of clay, etc.[7] These the Prophet learned probably from Mary, his Coptic concubine, as they are all contained in such Coptic books as the Gospel of St. Thomas.[8] Thus we have the descent of the Table from Heaven (derived no doubt from the table of the Lord's Supper); the promise by Jesus of a prophet to come, called Ahmed,[9] which was apparently caused by the mistake of περικλυτος for περικλητος; the notion that the resemblance only, and not the real person, of Christ was slain,[10] derived from the heretic Basilides, etc. Passing over much of interest, we may close our review of Christian sources by notice of the *balance*, briefly mentioned in the Koran,[11] but surrounded by a vast variety of Coptic tales. Two Egyptian books (one of ancient date placed in the tombs to be read by the dead) are quoted at length; ... and strange sights are given of Adam and Abraham in the heavens beyond.

Chapter V relates many things from ancient Zoroastrian and even Hindu writings. Persia, far ahead of Arabia, had a sensible influence upon it, and much of what is Oriental in the Koran and tradition is evidently derived from Pahlavi and other Eastern sources. Thus we have the marvels of the seven heavens, seen by the Prophet on his ascent from Jerusalem; the Houris; Azazil and other spirits coming up from Hades; the light of Muhammad, the bridge of Sirat, etc.—all illustrated by the author's marvellous knowledge of Eastern literature, beliefs, and history. The Prophet must have learned all these things from the foreigners who frequented Medina. Suspected of this, he indignantly replied that his tongue was not foreign, but pure Arabic alone.[12]

The concluding chapter tells us of a few inquirers in Arabia, called Hanefites, just before the time of Muhammad. There were four at Mecca, of whom one became a Christian, another a Muslim, and a third joined Caesar. The fourth, Waraqa, was first a Jew then a Christian. One of these, a pious devotee, worshipped yearly in a cave near Mecca, and no doubt influenced the Prophet, who used to visit the same place for quiet and lonely contemplation.

The sources of Islam, our author in conclusion shows, have been altogether human and misleading. They all passed through the Prophet's mind as he composed the Koran, which thus bears throughout the impress of his own heart and character. One good thing there is in it, namely, a thorough testimony to the Gospel and Torah; all true Muslims are accordingly invited to study both, and thus through our Savior Christ obtain the true promises of their father Abraham.

The *Sources* is a noble work, and reflects high distinction on the writer. Hitherto much labor has been spent in showing the falsity and errors of Islam, as has been ably done by Pfander and others. It has remained for our author not only to conceive a new, and perhaps more thorough and effective, mode of treating the so-called divine and eternal faith, but also in doing so to prove its sources to be of purely human origin; and that in so masterly and effective a way that it seems impossible for good Muslims to resist the conclusion drawn. And for all this the thanks of the Christian world are eminently due to the Rev. W. St. Clair-Tisdall.

W. MUIR

Translations

It appears to me of great importance that *The Sources of Islam* should be translated into Arabic, Urdu, and other languages of the East, and so made accessible to Muslim readers everywhere.

The Persian volume, of which the present forms but a partial and compressed translation, is remarkable for giving, *in their primitive tongues*, all the authorities quoted by our author, which are then followed by translations into Persian. Where the passages are in Arabic or other language *understood at the present time*, it will no doubt be proper in any new editions to continue printing them as they stand, with a translation into the common tongue of the country for which the edition is intended. But where they consist of quotations from primitive tongues (as Pahlavi, etc.) not now in use, the *originals* should I think be left out, and simply the translation given as above proposed. The great antiquity of some of the evidence which Mr. St. Clair-Tisdall has given in its ancient form, is no doubt a remarkable proof that certain of the sources of Islam have descended from time immemorial; and it may also be thankfully added, of the wonderful learning and research of the author. But in all new editions and translations these antique passages should I think be omitted in their original tongue, and the rendering alone given in the language of the day.[13]

The Church Mission is to be congratulated on this memorable treatise—bringing as it does so wonderfully to light, tho earthly sources of the Koran, in contradiction to the Muslim belief in its heavenly and eternal origin; and, in a very special manner, on its having come from the hands of one of their own distinguished missionaries. And the hope may be warmly expressed that the work will be widely distributed throughout the East, and lead many an earnest reader in Muslim lands to the faith of his Father Abraham, and the living sources of the Gospel of our Savior.

W. M.

Introduction

Since every religion must have had a source from which it sprung, so this last faith, Islam, must like all others have had its originating cause. Accepted neither by Jews nor Christians, many treatises have been written to controvert it. These have been answered by Muslims in such works as the *Mizan ool Mavazir*, but unfortunately the learning of the authors of these defenses of Islam has not been equal to their zeal. The object of the present work is to investigate the various theories which have been put forward as to the origin of Islam. The author first states briefly the Muslim view, and then examines the claim of those who hold that Islam has a human and not a divine origin.

In this new endeavor, it has been the author's object, by God's help, to show from whence the Muslim faith has risen, its foundation and origin, in other words, its source. And he trusts that those who study the following pages, having learned the origin of the faith, may not lose sight of those sources whence has arisen the vast stream which has overflowed so many nations of the East.

Chapter I.

Views of Muslim Divines as to the
Sources from Which Islam Sprang

Muslims hold that their faith came direct from heaven. The Koran and all their tenets were sent down by Gabriel from God himself to Muhammad. Much of their faith is also built upon *tradition* [Hadith] handed down by the Prophet's followers. But the Shias differ from the Sunnis as to much that is told us by tradition; and the author, therefore, has based his arguments mainly on the Koran which is accepted as divine by every Muslim, and on such tradition as is conformable thereto. As for the Koran, it is held to be of eternal origin, recorded in heaven, and lying as it does there upon the "Preserved Table" (sura lxxxv.21).[14] Thus God alone is held to be the "source" of Islam; and if so, then all effort to find a human origin for any part of it must be in vain. Now, if we can trace the teaching of the Koran, or any part of it, to an earthly source, or to human systems existing previous to the Prophet's age, then Islam at once falls to the ground.

It therefore behooves every true and earnest believer, with the utmost diligence, to test whether this claim be true or not. If their opponents can bring to light no human source, they may contend that by admission Islam is indeed divine; but if otherwise, they cannot but perceive what fatal conclusion must be drawn. Let us then test the assertions of those who hold to the existence of human sources and see whether any portion of the doctrines and tenets of Islam can be traced to other faiths or sources preceding the Prophet's age, or existing at the time.

Chapter II.

Certain Doctrines and Practices of the
Arabs in the "Days of Ignorance" Maintained in Islam

Some hold that these are its *initial* source. When the desire arose in the mind of Muhammad to draw his people from the worship of idols to that of God Almighty; and when he remembered that their forefathers in the days of Abraham believed in the divine unity; and further that they inherited many of the beliefs and customs of their pious forefathers; he was unwilling to force abandonment of them all, but desired rather to purify their faith, and to maintain such ancient practices as he thought good and reasonable. And so we find this passage in the Koran: "Who is better than he that resigneth himself to God, and worketh righteousness, and followeth the religion of Abraham the faithful? and truly God took Abraham for his friend" (sura iv. 124). And again: "Say, The Lord speaketh truth; follow ye, therefore, the faith of Abraham the righteous; for he was no idolator" (sura iii. 89). And yet once more: "Say, Verily my Lord hath directed me into the right way, the true faith, the religion of righteous Abraham, and he was no idolator" (sura vi. 89).

Hence it came to pass that (excepting the worship of idols, a plurality of gods, the killing of daughters, and other such evil practices), many of the ideas and customs subsisting among the Arabs from the time of Abraham were retained by the Prophet, and form part of his religion. Although some of the southern and eastern tribes became mixed up with the children of Ham, yet we learn, as much from the Torah as from Ibn Hisham, Tabari and others, that the north and west of the country was occupied by the progeny of Shem. Some tribes were descended from Joktan, others from Hagar, Ketura, and Ishmael. Among the latter was the tribe of the Quraish, itself among the descendants of Abraham. Now, although the children of Shem had greatly lost the purity of their faith from mixing with the tribes of Syria, yet when all the people of those parts, except the Jews, had altogether forgotten the unity of God, still the dwellers in the north and west of the peninsula retained a certain knowledge of the unity divine. There is every reason to believe that in the days of Job, the stars, sun, and moon were worshipped in those parts of Arabia;[15] and Herodotus, more than four centuries before Christ, tells us that the Arabs of his day had only two gods, *Orotal* and *Alilat*,[16] evidently meaning Allah-taala and Allat, though as a foreigner he was not exactly acquainted with the local form of the names. The term Allah itself is repeatedly found in the seven *Mu'allaqat*, whose authors lived before the ministry of Muhammad, and also in the *Diwan* of Labid.

Still more, we know that the Ka'aba was of old the holy *masjid* [mosque] of the Arab tribes at large; for we learn from Diodorus Siculus, sixty years before the Christian era, that it then existed (Bk. iii). From the use of *al* (or *the*) in *Allah* it is manifest that the unity of God was never forgotten by the Arabs. The Koran, indeed, calls them idolators for giving others gods the worship due to Him alone. But they never held those other gods on an equality with the great God above, whom by their adoration they sought specially to propitiate. The following story from early Muslim writers makes this all the more clear.

> Some of the Abyssinian refugees returned to Mecca when sura liii. was being read. Coming to the verse: "What think ye of Allat and Al-'Uzza and Manat the other, the third?" Satan cast these words into the reader's lips: "These three noble ones whose intercession is to be hoped for." When the sura ended, the whole company bowed down in adoration; and the idolaters together with them, thinking that their gods had been thus graciously acknowledged. The strange episode was spread abroad by Satan, and the refugees hastily returned to Mecca expecting to find the whole city converted.

Baidhawi and others are the more inclined to believe this tale from the words in sura xxii. 51: "Truly we have sent no Apostle or Prophet before thee, but then he read, Satan suggested some (error) in his reading; but God shall make void that which Satan suggested."

Along with the early spread of idolatry, there still survived throughout Arabia the consciousness of one true God. Shahristani tells us this, and gives a long list of the local deities, and also of the customs retained by the Prophet. Some denied a future life as well as a creator, while others admitted both.[17] He then mentions a variety of tribal gods, and gives the name and place of eleven, including 'Uzza of the Quraish, Hubal aloft on the Ka'aba, etc.; also angels, genii, and heavenly bodies adored by the Sabaeans. We are then informed of a variety of local customs in vogue among the heathen Arabs, some retained in Islam, as family restrictions in marriage, Hajj to the Ka'aba with its various practices, visiting Safa and Marwa, throwing stones in Wadi Mina, ablution, and several minor matters. Very similar is the testimony of Ibn Ishaq, and the *Sirat al-Rasul*, that notwithstanding the idolatry into which the Arabs fell when they lost the faith of Abraham and Isaac, yet throughout it all they never forgot the great God above all other gods. Thus at the new moon, the Bani Kinana and Quraish would cry aloud, "Labbeik, Allah Labbeik! Thou hast no Companion, but rulest over all," acknowledging thus the oneness of Him they called upon; and while joining their idols in worship with the Highest, they yet placed them all under his hand. Then the unity is thus expressed in the Koran: "Verily your Lord is God who created the heavens and the earth in six days, then ascended the throne to rule over all things. There is no intercession but by his permission. God is your Lord, wherefore serve Him. Ah! will ye not consider?" (sura x. 3).

From all this we perceive that while the Arabs up to the Prophet's time worshipped idols, they did so regarding them as intercessors with the great God whom they held supreme.[18] The truth was so well known in Muhammad's own household, that his father and uncle bore the names 'Abd-Allah and 'Ubaid-Allah,—*Al*, as we have seen, signifying *The* One. Hence we are sure that the unity was acknowledged long before the Prophet's mission, as well as the various Meccan customs still in current use. Circumcision also was practised from of old, as we learn from the epistle of Barnabas written about two centuries after Christ. Multitudes of idols being all around Mecca,[19] certainly little inspiration was needed to show how false the system was, and the task was well carried out by Muhammad. While so many of ancient places, rites, and customs were maintained, only one quasi-idolatrous practice has been kept up, namely, the kissing of the Black Stone, which was then worshipped as of heavenly descent; the habit was so loved by the people, that it could not be forbidden, and indeed is still observed.

In conclusion, then, we find that the first "source" of the Koran and tradition consisted of the notions, customs, and religious beliefs, existing around Muhammad. And we know of no other answer as to the adoption of these, than that they were assumed to exist in the time of Abraham, and therefore were continued by the Prophet. Now, although we are told in the Torah that the doctrine of unity, as well as circumcision, were of Abraham's time, yet in the Holy Scriptures we find no mention of Mecca, procession round the Ka'aba, the Black Stone, the other holy places, etc.; nor can there be any doubt that all these things were the gradual creation of idol worshippers, and had no connection whatever with the faith and tenets of Father Abraham.

It is interesting also to note that some verses of the Koran have without doubt been taken from poems anterior to Muhammad's assumption of the prophetic office, in proof of which two passages in the *Sabaa Mu'allaqat* of Imra'ul Qays etc. are quoted, in which several verses of the Koran occur, such as, "The hour has come, and shattered is the moon."[20] It was the custom of the time for poets and orators to hang up their compositions upon the Ka'aba; and we know the seven *Mu'allaqat* were exposed. We are told that Fatima, the Prophet's daughter, was one day repeating as she went along the above verse. Just then she met the daughter of Imra'ul Qays, who cried out: "O that's what your father has taken from one of my father's poems, and calls it something that has come down to him out of heaven"; and the story is commonly told amongst Arabs until now.

The connection between the poetry of Imra'ul Qays and the Koran is so obvious that the Muslim cannot but hold that they existed with the latter in the Heavenly Table from all eternity! What then will he answer? That the words were taken from the Koran and entered in the poem?—an impossibility. Or that their writer was not really Imra'ul Qays, but some other who, after the appearance of the Koran, had the audacity to quote them there as they now appear?—rather a difficult thing to prove!

In concluding this chapter, we have no difficulty in asserting with every confidence that the customs, rites, and beliefs of the ancient Arabs formed one of the most important sources of the Koran.

Chapter III.

How Far Some of the Doctrines and Histories in the Koran and Tradition Were Taken from Jewish Commentators, and Some Religious Customs from the Sabaeans

At the period when Muhammad was using the utmost endeavor to turn his people from idolatry to the faith of Abraham, the Arabs had no religious writings acknowledged in common by them all, so that it was a matter of extreme difficulty to make them see the evils of their native faiths. There were three religions in the peninsula—the Sabaean, Jewish, and Christian—each of which, as we hope to show, helped to nurse Islam, which at the first lay like an infant in its cradle.

The Sabaeans have disappeared. No trace of them anywhere remains, and even of their history but little is known. We are told by Eastern authorities[21] that they were the first of all peoples who inhabited Syria; that they derived their faith from Seth and Idris; and that they possessed a book called *Pages of Seth*, in which were inculcated righteousness, truth, bravery, care of the poor, and avoidance of evil. They had seven times for prayer, five of which were at the same hour as chosen by the Prophet. They prayed also for the dead, but without prostration; fasted thirty days from night to sunrise, and also if any new moon rose badly, for the remaining day of the month; observed Eed from the setting of their five stars; and venerated the Ka'aba. Hence we see that the Sabaeans kept many observances still in force among the Muslims.

We turn to the Jews. Of course it is known to all how numerous and powerful the race was in Arabia at the time of Muhammad, and especially before the Hegira. Amongst their chief tribes were the Bani Quraiza, Qainuqa'a, and Nadhir, having their three villages in the vicinity of Medina.

When it became manifest that the Jews would in no wise recognize the prophetic office of Muhammad, he fought several severe battles with them and, not without difficulty, either took them prisoners and slew them with the sword, or at last expelled them from the land. Now, although these Jews were an ignorant people, yet they possessed and carefully preserved the Torah, the Psalms, etc., and were called (as also the Christians) *The People of the Book*. Though the nation at large knew little or nothing of Hebrew, yet (like the Jews we see in Persia at the present day) they were familiar with the stories of the Talmud and the foolish tales which had come down from their ancestors, and which, being ignorant of their own sacred books, they regarded as holy and divine.

The ignorant Arabs of the day looked upon their neighbors the Jews with honor and respect as being of the seed of Abraham, and possessed of the word of God. Hence when the Prophet turned aside from idols as hateful to the Almighty, and sought to bring his people back to the faith of Abraham, he betook himself with the utmost care to learn in what the teaching, customs, and obligations of that faith consisted. Comparing these with the Koran and tradition, we find the closest similarity between the two. Thus the Koran throughout bears witness to the faith of Abraham, to the truth of the Jewish religion, and the heavenly origin of their divine books. The following passages will be found to that effect: "Dispute not with the People of the Book, but in the mildest way, excepting such as behave injuriously; and say, 'We believe in that which hath been revealed unto you; our God and your God is One, and to Him we are resigned.'" And again: "Say, We believe in God, and in that which was sent down unto Abraham and Ishmael, and Isaac and Jacob, and the Tribes; and in that which was delivered unto Moses and Jesus, and in that which was delivered to the Prophets from the Lord. We make no distinction between any of them; and to Him we are resigned." At this period, also, Muhammad made the Holy House (Jerusalem) the *qibla* of his followers, being then (as it has since remained) the *qibla* of the Jews.

To this it might be objected that Muhammad, as the "illiterate prophet,"[22] must have been unable to read, and how then could he have gained all this knowledge from Jewish literature? But even admitting it to have been so, it must still have been easy enough for him to have learned all about their beliefs and customs and tales from his companions, such as 'Ubaid-Allah, Waraqa, or even himself from his Jewish friends. For these people, though they had but an imperfect knowledge of the Old Testament Scriptures, yet well knew the foolish tales current among the Jewish nation. And now, if we compare the Koran with the tales in the Talmud and other books still current among the Jews, it becomes evident that although the Koran speaks of Abraham and many others whom we read in the Torah, still all the wild stories it tells us are taken from Jewish traditional sources. And we shall now give a few specimens to prove that it is so.

FIRST. *Cain and Abel.*—In sura v. 30-35 we have the following passage:

And tell them the story truly of the two sons of Adam. When they offered up their sacrifice, and it was accepted from one of them, and not accepted from the other, Cain said, "I will kill thee." Abel answered, "God accepteth (offerings) of the pious alone. If thou stretchest forth thine hand against me to kill me, I will not stretch forth my hand to kill thee; for I fear God, the Lord of all worlds. I desire that thou shouldest bear my sin and thine own sin, and become a dweller in the Fire, for that is the punishment of the oppressor." But the soul of Cain inclined him to slay his brother, and he slew him; then he became one of the destroyed. And God sent a raven which scratched the earth to show him how he should hide his brother's body. He said "Woe is me! I am not able to be like this raven"; and he became one of those that repent (v. 35). For this cause we wrote unto the children of Israel that he who slayeth a soul,—without having slain a soul or committed wickedness in the earth,—shall be as if he had slain all mankind; and whosoever saveth a soul alive, shall be as if he had saved all mankind.

Now this conversation and affair of Cain and Abel, as given above in the Koran, has been told us in a variety of ways by the Jews.[23] Thus when Cain, according to them, said there was no punishment for sin and no reward for virtue, Abel, holding just exactly the reverse, was killed by Cain with a stone. So also in the book *Pirke Rabbi Eleazer*, we find the source of the burying of Abel as described in the Koran, there being no difference excepting that the raven indicates the mode to Adam instead of to Cain as follows: "Adam and Eve, sitting by the corpse, wept not knowing what to do, for they had as yet no knowledge of burial. A raven coming up, took the dead body of its fellow, and having scratched up the earth, buried it thus before their eyes. Adam said, 'Let us follow the example of the raven,' and so taking up Abel's body buried it at once."

If the reader will look at the last verse [35] in the quotation above from sura v. of the Koran, he will see that it has no connection with the one preceding. The relation is explained thus in the Mishnah Sanhedrin, where in quoting from Genesis the verse, "The voice of thy brother's blood crieth unto me from the ground,"[24] the commentator writes as follows: "As regards Cain who killed his brother, the Lord addressing him does not say, 'The voice of thy brother's blood crieth out,' but 'the voice of his bloods'— meaning not his blood alone, but that of his descendants; and this to show that since Adam was created alone, so he that kills an Israelite is, by the plural here used, counted as if he had killed the world at large; and he who saves a single Israelite is counted as if he had saved the whole world." Now, if we look at the thirty-fifth verse of the text above quoted, it will be found almost exactly the same as these last words of this old Jewish commentary. But we see that only part is given in the Koran, and the other part omitted. And this omitted part is the connecting link between the two passages in the Koran, without which they are unintelligible.

SECOND. *Abraham saved from Nimrod's fire.*—The story is scattered over various passages of the Koran, chiefly in those noted below.[25] Now whoever will read these, as well as the traditional records of the Muslims,[26] will at once perceive that the tale as there told has been taken from one of the ancient Jewish books called *Midrash Rabbah*. To bring this clearly to view, we must first show the history as given in the Koran and Muslim writings, and then compare it with the Jewish tale in the above book.

In a work of Abdul Feda we have the Muslim story as follows.[27]

Azar, Abraham's father, used to construct idols, and hand them over to his son to sell. So Abraham would go about crying, "Who will buy that which will hurt and not benefit him?" Then when God Almighty commanded him to call his people to the divine unity, his father refused the call, and so did his people. Thus the matter spread abroad till it reached Nimrod, son of Cush, king over the country . . . who took Father Abraham, and cast him into a fierce fire; but the fire grew cool and pleasant unto Abraham, who came out of it after some days.

Again in the *Araish al-Majalis* we read:

Before this, when Abraham one night came out of his cave and saw the stars before the moon arose, he said: "This is my Preserver."[28] *And when the night overshadowed him, he saw a star, and said, "This is my Lord;" and when it set, he said, "I love not those that set." And when he saw the moon rising, he said, "This is my Lord;" but when it set, he said, "Verily if my Lord direct me not, I shall be of those that go astray." And when he saw the sun rising, he said, "This is my Lord; this is the greatest." But when it set, he said, "O my people! Verily I am clear of that which ye associate together with God. Verily I direct my face unto him who hath created the heavens and the earth. I am orthodox, and not one of the idolators."*

They say that Abraham's father used to make idol images and give them to Abraham to sell. So Abraham taking them about would cry: "These will neither hurt nor help him that buys," so that no one bought from him. And when it was not sold, he took an image to the stream, and striking its head, would say, "Drink, my poor one!" in derision, for his people and the heathen around him to hear. So when his people objected, he said, *"Ah! do ye dispute with me concerning God, and verily God hath directed me...." And this is our argument wherewith we furnished Abraham for his people. We raise the dignity of whom we wish, for thy Lord is wise and knowing.*[29] And so in the end Abraham overcame his people by such arguments. Then he called his father Azar to the true faith, and said: *"O my father, wherefore dost thou worship that which neither hears nor sees, nor yet doth profit thee in any way,"* and so on to the end of the story.[30] But his father refused that to which Abraham called him; whereupon Abraham cried aloud to his people that he was free from what they worshipped, and thus made known his faith to them. He said, *"What think ye? That which ye worship, and your forefathers also, are mine enemies, excepting only the Lord of the worlds."*[31] They said, "Whom then dost thou worship?" He answered, "The Lord of all the worlds." "Dost thou mean Nimrod?" "Nay, but he that created me and guideth me," and so on. The thing then spread abroad among the people, till it reached the ears of the tyrant Nimrod, who sent for him, and said: "O Abraham! Dost thou hold him to be thy god that hath sent thee; dost thou call to his worship and speak of his power to those that worship other than him? Who is he?" A. *"My Lord, he that giveth life, and giveth death."*[32] N. "I give life, and cause to die." A. "How dost thou make alive, and cause to die?" N. "I take two men who at my hands deserve death, one I kill who thus dies; the other I forgive, who thus is made alive." Whereupon Abraham answered, *"Verily God bringeth the sun from the East, now do thou bring him from the West."*[33]

Thereupon Nimrod was confounded, and returned him no reply. The people then went away to celebrate their *'id* [holiday], and Abraham, taking the opportunity, broke all the idols but the biggest, and then the story proceeds as follows:

When they had prepared food, they set it before their gods and said, "When the time comes we shall return, and the gods having blessed the meat we shall eat thereof." So when Abraham looked upon the gods, and what was set before them, he said derisively, "*Ah! ye are not eating*"; and when no answer came, "*What aileth you, that you do not speak?* and he turned upon them and smote them with his right hand.*[34] And he kept on striking them with a hatchet in his hand, until there remained none but the biggest of them, and upon its neck he hung the axe.[35] Now when the people returned from their *'id* to the house of their gods, and saw it in such a state, they said, "*Who hath done this to our gods? Verily he is a wicked one.*" *They answered, "We heard a young man speaking of them; they call him Abraham.* He it is, we think, who hath done it." When this reached the tyrant Nimrod and his chief men, *They said, "Bring him before the eyes of the people; perhaps they will bear witness* that he hath done this thing." And they were afraid to seize him without evidence.[36] So they brought him and said: "*Hast thou done this unto our gods, O Abraham?*" He answered, "*Nay but that big one hath done it*, he was angry that ye worshipped along with him these little idols, and he so much bigger than all; and he brake the whole of them into pieces. Now ask them if they can speak."[37] When he had said this, *they turned their backs,* and said (among themselves), "Verily it is ye that are the transgressors. . . . We have never seen him but telling us that we transgress, having those little idols and this great one." So they broke the heads of them all, and were amazed that they neither spake nor made any opposition. Then they said (to Abraham), *"Certainly thou knowest that they speak not."* Thus when the affair with Abraham was ended, he said to them: "*Ah! do ye indeed worship, besides God, that which cannot profit you at all, nor can it injure you. Fie on you, and on that which ye worship besides God! Ah, do ye not understand?*"

When thus overthrown and unable to make any answer, *they called out, "Burn him, and avenge your gods if ye do it."* Abdallah tells us that the man who cried thus was a Kurd called Zeinum; and the Lord caused the earth to open under him, and there he lies buried till the day of Judgment. When Nimrod and his people were thus gathered together to burn Abraham, they imprisoned him in a house, and built for him a great pile, as we read in sura Saffat: "*They said, Build a pile for him and cast him into the glowing fire.*" Then they gathered together quantities of wood and stuff to burn; and so, by the grace of God, Abraham came out of the fire safe and sound, with the words on his lips, "*God is sufficient for me*" (sura xxxix. 39);

and "*He is the best Supporter*" (sura iii. 37). For the Lord said, *"O Fire! Be thou cool and pleasant"* unto Abraham.[38]

Now, let us compare the story of Abraham as current amongst the Jews, with the same story in the Koran and tradition as given above, and see how they differ or agree. The following is from the Midrash Rabbah on Abraham brought out of Ur (Gen. xv. 7).

Terah used to make images. Going out one day, he told his son Abraham to sell them. When a man came to buy, Abraham asked him how old he was. "Fifty or sixty years," he replied. "Strange," said the other, "that a man sixty years of age should worship things hardly a few days old!" On hearing which the man, ashamed, passed on. Then a woman carrying in her hand a cup of wheaten flour said, "Place this before the idols." On which, Abraham, getting up, took his staff in his hand, and having broken the idols with it, placed the staff in the hand of the biggest. His father coming up, cried, "Who hath done all this?" Abraham said, "What can be concealed from thee? A woman carrying a cup of wheaten flour asked me to place it before the gods; I took and placed it before them; one said, 'I will eat it first,' and another, 'I will eat first.' Then the big one took the staff, and broke them all in pieces." His father: "Why do you tell such a foolish tale to me? Do these know anything?" He answered, "Does thine ear hear what thy mouth speaks?" On this his father seized and made him over to Nimrod, who bade him worship Fire. Abraham: "Rather worship Water that putteth out Fire." *N.* "Then worship Water." *A.* "Rather worship that which bringeth Water." *N.* "Then worship the Cloud." *A.* "In such case, let us worship Wind that drives away the Cloud." *N.* "Then worship Wind." *A.* "Rather let us worship Man that standeth against the wind." On this Nimrod closed: "If thou arguest with me about things which I am unable to worship other than Fire, into it I will cast thee; then, let the God thou worshippest deliver thee therefrom." So Abraham went down into the flames, and remained there safe and unhurt.

Comparing, now, this Jewish story with what we saw of it in the Koran, little difference will be found and what there is no doubt arose from Muhammad hearing of it by the ear from the Jews. What makes this the more likely is that Abraham's father is in the Koran called *Azar*,[39] while both in the Midrash and Torah he is called Terah. But the Prophet probably heard the name in Syria (where, as we learn from Eusebius, the name had somewhat of a similar sound), and so remembered it.

The Muslims, of course, hold that their Prophet gained the tale of Abraham's being cast into the fire neither from Jews nor Christians, but through Gabriel from on high; and as the Jews, being children of Abraham, so accepted it, the Koran, they say, must be right. But it could only have been the common folk among the Jews who believed it so; for those who had any knowledge of its origin must have known its puerility.

The origin of the whole story will be found in Genesis xv. 7: "I am the Lord that brought thee out of Ur of the Chaldees." Now *Ur* in Babylonian means a "city," as in *Ur*-Shalim (Jerusalem), "the City of Peace." And the Chaldaean Ur[40] was the residence of Abraham. This name Ur closely resembles in speech another word, *Or,* signifying light or fire. And so ages after, a Jewish commentator,[41] ignorant of Babylonian, when translating the Scripture into Chaldean, put the above verse from Genesis, as follows: "I am the Lord that delivered thee out of the Chaldaen fiery oven." The same ignorant writer has also the following comment on Genesis xi. 27: "Now this happened at a time when Nimrod cast Abraham into the oven of fire, because he would not worship the idols, that leave was withheld from the fire to hurt him"—a strange confusion of words—*Ur*, the city, for *Or*, light and fire. It is as if a Persian seeing notice of the departure of the English *post*, should put in his diary that an Englishman had lost his *skin*, not knowing that the same word for skin in Persian means *the Post* in English.

No wonder then that an ignorant Jew should have mistaken a word like this, and made it the foundation whereon to build the grand tale of Abraham's fiery oven. But it is somewhat difficult to understand how a Prophet like Muhammad could have given credence to such a fable, and entered it in a revelation held to have come down from heaven. And yet the evidence of it all is complete, as quoted above from the Jewish writer. Apart from this we know from Genesis that Nimrod lived not in the days of Abraham but ages before his birth. The name indeed is not in the Koran, though freely given in the Muslim commentaries and tradition. As if a historian should tell us that Alexander the Great cast Nadir Shah into the fire, not knowing the ages elapsed between the two, or that Nadir never was so thrown.

THIRD. *Visit of the Queen of Saba (Sheba) to Solomon.*—The story of Balkis, queen of Saba, as told at length in the Koran, corresponds so closely with what we find in the II. Targum of the Book of Esther, that it was evidently taken from it, as heard by Muhammad from some Jewish source. The following is from the sura of the Ant (xxvii. 17 *et seq.*):—

His armies were gathered together unto Solomon, consisting of genii, men and birds, and they were kept back.... Solomon smiled at the ant and said: "O Lord! may I do that which is right and well pleasing unto thee, so that thou introduce me amongst thy servants the righteous." And he viewed the birds and said, "Why is it that I see not the Hudhud (Lapwing)? Is she among the absent ones? Truly I will chastise her with a severe chastisement, or will put her to death unless she bring a just excuse." But she did not wait long, and said, "I have viewed a country that thou hast not seen: and I come unto thee from Saba with certain news. I found a female ruling over them, surrounded with every kind of possession, and having a magnificent throne. I found her and her people worshipping the Sun apart from God. Satan hath made their deeds pleasant unto them, and hath turned them aside from the right way, and they are not rightly directed,—lest they should worship God who manifesteth that which is in heaven and earth, and knoweth what they conceal and what they discover. God! there is no God but he, the Lord of the great throne!" Solomon said: "We shall see whether thou tellest the truth or art amongst the liars. Go with this my letter, and having delivered it to them turn aside, and see what answer they return." The queen having received it, said: "O ye nobles! verily an honorable letter hath been delivered unto me. It is from Solomon. It is in the name of the Most Merciful God;— 'Rise not up against me; but come ye submissive unto me.'" She said: "O ye nobles! advise me in the affair; I will not resolve upon it, until ye be witnesses thereof." They said: "We are men of strength and of great prowess; but the matter belongeth unto thee: see therefore what thou wilt command." She said: "Verily kings when they enter a city waste it, and abuse its most powerful inhabitants; and so will they do. But I will send gifts unto them, and wait to see what the messengers will return with." So when they went to Solomon, he said: "Ah! do ye present me with wealth? Verily that which God hath given unto me is better than that which he hath given you, but ye do rejoice in your gifts. Return unto them; we will surely come unto them with an army which they cannot withstand, and we shall drive them thence humbled and contemptible. O ye nobles (he continued), which of you will bring me her throne, before they come submissive unto me?" A giant of the genii cried, "I will bring it unto thee before thou gettest up from thy place, for I am strong in this, and to be trusted." And one who had knowledge of the Scriptures: "I will bring it unto thee before the twinkling of thine eye." Now when (Solomon) saw it placed before him he said: "This is a favor of my Lord, that he may try me whether I am grateful or ungrateful; he that is grateful is grateful for his own benefit; but he that is ungrateful, verily the Lord is rich and beneficent." And (Solomon) said: "Alter her throne, that we may see whether she be rightly directed, or be amongst those who are not rightly directed." And when she came, it was said, "Is this thy throne?" She said, "It is as if it were; and knowledge hath been bestowed upon us before this, and we are resigned (unto God)." But that which she worshipped besides had turned her aside, for she was of an unbelieving people. It was said to her, "Enter the Palace." And when she saw it, she imagined that it was a great surface of water, and she uncovered her legs, when (Solomon) said, "Verily it is a palace floored with glass." And she said, "Truly I have done injury to my own soul, and I resign myself, along with Solomon, unto God, the Lord of all creatures."[42]

Such is the account the Koran gives us of the queen of Saba. What it tells us of the throne differs but little from the Targum, where it is said to have belonged to Solomon, and to have had no other like it in any land. There were six steps of gold to ascend, and on each twelve golden lions, while twelve eagles of gold were perched around. Four-and-twenty other eagles cast their shadow from above upon the king, and when he wished to move anywhere, these powerful eagles descending would lift the throne and carry it wherever he wished. Thus they performed, according to the Targum, the same duty the Koran tells us the genii did. But otherwise in respect of the queen of Saba, her visit to Solomon, the letter sent by him to her, etc., there is a marvellous resemblance between the two, excepting this, indeed, that in place of the lapwing of the Koran, the Targum speaks of a redcock,—not a very vital difference after all! The whole story is told in the Targum as follows:—

At another time, when the heart of Solomon was gladdened with wine, he gave orders for the beasts of the land, the birds of the air, the creeping things of the earth, the demons from above and the genii, to be brought, that they might dance around him, in order that all the kings waiting upon him might behold his grandeur. And all the royal scribes summoned by their names before him; in fact, all were there except the captives and prisoners and those in charge of them. Just then the redcock, enjoying itself, could not be found; and King Solomon said that they should seize and bring it by force, and indeed he sought to kill it. But just then the cock appeared in presence of the king, and said: "O Lord, king of the earth! having applied thine ear, listen to my words. It is hardly three months since I made a firm resolution within me that I would not eat a crumb of bread, nor drink a drop of water until I had seen the whole world, and over it make my flight, saying to myself, I must know the city and the kingdom which is not subject to thee, my Lord King. Then I found the fortified city *Qitor* in the Eastern lands, and around it are stones of gold and silver in the streets plentiful as rubbish, and trees planted from the beginning of the world, and rivers to water it, flowing out of the garden of Eden. Many men are there wearing garlands from the garden close by. They shoot arrows, but cannot use the bow. They are ruled by a woman, called queen of Sheba. Now if it please my Lord King, thy servant, having bound up my girdle, will set out for the fort Qitor in Sheba; and having 'bound their kings with chains and their nobles with links of iron,' will bring them into thy presence." The proposal pleased the king, and the scribes prepared a despatch, which was placed under the bird's wing, and away it flew high up in the sky. It grew strong surrounded by a crowd of birds, and reached the fort of Sheba. By chance the queen of Sheba was out in the morning worshipping the sea; and the air being darkened by the multitude of birds, she became so alarmed as to rend her clothes in trouble and distress. Just then the cock alighted by her, and she seeing the letter under its wing opened and read it as follows: "King Solomon sendeth to thee his salaam, and saith, 'The high and holy One hath set me over the beasts of the field, etc.; and the kings of the four quarters send to ask after my welfare. Now if it please thee to come and ask after my welfare, I will set thee high above them all. But if it please thee not, I will send kings and armies against thee;—the beasts of the field are my people, the birds of the air are my riders, the demons and genii thine enemies,—to imprison you, to slay and to feed upon you.'" When the queen of Sheba heard it, she again rent her garments, and sending for her nobles asked their advice. They knew not Solomon, but advised her to send vessels by the sea, full of beautiful ornaments and gems, together with 6000 boys and girls in purple garments, who had all been born at the same moment; also to send a letter promising to visit him by the end of the year. It was a journey of seven years, but she promised to come in three. When at last she came, Solomon sent a messenger shining in brilliant attire, like the morning dawn, to meet her. As they came together, she stepped from her carriage. "Why dost thou thus?" he asked. "Art thou not Solomon?" she said. "Nay, I am but a servant that standeth in his presence." The queen at once addressed a parable to her followers in compliment to him, and then was led by him to the court. Solomon hearing she had come, arose and sat down in the palace of glass. When the queen of Sheba saw it, she thought that the glass floor was water, and so in crossing over lifted up her garments. When Solomon seeing the hair about her legs, cried out to her: "Thy beauty is the beauty of women, but thy hair is as the hair of men; hair is good in man, but in woman it is not becoming." On this she said: "My Lord, I have three enigmas to put to thee. If thou canst answer them, I shall know that thou art a wise man; but if not that thou art like all around thee." When he had answered all three, she replied, astonished: "Blessed be the Lord thy God, who hath placed thee on the throne that thou mightest rule with right and justice." And she gave to Solomon much gold and silver; and he to her whatsoever she desired.

In the Jewish statement, we see that the queen put several enigmas for Solomon to solve; and though this is not mentioned in the Koran, it is in the Muslim traditions. And so with the story of her legs; for in the *Araish al-Majalis* we find the following: "When the queen was about to enter the palace, she fancied the glass floor to be a sheet of water, and so *she uncovered her legs*, that is, to pass over to Solomon; and lo her legs and feet were covered with hair; which when Solomon saw, he turned his sight from her, and called out, 'The floor is plain glass.'"

Here we would ask whether there is any reality whatever in all this story. There is indeed so much as we find in the First Book of Kings, x. 1-11,[43] which is as follows:

> And when the queen of Sheba heard of the fame of Solomon concerning the name of the Lord, she came to prove him with hard questions. And she came to Jerusalem with a very great train, with camels that bare spices, and very much gold, and precious stones: and when she was come to Solomon, she communed with him of all that was in her heart. And Solomon told her all her questions: there was not anything hid from the king, which he told her not. And when the queen of Sheba had seen all Solomon's wisdom, and the house that he had built, and the meat of his table, and the sitting of his servants, and the attendance of his ministers, and their apparel, and his cupbearers, and his ascent by which he went up unto the house of the Lord; there was no more spirit in her. And she said to the king, "It was a true report that I heard in mine own land of thy acts and of thy wisdom. Howbeit I believed not the words, until I came, and mine eyes had seen it: and, behold, the half was not told me: thy wisdom and prosperity exceedeth the fame which I heard. Happy are thy men, happy are these thy servants, which stand continually before thee, and that hear thy wisdom. Blessed be the Lord thy God, which delighted in thee, to set thee on the throne of Israel: because the Lord loved Israel for ever, therefore made he thee king, to do judgment and justice." And she

gave the king an hundred and twenty talents of gold, and of spices very great store, and precious stones: there came no more such abundance of spices as these which the queen of Sheba gave to king Solomon.

Now these are the facts of the queen's visit, and all beyond mere fiction. The Jews themselves admit it to be so—excepting, indeed, Solomon's magnificent throne, though not its being carried aloft. The Koran account of Solomon ruling over demons, genii, etc., is in entire accord with what we have cited from the Targum; and it is curious to find, as learned Jews tell us, that the origin of the notion lay in the similarity of two Hebrew words,[44] with two kindred words signifying *demons* and *genii*, and the ignorant commentator confounding them together led to the strange error.

In concluding our notice of the fanciful tale which we have given from the Jewish Targum, we might say that it reminds one of such stories as we find in the "Arabian Nights." But strange that the Prophet could not have seen it so. Having heard it from his Jewish friends, he evidently fancied that it had been read by them in their inspired Scriptures, and as such introduced it, as we find, into the Koran.

FOURTH. *Harut and Marut.*—There are many other stories in the Koran taken from the fanciful details of Jewish writers; but we shall content ourselves with this one other before entering on more general questions. We shall first recite the tale of those two spirits as given in the Koran and tradition, and then compare it with the same as told by Jewish writers. The passage in the Koran is this: "Solomon was not an unbeliever; but the devils believed not. They taught men sorcery, and that which was sent down to the two angels at Babel—Harut and Marut. Yet these taught no man until they had said, 'Verily we are a temptation, therefore be not an unbeliever.' "[45]

The following is from the *Araish al-Majalis.*

The commentators say that when the angels saw the evil doings of mankind ascending up to heaven (and that was in the days of Idris), they were distressed and complained thus against them: "Thou hast chosen these to be the rulers upon earth, and lo they sin against thee." Then said the Almighty: "If I should send you upon the earth, and treat you as I have treated them, ye would do just as they do." They said, "O our Lord, it would not become us to sin against thee." Then said the Lord, "Choose two angels from the best of you, and I will send them down unto the earth." So they chose Harut and Marut; who were among the best and most pious amongst them.

Al-Kalby's version: The Almighty said: "Choose ye three": so they chose Azz (i.e. Harut), and Azabi, (i.e. Marut), and Azrael; and the Lord changed the names of the two when they fell into sin, as he changed the name of the Devil, which was Azazil. And God placed in their heart the same fleshy lust as in the sons of Adam; and sending them down to the earth, bade them to rule righteously amongst mankind, to avoid idolatry, not to kill but for a just cause, and to keep free from fornication and strong drink. Now when Azrael felt lust in his heart, he prayed to the Lord to relieve him, and was taken up to heaven, and for forty years was unable to raise his head for shame before his Maker. But the other two remained steadfast, judging the people during the day, and when night came ascending to the heavens, worshipping the name of the Almighty. Catada tells us that before a month had passed they fell into temptation; for Zohra, one of the most beautiful of women (whom Aly tells us was queen of a city in Persia), had a suit before them, and when they saw her they fell in love with her, and sought to have her, but she refused and went away. The second day she came again, and they did the same; but she said, "Nay, unless ye worship what I worship, and bow down to this idol, or kill soul, or drink wine." They replied, "It is impossible for us to do these things, which God hath forbidden"; and she departed. The third day again she came holding a cup of wine, and her heart inclined towards them; so when they desired her, she said the same as yesterday, but they replied, "To pray to other than God is a serious thing, and so is the killing of anyone; the easiest of the three is to drink the wine"; so they drank the wine, and becoming intoxicated fell upon her and committed adultery; and one saw it, and they slew him. And it is said that they worshipped an idol, and the Lord changed Zohra into a star. Aly and others tell us that she said, "Come not near me till you teach me that by which ye can ascend to the heavens." They said, "We ascend by the name of the great God." Again she said, "Come not near me till ye teach me what that is." So they taught her; and forthwith she, repeating it, ascended to the skies, and the Lord changed her into a star.

Turning now to the Jews, the same account is given in two or three places of the Talmud, especially in this extract from the Midrash Yalkut:[46]

Rabbi Joseph being asked by his disciples about Azael, told them as follows: After the Flood, idolatrous worship prevailing, the Holy One was angry. Then two angels, Shamhazai and Azael arose and addressing him said, "O Lord of the Universe, when thou createdst the world, did we not say to thee, 'What is man that thou art mindful of him?' and now we are anxious about him." The Lord relied: "I well know that if ye be sent to rule over the earth, your evil passions will have possession of you, and ye will become tyrants over mankind." They answered: "If thou wilt give us leave, and we shall dwell amongst them, thou shalt see in what wise we shall sanctify thy name." "Go then," he said, "and dwell amongst them."

Soon after, Shamhazai saw a beautiful maiden called Esther, and turning his eyes upon her to come and be with him, she said, "I cannot surrender myself to thee until thou teach me that great name by which thou canst ascend to the heavens above." He told her, and she having spoken it, ascended upwards undefiled. Then said the Holy One, "Since she hath kept herself clear from defilement, she shall be raised aloft amid the Seven Stars, there to give praise unto the Lord." Forthwith the two went forth and consorted with the beautiful daughters of men, and children were born unto them. And Azael adorned the women he was inclined to with all kinds of beautiful ornaments. [Azrael is the same as in the Talmud is called Azael.]

Now anyone comparing the two stories together must see that they agree, excepting that in the Muslim one the angels are called Harut and Marut, and in the Jewish, Shamhazai and Azael. But if we search whence the names in the Koran and tradition came, it will be seen that Harut and Marut were two idols worshipped far back in Armenia. For in writers of that country they are so spoken of, as in the following passage from one of them:

Certainly Horot and Morot, tutelary deities of Mount Ararat, and Aminabegh, and perhaps another not now known, were assistants to the female goddess Aspandaramit. These aided her, and were excellent on the earth.

In this extract, Aspandaramit is the name of the goddess worshipped of old in Iran also; for we are told that the Zoroastrians regarded her as the spirit of the earth, and held that all the good products of the earth arise from her. Aminabegh also was held by the Armenians to be the god of vineyards, and they named Horot and Morot the assistants of the spirit of the earth, seeing that they held them as spirits who had control over the wind so as to make it bring rain. They sat on top of the lofty mountain Ararat, and sent down showers that fertilized the earth; the two were thus rulers of the wind.[47] The Armenians—fancying that *Morot* came from *Mor*, genetive of *Mair*, "mother"—formed *Horot* in the same way from *Hair*, "father." When also it is said that the two angels came down to propagate mankind, the meaning is that they caused the earth to bring forth its produce for that end. Zohra in Hebrew reads as Ishtar or Esther, the same as of old was worshipped in Babylon and Syria as the goddess over the birth of children and promoter of passion and desire. In proof of all this, we find in the ruins between the Tigris and Euphrates the name Ishtar on the primeval tiles. The story of one Gilgamesh, with whom Ishtar fell in love but was rejected, has been deciphered in ancient Babylonian character upon these tiles. Ishtar came to him having the crown upon her head and asked him to kiss her, and with many loving words and gifts to be her husband, when he would in her palace have a quiet and happy life. Gilgamesh in derision rejected her offer, whereupon she ascended to the sky and appeared before the god of the heavens.[48] It is remarkable that idolators of Babylon are shown in this primeval story to have held that Ishtar, that is Zohra, ascended on high—exactly as is told us in Muslim tradition, as also in the Jewish commentaries.

Now if we search for the source of the above tale, we shall no doubt find it in what the Talmud says of the angels associating with women, in its commentary on the two verses in Genesis quoted below.[49] Speaking of the second verse, a Jewish commentator gives us the following interpretation: "It was Shamhazai and Uzziel who in those days came down from heaven." Hence we see that the whole imaginative tale has come out of the mistake of this and other ignorant commentators. For the word *giant*, as shown below, was misconstrued by them to signify not those who tyrannically "fell" on the poor people around them, but angels who "came down, or fell from heaven."[50] And this unhappy mistake has led to the spread of the strange idol-worship just narrated. Nor was there any apparent reason for the mistake; since in the Targum we find the name (*Nefilim*) explained in its right and natural sense as "giants." But by and by the Jews came to love the wild tales that spread abroad; and so in a counterfeit book ascribed to Enoch, we are told that 200 angels under Samyaza (i.e., Shamhazai) came down from the heavens to commit adultery on the earth, as we read:

> The angels of heaven having seen the daughters of men, fell in love with them, and said to one another, "Let us take for ourselves these women, the daughters of mankind, and beget children for ourselves." And

Samyaza, who was their chief, said . . . Azaziel taught men to make swords, daggers, and shields, and taught them to wear breastplates. And for the women they made ornaments of kinds, bracelets, jewels, collyrium to beautify their eyelids, lovely stones of great price, dresses of beautiful colors, and current money.

Let it be remembered also that we have mention of this in the Koran: "Men learned from these two (Harut and Marut) that by which to cause a division between a man and his wife; but they did not injure anyone thereby excepting by leave of God; and they learned that which would hurt them and not profit them."[51] This is similar to what we have seen above in the Midrash Yalkut, where we are told that Azael embellished the daughters of men with ornaments to make them lovely and attractive.

But enough has been said to show that the story of Harut and Marut, as we find it in the Koran and Muslim books, has been derived from Jewish sources.

FIFTH. *A few other things taken by Islam from the Jews.*—If time permitted, we could easily tell of many other narratives in the Koran, not in our Scriptures but taken from foolish tales of the Jews, about Joseph, David, Saul, etc.; but space will not permit, excepting for a few. Here, for example, is the account of "Sinai overhead" as we have it in sura vii. 172: "And when we raised the mountain over them, as though it had been a canopy, and they imagined that it was falling upon them, (we said) 'Receive that which we have sent unto you with reverence, and remember that which is therein, if may be that ye take heed;' " and we have two other passages (vv. 60 and 87) in sura Bakr to the same effect, the meaning being that when the Jews held back from accepting the Torah, the Lord lifted Mount Sinai over their heads to force their reception of it. The same tale is given by a Hebrew writer thus: "I raised the mount to be a covering over you, as it were a lid."[52] It need hardly be said that there is nothing of the kind in the Torah. The tale, however, may have arisen (Exodus xxxii. 19) from the fact that when Moses, returning from Mount Sinai, saw his people worshipping the calf, "his anger waxed hot and he cast the tables (of the Law) out of his hands, and brake them beneath the mount." The words "beneath the mount," simply mean that he cast the tables down at the foot of Mount Sinai. And hence all this wild fiction of the mountain being lifted over their heads! We can only compare it to a like Hindu tale of a mountain similarly lifted over the people's heads, very much resembling what we have in the Koran.

Here are one or two other tales of Moses in the wilderness; and first, that of the Golden Calf which came out of the fire kindled by the people at Sinai. The Koran tells us that "Sameri also cast (what he had into the fire) and brought out unto them a bodily calf which lowed."[53] The origin of this fiction we find in a Jewish writer,[54] as follows: "The calf having cried aloud, came forth, and the children of Israel saw it. Rabbi Yahuda says that Sammael from the inside of it made the cry of the calf in order to lead the Israelites astray." No doubt the Prophet in this matter got his information from the Jews; strange that he should have been led to adopt this baseless tale. But he has used the wrong name, al-Sameri. The name of the people, of course, occurs often in the Bible, and the Jews regarded the Samaritans as their enemies; but as the city of Samaria did not arise till some four hundred years after Moses, it is difficult to imagine how it came to be entered in this story.[55] We also note that in this matter the Koran is in opposition to the Torah, which tells us that Aaron was the person who for fear of the Israelites around him, had the molten calf set up. Another story, given us twice in the Koran,[56] is that when the Israelites insisted on seeing the Lord, they were punished by death, but eventually restored to life again; and to add to the foolish tale we are told that it was the Torah which appealed for help and thus obtained their revival.

SIXTH. *A few other Jewish matters.*—In the Koran are a number of Chaldaean and Syrian words which the Muslims have been unable rightly to explain, as *Torat, Jahannam,* and such like.[57] To know their meaning, it must be learnt from Hebrew, Chaldaean, and Syriac, for they are not genuine Arabic words.

The following ideas are common to both Jews and Muslims:

In the Koran we are told of there being seven heavens, and seven stories to hell, which we also find in Jewish writings.[58] Similar accounts of the heavens and the earth we have also in Sanskrit sources, and also from Muslim tradition; and also from such stories in Zoroastrian books as that there are seven climes, etc.

In sura xi. 9, we are told of God's *throne being above the waters*; and similarly the Jewish Rashi, commenting on Genesis i. 2, says: "the glorious throne stood in the heavens and moved over the face of the waters." Again, Muslims tell us that the Lord appointed an angel Malik ruler over Jehannam. Similarly the Jews speak of the Prince of Hell; only the Muslims call him Malik, following the ancient idolaters of Palestine, who worshipped the Ruler of Fire as *Molech.*

In sura vii. 44 there is mention of a wall or partition called *Aaraf* as separating paradise and hell, thus: "And between the two a Veil, and upon al-Aaraf (stand) men." So in the Jewish Midrash, when it is asked what the distance is between heaven and hell, the answer of one rabbi is "a wall," and of another "a span"; and again, "Our leaders tell us that the two are so close that a mere ray glances from one to the other." And so we find similar passages in the Avestic and Pahlavi writings, as, "the distance is but as that between light and darkness."

In three passages of the Koran,[59] we are told of Satan listening stealthily, and being driven away with stones; another idea taken from the Jews, in one of whose books we find it written of the Genii that "they listened behind the curtain" in order to gain knowledge of things to come.

In sura 1. 29, we read: "On the day we shall say unto hell, 'Art thou full?' and it shall reply, 'Is there yet anymore?' " Similarly in a Jewish author: "The Prince of Hell shall say, day by day, 'Give me food that I may be full.' "

In suras xi. 42 and xxiii. 27, it is said of the Flood, "The oven boiled over"; and in a Jewish work we have this: "The people of the Flood were punished with boiling water."

These similarities are interesting as showing the close connection between the Koran and Jewish remarks; but enough has been given of them.

SEVENTH. *Religious usages of Islam taken from the Jews.* There are many such, but it will suffice to mention two or three. We have seen that keeping the fast of Ramadan has been taken from the Sabaeans and not the Jews; still there is one point certainly coming from the latter, and that regards eating and drinking at night during the month. In sura ii. 83, we read: "Eat and drink until ye can distinguish a white thread from a black thread by the daybreak, then fulfil the fast." In a Jewish book[60] we find it similarly laid down that "the beginning of the day is at the moment when one can distinguish a blue thread from a white thread"—a striking coincidence.

Again, Muslims of all lands, at the fixed time of their five prayers, wherever they happen to be, whether in the house or in the street, perform their devotion on the spot—especially at places where people are passing by. This strange practice is entirely confined to them and would be seemly in no other religion. But in the days of the Prophet there were Jews in Arabia who used this habit; for many of them were descended from the Pharisees, of whom our Savior said: "They love to pray standing in the synagogues and in the corners of the streets, that they may be seen of men."[61] Thus the companions of Muhammad, looking upon the Jews as the

People of the Book and children of father Abraham, regarded such practices as having descended from him, and so adopted and have continued them to the present day, as we see, unchanged, though they are no longer kept up by the Jews themselves.

Does it not seem strange to the reader that although the Koran repeatedly attests our Scriptures as the Word of God, yet but one quotation is taken from them, viz., sura xxi. 105: "Verily we have written in the Psalms after the mention (of the Law) that my servants the righteous shall inherit the earth"—an evident reference to Psalm xxxvii. 11: "But the meek shall inherit the earth."

Two other matters borrowed from the Jews. Every Muslim thinks the Koran to have been on the heavenly table (*Lauh*) from before the creation of the world, as is mentioned in a passage already quoted: "Truly it is the glorious Koran, on a preserved table."[62] Now before saying anything about this table, one may ask, was the Book of the Psalms in existence before the Koran or not? For we have given above a verse in which is revealed the inheritance given by the Lord to his servants, as mentioned in the Psalms before the Koran was revealed. The Koran quotes from the Psalms: is it not clear, therefore, that the Psalms were before the Koran? How then could the Koran, produced so late in the world, have been placed on the heavenly table?

Now let us hear what tradition tells us about this table:

One tells us that the throne is made out of a pearl, as is also the preserved table, the height of which is 700 years' journey, and its breadth 300. All around it is adorned with rubies. The Lord commanded that there should be written upon it what he had wrought in Creation, and onwards till the Day of Judgment: "In the name of the Lord, the Compassionate and Merciful. I am God and there is none else beside me. He that accepts my decree, is patient at my punishment, and thankful at my mercies, I will write and place him along with the righteous; he that doth not accept my decree, let him go forth from beneath my heaven," etc.[63]

The source of this tale is to be found in Jewish books, but vastly exaggerated by Muslims. We find in the Torah that when God desired to give forth the Ten Commandments, he thus addressed Moses, who has himself given the account in Deut. x. 1-5:

At that time the Lord said unto me, "Hew thee two tables of stone like unto the first, and come up unto me into the mount, and make thee an ark of wood. And I will write on the tables the words that were in the first tables which thou brakest, and thou shalt put them in the ark." And I made an ark of shittim wood, and hewed two tables of stone like unto the first, and went up into the mount, having the two tables in mine hand. And he wrote on the tables, according to the first writing, the ten commandments, which the Lord spake unto you in the mount out of the midst of the fire in the day of the assembly: and the Lord gave them unto me. And I turned myself and came down from the mount, and put the tables in the ark which I had made; and there they be, as the Lord commanded me.

Elsewhere also we are told that the two tables were preserved in the Ark of the Covenant, made by Moses at the Lord's command.[64] But in the course of time the Jews imagined that all the books of the Old Testament, nay the Talmud itself, were deposited in the Ark on the tables. Muhammad hearing this of the Jewish Law and Scriptures, imagined the same of his own, and said (as we are told above) that the Koran also was placed on the preserved table; and his followers, not understanding of what heavenly table he spoke, swelled out the whole matter into the story given above.

The following is from the Jewish writer, Rabbi Simeon:

What is that which is written that the Lord said to Moses: Come up to me into the mount, and be there; and I will give three tables of stone, and a law, and commandments which I have written; that thou mayest teach them (Exodus xxiv. 12). The tables are the Ten Commandments; and the Torah the Law which is read; and the Commandments also mean the Mishnah; and "that which I have written" means the Prophets, and the Holy Writings; and "that thou mayest teach them" points to the Gemara. And from this we learn that all these were delivered to Moses on Mount Sinai.

No intelligent Muslim would for a moment credit this foolish story, knowing that the Mishna was not written till about the year 220 of the Christian era; the Gemara of Jerusalem in 430 C.E.; and the Gemara of Babylon about 530 C.E. But ignorant Muslims, believing it all, added their own Koran to the rest, and so comes this wretched story. The reader will not think it necessary, we are sure, that anything more of the above kind be added, excepting this, perhaps, that the Jews themselves hold the tables to be of date beyond time; for one tells us they were made "at the creation of the world at the sunset before the Sabbath day."[65]

The Mount Caf.—The origin of what the Muslims tell us about this mountain clearly originated from the Jews. Here is what the tradition of the Muslims tells us:[66]

> The Lord Almighty formed a great mountain from green chrysolite—the greenness of the sky is from it—called Mount Caf, and surrounded the entire earth therewith, and it is that by which the Almighty swore, and called it Caf (see sura 1. 1).

And again:

> One day Abdallah asked the Prophet what formed the highest point on the earth. "Mount Caf," he said. "And what is Mount Caf made of?" "Of green emeralds," was the reply; "and from hence is the greenness of the sky." "Thou hast said the truth, O Prophet; and what is the height of Mount Caf?" "A journey of five hundred years." "And round about it how far is it?" "Two thousand years' journey."

Now all these strange ideas are founded on the Jewish writing called Hagigah, where we meet with the following comment on the word *thohu* in Genesis i.2: "Thohu is a green *line* (*cav* or *caf*) which surrounds the whole world, and hence comes darkness." And so the companions of the Prophet hearing this explanation of the word *cav*, and not understanding what was meant, fancied it must be a mountain, or succession of great mountains, surrounding the world and making it dark.

From all that has now been said, it must be clear to the reader that the Jewish writings, and specially the fanciful tales of the Talmud, formed one of the chief sources of Islam. And now we must turn our attention to the similar influence on Islam exercised by the Christian religion, and especially by those foolish stories to which in the Prophet's day the heretical sects, with their forged and got-up tales, spread abroad.

Chapter IV.

On the Belief that Much of the Koran Is
Derived from the Tales of Heretical Christian Sects

In the Prophet's day, numbers of Christians in Arabia were not only an ignorant people, but belonged to heretical sects, which, on account of their dangerous influence, had been expelled from the Roman Empire, and thus had taken refuge beyond the border land. They had hardly any acquaintance with the Gospel or apostolic writings, but were conversant with heretical books and the extravagant tales they contained. Now our argument is that Muhammad having but an imperfect knowledge of the Gospel, learned from these people, who were all around them, what he believed to be the purport of the New Testament. It was his object to establish a faith which should embrace and unite all races of the peninsula, and the Christians among the rest. He therefore entered in the Koran very much of the teaching and vain imaginations of these ignorant sects. It is our object carefully to test whether this proposition is true—that is, whether it be the case that such stories form one of the sources of the Koran or not; and that we propose to make the subject of the present chapter.

I. *The Seven Sleepers, or Companions of the Cave.*

The tale as given in the Koran is quoted in full in the note section.[67] It is one of Greek origin to be found in a Latin work of Gregory of Tours[68] and may be described in brief as referring to the age of the Emperor Decius (249–251 C.E.), when Christians were terribly persecuted and every endeavor made to destroy the faith. To escape with their lives, seven men of Ephesus took refuge in a cave near their city, and fell asleep for two hundred years, till the reign of Theodorus II (447 C.E.). On awaking, one of them ventured into the city to see what in the interval had happened, and was overcome with amazement to find the Christian faith triumphant over all other religions. The cross, once the sign of shame and disgrace, now the crown of the emperor and the mark of the empire; and nearly the whole people of the land turned Christians. All this of course is a mere story, composed no doubt to illustrate the rapidity with which, by the grace of the Holy Spirit and shedding of martyr's blood, the faith had gained ascendency at last. No Christian ever dreamt that the tale was true, but such as the nurse tells her children of "the cat and the mouse," etc. But the

Prophet has entered it with all gravity in the Koran for the instructions of his followers. Is it needful for us to add that such a tale could never have been placed by the Most High upon the heavenly table and from thence sent down to the Prophet, but was learned by him from some of the ignorant Christians around him?

II. *The History of Mary.*—In sura Mariam we are told that after the birth of the Holy Child, the people came to her and said, "O Mary, now hast thou done a strange thing; O sister of Aaron, thy father was not a bad man, neither was thy mother a wicked woman."[69] According to Muhammad, therefore, Mary (Miriam) was the sister of Aaron, Moses' brother; which is all the plainer as elsewhere she is named *Mary daughter of Imran;*[70] and again, "We gave unto Moses the Book, and appointed him his brother Aaron as Vizier."[71] Hence it is clear that Imran, Moses, Aaron, and Mary (Mariam) are the same persons as are so named in the Torah, excepting only that in the Hebrew the name of the first is Amram; and in Numbers (xxvi. 59) we are told that "the name of Amram's wife was Jochebed, the daughter of Levi, who was born to Levi in Egypt, and she bare unto Amram, Aaron and Moses and Miriam their sister"; and also in Exodus (vx. 20) we read of "Miriam (Mary) the prophetess, the sister of Aaron." Now looking to the words in the Koran above quoted: "O Mary! O sister of Aaron," it is quite evident that Muhammad is speaking of Mary the sister of Aaron and daughter of Imram, as the same Mary who, some 1570 years after, became the mother of our blessed Savior! The commentators have in vain endeavored to explain this marvellous confusion of time and space. One attempt may be set down to the fabulous Jewish story regarding Mary the sister of Aaron, that "the angel of death had no power over her, that she passed away with the kiss of the Lord, and that no insect or worm could touch her person"—a strange conceit this: nor have any of the Jews ever said that she survived to the Christian era.

As regards Mary the mother of Jesus, we find many passages in the Koran opposed to the four Gospels, and taken evidently from the apocryphal writings of the heretical sects. For example, the following is from sura iii. vv. 31 and 32:—

> Then the wife of Imran said, "O Lord, I have presented unto Thee that which is in my womb as dedicated to thy service. Accept it, therefore, from me; for thou art he that both heareth and knoweth." So when she was delivered of the child, she said, "O Lord, truly I have brought forth a

female (and God knoweth what she had brought forth), and a male is not as a female. I have called her Mary; and I commend her unto thee, and her issue, against Satan the stoned one." Whereupon the Lord accepted her with a gracious acceptance, and caused her to bear an excellent offspring. And Zacharias took care of the child; and as often as Zacharias entered the chamber unto her, he found provisions laid beside her, and he said, "O Mary, whence hast thou this?" She answered, "This is from God; for the Lord provideth for whom he pleaseth without measure."

We read also in Baidhawi and other commentators that Imran's wife, who was aged and barren, one day saw a bird feeding its little ones and at once longed for a child herself, and cried: " 'O Lord, if thou wilt give me either a son or a daughter, I will present it unto Thee in the Temple, thy holy house.' The Lord heard her prayer; she conceived and bore a daughter, whom she called Mary." Jalal ud-Din also tells us that some years after, Mary's mother, called Hanna, taking the child to the temple, made her over to the priests, who in their turn made her over to Zacharias to take care of; and he placed her in a chamber shut off from anyone else to enter. But the angels came there to tend and nourish her.

Again, we read in the same sura, vv. 37–42:

Now when the angels said, "O Mary, verily God hath chosen thee, and purified thee, and hath chosen thee over all the women of the world: O Mary, be devout towards thy Lord, and worship, and bow down with those who bow down." This is a secret history. We reveal it unto thee, although thou wast not present with them when they cast their rods as to which of them should have the education of Mary; nor wast thou with them when they strove among themselves. When the angels said, "O Mary, verily God sendeth thee good tidings regarding the Word from himself; his name is Jesus the Messiah son of Mary honorable, in this world and in that to come, and one of these that approach nigh to the Almighty. And he shall speak unto men in the cradle, and when he is grown up, and he shall be one of the righteous." She said, "Lord, how shall I have a son, since no man hath touched me." He said: "Thus the Lord createth that which he pleaseth. When he decreeth a thing, he but saith unto it,—*Be*, and it is."

The notice here given of the "casting of rods" is thus explained by Baidhawi and Jalal ud-Din. Zacharias, with six and twenty other priests who sought to have the charge of Mary, went to the river, in order to choose which should be the favored one, and cast their rods into it. All sank but that of Zacharias, who thus became Mary's guardian. Regarding all this we read in sura xix. 16-31, as follows:

And in the Book make mention of Mary, when she retired from her people to a place towards the East, and took a veil, apart from them. And we sent unto her our Spirit, who appeared unto her as a real man. She said, "I flee for refuge from thee unto the Merciful, if thou fearest the Lord." He answered, "Verily I am the Messenger of thy Lord that I may give unto thee a holy Son." She said, "How shall I have a son, for no man hath touched me, and I am no harlot." He said, "So shall it be. Thy Lord saith, 'This is easy with me, and we shall make him a sign unto mankind, and a mercy from us; for it is a thing decreed.'" Whereupon she conceived him, and retired with him (in her womb) to a distant place; and the pains of childbirth came upon her by the trunk of a palm-tree. She said, "Would to God I had died before this, and had become a thing forgotten, lost in oblivion!" And one from beneath her called out: "Grieve not: verily thy Lord hath provided a rivulet under thee; and do thou shake the body of the palm-tree, and it shall let fall upon thee ripe dates ready gathered; so do thou eat and drink, and comfort thine eyes. Moreover, if thou seest any man, say, 'I have vowed a fast unto the Merciful, and I will speak to no man this day.'" So she came to her people, carrying the child in her arms. They said, "O Mary, thou hast done a strange thing: O sister of Aaron, thy father was not a bad man, neither was thy mother a harlot." Then she made signs to the child. They said, "How shall we speak to an infant in the cradle?" Whereupon the child said, "Verily I am a servant of God: He hath given me the Book and hath made me a prophet."

Such, then, are the tales regarding the Virgin Mary which we find in the Koran and ancient Muslim commentators. From whence did such strange fictions come? Clearly not from the true Gospel, but nearly all of them from the schismatic writings of ignorant men, spread abroad in ancient times amongst a people given to wild fictitious stories. To prove this, we now give full and satisfactory evidence. In the Protevangelium of James the Less, written in Hellenic Greek, we have the following:

Anna, looking upwards to the heavens, saw a sparrow in its nest, and sighed saying, "O me! O me! Would it were the same with me. O me! to what thing am I alike? Not like unto the birds of heaven, for the birds of heaven are fruitful before thee, O Lord...." And lo! an angel of the Lord from above spake thus unto her: "Anna, Anna! the Lord God hath heard thy cry, and thy seed shall be spoken of over the whole earth." Anna said, "As the Lord my God liveth, if a child, either male or female, be born unto me, I will offer it as a gift to the Lord my God, and it will be in his service all the days of its life...." And when her full time had come in the ninth month, Anna was delivered.... And she gave the breast to the child and called its name Mary.

In an Arabic apocryphal book, called the *History of our Holy Father the Aged, the Carpenter* (Joseph), there is given the following account of Mary as a child. Her parents took her to the temple when three years old, and she remained there nine years. Then when the priests saw that the Holy Virgin had grown up, they spoke among themselves, "Let us call a righteous man, one that fears the Lord, to take charge of Mary till the time of her marriage, that she may not remain in the temple." But before that time when her parents brought her, a new occasion had arisen, of which we read as follows in the Protevangelium:

The priest accepted the child, and having kissed and blessed her, spake thus to her: "May the Lord glorify thy name over all the races on the face of the earth. The Lord God will in the latter days manifest to thee the ransom of the house of Israel." And Mary remained like a dove in the temple of the Lord, and received food at an angel's hand. And when she was twelve years of age, the priests came together saying: "See now, Mary is twelve years old, and still in the temple of the Lord; what then shall we do with her? ..." And behold an angel of the Lord stood beside him and said: "Zacharias, Zacharias! come forth, and bring together all the widowers of thy people, and let each carry his rod, and whom the Lord God will signify, his wife shall she be." And the criers went over the whole land of Judaea, and proclaimed it by the trumpet of the Lord, and all flocked together; and Joseph also carrying his rod hurried to the synagogue. So having come together, they went to the priest who, gathering all their rods, went into the temple and prayed. Having finished the prayer, he came forth, and gave to each man his rod, but upon none of them was there any mark. Joseph's rod came to him last of all. And lo! a dove came out of the rod, and sat upon Joseph's head. Then the priest said to him: "Thou hast been chosen to take the Virgin of the Lord; take her therefore under thy protection."

And Mary, taking a pitcher went forth to fill it with water; and lo! a voice saying, "Hail thou highly favoured one: the Lord is with thee; blessed art thou among women." And she looked to the right and to the left to see whence the voice came; trembling she returned to her house, and putting down the pitcher, sat upon her seat.... And lo, the angel of the Lord from over her cried, "Fear not, Mary, for thou hast found favor with the Lord and shalt conceive by his word." Mary, hearing it, became anxious in her soul, saying, "Am I to conceive, as every woman doth, and bring forth?" And the angel said unto her: "Not thus, Mary, for the power of the Highest shall overshadow thee: therefore that Holy Child shall be called the Son of the Highest, and thou shalt call his name Jesus."

Anyone reading the above will see that it gives a close account of Mary's residence in the holy temple. We have pretty much the same in other books, such as the following from the Coptic book on the Virgin Mary:

When placed by Hanna in the temple, Mary was fed there like the doves, as the angels of the Lord brought her food from the heavens. When she worshipped the Lord in the temple, they did reverence to her, and often brought her fruit from the Tree of Life, which she did eat with cheerfulness.[72] ... Mary lived in the temple, a pure and holy worshipper, till twelve years of age. She had been her first three years in her parents' home, and nine years in the temple. Then the Priests, seeing that she was growing up a virtuous and God-fearing maiden, consulted together, saying: "We must seek for a righteous God-fearing man to whom she may be given in marriage." And so having summoned the tribe of Judah together, they chose twelve men according to the names of each of the twelve tribes of Israel, and the lot came out upon that good old man Joseph.[73]

Then when she became with child, Mary was summoned with Joseph before the High priest, who thus addressed her: "O Mary, what is this thou hast done, and debased thy soul: thou who in the Holy of Holies feddest from the hand of an angel, and heardest their hymns,... what is this thou hast done?" Weeping bitterly she answered: "By the living God I swear that I am pure before him and have known no man."[74]

After that we have the account of Joseph and Mary leaving Nazareth for Bethlehem, where they rested in a cave, and there Jesus was born:

And Joseph having found a cavern, brought Mary into it ... And he tells us: "I looked up to the heavens, and saw the heavenly vault standing still, and the birds of the air trembling; then looking down upon the earth, I beheld a dish laid, and the workers sitting at meat around it, their hands therein, yet not taking out anything, or putting a morsel to their mouths, but their faces all looking upwards. And I saw sheep being driven, but they stood still, and the shepherd raised his crook to strike them, but his hand remained raised. And by the bed of the river I saw kids with their mouths as it were touching the water, but stopped from drinking. All things in fear and alarm."[75]

Referring now to what is told us in a quotation from the Koran given above, regarding Mary, the Palm-tree, etc., we give an extract from an apocryphal book called the *History of the Nativity of Mary and the Savior's Infancy.*

Now on the third day after she had set out, Mary was wearied in the desert by the heat, and asked Joseph to rest for a little under the shade of a palm-tree. So he made haste and made her sit down beneath it. Then Mary looking up and seeing its branches laden with fruit, said, "I desire if it were possible to have some of that fruit." Joseph answered: "I wonder at what thou sayest, since thou must see how lofty the branches of the palm-tree are; and besides, I am anxious to get water, for all in my vessel is done, and there is none anywhere about to fill it with." Just then the child Jesus, looking up with a cheerful smile from his mother's bosom, said to the palm-tree: "Send down thy branches here below, that my Mother may eat fresh fruit of thee." Forthwith it bent itself at Mary's feet, and so they all ate of its fruit. When they had gathered all the fruit, it still remained bent, waiting for orders to arise. Then Jesus said: "O palm-tree, arise with cheerfulness, be one of my Father's trees in Paradise; but with thy roots open the fountain beneath thee; and bring me here for my refreshment some of the water flowing from that fount." At once the tree became erect, and began to pour from its roots water beautifully clear and sweet before them. So when they saw the water, they were all filled with delight, and drank of it with their cattle and servants, till they were satisfied and praised the Lord.

Between this story, as told here and in the Koran, there is just this divergence, that with the latter the Palm-tree appears at the time of the Messiah's birth, whereas this ancient Christian tale belongs to a somewhat later period, namely, after the journey of Joseph and Mary into Egypt.

III. *The Childhood of Jesus.*—In the Koran we are told that the angels, before the infant's birth, thus addressed Mary: "And he shall speak to men in the cradle.... And he shall say, 'Verily I come unto you with a sign from your Lord, for I shall make unto you of clay the figure as it were of a bird; then I will blow thereon and it shall become a bird, by permission of God.'"[76] And again in another sura:

> When God said, "O Jesus son of Mary! remember my favor towards thee, and towards thy Mother; when I strengthened thee by the Holy Spirit, that thou shouldest speak unto men in the cradle, and when grown up; and when I taught thee the Book and wisdom, and the Torah, and the Gospel; and when thou createdst of clay as it were the figure of a bird by my permission, and didst breathe thereon, and by my permission it became a bird. And when thou didst heal one born blind, and the leper, by my permission; and didst raise up the dead by my permission; and when I held back the children of Israel from thee at the time thou camest unto them with evident miracles; and when such of them as believed not said, 'This is nothing but manifest sorcery.'"[77]

It need not be repeated that tales of our Savior's childhood such as these have nothing to do with the Gospel, but like those before of the cradle, palm-tree, etc., have been taken from imaginary and fabulous Christian writings, such as the following from a Greek storybook called *The Gospel of Thomas the Israelite:*

> The child Jesus, when five years of age, was playing on the road by a dirty stream of running water; and having brought it all together into the ditches, immediately made it pure and clean; and all this by a single word. Then having moistened some earth, he made of it twelve sparrows. And it was the Sabbath day when he did these things. There were many other children playing with him. Now a Jew, seeing what Jesus did, that he was playing on the Sabbath day, forthwith went his way to his father Joseph; "Behold," he said, "thy son is at the stream of dirty water, and having taken up some mud, hath made of it twelve sparrows, and hath thus desecrated the Sabbath." On this Joseph went to the spot, and cried out: "Why dost thou do these things on the Sabbath day which it is not lawful to do?" Whereupon Jesus, clapping his hands at the sparrows, cried aloud to them, "Go off!" So they, clucking, flew away. The Jews seeing it were astonished, and went and told their rulers what they had seen Jesus do.

In the Arabic *Gospel of the Infancy*, the whole story is found twice over, in chapter 36, and again in a different form in chapter 46, because the latter part of the book is taken from *The Gospel of Thomas the Israelite.*

In reference to the supposed fact that Jesus spoke when an infant in the cradle, we find it said in the Koran (sura xix. 29-31) that when the Virgin Mary's people reproached her, she pointed to Jesus, implying that they should ask him about the matter. And when they asked her, "How can we speak to a child in the cradle?" then Jesus answered them and said, "Verily I am the servant of God, who hath given the Book, and made me a Prophet." So also in the *Gospel of the Infancy*, chapter 1, it is thus written:

> In the Book of Josephus, High Priest, who lived in the time of the Messiah (and men say he was Caiaphas), we find it said that Jesus spake when he was in the cradle, and called out to his mother Mary: "Verily I am Jesus, the Son of God, the Word, whom thou hast given birth to according to the good tidings given thee by the angel Gabriel, and my Father hath sent me for the salvation of the world."

Now if we compare the above, taken from this ancient Arabic work on the infancy of our Savior, with the Koran, it will be at once apparent that Muhammad has adopted the story, with its very words, changed only so far as to bring them into accord with his own belief and teaching; and doubtless it was all taken from this ancient apocryphal treatise. Should anyone ask, How could this have been?—the answer is that this book of the childhood was translated into Arabic from the Coptic original, and must have been known to the Prophet's Coptic handmaiden, Mary. From her he must have heard the tale, and believing it to have come from the Gospel, adopted it with some little change, and so entered it into the Koran. Now it is clear that such stories of infantile miracles are altogether opposed to what is written in the Gospel of St. John (ii.) regarding the turning of water into wine, where it is recorded that "This beginning of miracles did Jesus in Cana of Galilee and manifested forth his glory." Jesus was then over thirty years of age; and it is clear that before this no miracle had been done by him. But all the miracles noted in the Koran, beyond what have been mentioned above, and that of the table to be spoken of below, were undoubtedly true and beyond question, as they correspond with what we read of in the four Gospels.

Now as to the *table*, the following is the account given in the Koran (sura v. 112-115):—

When the apostles said, "O Jesus Son of Mary! is thy Lord able to cause a table to descend unto us from heaven?" He said, "Fear God if ye be true believers." They answered, "We desire to eat therefrom, and that our hearts may rest at ease, and may know that thou hast told us the truth, and that we may be witnesses thereof." Jesus Son of Mary said, "O God our Lord! Cause a table to descend unto us from heaven, that it may become an *'id* (day of festival) to the first of us and unto the last; and a sign from thee; and do thou provide food for us, for thou art the best Provider." God said, "I will send it down unto you."

This miracle is not mentioned in any Christian book. So strange an imagination never could have had reality; but its origin is no doubt to be found in the supper which Jesus partook of with his disciples the night before his death. This *Lord's Supper*, which has ever since been observed by Christians as a sacred ordinance according to Christ's command, is described in each of the four Gospels.[78] It is also mentioned in Luke (xxii. 30), where Jesus promises his disciples "that ye may eat and drink at my table in my kingdom and sit on thrones, judging the twelve tribes of Israel."[79]

We pass on to other notices in the Koran regarding Jesus and his mother, that we may observe the sources from which they were derived. Thus, in sura v. 116: "When God shall say unto Jesus at the last day, O Jesus Son of Mary! hast thou said unto men, Take me and my Mother for two gods, besides God?" And again, in sura iv. 169:

O ye people of the Book! Exceed not the just bounds in your religion; neither say of God other than the truth. Verily the Messiah Jesus Son of Mary is the apostle of God, and his Word which he placed in Mary, and a Spirit, from him. Believe, therefore, in God and his apostles, and say not there are three (Gods); forbear this; it will be better for you. Verily God is one God. Far be it from him that he should have a son. To him belongeth whatever is in heaven and earth; and he is a sufficient advocate.

And once more, sura v. 77:—

They are very unbelievers who say, "God is the third of three"; for there is no God but the one God. And if they refrain not from what they say, a dreadful torment shall surely be inflicted on such of them as disbelieve.

From these verses it is evident, as Jalal ud-Din and Yahya say, that the Prophet must have heard from some of the heretical Christian sects that they held the Almighty to be three, namely, God, and Mary, and Jesus; and to oppose this evil teaching, it is over and again repeated in the Koran that God is one. Whoever may read the Torah and the Gospel must know that unity of the Almighty is at the foundation of the Christian faith; as we read in Deut. vi. 4: "Hear O Israel, the Lord our God is one Lord"; a text quoted and enforced by Jesus himself, Mark xii. 29. The godhead of Mary is held by no real Christian. It is, alas, true that several churches do worship her—which is nothing short of idolatry, and altogether opposed to the teaching of the Holy Scriptures; yet it is in accordance with what many of the heretical works contained regarding Mary; and from them no doubt Muhammad learned the strange story he has put in the Koran.

In sura iv. 156 we find it written that the Jews said: "We have slain Jesus son of Mary, the Apostle of God. Yet they slew him not, neither crucified him, but a likeness was given unto them. . . . They did not really kill him; but God took him up unto himself, and God is mighty and wise." It need hardly be said that this doctrine of the Koran is entirely opposed to the writings of the prophets and apostles, but it is in agreement with the teaching of some of the early heretics. Thus the ancient writer Irenaeus tells us that Basilides, one of their chief men, held this view, for he wrote of Jesus as follows:

> He suffered not; but Simon of Cyrenian was compelled to carry the cross for him; and he through error and ignorance was crucified, being transfigured by him, that it might be thought that he was Jesus himself.

It is evident then that Muhammad learned this story as propagated by the disciples of Basilides—a story every one must know to be opposed to the writings of the prophets, who said that the Messiah would come as a sacrifice for the redemption of mankind and to the testimony of the apostles, who with their own eyes saw our blessed Redeemer on the cross. Muhammad, however, failed to see that the object of this heretic was to hold up the vain imagination that Jesus was not clothed with manhood proper, but had only the semblance and not the reality of it. If so, it was not possible that he could have been born of the Virgin and suffered on the cross, but that men were deceived into thinking that these things happened to him. Now all this heretical teaching is entirely opposed not only to the

Gospel, but to the Koran itself. Accordingly, it did not become Muhammad to accept part of the wild imaginations of Basilides and reject a part; for if the basis of a heretic's teachings is false, how can the notions and doctrines derived therefrom be true? And yet we see that the Prophet did so, in accepting the vain imagination of the heretic as given in the verse of the Koran quoted above.

The Muslims hold that Christ announced to his followers that they were to expect a prophet named Ahmed; and in proof they adduce the following verse from the Koran, S.1xi. 6: "And when Jesus Son of Mary said, 'O children of Israel, I am the apostle of God unto you, confirming that which was delivered unto me in the Torah, and bringing good tidings of an apostle who shall come after me, named Ahmed.'" This passage refers no doubt to the Comforter, the Paraclete promised in the Gospel of John.[80] But anyone who attentively reads what is said in the passages on the subject, will perceive that they make no promise of any prophet's advent, but of the coming of the Holy Ghost—a promise fulfilled shortly after our Savior's ascent to heaven by the descent of the Holy Spirit, as described in Acts ii. 1-11.

The origin of the misapprehension in the Koran came from the Arabs not knowing the meaning of Paraklete (Faraclete), and fancying it to signify Ahmed, or "the praised one"; while the real sense of the name is the Comforter. But there is in Greek another word which to the ear of a foreigner would have a nearly similar sound, namely, Periclete (praised or celebrated); and it is extremely probable that the people of Arabia, not familiar with Greek, mistook its meaning thus and named the promised one Ahmed, or "the praised."[81]

We read in ancient times of one Mani[82] in Iran, who fancied himself a prophet, and claimed to be the Paraklete promised by the Messiah. But he was rejected by the Christians of Persia, who, being well acquainted with the Gospel, knew that our Savior made no promise of any prophet to come.

We have it in tradition that Muhammad said Jesus would descend upon earth, there live forty years, and become married.[83] Anyone acquainted with the Bible will understand how this strange imagination arose; for in Rev. xix. 7–9, we read as follows:

> Let us be glad and rejoice, and give honor to him: for the marriage of the Lamb is come, and his wife hath made herself ready. And to her was granted that she should be arrayed in fine linen, clean and white: for the

fine linen is the righteousness of saints. And he saith unto me, "Write, Blessed are they which are called unto the marriage supper of the Lamb." And he saith unto me, "These are the true sayings of God."

And if it be asked, Who is the bride spoken of here? the answer is in ch. xxi. 2: "And I John saw the holy city, new Jerusalem, coming down from God out of heaven, prepared as a bride adorned for her husband." We see then that the bride spoken of here is the Christian Church which will be on the earth at the second coming of Jesus; and their "marriage" is simply the symbol of the perfect union, love, and devotion that will subsist between the two, as between a husband and his wife. The whole story of the commentators is but a foolish myth.[84]

Again we read in sura iii. 48: "O Jesus! I will cause thee to die," the meaning being that after his return to this earth Jesus will die. This is entirely opposed to the Scriptures, for in Revelation i. 17, 18, Jesus says, "I am the first and the last: I am he that liveth, and was dead: and, behold, I am alive for evermore, Amen; and have the keys of hell and of death." The story has arisen from a passage in a traditional book[85] regarding Enoch and Elias, who ascended without dying to the heavens and of whom we are told: "It will happen to them that they will return to the world in the last time, in the day of grief and fear and distress, and then will die." And in the Coptic tale of the falling asleep of Mary, it is said of Enoch and Elias, "Of necessity both of these will at the last taste of death." So when the companions of the Prophet had such foolish notions in their heads, they no doubt concluded that Jesus too, like Enoch and Elias, would eventually be made to taste of death; and moreover, knowing that he had ascended up to heaven, they thought that his death would follow his return at the Second Coming. Hence the way in which they tried to illustrate the above text. It may be noticed also that in other suras we find it written that "Every soul shall taste of death."[86]

IV. *Some Other Stories from Christian or Heretical Writers.*—When God would create Adam he sent angels and archangels, one after another, to bring a handful of earth. At last Azrael, having descended, brought a handful gathered from every quarter, and said, "O Lord, thou knowest whence I have brought it."[87] Abul Feda, quoting from Ibn Athir, gives us this account:—

The Prophet said that God created Adam from a handful of earth gathered from all round the world . . . and that he was called Adam as formed out of the earth *below* (i.e., *adim*).

The following is also taken from the heretic Marcion, who is quoted by an old Armenian writer as follows:

> The God of the Law seeing the earth fair to look upon, desired to make man out of it, and having descended to Matter, *Hyle* [ὕλη] on the earth, he said, "Give me some of thy soil, and I will from myself impart to it a soul." ... So when Matter had given to him some of the earth, he created man and breathed into him a soul; and for this reason he was called Adam, because he was made out of the earth.

According to the heretic Marcion, he whom they name "the God of the Law," who got earth for the creation of man, was only an angel; for they say that the Law came down from one of the angels hostile to the great God. And that angel they call lord of the universe, creator of all things, and prince of this world. This last is taken from the Gospel of John, where the devil is so called.[88] Marcion tells us that this angel was an inhabitant of the second heaven, and at first knew nothing of the great God; but when he came to know of his existence, then he turned out to be an enemy of "the unknown God," and sought that mankind should neither know nor worship him.

This imaginative story of the creation is in entire accord with what the Muslims say regarding Azazil, who came to dwell in the second heaven. But the rest of the tale about him belongs to the Zoroastrian books, which will be noticed in our fifth chapter.

In sura xix. vv. 69-73 we have the following passage:

> By the Lord! we shall surely assemble them round about hell on their knees. Then will we draw forth from every sect such of them as shall have been most rebellious against the Merciful; and we best know which of them are the more deserving to be burned therein. There are none of you but shall descend into the same. It is an established decree with thy Lord. Then we will deliver the pious ones; but will leave the wicked ones therein upon their knees.

In explaining this passage tradition varies. Some say that all believers will descend into hell, but will not be touched by the flames; others that it refers to the Bridge Sirat, over which all must pass, and which is over Jehannam. It is just possible that the words, "There are none of you but shall descend into it," may be borrowed from the way in which some ignorant Christians interpreted the "Trying with fire," mentioned in the

Gospel,[89] as if it meant that they were thus to be purified of their sins. But if the Koran here refers to the Bridge Sirat, the idea cannot be from any of them, but from the Zoroastrian books, to be noticed below.

The *balance* is mentioned in two passages of the Koran, sura xlii. 16: "It is God who hath sent down the Scripture with truth, and the balance; and what shall inform thee whether the time be near at hand?" And sura ci. 5, 6: "Moreover, he whose balance shall be heavy will lead a pleasing life; but he whose balance shall be light, his dwelling-place shall be hell."

We need not enter into the vast store of tradition devoted to this great balance, but simply enquire whence the notion arose. There is a fictitious work called "The Testament of Abraham," written originally in Egypt, and thence translated into Greek and Arabic; and what is there said of the weighing of deeds, good and bad, we shall compare with what is in the Koran. In this book we are told that when the Angel of Death wished to seize the soul of Abraham, the patriarch desired that before his death he might see the wonders of the heavens and of the earth. Having obtained permission, he ascended and beheld all the scenes around him. After a time he ascended the second heaven, and there saw the balance by which angels try the deeds of mankind. The following is an extract from this work:

> Betwixt the two doors there stood a throne...and upon it was seated a wonderful man.... Before him stood a table, like as of crystal, all covered with gold and linen. And upon the table a book lay, its length six fingers, and breadth ten fingers. On the right hand of it and on the left, stood two angels having paper and ink and pen. In front of the table sat a brilliant angel, holding in his hand a balance. On the left sat an angel, as if it were all of fire, merciless and stern, having in his hand a trumpet, in which was flaming fire, the touchstone of sinful men. The wonderful man seated on the throne was judging the souls and passing sentence upon them. And the two angels on the right and on the left were writing down, the one on the right, righteous deeds; and he on the left, sinful ones. And he that stood before the table holding the balance was weighing the souls, and the angel holding the fire, passing judgment upon them. And so Abraham asked Michael, the captain of the host, "What is all this that we see?" He answered, "That which thou seest, holy Abraham, is the Judgment and Retribution."

Thereafter we are told that every soul whose good deeds equalled its evil ones was reckoned neither as one of the saved nor as one of the condemned, but put in a position between the two, like what is told us in the Koran already quoted, "Between the two a veil, and men upon al-Araf."

From the above it is clear that what Muhammad mentions about the balance in the Koran was derived from this fictitious "Testament of Abraham," written in Egypt some four hundred years before the Hegira, and of which an account was probably given him by his Coptic concubine Mary.

But what is there mentioned about the balance belongs to a far earlier source, namely, to a book called "The Book of the Dead." Many copies of this primeval work have been found in the sepulchres of the ancient idolatrous Egyptians, placed there because supposed to have been written by one of their gods called *Thoth*, and with the notion that they would be read by the dead buried there. In it is a strange picture illustrating the Judgement hall of Osiris,... There are in it two deities on opposite sides of a balance. One of these is weighing the heart of a good man placed in a vessel on a scale, and in the corresponding scale opposite is an idol called *Ma* or truth. The great god is recording in ancient Egyptian the fate of the departed: "Osiris the justified is alive; his balance is equal in the midst of God's palace; the heart of Osiris the justified is to enter into its place. Let the great god, Lord of Hermopolis, say so." Over some of the idols are their names; and above a savage figure, the words, "Conqueror of his enemies, god of *Amenti* (Hades)"; several times also are repeated the words, "Life and peace to Osiris."...

From all this it is clear that what we have in the Koran about the balance was learned by the Prophet from such sources as the above.

As regards the ascent to heaven, tradition tells us that Muhammad there saw Father Adam, at times weeping and groaning, at times happy and rejoicing; of which in the Mishkat we have this account:

> When he opened, we went up to the lower heaven. Lo! a man seated, on his right hand were dark figures, and on his left dark figures. When he looked to his right, he laughed; when to the left, he wept. And he said, "Welcome to the righteous Prophet, and to the excellent Son." I then asked Gabriel, "Who is this?" "It is Adam," he said, "and these dark figures on his right, and on his left, are the spirits of his sons. The people on his right hand are the inhabitants of Paradise; and the dark figures on his left are those of the Fire; when he looks to his right. he smiles; and when he looks to the left, he weeps."

The same tale we find in the ancient "Testament of Abraham," as follows:

> So Michael turned the chariot, and took Abraham towards the east through the first gate of heaven. There Abraham saw two roads; one straight and difficult, the other wide and easy. He beheld also two gates, one wide like its road, and another narrow like the other road. Outside the two gates they beheld a man sitting on a golden throne, his aspect terrible like unto the Lord. They saw a multitude of souls driven by the angels through the wide gate, but few souls led by the angels through the narrow one. And when the great man seated on the golden throne saw but few passing through the narrow gate, and so many through the wide gate, forthwith he grasped the hair of his head and his beard on either side, and cast himself weeping and groaning from his throne upon the ground. But when he saw many souls entering in by the narrow gate, he arose from the ground, and with joy and rejoicing seated himself again upon the throne.
>
> Then Abraham asked the captain of the host: "My Lord Commander! Who is that great man adorned with so much grandeur, who sometimes weeps in great distress, and sometimes rejoices and is glad?" Then the Spirit (Michael) answered: "This is Adam, the first created man, adorned with so much glory; and here he beholds the world and the multitudes who derive their existence from himself. When he beholds many souls passing the narrow gate, then rising up he seats himself upon his throne in joy and gladness, because the narrow gate is for the righteous and leadeth unto life eternal. Those passing through it are on the way to Paradise, and hence the first created Adam rejoiceth, because he seeth souls that are saved. But when he beholds many passing through the wide gate, then he seizes the hair of his head, beats and casts himself to the ground crying bitterly. For the wide gate leadeth the wicked to everlasting destruction."

It were easy to show that many other passages in the Koran are in close accord with the tales of ignorant Christians, or of heretical writers, anterior to the Prophet; but the examples given above may amply suffice. Before closing the chapter, however, it seems proper to ask whether Muhammad, having borrowed so much from fictitious works, has taken anything at all from the Gospel, or apostolic writings. In answer to this serious question we reply that throughout the Koran only one verse is quoted from the Gospel, and by a well-known traditionist possibly one verse from St. Paul.

First. In sura vii. 38 it is written: "They that charge our signs with falsehood and proudly reject them, the gates of heaven shall not be opened to them, nor shall they enter Paradise until a camel pass through the eye of a needle"; compared with this in three of the Gospels: "It is easier for a camel to go through the eye of a needle than for a rich man to enter into the kingdom of God."[90]

Second. Abu Hureira tells in the Mishkat of the Prophet having stated that God Almighty had said as follows: "I have prepared for the righteous what eye hath not seen, nor ear heard, nor hath entered into the heart of man." See similar words in 1 Cor. ii. 9.

But this absence of actual quotation does not detract from the second-hand, and in many respects fictitious, knowledge of the Christian past. And we conclude that the Gospel, and especially some of the ancient heretical works, were clearly among the sources of Muslim teaching, a conclusion altogether beyond question.

Chapter V.

Some Things in the Koran and Tradition Derived from Ancient Zoroastrian and Hindu Beliefs

We learn form Arabian and Greek historians that previous to Muhammad's birth, and during his life, many parts of the peninsula were ruled over by Persian kings. For example, Kesra Nousherwan, having sent an army to Hira, put down Harith the king, and in his room placed the subservient Mandzar on the throne. He also sent an army to Yemen, and having expelled the Abyssinian invaders, restored the old king, whose progeny followed him in the government of the land. Abulfeda tells us that "the family of Mandzar, and race of Nasr, son of Rabia, were the Kesra's governors over the Arabs of Iraq"; also that after the Himyarites, "there were four Abyssinian governors of Yemen, and eight Persians, and then it became ruled over by Islam." It is clear, then, that both in the time of Muhammad and previously, the Persians had constant intercourse with Arabia; and being incomparably more learned than its ignorant people, must have had an important influence on their religion, on their customs, and on their knowledge at large. Both history and Koranic commentaries show that the tales and songs of Iran were spread abroad among the tribes of Arabia. Thus Ibn Hisham tells us that in the days of the Prophet, stories of Rustem, Isfandiyar, and the ancient kings of Persia were not only current

at Medina, but that some of the Quraish used delightedly to compare them
with the similar tales in the Koran. He adds as follows:

> The Prophet of the Lord, when he sat in the assembly, used to pray there
> to the Almighty, read to them from the Koran, and warn the Quraish of
> what in times past had happened to the unbelieving nations. It so came
> to pass that one day after he had left, Nadhr, son of al-Harith, came in
> and told them stories of the great Rustem and of Isfandiyar and the kings
> of Persia. Then he said, "I swear by the Lord, that the stories of
> Muhammad are not better than my own; they are nothing but tales of the
> past which he hath written out, just as I have written mine out." Then
> descended this passage: "They say these are fables of the ancients which
> he hath caused to be written down, dictated by him morning and evening.
> Say, He hath revealed the same who knoweth the sacred things in heaven
> and earth; verily he is gracious and merciful.[91] ... When our verses are
> recited unto him, he saith, 'Fables of the ancients.'[92] Woe unto every
> lying and wicked one that heareth the verses of God read unto him, then
> proudly resisteth, as if he heard them not; wherefore denounce unto him
> a fearful punishment."[93]

These stories of Rustem, Isfandiyar, and other ancient kings of Persia
are similar to what Firdausi, some centuries after the Prophet, turned into
song in his *Shah Nama*. Certainly as the Arabs used to read of the ancient
sovereigns, they could not have been ignorant of stories such as those of
Jamshid, the ascent of Ahriman out of darkness, Arta Viraf, the bridge
Chinavad, and such like. Our object is by careful search to ascertain
whether these stories and the like had any effect on the Koran and tradition. We are sure that they had, and that Perisan tales and doctrines form
one of the sources of Muslim faith. Many also of the stories, literary,
imaginative, and religious, were not confined to Iran, but were current
among the Hindus in India, and spread abroad amongst the people travelling by Herat and Merve, and so westward. It will be asked what our proof
of all this is; and we propose accordingly to quote some passages from the
Koran and tradition, and then to compare these with what may be found in
ancient Zoroastrian and Hindu writings.

We begin with *the ascent,—Miraj—of the Prophet.* The following account
of it is in sura xvii. 1: "Praise be to him who transported his servant by
night from the sacred temple (of Mecca) to the farther temple (Jerusalem)
the surroundings of which we have blessed, that we might show him some

of our signs, for he is both the hearing and the seeing One." In the interpretation of this verse the greatest difference has prevailed. Thus Ibn Ishaq gives this account from 'A'isha: "The body of the Prophet did not disappear, but the Lord carried off his soul by night." Tradition also tells us that the Prophet himself said: "Mine eyes slept, but my heart was awake."[94] Muhyi ad-Din [ibn al-'Arabi] is of the same opinion; writing of the ascent and night journey, he says, in explanation of the above passage:

> Praised be he that transported his servant; that is, released him from material surroundings, and caused a spiritual separation without any change of the body. *By night,* i.e., in darkness surrounding the physical frame; for the ascent could only be carried out spiritually through the inner senses of the body. *From the holy Masjid;* that is, from the center of a sacred heart, free from bodily corruption and sensual coverings. *To the further Masjid;* that is, the fountain of the spirit, far removed from the corporeal world, and close to the manifestation of the Almighty's glory, in order that he might the better understand that which, "We might show him some of our signs," even if they be within the heart, which can only be done in all their glory and grandeur by spiritual discernment within the soul; namely, that we can show him of our nature and perfection.

Hence, if we accept the above, together with the witness of 'A'isha, and what the Prophet himself is reported to have said, the ascent was not in body, but in spirit. But the view of others is altogether different. Thus Ibn Ishaq tells us that, according to what Muhammad said, Gabriel awoke him twice; but he went to sleep again:

> "And he came to me the third time, and made me stand up and go with him to the gate of the mosque, where, lo! there was a white steed, in appearance between a pony and an ass. Then with his hand he helped me upon it, neither of us preceding the other." (Then follows a quotation from Cotada.) The Prophet said: "When I tried to mount on Buraq he became refractory; then Gabriel touched his mane and said: 'Buraq, knowest thou what thou art doing? for, by the Lord! no servant of God hath ever mounted thee more blessed from heaven than Muhammad.' Whereupon Buraq became so ashamed that sweat poured like water from him. Then he stood still, and I mounted him." After that, (Hasan tells us) the Prophet went forward and Gabriel with him, till they reached the holy temple at Jerusalem, and there found Abraham, Moses and Jesus, with a company of prophets, whom the Prophet led in prayer. Then were

brought two vases; in one was wine and in the other milk. So the blessed Prophet took that with milk, and drank of it, and left the vase of wine alone. Then Gabriel said: "Guide unto temperance, and teach thy people so, O Muhammad, for wine is forbidden unto you." Then the Prophet returned to Mecca; and in the morning, meeting the Quraish, he told them all that happened. "By the Lord!" said the people, "what a marvellous thing. It takes our caravans a whole month to reach Syria from this, and a whole month to return; yet Muhammad has gone it all in a single night, and in the same returned!"[95]

The following is another account given by the Prophet of his night journey, as heard by Cotada:

While I was asleep, lo one came to me, close as the hair is to the skin, and took out my heart. He then brought a golden vase filled with faith, in which my heart was placed, and my stomach cleansed in the water of Zemzem, so that I was filled with faith and wisdom. Thereupon Gabriel mounted me upon Buraq (as in the previous account), and having carried me upwards to the lowest heaven called out to open the gate. "Who is this?" one cried. "It is Gabriel." "And who is with thee?" "It is Muhammad." "Was he summoned?" "O yes!" was Gabriel's answer. "Then welcome to him; how good it is that he hath come." And so he opened the gate. Entering, Gabriel said, "Here is thy father Adam; make thy salutation to him." So I made to him my salaam, and he returned it to me; on which he said, "Welcome to an excellent son and to an excellent Prophet." Then Gabriel took me up to the second heaven, and lo there were John (the Baptist) and Jesus.[96] In the third heaven there was Joseph; in the fourth Idris; in the fifth Aaron; and in the sixth Moses. As he returned the salutation of the Prophet, Moses wept, and on being asked the reason said: "I mourn because more of the people of him that was sent after me do enter Paradise than of mine." Then we ascended the seventh heaven. "This is thy father Abraham," said Gabriel, and salutation was made as before. At the last we made the final ascent, where there were beautiful fruits and leaves like the ears of an elephant. "This," said Gabriel, "is the last heaven"; and lo! four rivers, two within, and two without. "What are these, O Gabriel?" I asked. "Those within," he said, "are the rivers of Paradise; and those seen without, are the Nile and the Euphrates." Then a dwelling-place was prepared for me; and then they brought me vessels of wine and milk and honey. So I took the milk, and he said, "This is food for thee and thy people."[97]

Much more of the same kind of Muslim stories, as of Adam wailing, etc., might be given; but enough and to spare has been quoted for comparison with the sources which follow, from which it has all been derived.

I. And first as to Muhammad's *Miraj* or ascent to heaven. We begin with a Pahlavi book called *Arta Viraf Namak*, written in the days of Ardashir, some four hundred years before the Hegira. We are there told that, the Zoroastrian faith fading away, the Magi of Persia sought to revive it in the people's hearts, by sending a Zoroastrian of the above name up to heaven, with the view of bringing down tidings of what was going on there. This messenger ascended from one heaven to another, and having seen it all, was commanded by Ormazd to return to the earth, and tell it to his people. The result is contained in the above-named book, of which we shall briefly quote a few passages, freely translated, to show how far the Muslim account corresponds with the imaginary details below:

Our first advance upwards was to the Lower heaven; ... and there we saw the angel of those Holy Ones, giving forth a flaming light, brilliant and lofty. And I asked Sarosh the holy and Azar the angel: "What is this place; and these, who are they?" ... We are then told that Arta ascended similarly to the Second and Third heavens, and to many others beyond.[98]

Rising from a gold-covered throne, Bahman the archangel led me on, till he and I met Ormazd with a company of angels and heavenly leaders, all adorned so brightly that I had never seen the like before. My leader said: "This is Ormazd." I sought to salaam him, and he said he was glad to welcome me from the passing world to that bright and undefiled place. Then he bade Sarosh and the Fire-angel to show me the blessed place prepared for the holy, and that also for the punishment of the wicked. After which they carried me along till I beheld the archangels and the other angels.

At the last, says Arta, my guide and the Fire-angel having showed me Paradise, took me down to Hell; and from that dark and dreadful place, carried me upward to a beautiful spot where were Ormazd and his company of angels. I desired to salute him, on which he graciously said: "Arta Viraf, go thou to the material world; thou hast seen and now knowest Ormazd, for I am he; whosoever is true and righteous, him I know." When Ormazd began thus to speak, I became confused in mind, because I saw a brilliant light but no appearance of a body, and forthwith I perceived the unseen must be Ormazd himself.

There is no doubt a singular resemblance between the ascent of this Magian messenger, and that also told of Muhammad, to the heaven above. In the fabulous Zerdashtnama there is also an account of Zoroaster having ages before ascended to the heavens, after having received permission to visit hell, where he found Ahriman (the devil). It is remarkable that similar tales are not confined to Persia, but extend to India, where they are recorded in the Sanskrit poems. Thus Arjuna was shown over the heavens, and there saw Indra's palace, its garden with rivers and fruits, and a tree of which if one eats, he never dies, but lives in delight and enjoys all his heart desires.[99]

Many such tales are to be found not only in Zoroastrian books, but also in works of heretical Christian sects, such as "The Testament of Abraham" already noticed. The Apostle is there said to have ascended, at the bidding of one of the Cherubim, to the heavens, and there to have seen all the sights around him. Of Abraham also we have the following account:

> The archangel Michael, having descended to the earth, took Abraham in a cherub's car, raised him aloft on the cloud, with sixty angels; and from the same car showed him the whole world beneath.

This is no doubt the origin of the Buraq (ethereal horse) tradition; something like which is to be found in the Book of Enoch, where also is notice of the heavenly tree, and the four rivers of Paradise. The Jews hold that the Tree of Life in Eden is so high as to take five hundred years to reach its top,[100] and tell us numberless other stories of a similar kind.

The Muslims believe that the Garden of Eden was in the heavens above, an idea taken from many of these fictitious writings, specially that called *Visio Pauli*. Perhaps also such stories may have been derived from Zoroastrian or Hindu sources, or these from them; at any rate they are altogether imagery. If it be asked whether there is any foundation for such tales, the answer must be that there is none whatever. They must have arisen from ignorant and imaginative people seeking to amplify what we find in the Bible of the ascent of Enoch and Elias, and also of our Savior Christ, and also what Paul saw in his sleep, or Peter in his vision at Caesarea. But anyone reading these in our Scriptures will see that to compare them with the wild and fanciful tales of the East would be as sensible as to compare heaven with earth, or the fabulous *Shah Nama* with the history of the great Nadir. The origin of the Jewish and Christian fancy about the heavenly tree, the four rivers, etc., has evidently been the passage in Genesis about the Garden of Eden,[101] which the wild imagination of these people pictured as if in heaven, not knowing that the spot lay near to Babylon and Baghdad; and thus they changed the truth of God into a lie, and the divine history into childish, foolish fancies of their own.

II. *What the Koran and Tradition Tell Us Regarding Paradise*, with its houris and youths, the King of Death, etc. As our Muslim friends know well about all such matters, it is unnecessary to go into any detail about them here. Their origin is to be found altogether in Zoroastrian sources. Not a syllable is mentioned about them in the Bible, which tells us simply of the rest and peace provided for the true believer on the breast of Abraham, and the blessed place named Paradise in heaven; but not a word have we in the pages of any Jewish prophet, or New Testament writer, of houris or youths of pleasure there. The books of the Zoroastrians and Hindus, however, are full of them; and these bear the most extraordinary likeness to what we find in the Koran and tradition. Thus in Paradise we are told of "houris with large black eyes, resembling pearls hidden in their shells."[102] And just so the Zoroastrians speak of fairies—*paries* (Pairkan)—spirits in bright array and beautiful, to captivate the heart of man. The name *houry* too is derived from an Avesta or Pahlavi source, as well as *jinn* for genii, and *bihisht* (Paradise), signifying in Avestic "the better land."[103] We also have very similar tales in the old Hindu writings, of heavenly regions with their boys and girls resembling the houris and *ghilman* of the Koran. The account before given of the Prophet when he beheld Adam rejoicing at the righteous entering Paradise, and weeping at the destruction of the wicked, is also given in "The Testament of Abraham"; but with this difference that it relates to the spirits of the dead, and in the other to the spirits of those not yet born. The latter are called by the Muslims "existent ants or motes"; and though the term is Arabic, the idea is no doubt Zoroastrian, and may possibly have been taken by them from the Egyptians; but in any case the Arabs must have gained it from Persia.

We have already seen that the "Angel of Death" is a name that must have been borrowed by the Muslims from the Jews, that being his title in Hebrew. There is, however, this difference, that the Jews name him *Sammael*, and the Muslims Azrael:[104] neither word is Arabic, but Hebrew. Since, however, the idea nowhere occurs in the Bible, the Jews must have got it elsewhere, and a possible origin we may find in the Avesta, where we are told that if anyone falls into the water or fire, his death is not from the fire or water, but it is the Angel of Death that destroys him.

III. *Story of Azazil Coming Forth from Hell.*—Muslims take this name from the Jews, who call the evil spirit by the same name; but the Arabs have received the story from the Zoroastrians. According to Muslim tradition, God created Azazil, who in the seventh hell worshipped the Almighty for a thousand years; he then ascended, spending a similar term at each stage, till he reached the earth. Elsewhere we read that the devil (i.e., Azazil) stayed three thousand years close by the gate of Paradise, with hostile intentions against Adam and Eve, of whom he entertained the utmost jealousy.

In a Zoroastrian book[105] we have the following account of the devil, by name Ahriman:—

> He remained in the abyss, dark and ignorant, there to commit hurt and injury, and such mischief and darkness is the place that they term it the dark region. Ormazd, who knew all things, was aware of Ahriman's existence and designs.... Both remained thus for 3000 years, without change or action. The evil spirit was ignorant of Ormazd's existence; but eventually rising out of the pit, at last beheld the light of Ormazd.... Then, filled with hostility and envy, he set to work to destroy.

There is no doubt some difference between the two accounts: the Muslims holding that Azazil worshipped the Almighty, while the Zoroastrians say he knew him not. Still the similarity is obvious, for according to both, he came forth from the pit to destroy God's creation.

Before leaving Azazil, there is another tale of which comparison may be made between the Muslims and Zoroastrians, namely, the story of the peacock. The following is the Muslim tradition:

> Azazil kept sitting at the gate of Paradise, anxious to enter. The peacock also was there seated on a pinnacle, when he saw one repeating the mighty names of God. "Who art thou?" asked the peacock. "I am one of the angels of the Almighty"; "But why art thou sitting here?" "I am looking at Paradise and wish to enter." The peacock said, "I have no command to let anyone enter as long as Adam is there." "If thou wilt let me in," said the other, "I will teach them a prayer which if anyone repeat, three things will be his—he will never grow old; never be rebellious; nor will anyone ever turn him out of Paradise." Then Iblis (the devil) repeated the prayer. The peacock also from his pinnacle did the same, and forthwith flew up to the serpent and told him what he had heard from Iblis. We also learn that when God cast down Adam and Eve with the devil (Iblis) from Paradise, the peacock also was expelled along with them.[106]

The old Persian account of the peacock differs from the above; but they too associate him with Ahriman, for Eznik in his book *Against Heresies* writes as follows:

> The Zoroastrians tell us that Ahriman spake as follows: "It is not the case that I am unable to do anything good myself, but that I do not wish it; and to make this thing certain, I have produced the peacock."

So the peacock having been the creation of Azazil, it is quite consistent with the Muslim tradition that he should be his assistant, and with him have been cast down from Paradise.

IV. *The Light of Muhammad.*—Muhammad is reputed by tradition to have said: "The first thing created by the Almighty was my light."[107] Again:

> When Adam was created, the Lord having placed that light upon his forehead, said, "O Adam, this light which I place upon his forehead is that of the greatest and best of thy descendants, the light of the chief of prophets that shall be sent. This light descended from Adam to Seth, and then in successive generations to Abdallah, and from him to Amina at the time of Muhammad's conception."[108]

We are further told by the traditionists that the Prophet is reputed to have spoken thus:

> The Almighty parted that light into four sections, from which he made the heavens, the pen, Paradise, and believers; each of these four he again divided into four: from the first he formed me, who am the Prophet; from the second he formed reason placed in the believer's head; from the third modesty within the believer's eye; and from the fourth love within his heart.[109]

Let us compare this with the Zoroastrian views:—

> In a very ancient book, Ormazd is represented as having created the world and the universe, angels and archangels, and the heavenly intellect, all out of his own light, with the praise of boundless time.[110]

Again, from a still much older work, we quote as follows:

> A grand and royal halo long attached itself to Jamshid, lord of the good flock, while he ruled over the seven climes—demons, men, fairies, wiz-

ards, sorcerers, and evil-doers.... Then when he approved of that false and baseless word, the visible halo departed from him in the form of a flying bird.... When Jamishid, lord of the good flock, no longer saw that halo, he became devoid of joy, and in distress gave himself up to making enmity upon earth. The first time that halo was removed from Jamshid, it departed from Jam, son of Vivaghan (the sun), in the form of a Varagh bird, and Mithra seized the halo. When a second time the halo was removed from Jamshid, it departed as before in the form of a bird; then Faridun the brave took that halo.... When that halo departed the third time from Jamshid, it was taken by Keresaspa (Garshasp), that great and powerful man.[111]

Now if we bring these two accounts together, and remember that according to the Avesta, Jamshid was the first man created by God upon earth, and therefore the same as Adam, the father of mankind, we see at once that the light which from Jamshid descended on the best of his posterity agrees with what tradition speaks of as the light of Muhammad, which Muslims appear thus to have borrowed from the Zoroastrians. We also gather that what appears in the Zoroastrian book about Jamshid ruling over men, genii, giants, etc., is very similar to what the Jews write of Soloman, evidently from the same source, and taken from them by the Muslims, as indeed has been seen in our third chapter. Also what the Muslims write about the division of the Prophet's light, coincides closely with what appears in a Zoroastrian book,[112] and was evidently taken from that source.

V. *The Bridge Sirat.*—Muslims tell us the Prophet held that at the last day after the Judgment, all mankind will pass over this bridge, which is finer than a hair, and sharper than a sword; and that the wicked will fall from it into hell. Now what is the origin of the name Sirat? Though adopted into Arabic, it is of Persian origin, and called by the ancient Zoroastrians *Chinavad*,[113] and its history is also derived from them, as will be seen from the following account taken from one of their ancient writings:

I flee from much sin and I keep my conduct pure. The keeping pure of the six vital powers—conduct, speech, thought, intellect, reason, wisdom—according to thy will, O author of the power to do good works, with justice do I perform it, that service of thine, in thought, speech, and deed. It is good for me to abide in the bright way, lest I arrive at the severe punishment of hell, that I may cross over Chinavad and may reach the blest abode, full of odor, entirely delightful, always bright.[114]

The meaning of the Persian name is "the connecting link," the bridge being that which joins earth with Paradise.

VI. The Muslims say that each prophet before his death gives notice of the next to follow, as Abraham did of Moses, Moses of David, and so on. Nothing of this sort, however, is in the Bible; on the contrary the prophets from first to last gave notice of the coming of the Messiah, and nothing more. As they could not therefore have got this notion from the Scriptures, from whence then could it have come? There is a work[115] believed by the Zoroastrians to have been written in the language of heaven, and, about the time of Khusru Parwez, to have been translated in the Dari tongue.[116] It comprises fifteen books said to have descended upon fifteen prophets; last of all came the sixteenth, Zoroaster himself. At the end of each book, the name is given of the prophet that is next to follow. These books no doubt are an ancient forgery, but apparently the Muslim traditionists took their idea of the anticipated coming of each prophet from them. Again, the second verse in each of these books opens with: "In the name of God, the Giver of gifts, the Beneficent"; similar to the words at the opening of all the suras,[117] "In the name of God the Merciful and Gracious." We also find the first words in another Zoroastrian book[118] to be very similar, namely, "In the name of Ormazd the Creator." We have already noticed that the five times of Muslim prayer are the same as five of the seven common to the Zoroastrians and Sabaeans, no doubt taken from them.

Many other things might have been added common to the two systems; but it would have swelled our pages beyond reasonable dimensions; and we must be content with what has been give,

VII. Some may hold it difficult to understand how Muhammad could have obtained such stories and matters as we find in the Koran and tradition from Zoroastrian sources; and further, how it was possible for the "unlearned" Prophet to have become informed of them. But tradition[119] tells us as follows: "It was his practice to converse in their own tongue (so we read) with people of every nation who visited him; and hence the introduction of some Perisan words into the Arabic language." Again, as the Prophet introduced Jewish tales, and also the stories and customs of Arabian heathen, into the Koran, what wonder that he should do so likewise with Perisan tales? Many of these, moreover, were current among the Arabs, as al-Kindy tells us: "Suppose we relate to thee such fables as those of Ad, Thamud and the She-camel, the Companions of the Elephant, and such like, it would only be the way of old women who spend their days and nights in such foolish talk."

In the *Sirat al-Rasul*,[120] we learn that Muhammad had among the companions a Persian called Salman, who at the siege of Medina advised him to surround the city with a trench, and when fighting with the Thaqif helped the Muslims with a catapult. Now it is said that some of the Prophet's opponents spoke of this person as having assisted him in the composition of the Koran, an accusation noticed in sura xvi.105, as follows: "And, verily, we know that they say, 'Truly a certain man teacheth him'; but the tongue of him unto whom they incline is a foreign one, while this is the tongue of perspicuous Arabic." Now if these objectors simply spoke of this Persian helping in the style of the Prophet's composition, the answer would have been sufficient. But when we find that much of the Koran and tradition has the closest resemblance to the contents of the Zoroastrian books, the answer is of no value whatever. On the contrary, the above verse shows, by the admission of the Prophet himself, that he was assisted by the Persian Salman. Hence even from this story it is clear that the Zoroastrian writings formed one of the sources of Islam.

Chapter VI.

The Hanefites: Their Influence on Muhammad and on His Teaching

Before the time of Muhammad, there were a few inquirers from amongst the Arabs who had a strong aversion from idolatry, and who accordingly sought to find relief in a better faith. Amongst the Jews, and possibly from ancient tradition still surviving, it was known in Arabia that Abraham was a worshipper of the one true God. Hence both at Mecca and Medina, and also at Tayif, we find that there were men who, seeking after the truth, had abandoned the worship of idols; and these were called Hanefites. The names of six of these are given in the margin, some having also followers of their own. Now we hold that these inquirers, and especially Zaid ibn Amr, had a very marked effect, by their conceptions, conversation, and example, upon the Prophet, as we find from the contents of the Koran. Of all the authorities on the subject, that of the Ibn Ishaq and Ibn Hisham as contained in the *Sirat*,[121] is by far the oldest, and being nearest Hegira, the most reliable that we have. The details of this work were learned from Zohry (d. A.H. 124), who knew a succession of the companions, and in

Abu Amir .... Medina	
'Ummeya .... Tayif	
Waraqa ⎫	
'Ubaidallah ⎬ .... Mecca	
'Uthman ⎪	
Zaid ⎭	

especial Orva, a relation of 'A'isha. Zohry's book no longer exists, but much has been preserved in that of his pupil, Ibn Ishaq (d. A.H. 151), from which we have quotations in the *Sirat* of Ibn Hisham (d. A.H. 213). No doubt in these writings there is a vast amount of the fanciful and exaggerated; but much also is valuable as giving men's impressions, and memory of facts, as they existed at the time. We take, therefore, from the *Sirat* the following account of the Hanefites:

The Quraish were once gathered together during their *'id* [holiday] beside one of their idols, slaying sacrifices, praying, and making circuits around it, as they used to do at this festival every year. Just then four friends stood apart, and spoke secretly to one another in righteous terms. These were Waraqa, 'Ubaidallah, grandson of Abdal Mutalib, 'Uthman and Zaid ibn Amr. They said: "By the Lord! our people have nothing left of the faith of Abraham. What is this stone that we should encircle it? It can neither hear nor speak, neither hurt nor help. O our people! look out for your souls, for by the Lord ye are altogether wanting." Then they separated and departed into various lands to find out the true faith of Abraham. *Waraqa* embraced the Christian religion, and studying the books of its people, became fixed in their faith. *'Ubaidallah* remained in his doubts, but at last embraced Islam; then with a party of the Muslims he emigrated to Abyssinia along with his wife Umm Habibah, daughter of Abu Sufyan and also a believer. There, however, he afterwards became a Christian, and perished. When he was converted to Christianity, he said to his companions: "We see, but ye are only blinking"—that is, cannot see plainly, like a whelp trying to open its eyes. The Prophet himself married his widow, Umm Habibah, sending over a follower for that purpose to the Najashy, who himself concluded the marriage ceremonial—the dower being 400 dinars, which formed a precedent for time to come. Now as to *'Uthman*, he repaired to the court of the emperor of Byzantium, where he obtained high rank and embraced the Christian faith. . . .

Last of all we come to *Zaid*, who stood fast, joining neither the Jewish nor the Christian religion. He broke off from his own people's faith, and gave up idols, the eating of carrion, blood, the slaughter of animals for the gods, and the putting of daughters to death. He said: "I worship the God of Abraham"; but he blamed his people for having chosen evil ways. There is a tradition from Amina, daughter of Abu Bakr that she once saw Zaid, then very aged, leaning with his back on Ka'aba, and thus addressing the people: "O Quraish! by Him in whose hand is the life of Zaid ibn Amr I swear, that not one of you professeth the faith of Abraham, but me alone." Then he prayed: "O Lord! if I but knew what way was most pleasing unto thee, I would worship thee in that manner; but I know it not." Then putting the palms of his hands to the ground, he bent his body down in worship. We are also told that Muhammad being asked by his relations to pray that Zaid might be forgiven, consented, "for he shall be raised up alone, like a community."[122] Zaid wrote the following lines regarding his parting with his people's faith, and what happened to him therefrom—

Am I to worship one or a thousand
I have altogether forsaken Lât
    and 'Uzza,
Hence I neither worship 'Uzza nor her
    two daughters,
Neither do I worship Ghanam,

I was astonished, and had strange
    thoughts in the night seasons.
Since the Lord destroyeth multitudes
And many others he preserveth for
    their goodness,
Are Divine affairs divided thus?
Thus should every brave and
    thoughtful man.
Nor the two idols of the Beni Amr,
    nor do pilgrimage unto them.
Though I did regard him my Lord,
    when I had little understanding.
And in the daytime the seeing will
    understand.
Because their works are evil;
And cherisheth the little ones.

Amongst us, one day man will
    stumble;
But I now worship my Lord Most
    Merciful;
Therefore observe the fear of the
    Lord your God;
Thou shalt see the home of the pure
    in the Gardens;
During this life disgrace,

And the next, he will be as the branch
    fed by the rain.
That the Compassionate Lord may
    pardon my sin.
So long as ye do so, ye shall not
    perish;
But for the unbelievers, flaming hell-
    fire;
And after death that which shall
    bitterly cramp their breasts.

We further learn from Ibn Hisham that Zaid was expelled from Mecca; and being forbidden to remain there, had to live on Mount Hira, opposite the city. The Prophet himself in the summertime used every year to retire, as the Arabs used to do, into a cave in the sacred mount for solitary meditation; and so we believe that he must often have met his relative Zaid there. For he used still to go after his call to be a Prophet, as we learn from Ibn Ishaq: "Gabriel by the mercy of the Lord came to him at Hira in Ramazan...This he did every year, according to the custom of the Quraish in the days of ignorance, to be alone and refresh their souls." Now everyone acquainted with the Koran and tradition cannot but perceive how alike is the teaching of both, and that they must have had the greatest influence on each other, in their views about such things for instance as idol worship, the burying alive of infant girls, the unity of God, Paradise and Hell, and calling God "the Lord most Merciful and Compassionate." Again, Zaid and the Hanefites, like the Prophet, followed Abraham, calling him by the same name (Hanif) as their own, in illustration of which we may quote sura iv. 126: "Who is of better religion than he who resigneth himself unto God, and followeth the faith of Abraham the Orthodox" (Hanif)....And again, sura iii. 89: "Say, The Lord hath said truly, 'Follow the faith of Abraham the Orthodox (Hanif), for he was not one of the idolators.'" And again, sura vi. 162: "Verily the Lord hath guided me into the right way, the true faith, the religion of Abraham the Orthodox" (Hanif). And thus we see the Prophet calls himself and his people by the name Hanif. The word, indeed, originally signified "unclean" or "apostate," and was so used by the idolatrous Arabs of Zaid, because he abandoned the worship of their gods. The name pleased the Prophet and was used by him in a good sense. We must not forget, however, that all the four Hanefites were themselves, as already said, nearly related to the Prophet— 'Ubaidallah being nephew to Muhammad who took his widow 'Umm Habibah to wife, while Waraqa and 'Uthman were sons of two aunts of Khadija. Hence the views, sayings, and teaching of these Hanefites cannot but have had decided influence on the Prophet. We may also remember that though the Prophet is believed to have said that he had no right even to pray for the salvation of his own mother, yet he did so for Zaid and his blessedness hereafter. From all this we see that the Prophet recognized his principles, and attested them as right.

But now some of our objectors may say, Suppose we accept as true all that you have told us of the various sources from which Islam is derived; then it would prove that Muhammad himself had personally no influence on the faith—a thing hard to believe. Certainly, we reply, it is impossible to imagine that as Muhammad himself was the author of the faith, his own purpose and mind had no effect in the structure; just as in a building the use of stones, etc., in its erection, does not detract from the skill and ability of the architect, without whom they would be of no possible use. And in like manner, as the edifice of Islam has its own established character, and differs from all other religions, it is clear that it is the work of one possessed of the highest gifts and power; and, from the beauty of the composition of the Koran we see that he was singularly wise and eloquent. Moreover, from his life as given in tradition, and the history of his time, the personality of the Prophet is manifest in the Koran. Thus before his flight to Medina, being a mere ordinary citizen of Mecca, he made no mention in the passages given forth there, of force or war for the extension of the faith.

But, *first*, after the Hegira, when he had gained the powerful body of the Ansars for his followers, he gave them leave to defend themselves and beat off their opponents. Thus in sura xxii. 40: "Permission is given to them to fight, because they are persecuted...those who have been turned out of their houses without just cause other than they say, Our Lord is God"; and it is allowed by the commentaries, that this was the first revelation giving permission to fight.

Second, some time after, when Muhammad had gained victories over his enemies, this simple permission was changed into command, as we find in sura ii. 212, 214: "War is enjoined you, but it is hateful unto you. . . . They will ask thee concerning the sacred month, whether they may war therein. Say—To war therein is grievous, but to obstruct the way of God, and infidelity towards him and the holy Masjid, and to drive out his people from thence, is more grievous in the sight of God; and temptation (to idolatry) is more grievous than to kill." The instruction in this passage being that the Muslims should war against the Quraish even in the sacred months, because they prevented them from visiting the Ka'aba.

Third, when in the sixth year of the Hegira, the Prophet had conquered the Bani Quraiza and other tribes, he issued still sterner commands against his adversaries, as we find in sura v. 37: "The recompense of those who fight against God and his Apostle, and study to act corruptly on the earth, is that they shall be slain or crucified, or have their hands and their feet cut off on the opposite sides (of the body), or be banished from the land. Such shall be their disgrace in this world, and in the next they shall suffer a grievous punishment." The commentators hold that this terrible command relates to idolators only, and not to Jews and Christians.

Fourth. But towards these also, the attitude of the Prophet towards the end of his life entirely changed; and so we read in the last revealed sura (ix. 5, 29) that after the four sacred months had passed, they should again commence war, as follows: "And when the sacred months are ended, kill the idolators wheresoever ye find them, take them prisoners and beseige them, and lay wait for them in every convenient place. But if they repent, and offer up the appointed prayers, and pay the legal alms, then dismiss them freely, for God is gracious and merciful.... Fight against those who believe not in God, nor in the last day, nor forbid that which God and his apostle have forbidden, and profess not the true religion, namely, of those to whom the Scriptures have been given, until they pay tribute by the hand, and be reduced low."

And so we learn from these successive passages in the Koran, that the great and unchanging Almighty God, step by step, allowed his divine law to be altered as the Prophet and his followers gradually gained successive victories by the sword. Not only so, but we see the same liberty of change permitted in respect of certain passages in the Koran to be cancelled by other passages; thus in sura ii. 100: "We abrogate no verse, or cause it to be left out, but we bring in its place a better, or one like unto it. Ah! dost thou not know that God is over all things almighty?"

Hence so long as Muhammad entertained the hope of bringing together both Jews and Christians, and also the Arab tribes, by the retention of some of their national practices, there seemed to him the possibility of uniting all Arabia in one grand religion. But when he found this to be impracticable, then it remained for him either to abandon and eventually destroy the two former, or else lose the native Arabs as a whole. The objects and the mind of the Prophet are manifest throughout his prophetic life. Thus, to take an instance, the marriage with Zainab, wife of his adopted son Zaid, as justified in the Koran,[123] shows how much the revelation and whole system of the day was permeated by the objects of his hourly life and personal surroundings which indeed is manifest in a multitude of other matters in the Koran itself and in tradition. And certainly, when we look at the variety of teaching and of interests embodied in these, we gain a wide and extensive survey of the thousand rills which run along to form the vast Muslim river—sources they all are of Islam, but every one affected by the intellect, the nature, and the personal aims and objects of the Prophet himself.

We readily admit the many precious truths and lessons taught in the Koran, above all the unity of Almighty God; and, among such stories as those about the table, paradise, the tree Tuba, etc., we often find good and valuable teaching. But anyone who has drunk of the pure and sparkling stream, will turn from all others, especially if turbid anywhere, and seek refreshment in the water of life, so often borne testimony to in the Koran itself; and what is that blessed fountain but the writings of the prophets and apostles, to which Muhammad in the following passages himself bears such remarkable testimony: "Verily we have sent down the Torah, in which are direction and light.... And we caused Jesus, son of Mary, to follow in their footsteps, confirming that which was in his hands of the Torah, and we gave him the Gospel in which is guidance and light and attestation of that which was revealed before it of the Torah, and a direction and admonition to the pious."[124]

Whosoever, then, desires to know what was the faith of Father Abraham, the friend of God, let him diligently read the Torah of Moses, so strongly borne testimony to in the above verses of the Koran; and there he will find the blessed promise given him by the Almighty, that the one divine savior, the Lord Jesus Christ, was to come of the descendants of Abraham and of his son Isaac. The patriarch accepted the promise, and believed in the coming Messiah, as we see in a passage of the Torah, where God spoke thus to Abraham: "And God said, 'Sarah thy wife shall bear thee a son indeed; and thou shalt call his name Isaac: and I will establish my covenant with him for an everlasting covenant, and with his seed after him.'"[125] The same promise is repeated again in the Book of Genesis to Abraham: "And in thy seed shall all the nations of the earth be blessed, because thou hast obeyed my voice."[126] And Jesus himself refers to this promise when he said to the Jews: "Your father Abraham rejoiced to see my day; and he saw it and was glad."[127] The apostle Paul also makes mention of the same expectation: "To Abraham and his seed were the promises made. He saith not,—And to seeds, as of many; but as of One, And to thy seed, which is Christ"; and again: "If ye be Christ's, then are ye Abraham's seed, and heirs according to promise."[128]

May the gracious and compassionate Lord, who hath in his infinite mercy fulfilled this his eternal covenant, grant that the humble writer and the kind reader of these pages, may, along with the blessed patriarch, be made partakers of the heavenly inheritance thus promised through our Savior Jesus Christ. And to his name be glory.

Amen, so let it be!

13.

The Jewish Foundation of Islam
Charles Cutler Torrey

Allah and Islam

*T*HE LESSONS WHICH MUHAMMAD LEARNED, in one way or another, from the Israelites of Mecca gave him a new horizon. The idea of the Prophet and his mission and authority, and the picture of the chosen people holding the religious leadership of the nations of the earth, illustrated in the written records of the past from the very beginning, meant more to the Meccan tradesman than any other of his acquisitions. He not only gained a new conception of human history, but began to see that it is all religious history, directed in its successive periods by Allah and his prophets. The choice of the Arabs was one link in a continuous chain, and the revelation given to them through their Prophet was the last stage in a process which began with Adam. Moreover, the thought of "Islam" (whenever this took shape in Muhammad's mind) must take in not only the Arabs, but also the other peoples of the earth. Allah had not simply transferred his interest from the children of Israel (i. e., the Jews and Christians) to the children of Ishmael; he was the "Lord of the Worlds," holding all races in his hand. The preferred people has a certain responsibility for its

Originally published as the third and fourth lecture in *The Jewish Foundation of Islam* (New York: Jewish Institute of Religion Press, Bloch Publishing Co., 1933), pp. 62–126.

fellows. The Hebrew scriptures took account of foreign nations, and assigned them to their places with authority; the prophets were much concerned with them; Jonah was sent to Nineveh to convert its population. The great table in the tenth chapter of Genesis (of which Muhammad certainly had some knowledge) classified the races of the earth according to their genealogy.

All this was food for the Arabian Prophet's thought, but not material for his use. He had neither the knowledge of the outside world nor the interest in it which would lead him to make his Koran range abroad. The idea of a sketch of religious history, connected or disconnected, could hardly have occurred to him, nor would any such undertaking have served his purpose. His concern was with the Arabs, with the Israelites whose inheritance they had received, and especially with the Hebrew prophets as his own predecessors. The one and only place in which the Koran ventures outside Arabia, either in connection with events of its own day, or in prophecy of the future, is the remarkable passage at the beginning of the thirtieth sura, where the Prophet takes momentary notice of a contemporary event in Syria, a military incident in the Greco-Persian war about which some information had reached Mecca: "The Greeks are beaten, in a near part of the land; but after their defeat they themselves shall conquer, in a few years." This singular prediction is probably not a *vaticinium ex eventu* (though the Greeks *did* ultimately conquer), but the expression of the Prophet's conviction that the "people of the Book" were bound to triumph over the unbelievers.

The "history" contained in the Koran consists mainly of bits of narration taken from the Old Testament and the Jewish Midrash. This fragmentary material, usually scattered along in the most casual way, occupies a large portion of the growing volume, especially the part produced in the middle years of the Prophet's public career. The earliest suras, prevailingly brief, consist chiefly of impassioned exhortation. Muhammad is here the preacher, proclaiming, warning, and promising. In the last years of his life, at Medina, he is so occupied with legislation and other practical matters as to leave little room for storytelling, even if that which he regarded as essential had not already been provided. It is during the latter years of his Meccan ministry, especially, that he gives a large amount of space to the "old stories" (as his skeptical countrymen impolitely termed them). He himself was highly interested in the tales of the ancients, the wonders which Allah wrought among them, the deeds and experiences of their famous men, from Adam and his family down to the seven sleepers of

Ephesus and the martyrs of Nejran. The Arabs must now be told all this, and learn it as the preliminary stage of their own religious history. Moreover, the stories would help him to gain a hearing. Thus he says at the beginning of the twelfth sura, dealing with Joseph and his fortunes, "We now narrate to you a most beautiful tale."[1] And in fact, these little anecdotes of prophets and heroes undoubtedly led many to listen who otherwise would have paid no attention to the new teacher.

Muhammad was both sincere and wise in his effort to give the new religion of the Arabs its secure foundation in the past, and to claim its affiliation with the great religions which had preceded. And he had in mind, in his constant reference to biblical personages and incidents, not merely the instruction and inspiration of his countrymen, but also the effect on another audience. The ideas which had awakened him and changed his whole view of life were not his own discovery, but were the fruits of his intercourse with the Jews of Mecca, possibly (though not probably) also with Christians, either at home or abroad. These counselors should hear the revelation now given by Allah to his Arabian Prophet. In Muhammad's thought, Islam was not at all a new religion, but merely a continuation. The Koran, he declares many times over, "confirms" the scriptures already existing. Jews and Christians (he hardly distinguished between them at first) would be glad to hear more about Moses and Solomon and Jesus. He felt that he was giving them support, and expected them to support him in return.

There was another consideration which weighed heavily. The history of the past, from beginning to end, was the story of his own predecessors. He was filled with the thought of those favored men who stood so near to the One God, and by him had been commissioned to teach their people. They were "prophets" (*nebiyim, anbiya'*) one and all, and the fact ever foremost in his mind was the way in which their message had been received, or rather rejected, by the most of their contemporaries. His own experience, as soon as he had fairly begun preaching to the people of Mecca, showed him very clearly what opposition a prophet is likely to encounter. The new teaching is not received with gratitude and awe; it is laughed at. Thus Noah was ridiculed by his people, until they were drowned in the flood. So the men of Sodom and Gomorrah jeered at Lot, until the fire came down from heaven. The Israelites of the exodus from Egypt would not submit to the authority of Moses but rebelled against him; and for their obduracy they perished in the desert. In general, the Hebrew prophets were very badly treated; so Muhammad's informants told him. It is easy to see why the Koran abounds in passages dealing with the heroes and patriarchs of the Old Testament. There are lessons here "for those who have intelligence," the Meccan Prophet keeps reiterating. The truth prevailed, in spite of opposition; the unbelievers roasted in Gehennama; and—most important of all—the religion proclaimed by these ancient mouthpieces of God is precisely the one which is now announced, in its final and most perfect form, to the people of Arabia.

There were also lessons from Arabian history. Muhammad and his fellow-countrymen had seen the ruins of vanished cities, and had heard of many others. There were traditions of the *sail al-'arim* (34:15),* the bursting of the great dam at Ma'rib in Yemen, and the destruction of the city by the resulting flood. This was a judgment from heaven. Far more striking were the signs of vanished splendor, of a high civilization now utterly obliterated, in the regions north of the Hijaz. The tribes of Ad and Thamud, and the cities of Midian had perished, leaving behind only a few very impressive traces. Why were these prosperous peoples wiped out of existence? Muhammad's imagination gave the answer. Each one of them had its prophet, who preached Islam. They would not hear, and therefore God destroyed them. But the Koranic narratives dealing with these events were, after all, of secondary importance. Islam was for the world, and the emphasis must be laid on persons and events which were known and acknowledged the world over. The three rejected prophets of the northern desert and Sinai were indeed important in Muhammad's scheme of religious history, but they were small links in a great chain. When the merchants of Quraish traveled into Egypt, Syria, Mesopotamia, and Abyssinia, they would meet no one who had ever heard of Hud, or Salih, or Shu'aib; but in every city where they halted they would find multitudes to whom the names of Noah, Abraham, Joseph, David, Elijah, and "Jesus the son of Mary" were perfectly familiar.

A very striking feature of the Koranic scraps of Israelite history is the rabbinic element—gleanings from Talmud and Midrash—so frequently in evidence. This has always been the subject of comment and conjecture. Thus H. P. Smith, *The Bible and Islam*, p. 77, says of Muhammad's story of Moses, "From Jewish tradition he asserts: that Moses refused all Egyptian nurses; that the people at Mount Sinai demanded to see God, and on seeing him fell dead, but were revived by divine power; and that they refused to

---

*Refers to the sura and verse number of the Koran.

accept the covenant until the mountain was lifted up bodily and held over them (28:11; 2:53, 60; 7:170). The information that the golden calf, through the magic of its maker, *bellowed,* is found in rabbinical sources." Geiger, *Was hat Muhammad ... aufgenommen?,* pp. 154–172 [see chapter 11 of this volume], had discussed these and other similar features of the story. The remark is made in Nöldeke-Schwally, p. 8, that the source of Muhammad's knowledge of biblical characters and events was less the Bible than the extracanonical literature. This, I think, states the matter not quite correctly, for even in the stories where Muhammad makes largest use of the Haggada there is frequent evidence that he knew also the canonical account. Wellhausen, *Reste* (1st ed.), p. 205, in his argument for the Christian origin of Islam, handles this Jewish Haggada in a very gingerly manner. "Es ist wahrscheinlich, dass Muhammed denselben durch jüdische Vermittlung zugeführt bekommen hat, wenngleich man dessen eingedenk bleiben muss, dass derselbe Segenstoff auch bei den orientalischen Christen im Umlauf war, und dass die Haggada ihre Quelle grossenteils in apokryphen Schriften hatte, die wenn sie auch jüdischen Ursprungs waren doch seit dem zweiten Jahrhundert immer ausschliesslicher in christlichen Besitz übergingen."* I confess myself unable to see light in this argument, nor do I know any sound reason for doubting that Muhammad received his Haggada directly from Jews. Wellhausen felt this to be a weak point; for he at once proceeds to draw a line between the religious material of the Koran and the *stories,* which he would have us believe to be merely the fruit of the prophet's intellectual curiosity. It therefore, he declares, is a matter of very little importance, whence Muhammad obtained the legends; and the fact that some "chance" brought him into contact with a man who was acquainted with Jewish lore is not really significant. To this, an advocate of the contrary view would reply, that the legends are the *Vorgeschichte* of Islam; the account of Allah's dealing with men in the past, from which may be learned something in regard to his dealing in the present; the indispensable fabric of the doctrine of "the prophet of Allah." And if it was by mere "chance" that Muhammad was given Israelite instruction, it was a chance that lasted many years, and gave the Koran the most, and the best, of its material.

---

* "It is probable that Muhammad was introduced to the same material through Jewish intermediaries, even though one must keep in mind that the same sacred material was also in circulation among eastern Christians and that the Haggada has its source for the most part in apocryphal writings; even though these were also of Jewish origin, they were in the exclusive possession of Christians since the second century."

Muhammad's heroes of the past are almost all designated by him as "prophets"; they received the truth from Allah, and taught it to their children and their contemporaries. Adam was a prophet (20:120; 3:30); so were Ishmael, and David, and Job. In all, twenty-five are named; among them are the three Arabian prophets, Hud, Salih, and Shu'aib, and the three from the Gospel: Zachariah, John the Baptist, and Jesus. All the rest are from the Old Testament. A list of eighteen, containing only biblical names, is given in sura 6:83–6. In 33:7 there is an instructive list of the most important of the prophets, those with whom Allah made a special covenant. The names are these: Muhammad, Noah, Abraham, Moses, and Jesus. (The fact that Muhammad is named first is due merely to the literary form of the passage.) It is very noticeable that the Koran knows nothing of Isaiah, Jeremiah, and Ezekiel, nor has knowledge of any of the minor prophets with the exception of Jonah. This certainly does not mean that the books of these prophets were wanting at Mecca, but simply, that they were utterly beyond Muhammad's comprehension and outside his interests. His instructors knew better than to try to introduce him to these abstruse writings. Jonah, the little storybook, was in a class by itself. We might indeed have expected to find some mention of Daniel; but he also, it seems, did not enter Muhammad's horizon.

It must always be borne in mind that we cannot tell with certainty, from the Koran, what portions of the Old Testament the Prophet had heard. He makes use only of what is important for his purpose, as we learn from an occasional allusion to persons or events not otherwise treated. As a matter of fact, he shows some acquaintance with each of the five books of the Torah, and with the "historical books" from Joshua to 2 Kings. The book of Joshua, indeed, is represented only in the person of the prophet Dhu 'l-Kifl, who will receive notice presently; while a bit of the book of Judges, taken from the story of Gideon, has strayed into the narrative of "Saul and Goliath" (see the fourth lecture [next section]). Barely mentioned, for instance, are Azar, named in 6:74 as the father (!) of Abraham (evidently el-Azar, derived from the Eliezer of Gen. 15:2); 'Imran (Amram), named as the father of Moses, Aaron, and Miriam (identified with the Virgin Mary); Samuel, introduced without name as the prophet who anointed Saul as king; Elijah and Elisha. Also the wives of Noah, Lot, and Pharaoh, of whom the first two are assigned to everlasting fire. The influence of the Jewish Haggada constantly appears. Rabbinical sources for the Koranic narratives of Cain, Noah, Lot, and Aaron have been pointed out by Geiger, and others are soon to he mentioned. For a few interesting bits of legend which sound like Jewish lore—the incident of the breakers of the Sabbath, who were changed to apes (2:61; 4:50; 5:65; 7:166); David's invention of coats of mail (21:80); and how Job produced a spring of cool water by stamping on the ground, and thereafter was permitted to fulfill his hasty oath by beating his wife with a bundle of leaves instead of with a rod (38:41–43)—no Haggadic source is known.

Muhammad did his best with *Arabian* religious history, though he had little at hand that he could use. He thought of Hud, the prophet of the people 'Ad, Salih, the prophet of Thamud, and perhaps especially Shu'aib, the prophet of Midian, as preachers sent to peoples very closely related to the Arabs; and he introduces them frequently, sometimes in passages of considerable length, in the suras of the Meccan period. The incident of the elephant brought to the neighborhood of Mecca by the army of Abraha, the Abyssinian viceroy of Yemen, at about the middle of the sixth century, is made the subject of the very early sura 105, as an example of the might of Allah, who "brought their cunning plans to nought." In another sura of about the same time there is mention of "the men of the ditch, of the blazing fire; when they sat above it, witnessing what they were doing to the believers" (85:4–7). I have no doubt, in spite of the arguments of Geiger (p. 189) and Horovitz (pp. 92 f.), that this refers to the persecution of the Christians of Nejran by the Yemenite Jewish ruler Dhu Nuwas, shortly before the time of the viceroy Abraha.[2] It seems quite plain that the Koran is dealing here with a historical event, and persecution for religious faith is clearly stated in vs. 8. Muhammad treats the story as something well known in Mecca.

There is another feature of Arabian history, seemingly remote from Israelite influence, which occupied Muhammad's attention. There were certain ancient practices, religious and social, which were deeply imbedded in the life of the people; the property not merely of the Hijaz, but of the Arabian peninsula. The customs and ceremonies connected with the Ka'ba at Mecca had much to do with the commercial and friendly intercourse of the tribes, and the "house" itself was venerated far and wide. We may be sure that Muhammad intended, from the first, to preserve every time-honored element of the native "paganism" which did not involve idolatry. Neither the people of Mecca and Yathrib and Ta'if, nor the Bedouin tribesmen, would have been willing to abandon their ancestral rites and practices for no obviously compelling reason; and Muhammad would have been the last man to wish them to do so. It was imperative for his scheme of things to plant the new religion as deeply in the soil of Arabia as in that of the Hebrew and Christian revelations. This he could do by the help of the patriarch Ishmael, as will appear.

It is not necessary to review here the long list of personages of ancient history whose names and deeds play so important a part in the Koran. A considerable part of the Hebrew history and haggadic legend thus reproduced will be touched upon in the course of the next lecture, dealing with the Koranic narratives. At that time (if Allah wills) a goodly number of biblical characters (including Alexander the Great) will be introduced in their Arabian dress; so that sooner or later all the members of the "long list" shall have received mention, at least by name. Some of this Jewish-Muslim material has been well treated by Geiger, other writers have occupied themselves chiefly or wholly with the post-Muhammadan legends, as for example Weil's *Biblische Legenden der Muselmänner,* 1845 (also translated into English), and the important essays by Max Grünbaum and Israel Schapiro. The proper names in the Koran have been admirably treated by Josef Horovitz in his article, "Jewish Proper Names and Derivatives in the Koran," in the *Hebrew Union College Annual,* II (1925), 145–184, and again in the second part of his *Koranische Untersuchungen* (1926).

The present lecture will pay special attention to two subjects which are of prime importance for our understanding of the foundations of Islam: the source of Muhammad's ideas regarding Jesus and the Christian religion, and the place occupied by Abraham and Ishmael in his conception of the revelation to the Arabs. Before dealing with these three "prophets," however, I shall notice very briefly a few others, for whom the mere mention by name seems, for one reason or another, hardly sufficient.

It is perhaps needless to say, that the Hebrew chronology of the Koran is not one of its strong points. Muhammad had some idea of the long time that must have elapsed since Moses; though he certainly knew nothing of the complete line of descent which the Muslim genealogists carried back from his family, and from the Arab tribes generally, to Adam and Eve. He knew, as early (at least) as the thirty-seventh sura, something of the succession of Hebrew heroes, and was aware that the prophet-kings, Saul, David, and Solomon, were subsequent to the patriarchs; however hazy his ideas were as to the order of the other prophets and the time at which they lived. He had fantastic notions (as others have had) in regard to Ezra, and evidently had no idea where to locate him. Elijah and Elisha, Job, Jonah, and "Idris," are left by him floating about, with no secure resting place. He had heard nothing whatever as to the genealogy of Jesus (the claimed descent from David), nor of his contemporaries (excepting the family of John the Baptist), nor of any Christian history. He associated Moses with Jesus, evidently believing that very soon after the revelation to the Hebrew law-giver there had followed the similar revelation which had produced the Christians and their sacred book. This appears in his identification of Mary the mother of Jesus with Miriam the sister of Moses and Aaron, plainly stated in more than one place. In all this there is nothing surprising, when it is remembered how the Prophet received his information.

A Few "Minor" Prophets. The incident in the life of *Adam* which is oftenest dwelt upon in the Koran is the refusal of the devil (*Iblis, Shaitan*) to obey the divine command to the angels to fall down before this newly created being. The account is best given in 38:73–77, and appears only less fully in six other passages. Geiger, p. 98, doubts whether this can have come to Muhammad through Jewish tradition, on the ground that the command to worship any other than God would have seemed to any Israelite inconceivable. Grünbaum, *Neue Beiträge zur semitischen Sagenkunde,* pp. 60 f., follows Geiger. The Koran does not speak of *worshipping,* however, but merely of approaching a personage of high rank in a truly oriental way. See, for example, the use of the verb in the last verse of 'Amr ibn Kulthm's *mu'allaqa* (Arnold's *Septem Mo'allakat,* p. 144), where the action is one of purely human homage. The passages which Geiger cites, *Sanhedrin* 59 b (not "29") and *Midr. Rabba* 8, are a sufficient parallel to the Koran. See also the "Life of Adam and Eve" (Charles, *Apocrypha and Pseudepigrapha*), chaps. 12–17. As for Iblis and ash-Shaitan, the former name seems to have come down into Arabia from the north, while the latter is evidently a fruit of the long contact with the Abyssinians; both names were doubtless current among the Jews of the Hijaz before Muhammad's time. The identification of the serpent with Satan would seem to be implied in the passage *Ber. Rabba* 17, which Geiger quotes. See also Ginzberg, *Legends of the Jews,* V, p. 84.

The prophet *Shu'aib,* who was sent to the Midianites, is generally recognized as identical with the biblical Jethro. The name was hardly invented by Muhammad; it is far more likely that it was brought into use by the Arabian Jews. Its origin is obscure, but it is natural to suppose that there was some etymological reflection behind it. These Midianites, from whom Moses took his wife (the daughter of a priest), were in their origin very closely related to the Hebrews, though *their main body* became a persistent and dangerous enemy. Might the name Shu'aib, "little tribe," have been the result of thinking of *Jitro* [Jethro] ("rest of it") as representing the faithful "remainder" of a larger Hebrew tribe?

The prophet *Dhu 'l-Kifl* presents another problem. I think that here again the solution is to be found in the long association of the Arabs with the Abyssinians, in the traffic on the Red Sea. The word *kefl* appears frequently in the Ethiopic version of Joshua in speaking of the "division" of the territory among the Hebrew tribes, which is the central feature of that book. I believe that Joshua is "Dhu 'l-Kifl," that is, the one who effected the division. It is very noticeable that he does not receive mention in the Koran, unless under this name.

'Uzair ("little Ezra") is made by Muhammad the subject of a very singular accusation aimed at the Jews. In one of the latest suras, and in a context dealing harshly with all those who are not Muslims, occurs this passage (9:30): "The Jews say, Ezra (*'Uzair*) is the son of God, and the Christians say, al-Mesiah is the son of God." (This might make Ezra turn in his grave—if he had one.) Muhammad here seems to be trying to believe what some enemy of the Jews had told him. He is bound to claim pure monotheism for the Muslims alone in his day. The use of the unpleasant diminutive, "*little* Ezra," is probably his own invention. The name occurs nowhere else; and this great figure in Jewish legend has no other mention in the Koran, unless under the name which here follows.

If I am not mistaken, Ezra has his double in the Koran, in the person of the prophet *Idris* (19:57 f., 21:85), of whom we are told only this, that he was given a high place of honor. The name has generally been derived from Εσδρας; and indeed, it could hardly be anything else. Various other suggestions have been made, from Nöldeke's "Andreas" (*Zeitschrift für Assyriologie,* vol. 17, 83 ff.) to Toy's "Theodore of Mopsuestia." But any Andreas seems utterly remote from Muhammad's horizon. On the other hand, it would be very easy for the Greek name of the famous Ezra to make its way down into Arabia, there ultimately to be picked up by the Arabian Prophet. The latter could of course not be expected to know, or to find out, that it was only another name for his *'Uzair.*

'Isa ibn Maryam. The treatment which Jesus and his work receive in the Koran is of especial importance in the attempt to determine the principal sources of Muhammadanism. It is a patent fact that the prophet knew next to nothing about Jesus; also, that there are no distinctly and peculiarly Christian doctrines in the sacred book. All those who have studied the matter know and declare that the great bulk of the Koranic material is of

Jewish origin; and we have certain knowledge that Muhammad resorted habitually to learned Jewish teachers. Have we any good reason for supposing that he also received personal instruction from a Christian? I believe that it will eventually be recognized that whatever knowledge (or pseudoknowledge) he possessed in regard to the person and life of Jesus was derived from two sources: *first*, the facts and fancies which were common property in the Hijaz and elsewhere in Arabia; and *second*, a small amount of information supplied to him by his Israelite mentors.

The form of the name is remarkable, in comparison with Yeshu'. The Christian Arabs of northern Arabia had the form Yasu',[3] which is just what would be expected; "'Isa" makes its first appearance in the Koran. It has been explained by Nöldeke and others as a Jewish pleasantry of which Muhammad was the innocent victim, the name of *Esau*, the typical enemy, being in fact substituted for that of Jesus.[4] There is indeed complete formal identity, and the symbolic transfer is certainly characteristic. The Meccan Israelite who might be supposed to have had this happy thought can of course have had no idea that the substituted name would go beyond Muhammad ibn 'Abdallah and his few adherents. There is another explanation, which in recent years has frequently been adopted. The pronunciation of the name in Nestorian Syriac is *Isho'*. It is surmised that when this pronunciation came (in some way) to Muhammad's ear, he altered it by transposing the guttural and changing the final vowel, in order (for some reason) to give it assonance with the name Musa (Moses).[5] This theory, while neither simple nor free from difficulties, is not quite impossible, and the student may take his choice.

If the hypothesis of the Syriac origin of the name is entertained, it certainly is permissible to give it connection with that one of Muhammad's habitual instructors (the only one concerning whom we have any *definite* information) who seems to have come to Mecca from the Persian or Babylonian domain. This man has been mentioned several times in the preceding lectures. His language was *'ajami*. He was certainly a learned man, probably a Jew, certainly not a Christian (see below). The passage in which he is mentioned (16:105) is late Meccan, and it is evident that Muhammad had for some time been under his instruction. A number of Koranic properties which seem to have come from Mesopotamia make their appearance at about this time. Such are the Babylonian angels Harut and Marut, the pair Yajuj and Majuj (both pairs already noticed), the mention of the Sabians, and the collection of Mesopotamian-Jewish legends utilized in the

eighteenth sura; see especially the fourth lecture. It is at least very noticeable that the first mention of 'Isa in the Koran, in the nineteenth sura, dates
from this same period.

Rudolph, p. 64, remarks on the strange circumstance that the earliest
occurrence of the name of Jesus in the Koran comes so late. It is indeed
significant! In general, it is not safe to conclude that the Prophet's first
knowledge of a biblical personage or conception of an idea may be dated
from the Koran, and chronological tables assigning such matters to successive periods are likely to be of slight value. But if, as Rudolph supposes,
Muhammad had received his earliest and most important religious en-
lightenment from Christians, it is nothing short of amazing that his only
allusion to anything specifically Christian, prior to the second Meccan
period, should be an incidental rebuke of the worship of two gods. He had
of course from the first some knowledge of the Christian sect (as he would
have termed it), and may have heard the name of its founder. In one of his
early suras (112) he attacks the worship of "Allah's son," but the doctrine
was too remote to give him any real concern, and he exhibits no further
interest in it until the later period when he began to hear more about this
"prophet" and his history. And even in the suras of the Medina period it is
evident that the Christians, with their founder and their beliefs, were only
on the outer edge of his horizon, not at all important for the basal doctrines
of Islam, and chiefly useful in the polemic against the Jews.

Wellhausen, in his too hasty contention that the Arabian Prophet
received his first and chief impulse from Christianity, made the strange
claim that Muhammad assigned to Jesus the supreme place in the religious
history of the past. "Jüdische Gesinnung verrät es nicht, dass Jesus im
Quran hoch über alle Propheten des Alten Testamentes gestellt wird"*
(*Reste*, 1887, p. 205). This assertion evidently rests on a slip of the memory,
or on forced interpretation, for there is in the Koran nothing that could
substantiate it. On the contrary, in 2:130, a passage belonging to the
Medina period, where the prophets, Jesus among them, are enumerated by
name or collectively, the words are added: "We make no distinction among
them." That is, in rank; certain prophets, or groups of prophets, were
endowed with special gifts or distinctions not shared by their fellows
(2:254). Abraham was given Islam (2:126; 22:77); Moses was given *The Book*

---

* "Jewish sensibilities do not admit to the fact that Jesus in the Koran is ranked high
above all the prophets of the Old Testament."

(2:81); David was given the Psalms (4:161); Jesus was given the wondrous signs (*bayyinat*) and "the Spirit" (2:81, 254). The five prophets with whom Allah made a special covenant—Jesus among them—have already been named (sura 33:7). Nowhere in the Koran is there any trace of a wish to give 'Isa ibn Maryam especially high rank among the prophets; he simply had his very honorable place (chronologically somewhat vague!) in the long line. *Later*, in the early caliphate, when Muslims and Christians were closely associated, especially in Syria and Egypt, Jesus was indeed placed "high above the prophets of the Old Testament," and the attempt was made to interpret the Koran accordingly, as anyone may learn by reading the native commentators.

Muhammad did his best to specify the particular distinctions which Jesus had been given, as a prophet; and he had cogent reason for so doing, quite aside from any polemic against the Jews. The fact of a great Christian world outside was perfectly familiar in all the cities of Arabia. The purpose of the newly arisen Arabian Prophet was, from the first, to gain the support of the Jews and the Christians, by no means to make them his enemies. His program was obviously and necessarily this, to declare that these faiths, in their beginnings and as promulgated by their founders and divinely appointed representatives, were identical with his own teaching. Only in their later development had they strayed from the right path. The time had come for a new prophet to call these peoples back to the true religion. This could only be done by exalting their teachers and claiming to build on their foundation. Many since Muhammad's time have conceived the same plan, though lacking his energy and his unique opportunity. During the first years of his public teaching, however, as has already been said and many scholars have remarked, he seems to have known so little about the Christians that he could simply class them as Israelites who had gone their own peculiar way.

It was with Abyssinia especially that the Meccans associated the Christian faith. Arabs and Abyssinians were, and from ancient time had been, partners in the Red Sea traffic; and, as we have seen, scraps of Abyssinian speech and religious terminology had made their way all over the peninsula. It was very well known that the Christians worshiped *al-Masih*. This name is attested in Arabia before Muhammad's time, all the way from Nejran in the south to Ghassan in the north (Horovitz, pp. 129 f.); and he eventually employs it frequently in the Koran. Accompanying this term was another, *ar-Ruh*, "the Spirit," associated in some way with the worship of Jesus and regularly mentioned along with him. Muhammad was utterly bewildered by the term (and so, of course, were the Arabs generally, in so far as it was known to them), and he plays with it in the Koran in several very different ways. Stories of the *miracles* of Jesus, including the raising of the dead, we should suppose to have been what the Arabs heard first and oftenest from their Abyssinian associates, and indeed from all other Christians with whom they came in contact. The fact that the Koran has no mention of these "*bayyinat*" until the second Meccan period is merely another indication of the comparative remoteness of the Christians and their doctrines from the prophet's earlier thinking. When at length they became somewhat more real to him, he picked up the few Christian terms that were lying ready to hand, and used them over and over, with only the vaguest ideas as to their meaning. (Even Rudolph, p. 65, reaches a similar conclusion: "Bei den dürftigen Kenntnissen, die er speziell von Jesus hat, bekommt man den Eindruck, dass er sich seine Anschauung aus Einzelheiten, die er da und dort erfuhr, selbst zusammengemacht hat.")[*]

As to the *time* when the prophet began to feel more directly concerned with the claims of the Christians, it is a plausible conjecture that it coincided with the so-called "Abyssinian migration" which took place about five years after the beginning of his public activity. Ahrens, p. 150, thinks that this shows that Muhammad felt himself in closer sympathy with Christianity than with Judaism: "Hätte er sich dem Judentume näher verwandt gefühlt, so lag für ihn der Anschluss an die Juden von Jathrib oder Khaibar näher."[†] On the contrary, the reason for Muhammad's choice is obvious; namely, that while still in Mecca he had been shown very clearly that the Jews were much more likely to be his enemies than his friends. The time had come when he and his followers needed to see what support could be had from the Christians; but it is hardly likely that the envoys— or fugitives—went with high hopes. While the Muslim accounts are utterly incredible in the most of their details, the main fact seems well established, namely, that a company of Muhammad's adherents took temporary refuge in Abyssinia; partly in protest against the treatment which they had received in Mecca, partly also, no doubt, in the hope of receiving some

---

[*] "From the meager knowledge that he had of Jesus specifically, one gets the impression that he himself constructed his view (of Christianity) from the particulars that he picked up here and there."

[†] "If he had felt a greater affinity with Judaism, then an alliance with the Jews of Jathrib or Khaibar would have been natural."

support—at least moral support—from these time-honored allies. It was a most natural proceeding, and it doubtless made an impression in Mecca, though not in Abyssinia. The gain which the Koran made from it seems to have been merely what has just been described, an awakening of interest which led the Prophet to gather up such Christian scraps as he could use. One of the new catchwords was *"Injīl"* (Evangelium), which in Muhammad's mouth—as Rudolph, p. 80, remarks—meant simply the Christian book of revelation preserved in heaven; he seems to have known nothing about separate gospels or evangelists. He took up the shibboleth of the virgin birth (21:91; 66:12); this also he could concede to the Christians without difficulty, and he maintains it stoutly in opposition to the Jews (4:155). Nevertheless Jesus was a mere man like other men (16:45; 21:7); the Koran says this in different ways, in numerous passages. Whether "the Word" (*kalima*, λογος) as a designation of Jesus, 3:40 and elsewhere, was only another catchword which Muhammad could of himself pick up in Mecca or Medina may be strongly doubted. He had among his teachers in Mecca a man of letters who had read at least some portion of the Gospels and was familiar with the popular legends regarding Jesus which were current in Christian lands; and it was from him, in all probability, that he heard the theological term. This man was a learned Jew, as I think the evidence plainly shows.

It has sometimes been said, e.g. recently by Rudolph, pp. 65 f., and Ahrens, p. 153, that a Jewish teacher, if he could have consented to say anything to Muhammad about Jesus, must have ridiculed and vilified him. "Hätte jüdischer Einfluss auf Muhammad bestimmend eingewirkt, so hätte er entweder über Jesus schweigen oder ihn beschimpfen müssen. Palästinische Rabbinen, die in völlig christianisierten Städten wohnten, brachten es fertig, über Jesus völlig zu schweigen—das Schweigen des Hasses und der schimpflichen Nichtachtung; und der Talmud redet in den dürftigen Stellen, an den er auf Jesus zu sprechen kommt, nur mit beschimpfenden Worten von ihm."[*] This, I think, hardly deals fairly with the Jews, nor sees clearly what sort of teaching was natural—one might even say necessary—under the circumstances now before us. The cus-

---

[*] "If Jewish influence had had a decisive effect on Muhammad, then he would either have been silent about Jesus or he would have insulted him. Palestinian rabbis who lived in fully Christianized cities managed to maintain complete silence regarding Jesus—the silence of hatred and of insulting disrespect; and the Talmud speaks of him, in the few places in which Jesus is mentioned, only with insulting words."

tomary *Schweigen* ["silence"] in Jewish works written in Christian cities was a matter of course, and the attitude of the Talmud is also perfectly defensible. On the other hand, there was never lack of Jews, all through the Middle Ages, who spoke appreciatingly of Jesus, while rejecting the Christian dogmas. In the present case, whatever the teacher's preference may have been, Muhammad's own intention must have been the deciding factor. He knew the Jews to be a minority, and on the other hand was profoundly conscious of the religion of the Abyssinians and of the great Christian empire whose center was at Byzantium.[6] He was bound to make Christian allies, not enemies. Any vilification of Jesus would have led him to reject his teacher as untrustworthy. The latter of course knew this, and took care to keep the teaching in his own hands. There was certainly reason to fear what a Christian would teach in regard to the Jews. Now that the time had come for Muhammad to ask, from one who evidently knew: "What does the 'Book' of the Christians tell about 'Isa ibn Maryam?" the answer was given in good faith, as far as it went. That which Muhammad already knew was confirmed and supplemented, and numerous interesting details, chiefly from folklore, were added. The informant was certainly acquainted with the Gospels, but no particle of gospel information concerning the grown man Jesus, or his reported lineage, or his activities (excepting that, as Muhammad must already have heard, he performed miracles), or his teaching, or his followers, was given forth. The doctrine of the virgin birth, the most prominent of all the Christian shibboleths at that time, could be acquiesced in—it cost nothing; and it could not possibly have been combated!

What, according to the Koran, was the mission of Jesus? Numerous passages give the same vague answer: He was sent to confirm the Israelites in the true doctrine, in the teachings of the Torah (3:43 f.; 5:50; 43:63 f.; 57:27; 61:6), to insist on the worship of only one God (5:76), to warn against straying from the faith of Abraham and Moses and forming new sects (42:11)! It is very difficult to believe that any one of the verses here cited could have been written by Muhammad if he had ever talked with a Christian, orthodox or heretical; but they contain exactly what he would have acquired from the teaching which I am supposing. He knew that the followers of Jesus had ultimately chosen to form a separate sect, and that Jews and Christians were in controversy, each party declaring the other to be mistaken (2:107); but *why* the new sect had been formed, he did not at all know. He says in 3:44 that Jesus "made lawful" some things which had been prohibited. This may have been given him by his teacher, or it may be the reflection of his own doctrine (useful for his legislation), that some foods were forbidden the Israelites in punishment for their sins; see 4:158 and 3:87.

The passage 19:1–15 is of great importance as evidence of the source of Muhammad's information in regard to the prophet 'Isa. Here is an extended *literary* connection with the Christian scriptures, the one and only excerpt from the New Testament, namely an abridgment of Luke 1:5–25, 57–66. This was discussed in the second lecture, and the details need not be repeated here. The account of the aged and upright Hebrew priest and the birth of his son in answer to prayer, reading like a bit of Old Testament history, would appeal to any Israelite of literary tastes as interesting—and harmless. But as soon as the account of the birth of *Jesus* is reached, the gospel narrative is dropped as though it were redhot, and Muhammad is left to flounder on alone, knowing only the bare fact that John was the kinsman and forerunner of Jesus, and the dogma of the virgin birth; things which his people had long ago learned, especially from the Abyssinians. It seems possible to draw two conclusions with certainty: *first*, Muhammad was told the story of Zachariah and John by a learned man; and *second*, the man was by no means a Christian.

Horovitz, p. 129, declares that he can see no Jewish influence in the Koranic utterances regarding Jesus. It may, however, be possible to recognize such influence from what is withheld, as well as from what is said. The instructor, in this case, certainly knew what was told about Jesus in the four gospels; but not a word of it came to the ear of Muhammad. On the contrary, the bits of personal and family history of Jesus which appear in the Koran are all derived from fanciful tales which were in popular circulation; tales which a literary rabbi would certainly have known, and which, from his point of view, were perfectly harmless. We at the present day have some knowledge of them from surviving fragments of the "apocryphal gospel" literature. See, in the Koran, 3:32, 39, 43, and 5:110. The nature of the teaching with which Muhammad had been supplied appears most clearly in the suras (especially 3, 4, and 5) revealed at Medina, during the time when the attitude of the Prophet toward the Jews was one of bitter hostility. It is evident that he then tried to make much of Jesus and his history and his importance as a prophet, and to remember all that he could of what he had formerly been told; but what he had at his command was next to nothing. Any arguments or accusations that he could have used against the Jews he would have been certain to employ, and any Christian, lettered or unlettered, would have supplied him with plenty of material; but he had in fact no ammunition beyond what the Jews' own tradition had given him. In one very late utterance, 5:85, he makes a valiant attempt to put the Christians high above the Jews: the latter are the chief enemies of Islam, the former are its greatest friends. But he very unwisely attempts to tell wherein the excellence of the Christians consists, and can only specify their priests and monks—of whom recently (in 57:27) he had expressed a low opinion!

Muhammad did not know that 'Isa had met with opposition from his people other than that which his predecessors had endured, and this is most significant. If he had known the fact, he could not have failed to make use of it; but it had not been told him. It was a mere matter of course that 'Isa's contemporaries tried to kill him; the Hebrew people had been wont to kill their prophets (2:81, 85), as their own scriptures and popular traditions declared (see the Strack-Billerbeck comment on Matt. 23:35–37). That any special significance had been attached, by the Christians or others, to the death of 'Isa, or to his ascension, Muhammad never had heard. For the docetic doctrine which he gives forth (4:156), asserting that it was not Jesus who was executed, but another who was miraculously substituted for him, it is quite superfluous to search for a heretical Christian or Manichaean (!) source. The heresy was old, and very widely known, though of course rarely adopted. *It precisely suited the purpose of Muhammad's Jewish instructor.* 'Isa, thus escaping the fate intended for him, was taken up to heaven (3:48), as numerous others had been taken. No Christian doctrine was more universally held and built upon than the *Second Coming.* The Arabian Prophet could easily have fitted it into his scheme of things, if he had known of it; at least to the extent of giving the Christian prophet some such important place in the Day of Judgment as he holds in the later Muslim eschatology; but there is nothing of the sort in the Koran.

The conclusion to be drawn from all this is evident, and certain: Muhammad derived his main impression of the prophet " 'Isa" and his work from Jewish teaching, very shrewdly given.

In support of this conclusion a word may be added in regard to the various indications of Christian influence which some have claimed to find in the Koran, especially in recent years. Nöldeke's pioneer work, his *Geschichte des Qorans* (1860), recognized hardly any Christian element. He declared (p. 2): "Gewiss sind die besten Theile des Islams jüdischen Ursprungs";* and

---

* "The best parts of Islam are certainly of Jewish origin."

again (p. 5): "Die Hauptquelle der Offenbarungen … bildeten für Muhammed die Juden. … Viel geringer ist dagegen der Einfluss des Christenthums auf den Qoran."* On the contrary, in Schwally's revision of this work we are given the impression of a strong Christian element in Islam at its very beginning. We read (p. 8) that in numerous particulars the influence of Christianity is "beyond any doubt" (*ausser allem Zweifel*), and the following are specified: the institution of vigils;[7] some forms of the prayer-ritual; the use of the "Christian" term *furqan* "to mean revelation"; the central significance of the conception of the Last Day; and the superiority assigned to Jesus above all the prophets. The conclusion is (ibid.), that "Islam might be regarded as the form in which Christianity made its way into all Arabia."

The items in the above list are all taken over from Wellhausen, *Reste* (1887), 205–209, and have been repeated by others, e.g. by Rudolph, p. 63. Each one of these claims is considered elsewhere in the present lectures, and it will suffice to say here that not a single one of them is valid. The conclusion expressed seventy years ago by Muir in his *Life of Mahomet*, II, 289, is still very near the truth if it is limited to Muhammad and the Koran: "We do not find a single ceremony or doctrine of Islam in the smallest degree moulded, or even tinged, by the peculiar tenets of Christianity."[8]

Ibrahim and Isma'il. The importance of these two patriarchs in the genesis of Islam has not been duly appreciated. We must first bear in mind the ethnic relationship which gave such encouragement to Muhammad in his wish to consort with the Jews and his attempt to gain their support. The Arabs were Ishmaelites, according to the Hebrew tradition. God said to Abraham (Gen. 17, 20): "As for Ishmael, I have heard thee; behold, I have blessed him, and will make him fruitful, and will multiply him exceedingly; twelve princes shall he beget, and I will make him a great nation." The twelve princes, subsequently named (25, 13 ff.), represent Arabian tribes or districts; notice especially Kedar, Duma (Dumat al-Jandal), and Teima. The "great nation" is the people of Arabia. Ishmael was circumcised (17, 26), was with his father at the time of his death, and assisted Isaac in burying him (25, 9). The Arabs were rightful heirs of the religion of their father Abraham, though they chose paganism instead.

On this foundation Muhammad built his tales of Abraham and Ishmael at Mecca. In the fourteenth sura, which bears the title "Abraham," he

---

* "The main source of the revelations … for Muhammad were the Jews. … Much less, however, is the influence of Christianity on the Koran."

introduces, in a characteristically casual and obscure manner, his association of Ishmael with the Ka'ba. I say "his association," but it is quite likely
that he himself did not originate the idea. The Arabs cannot possibly have
remained ignorant of the fact that the Hebrew scriptures declared
Abraham and Ishmael to be their ancestors. It was then most natural that
they should have been associated, in popular tradition, with the ancient
sanctuary. In verses 38–42 we read:

> Remember the time when Abraham said, Lord, make this land[9] secure,
> and restrain me and my children from worshipping idols. Lord, they have
> led astray many men; whoever then follows me, is mine; and if any dis-
> obey me—thou art forgiving and merciful. [Here he refers to the chil-
> dren of Ishmael, the unbelieving Arabs.] O our Lord, I have caused some
> of my offspring to settle in an unfruitful valley, at the site of thy holy
> house; thus, Lord, in order that they may offer prayer. Grant therefore
> that the hearts of some men may be inclined toward them; and provide
> them with the fruits of the earth, that they perchance may be
> grateful.... Praise to God, who gave me, even in old age, Ishmael and
> Isaac; verily my Lord is one who hears prayer.

This passage, together with the majority of those which mention Ishmael, I should assign to the Prophet's later Meccan period. (This is not,
however, a generally accepted conclusion, as will presently appear.) In general, Muhammad has very little to say about Ishmael; and there was good
reason for his reticence. He did not himself read the Old Testament, but
merely built upon what he had been told. The episode of Hagar was of no
value for his purposes; in fact, he never mentions Hagar at all.[10] The early
Jewish narrators seem to have felt little interest in the disinherited elder
son of Abraham, and left him at one side.

After Islam had become a great power in the world, new light dawned,
and the storytellers, both Jewish and Muhammadan, found that they knew
more about Ishmael and his family. An early example is the picturesque
tale, found in the Jerusalem Targum and apparently alluded to in the Pirqe
Rabbi Eliezer, of Ishmael's two wives, so very different in character and
disposition; and of the visits of the "very old man" Abraham to the tent of
his nomad son, far away in the Arabian desert. The names of the two wives
(otherwise "tent-pins"), Ayesha and Fatima, make it quite certain that this
legend was not known to Muhammad and his contemporaries.

The famous well, Zemzem, at Mecca is also brought into connection with the biblical history. According to Pirqe Aboth, one of the ten things created..., that is, between the sixth day of creation and the following day of rest, was "the mouth of the well." This refers, as all interpreters agree, to the miraculously traveling well of the Israelites ("the spiritual rock that followed them," I Corinthians 10, 4), mentioned in Ex. 17 and Num. 20 and 21, in the account of the journey from Egypt to the promised land. Here again the Jerusalem Targum and the Pirqe Rabbi Eliezer bring in the story of Ishmael, by including also the well which appeared to Hagar (Gen. 21, 19). The Muhammadan orthodox tradition (*hadith*) then puts the capstone on all this by making Zemzem the well which saved the lives of Hagar and her son.[11] This, to be sure, would mean that the mother and child had walked some 600 miles on the occasion described. Such sages as Abu Huraira and Ibn 'Abbas were not troubled by considerations of geography; and inasmuch as this improvement of the legend is early Muslim tradition, it might be termed a doctrine of primitive Islam. But Muhammad knew better; at least, he says not a word in the Koran about the sacred well at Mecca.

The highly significant passage in which Abraham and Ishmael are associated in the founding of the Ka'ba at Mecca is 2, 118–123. "When his Lord tested Abraham with certain commands, which he fulfilled, he said, I make thee an example for mankind to follow. Abraham said, And those of my posterity? God answered, My compact does not include the evil-doers." This refers to the pagan Arabs, the descendants of Ishmael; like the verse 14:39, already cited. The passage proceeds:

> Remember the time when we made the house [that is, the Ka'ba] a place of resort and of security for mankind, and said, "Take the 'station of Abraham' [also 3:91] as a place of prayer"; and how we laid upon Abraham and Ishmael the covenant obligation, saying, "Make my house holy [cf. 80:14 and 98:2] for those who make the circuit, for those who linger in it, those who bow down, and prostrate themselves in devotion." And when Abraham said, "Lord, make this land secure, and nourish its people with the fruits of the earth; those among them who believe in God and the last day"; he answered, "As for him who is unbelieving, I will provide him with little; and thereafter I will drive him to the punishment of hell-fire; it will be an evil journey" [a warning to the men of Mecca, and to all the Arabs, the faithless Ishmaelites].

Then comes the important statement regarding the founding of the
Ka'ba; important, because it plainly contradicts the orthodox Muslim tradition.

> And when Abraham with Ishmael was raising the foundations of the
> house, he said, "Lord, accept this from us;...make us submissive to thee,
> and make of our offspring a nation submissive to thee; and declare to us
> our ritual....Lord, send also among them a messenger of their own, who
> shall recite to them thy signs and teach them the book and divine
> wisdom, and purify them; verily thou art the mighty and wise."

According to the later Muslim doctrine, the Ka'ba was first built by
Adam; the station (or standing place) of Abraham is the spot inside the
sanctuary where his footprint in the rock is still to be seen; the command
to the two patriarchs, "Make my house clean," meant "Cleanse it of idols."
But the meaning of the Koran is plain, that the holy station and the holy
house began with Abraham and his son.

In the verses which immediately follow, it is expressly said that the true
and final religion, Islam, was first revealed to the family of the patriarch.
Verse 126: "Abraham and Jacob gave this command to their sons: 'God has
chosen for you the (true) religion; you must not die without becoming Muslims.'" We could wish to know how important in Muhammad's thought this
conception of the genesis of Islam was, and how early it was formed in his
mind. I shall try to answer the question at the close of this lecture.

In so far as we are reduced to conjecture, there are certain known factors in the Meccan Prophet's religious development that would lead us to
suppose, if nothing should hinder the supposition, that he attached himself very early and very firmly to Abraham's family when he sought (as he
must have sought) support in the past for the faith which he set himself to
proclaim. We have seen how essential to all his thinking, from the very
first, was the idea of the written revelation, the scriptural guidance given
by God to men. Jews and Christians alike were "people of the Book"; in
each case a book of divine origin. But Jews and Christians were in sharpest
disagreement. As the Koran puts it in sura 2, 107, and as Muhammad had
known long before he began his public ministry, "The Jews say, 'The Christians are all wrong' [lit., rest on nothing]; and the Christians say, 'The Jews
are all wrong; and yet they read the scriptures!'" Now Muhammad knew
that these two religions were branches from the same stock; that the Chris-

tian sect had its beginnings in Judaism; and that the Christians held to the Hebrew scriptures, and claimed for themselves the prophets and patriarchs. The Hebrew people were the children of Abraham; so also, then, were the Christians, even though they attached no importance to this origin. Did not these facts point clearly to the starting point of the *final* religion? Here also the Arabs, the sons of Ishmael, came in for their long-lost inheritance. Muhammad could only conclude that Jews and Christian alike had been led away from the truth. The right way was now to be shown to them, as well as to the Arabs. This belief he expresses at first confidently, at length bitterly, at last fiercely.

It is not always easy to determine, from the Koran, either the relative age or the relative importance of Muhammad's leading ideas. We have seen the reasons for this. On this very point, the place occupied by the Hebrew patriarchs in the development of the prophet's religious doctrine, there has been some difference of opinion.

According to early Muslim tradition, there were in Arabia, not only in Mecca and Medina but also in a few other cities, before the time of Muhammad's public appearance as a prophet, certain seekers after truth, who revolted against the Arabian idolatry. They called themselves *hanifs*, and professed to seek "the religion of Abraham," their ancestor. Now Muhammad in the Koran repeatedly applies to Abraham the term *hanif* as descriptive of his religion. Where and how he got possession of the term cannot be declared with certainty, but may be conjectured, as we have seen. Certainly it came originally from the Hebrew *hanef*, and probably its employment by him as a term of praise, rather than of reproach, indicates that in his mind it designated one who *"turned away"* from the surrounding paganism. Be that as it may, his use of the word seemed to give support to the tradition just mentioned, until a thorough investigation of the latter showed it to be destitute of any real foundation.

The conclusive demonstration was furnished by Snouck Hurgronje, in his brilliant and searching monograph entitled *Het Mekkaansche Feest* (1880). Snouck made it clear to all who study his argument that Muhammad himself had no knowledge of any Arabian *hanifs*, and that the tradition had its origin in a theory of later growth. The conclusion at which he arrived went still farther than this, however, for he denied that the prophet had any special interest in the Hebrew patriarchs in the earlier part of his career. This is a matter which seems to me to be in need of further investigation.

Sprenger, *Das Leben und die Lehre des Muhammad*, Vol. II (1862), pp.

276–285, gave at some length his reasons for believing that Muhammad himself invented the association of Abraham with the Ka'ba, that he for some time supposed Jacob to be the son of Abraham, that he learned of Ishmael's parentage only at a comparatively late dare, etc.; all this very loosely reasoned, and arbitrary in its treatment of the Koran. Snouck, starting out from the plausible portion of Sprenger's argument, developed thoroughly and consistently the theory that the Prophet's especial interest in the Hebrew patriarchs arose in Medina, as a result of his failure to gain the support of the Jews. That is, in his reaction against the religion of Moses (?), he turned back to those earlier prophets to whose family he could claim to belong. Accordingly, after removing to Yathrib and suffering his great disappointment there, he began to make great use of the two patriarchs Abraham and Ishmael, to whom while in Mecca he had attached no especial importance.

The complete argument will be found in the reprint of Snouck's *Mekkaansche Feest* in his *Verspreide Geschriften,* I, 22–29; repeated also by him in the *Revue de l'histoire des religions,* vol. 30 (1894), pp. 64 ff. His principal contentions are the following: (1) In the Meccan suras Abraham is merely one among many prophets, not a central figure. (2) The phrase *millat Ibrahim* "the religion of Abraham," as the designation of Islam, is peculiar to the Medina suras of the Koran. (3) It was only after leaving Mecca that Muhammad conceived the idea of connecting Abraham and Ishmael with the Ka'ba. (4) In several comparatively late Meccan suras the Prophet declares that before his time "no warner" had been sent to the Arabs (32:2; 34:43; 36:5). Yet at this same time Ishmael is said by him to have "preached to his people" (19:55 f.). Does not this show that the Prophet while in Mecca had not associated Ishmael with the Arabs?

These conclusions are accepted, as proven, in the Nöldeke-Schwally *Geschichte des Qorans* (see especially pp. 146f., 152), and have been widely adopted. I think, however, that the argument will not bear close examination, in the light of present-day estimates of the Arabian Prophet's equipment. Muhammad's knowledge of Hebrew-Jewish lore in general, and of the Pentateuchal narratives in particular, is appraised considerably higher now than it was in 1880, and this is true also of Arabian culture in the Hijaz. Whether or not the Meccan Arabs had known that the Hebrew patriarch Ishmael was their ancestor, Muhammad must have known it and have been profoundly impressed by the fact very early in his course of instruction. The Koran, as I shall endeavor to show, testifies clearly to this effect. Muhammad certainly could not cut loose from the Jews by adopting Abraham! If he had wished to "emancipate Islam from Judaism," *and had found himself free to make his own choice,* he could easily and successfully have denied the Ishmaelite origin of the Arabs, falsely reported by the Jews. The founding of the Ka'ba could equally well have been ascribed to Noah, or "Idris," or some other ancient worthy. There is not a particle of evidence to show that the Koran gave less weight in Medina to Moses and his ordinances than had been given in Mecca. The fact is just the contrary; and the Prophet not only leans heavily on Moses, but openly professes to do so (e.g., in 5:48f.!). And finally, Snouck's theory is not supported by the Koran unless the text of the latter is reconstructed by the excision and removal from Meccan contexts of certain passages which, as they stand, would be fatal to the argument.

In reply to the principal contentions listed above: (1) In one of the very early Meccan suras Abraham is emphatically a "central figure" in the history of the world. In the closing verses of sura 87 we read of "the primal books, *the books of Akraham and Moses.*" Whatever the Prophet's idea may have been as to the contents of these "books," Abraham is here made the *father of the written revelation of God to mankind.* He instituted "The Book," of which Muhammad stood in such awe. In another early sura, 53, these "books" are again mentioned, and in the same connection Abraham is characterized in a significant way; vs. 38, "(the book) of Abraham, *who paid in full.*" This last phrase is elucidated in 2:118, where it is said: "When his Lord tested Abraham with certain commands, which he fulfilled, he said, 'I make thee an example for mankind.'" The command to the patriarch to sacrifice his own son is of course the one especially in mind, and it is plain that Muhammad had essentially the same idea of Abraham in the two passages.

The account of the attempted sacrifice which the Koran gives, in 37:99–113, is important for our knowledge of Muhammad's attitude toward the Jews in the early part of his career at Mecca. Abraham is given tidings of the coming birth of his "mild son"[12] (vs. 99). The boy grows up, and is rescued from the sacrificial knife by divine intervention (vss. 103–107). *Thereafter* (vs. 112), *the birth of Isaac is foretold to Abraham.* This seemed to Snouck (pp. 23 f.) to show that Muhammad had become confused and uncertain in regard to the story—unless vss. 122 f. could be regarded as an interpolation. But the Prophet, far from being confused, shows here both his acquaintance with the Old Testament narrative and also his practical wisdom. Why does he not name the elder son? The answer is plain. Muhammad was perfectly aware, even before he began preaching in public, that Abraham's first-born son, Ishmael, was the father of the Arabs. In the Hebrew narrative he is an utterly insignificant figure, an unworthy son of the great religious founder. The Arabian Prophet, instituting a religion centering in Arabia, saw his opportunity to improve this state of things. It is very significant that he employs three verses of his very brief narrative (101–103) to show that Abraham's son was informed beforehand of the intended sacrifice and *fully acquiesced in it*—a most important touch which has no counterpart in the biblical story. Ishmael was a true "Muslim." He leaves out the name, but this is not all. The mention of Isaac is introduced *after* the concluding formula (vss. 109–111) which runs through the chapter, and without any adverb of time (such as *thumma*); and thus he completely avoids unnecessary trouble either with the Jews who were his instructors or with his own few followers. The whole passage is a monument to his shrewd foresight, a quality which we are liable constantly to underestimate in studying his method of dealing with the biblical narratives.

(2) As for the *millat Ibrahim*, "the religion of Abraham," the single passage 12:38, of the Meccan period, is sufficient to nullify the argument. Could anyone suppose that Muhammad meant by the *milla* of Abraham, Isaac, Jacob, and Joseph any other religion than Islam? Ishmael could not have been mentioned here, since Joseph is enumerating his own ancestors. More than this, there are two other Meccan passages (16:124 and 22:77) in which the phrase *millat Ibrahim* occurs. These shall receive further notice presently.

(3) I have already expressed the opinion that the association of Abraham and Ishmael with the sanctuary at Mecca is pre-Islamic (see also Schwally, 147, note 3). As for Muhammad himself, he sets forth the doctrine fully in sura 14:38–42. The whole chapter is Meccan, and has always been so classed; and there is no imaginable reason why an interpolation should have been made at this point. Yet Schwally, p. 152, cuts out these verses from the sura on the sole ground that Snouck's theory requires their excision. The latter treats the passage, on p. 29, quite arbitrarily. It is obvious why the patriarch here names Ishmael and Isaac, not Isaac and Jacob. Verse 37 had just spoken of the countless favors of Allah, who *"gives you some portion of all that you ask of him."* This introduces the mention of Abraham, who in vs. 41 praises Allah for giving him *two sons* in his old age, and adds, "verily my Lord is the hearer of prayer!" Could anyone ask for a

better connection? The verses are Meccan, and always occupied this place in the sura.

(4) The passages which mention the "warner" give no aid whatever to the theory. The Prophet would at all times have maintained that the Arabian peoples had never had a "messenger" sent to them. The only passage in which there is mention of admonition given by Ishmael is 19:56, where it is said that he commanded "his family" (this, unquestionably, is what *ahlahu* means) to pray and give alms. As "a prophet and messenger" he must have done this much. But it is made perfectly plain in the Koran—the principal passages have already been discussed —that his children paid no attention to the admonition. Long before Arabia began to be peopled with the Ishmaelite tribes, the disobedient sons had passed away, along with the instruction given to them. No Arabian tribe had ever heard a word in regard to the true religion.

The Question of Composite Meccan suras. Some brief space must be given here to a matter which really calls for a monograph. A moment ago, I claimed as Meccan utterances of the Prophet two passages (16:124 and 22:77) which by occidental scholars are now quite generally regarded as belonging to the Medina period. The sixteenth sura is Meccan, as no one doubts. Of its 128 verses, Schwally assigns 43, 44, and 111–125 to Medina; at the same time combating, on obviously sufficient grounds, the opinions of those who would assign to Medina numerous other passages. In regard to sura 22 Nöldeke had declared (p. 158), that "the greater part of it" was uttered at Mecca, but that its most significant material came from the Medina period. It accordingly is now classed as a Medina sura in the standard treatises and in Rodwell's Koran; see also Nicholson's *Literary History of the Arabs*, p. 174. In the course of the argument concerning the association of Abraham and Ishmael with the Ka'ba I discussed a supposed insertion in sura 14, with the result of showing that the theory of interpolation is at least quite unnecessary. These are merely single examples out of a multitude. The accepted working hypothesis as to the composition of the Koran recognizes a considerable revision, after the Hijra, of the later Meccan suras by the insertion of longer or shorter passages, which certain criteria enable us to detect. Of course the theory has its apparent justification; the question is, whether it has not run wild.

The Koran is a true *corpus vile*; no one cares how much it is chopped up. The Arabs themselves have been the worst choppers. Their ancient theory of the sacred book led to just this treatment. It was miraculously revealed, and miraculously preserved. Muhammad, being "unable to read and write," left no copy behind at his death; so when it became necessary to make a standard volume, its various portions were collected "from scraps of paper, parchment, and leather, from palm-leaves, tablets of wood, bones, stones, and from the breasts of men." This is something like Ezra's restoration, from memory, of the lost Hebrew scriptures, twenty-four canonical and seventy apocryphal books (4 Ezra, 14:44ff.), and the two accounts are of like value for historical purposes. The Muslim commentators found no difficulty in seeing—as they did see—oracles of Mecca and Medina wonderfully jumbled together in many suras. Their analysis of the chapters which they themselves pronounced Meccan was based either on fancied historical allusions or on fundamentally mistaken notions as to the activities and associations of the Prophet in the years before the Hijra. The disagreement of these early interpreters, moreover, was very wide.

Muhammad himself wrote down the successive suras; and he gave them out as complete units, a fact which is especially obvious in such a group as the *Ha-Mim* chapters, 40–46, but is hardly less evident throughout the book. It might also be inferred from the challenge to his critics to produce "ten suras," in 11:16. He had his amanuenses, who made some copies for distribution. He himself supplemented a number of the completed suras, after they had been for some time in circulation, making important insertions or additions, obviously needed, and generally indicated as secondary by their form. Thus, 73:20 is an easily recognizable Medina appendage to a Meccan sura. The cautious addition in regard to Jesus in the nineteenth sura (vss. 35–41, marked off from their context by the rhyme) is another well known example. In 74:30, the Prophet's "nineteen angels" (numbered for the sake of the rhyme) called forth some ridicule, which he thereafter rebuked in a lengthy insertion, quite distinct in form from the rest of the chapter.[13] In such cases it certainly is the most plausible supposition that Muhammad made the alteration in writing, with his own hand.

It might at the outset seem a plausible hypothesis that the Prophet would make numerous alterations, in the course of time, in the suras which he had composed, as his point of view changed and new interests came into the foreground. The loose structure of the Koran in nearly all of its longer chapters rendered interpolation singularly easy. The kaleidoscope is constantly turning, and the thought leaps from one subject to another, often without any obvious connection. Since the verses are separate units, each with its rhymed ending (often a mere stock phrase), nothing could be easier than to insert new verses in order to supplement, or explain, or qualify; or even in order to correct and replace an objectionable utterance, as was done (according to an old tradition) in the middle of the fifty-third sura. It is important to note, however, that we should not be able to recognize any such insertions, unless the Prophet called attention to them in some striking way. Did Muhammad, in fact, freely revise his (i. e., Gabriel's) revelations? There is a doctrine clearly stated by him, and well illustrated, that certain utterances are "annulled" by subsequent outgivings. The latter, however, are never put beside the former, nor given specific reference to them, but merely make their appearance wherever it may happen—that is, when and where Gabriel found the new teaching desirable. In like manner, the supposed insertions now under discussion, "Medina additions to Meccan suras," are as a rule given no obvious motive by anything in their context, but seem purely fortuitous. If they really are insertions, and were made by the Prophet, it was not with any recognizable purpose.

For one reason in particular it is not easy to suppose any considerable amount of alteration in the divine oracles, after they had once been finished and made public. From the first they were learned by heart and constantly recited by those who had committed them to memory. As early as sura 73:1–6 the Prophet urges his followers to spend a part of the night in reciting what they have learned, and it is implied that the amount is already considerable. The acquisition was very easy, and before the Prophet's death, the number of those who could repeat the whole book without missing a word cannot have been very small. Under these circumstances, any alteration, especially if made without apparent reason, could not fail to be very disturbing. The few which (as we have seen) the Prophet himself made were doubtless explained by him; and we may be sure that he would have permitted no other to change the divine messages! After his death, the precise form of words was jealously guarded; and when, through the unforeseen but inevitable accidents of wider transmission, variant readings crept in, so that copies in different cities showed some real disagreement, a standard text was made, probably differing only in unimportant details from the form originally given out by Muhammad. In the early subsequent history, indeed, minor variations in the text, consisting mainly of interesting differences of orthography and peculiarities of grammatical usage, amounted to a large number; see the very important chapter on the history of the text in

Nöldeke's *Geschichte des Qorâns*. But whoever reads the Koran through must feel that we have the Prophet before us in every verse.

The *dating* of the suras of the Koran, as of Mecca or Medina, is generally, though not always, an easy matter. Any chapter of considerable length is sure to contain evidence clearly indicating the one city or the other as the place of its origin. The simple classification of this nature which was made by the best of the early Muhammadan scholars is nearly everywhere confirmed by modern critics. Even in the case of the briefer suras there is not often room for doubt. The possibility of dating more exactly, however, is soon limited. The career of the Prophet in Medina, covering ten years, is well known to us in its main outlines. Since a number of important events, chronologically fixed, are plainly referred to in the Koran, about one-half of the twenty or more Medina suras can be approximately located. Not so with the twelve years of the Meccan revelations. Here, there is an almost complete lack of fixed points, and we have very inadequate information as to Muhammad's personal history and the development of his ideas and plans. It is possible to set apart, with practical certainty on various grounds, a considerable number of suras as *early;* and a much smaller number can be recognized with almost equal certainty as coming from the last years of the Meccan period. Between the arbitrary limits of these two groups a certain development, partly in the literary form and partly in the relative emphasis given to certain doctrines, can be traced in the remaining suras; but with no such distinctness as to make possible a chronological arrangement. This is true of all three of the conventional "Meccan periods."

The native interpreters, as already observed, analyzed the Meccan suras to their heart's content; recognizing allusions to very many persons, events, and circumstances, and accordingly treating this or that sura without regard to considerations of literary or chronological unity. Modern occidental scholars saw that these hypotheses as to actors and scenes were generally either purely fanciful or else plainly mistaken; in Nöldeke's treatise, for example, they meet with wholesale rejection. The underlying theory, that of casually composite chapters, in which oracles from widely difficult periods might stand side by side without apparent reason for their proximity, was nevertheless adopted. The criteria employed by the Muslim scholars in identifying Medina verses in Meccan suras were also, in considerable part, taken over as valid. These consist of single words and phrases, often arbitrarily interpreted, and also of allusions to conditions supposed to be characteristic of the Medina period but not of the earlier time.

Here the critic is on slippery ground. That which Muhammad gave forth from time to time was largely determined by the immediate circumstances, concerning which it is likely to be the case that we either are not informed at all, or else are wrongly informed by the guesses of the native commentators. Ideas which (in the nature of the case) must have been in the prophet's mind from the very beginning may happen to find their chief expression only at a late date. Certain evils existed for some time before they became very serious. There were "hypocrites" in Mecca as well as in Medina. Such words as "strive," "contend," and "victory" gained great significance after the battle of Badr; but they ought not to be forbidden to the Prophet's Meccan vocabulary. In sura 29, for example, which unquestionably in the main was uttered before the Hijra, many of the Muslim authorities assign the first ten verses to Medina, and Nöldeke follows them.[14] Verse 45 is similarly treated—in spite of 6:153, 16:126, and 23:98! In fact, there is no valid reason for such analysis; the whole sura is certainly Meccan, and so not a few scholars, oriental and occidental, have decided. Another example of the forced interpretation of single words is to be seen in the treatment of the very brief sura 110. If Muhammad believed himself to be a prophet, and had faith in the ultimate triumph of the religion which he proclaimed, it is far easier to suppose that this little outburst came from the time when he first met with serious opposition than to imagine it delivered late in the Medina period, as is now commonly done. The word "victory" is no more remarkable here than it is in the closing verses of sura 32.

Another mistake made by the early commentators has had serious consequences. Having little or no knowledge of the presence of Jews in Mecca, and with their eyes always on the important Jewish tribes of Medina and the prophet's dealings with them, they habitually assigned to the Medina period the allusions to Jewish affairs which they found in Meccan suras; and in this they sometimes have been followed by modern scholars. It is one principal aim of the present lectures to show that Muhammad's personal contact with the Jews was closer (as well as much longer continued) before the Hijra than after it. By far the most of what he learned of Israelite history, literature, customs, and law was acquired in Mecca. It is also a mistaken supposition that he met with no determined opposition from the Jews, resulting in bitter resentment on his part, before the Hijra.[15] On the contrary, he was perfectly aware, before leaving Mecca, that the Jews as a whole were against him, though some few gave him support. After the migration to Yathrib, when his cause seemed to triumph, he doubtless cherished the hope that now at length the Jews would acknowledge his claim; and when they failed to do so, his resentment became active hostility.

It is not difficult to see why the Muslim historians and commentators habitually assign to Medina those passages in the Koran in which Muhammad is given contact with Jewish affairs, in default of any definite allusion to Mecca as the scene. The latter city was the Muslim sanctuary par excellence, from the Prophet's day onward, and unbelieving foreigners were not welcome. As for the Jews themselves, they of course realized, after seeing how their compatriots at Yathrib had been evicted or butchered, that Mecca was no place for them. Their exodus began during Muhammad's lifetime, and must soon have been extensive. After this emigration, their former influence in the holy city, as far as it was kept in memory, was at first minimized, and then ignored; eventually it was lost to sight. The Prophet's close personal association with Meccan Jews, and especially his debt to Jewish teachers (!), was of course totally unknown to the generations which later came upon the scene. On the other hand, they had very full knowledge of his continued contact with the Jews of Yathrib; and they very naturally interpreted the Koran in the light of this knowledge. Modern scholars have been far too easygoing in giving weight to these decisions of the native commentators, and the mistaken analysis of Meccan suras has too often been the result.

It would be fruitless to attempt to collect here the many "Medina" verses which have been found by Muslim scholars in the Meccan chapters merely because of the mention of Jews. Some similar criticism may be found in Nöldeke-Schwally in the comments on 6:91, 7:156, and 29:45 (already mentioned), as well as in the passages about to be considered. It must be clear, from what has thus far been said, that the only sound and safe proceeding in the "higher criticism" of the suras recognized as prevailingly Meccan is to pronounce every verse in its original place unless there is absolute and unmistakable proof to the contrary. I know of no later additions to Meccan suras, with the exception of the few which Muhammad himself plainly indicated.[16]

All this has led up to the consideration of the two passages previously mentioned, 16:124 and 22:77, in which Islam is termed "the religion (*milla*) of Abraham." Both passages are now generally assigned to the Medina period, but for no valid reason. Both suras are "in the main" Meccan, as few would doubt. In sura 16, verses 43 f. and 111 would naturally be supposed to refer to the migration to Abyssinia. Since however the latter verse speaks of "striving," an allusion to the holy war is postulated, and all three verses are referred to the Hijra; but the third stem of *jahada* was well known even in Mecca! Verse 119 is given to Medina on the ground that it probably refers to 6:147. If it does, this merely shows that 6 is earlier than 16, a conclusion which is opposed by no fact. Verse 125 is suspected of coming from Medina on the ground that "it deals with the Jewish sabbath." It is thus rendered natural (Schwally, p. 147) to assign the whole passage 111–125 to Medina; and Abraham, in vs. 124, is accordingly counted out. But unless better evidence than the foregoing can be presented, the whole sura must be pronounced Meccan.

Sura 22 affords the best single illustration of the fact that the latest Meccan revelations closely resemble those of Medina not only in style and vocabulary but also in some of the subjects which chiefly occupied the Prophet's attention. Considerable portions are now declared to be later than the Hijra; see Nöldeke-Schwally, pp. 214 f. These shall be considered in as brief compass as possible.

Vs. 17 is by no means "a later insertion"; it has its perfect connection in the concluding words of the preceding verse. Vss. 25–38 give directions in regard to the rites of the *Hajj*, at the sacred house. Does this remove them from their Meccan surroundings? Did not Muhammad (and his adherents) believe in the duty of the Pilgrimage before they migrated to Yathrib? Probably no one will doubt that they did so believe. It is very noticeable that the whole passage, as well as what precedes and follows it, is *argumentative*; addressed quite as plainly to the "idolaters" as to the Muslims. This is the tone of the whole sura. Notice especially vss. 15 (and in Medina would certainly have been written: "Allah will help *his Prophet*"); 32–36 (in the latter verse observe the words: "those who endure patiently what has befallen them"); 42–45; 48–50; 54–56; 66–71. In the last-named verse we see that the idolaters, among whom Muhammad is living and whom he is addressing, occasionally hear the Koran recited, and threaten to lay violent hands on those who recite it! The passage in regard to the *Hajj* is not mere prescription, for the instruction of the Muslims; it is designed to inform the Meccans that Muhammad and his followers mean to observe the rites in the time-honored way, and that they have been unjustly debarred from the privilege. The Prophet is thoroughly angry, and

expresses himself in a way that shows that some sort of a *hijra* must soon
be necessary. In vs. 40 formal permission is given to the Muslims to "fight
because they have been wronged"; from which we may see what a pitch the
Meccans' persecution had reached. The description of the whole situation
given in Ibn Hisham, 313 f., is generally convincing, as well as perfectly
suited to this most interesting sura.

The strongest support of the theory of later insertions in the chapter
seemed to be given by vs. 57. Nöldeke saw here the mention of certain true
believers, who after migrating from Mecca had been killed in battle; and he
therefore of necessity pronounced the passage later than the battle of Badr.
The view that a general supposition was intended, rather than historical
fact, seemed to him to be excluded by grammatical considerations. His foot-
note, repeated by Schwally, says: "If the reading were *man qutila,* 'if any one
is killed,' then the verses could have been composed before the battle; but
alladhīna qutilū excludes the conditional interpretation, and shows merely
the completed action: 'those who were killed.'" It is evident that Nöldeke
completely overlooked the passage 2:155 f., which is strikingly parallel in its
wording, while fortunately there can be no difference of opinion as to the
interpretation. In both cases we have merely a general hypothesis.
Muhammad is not always bound by the rules of classical Arabic grammar
(probably it would be more correct to say that his imagination was so vivid
as to make the supposition an actual occurrence), and he frequently
employs *alladhī* and *alladhīna* in exactly this way. The passage in our sura
refers to some lesser migration (or migrations) before the Hijra, and to
Muslims who may die, or be killed, after this clear proof of their devotion
to the cause of Allah. (Nothing is said of being killed *in battle.*)

Finally, vss. 76 ff. are said to have originated in Medina, because "they
enjoin the holy war," and because of the mention of the "religion of
Abraham." The interpretation of the first words of vs. 77 as referring to *the
holy war* is not only unnecessary, however, but also seems out of keeping
with what is said in the remainder of the verse. The believers are exhorted
to strive earnestly for the true faith; compare the precisely similar use of
this verb in the Meccan passages 25:54 and 29:69. The saying in regard to
Abraham is important for the history of the term "Islam," as will be seen.
To conclude, sura 22 is thoroughly homogeneous, containing no elements
from the Medina period. And (as was said a moment ago) much stronger
evidence than has thus far been offered must be produced before it can be
maintained that Meccan suras were freely interpolated after the Hijra.

The Origin of the Term "Islam." The theory propounded by Professor Snouck Hurgronje and discussed in the preceding pages has, I think, helped to hide from sight the true source of the name which Muhammad gave to the faith of which he was the founder. The one thing which we usually can feel sure of knowing as to the origin of a great religion is how it got its name. In the case of "Islam," the only fact on which all scholars would agree is that the name was given by Muhammad. The formal title appears rather late in the Koran, but is virtually there very early, for the true believers are termed "Muslims" in the suras of the first Meccan period. There has been considerable difference of opinion as to what the word means. The great majority have always held that this verbal noun, *islam*, was chosen as meaning "submission"; that is, submission to the will of God; but not a few, especially in recent years, have sought another interpretation. It is not obvious why the Prophet should have selected this name, nor does ordinary Arabic usage suggest this as the most natural meaning of the fourth stem of the very common verb *salima*.

Hence at least one noted scholar has proposed to understand the Prophet's use of this verb-stem as conveying the idea of coming into the condition of security (Lidzbarski, in the *Zeitschift für Semitistik* I, 86). The meaning of *Islam* would then be "safety"; and in view of the long catalogue of unspeakable tortures in Gehenna which are promised to the unbelievers, this might seem an appealing title. The interpretation is far from convincing, however, in view of several passages in the Koran. Professor Margoliouth of Oxford, one of the foremost Arabists of our time, offered the theory that the Muslims were originally the adherents of the "false prophet" Musailima, who appeared in central Arabia at about the time of Muhammad. This theory, as might be expected, was not received with favor.

It has been doubted by some whether the term is really of Arabic origin; see Horovitz, *Untersuchungen,* p. 55; Nöldeke-Schwally, p. 20, note 2, and the references there given. The attempt to find a real equivalent in Aramaic or Syriac has failed, however, and I, for one, can see no good reason for doubting that we have here genuine native usage. Moreover, the only meaning of the term which suits all the Koranic passages is the one which has generally been adopted.

But why *submission?* This was never a prominently appearing feature of the Muslim's religion. It is not an attitude of mind characteristic of Muhammad himself. It is not a virtue especially dwelt upon in any part of the Koran. It would not in itself seem to be an attractive designation of the Arab's faith. Why was not the new religion named "Faith," or "Truth," or "Safety," or "Right-guidance," or "Striving," or "Victory"? —since these are ideas prominent in the Koran. Why "Submission"?

I believe that the origin of the name is to be found in a scene in the life of Abraham and Ishmael depicted in the Koran and already mentioned in this lecture, and that the choice was made by Muhammad because of his doctrine that the final religion—or rather, the final form of the true religion—had its inception in the revelation given to Abraham and his family. The Koran knows of no "Muslims" prior to these patriarchs. We have seen that one of the very early suras speaks of "the books of Moses and Abraham" (87:19). In another sura of the same period we find the earliest occurrence of the designation "Muslims" (68:35). In what probably is the very last Meccan utterance of the Prophet (22:77), Abraham and the naming of Islam are mentioned in the same breath: "God gave you the faith of your father Abraham and named you Muslims." The collocation is certainly significant.

The Meccan Arabs knew, and probably had known before the time of Muhammad, that according to the Hebrew records they were the descendants of Ishmael. Because of their tribal organization, with all its emphasis on family history, we should suppose them to have been pleased with the gain of a remote ancestor, even if they felt little or no interest in his person. To Muhammad, the fact was profoundly significant. At the time when he first became aware of great religions outside Arabia, he heard of that ancient prophet Abraham, who through his second son, Isaac, was the founder of both the Israelite and the Christian faith, and through his elder son, Ishmael, was the father of the Arabian peoples. It may have been through meditation on this startling fact that he was first led to the conception of a new revelation, and a new prophet, for his own race. The Arabs were rightful heirs of the religion of Abraham; although, as he repeatedly declares, they had rejected the truth and fallen into idolatry.

It may be regarded as certain, however, that Muhammad did not believe his call to the prophetic office to be in any way the result of his own reflection on what ought to be. On the contrary, he was called by Allah, and the revelation for the Arabs was new, never previously given to anyone. In some true sense he himself was "the first of the Muslims" (39:14). But when at length, after the Koran was well advanced, he turns to the Hebrew patriarchs, he claims them as a matter of course and speaks of them in no uncertain terms. "Abraham said, 'Lord, make this land [the neighborhood of Mecca] safe, and turn me and my sons away from worshipping idols.... Lord, I have made some of my seed dwell in a fruitless valley, by thy holy house [the Ka'ba].... Praise to Allah, who has given me, even in my old age, Ishmael and Isaac'" (14:38 ff.). "When his Lord tested Abraham with certain commands, which he obeyed, he said, 'I make thee an example for mankind to follow.'"... "We laid upon Abraham and Ishmael the covenant obligation" [namely, to make the Ka'ba at Mecca a holy house, the center of the true Arabian worship, the beginning of a new stage in the religion of the world].... "And when Abraham, with Ishmael, was raising the foundations of the house, he said, 'Lord, accept this from us, ... make us *submissive to thee,* and make of our offspring a nation *submissive to thee,* and declare to us our ritual.... Lord, send also among them a messenger of their own, who shall teach them the Book and divine wisdom'" (2:118 ff.).

In the verses which immediately follow it is clearly implied that the true and final religion, Islam, was first revealed to the family of the patriarch. Vs. 126: "Abraham and Jacob gave this command to their sons: 'God has chosen for you the true religion; you must not die without becoming Muslims.'" All this plainly shows that the *submission* was originally associated in Muhammad's mind with Abraham; it was from his action, or attitude, that the religion received its name. "He obeyed the commands with which Allah tested him" (53:38 and 2:118).

There was one supreme test of Abraham's submission to the divine will, and it is described in an early passage in the Koran; namely, the attempted sacrifice of Ishmael (why *Ishmael,* not Isaac, has already been explained). sura 37:100 ff.: "When the boy was old enough to share the zeal of his father, Abraham said, 'My son, in a vision of the night I have been shown that I am to slaughter you as a sacrifice. Say now what you think.' He replied, 'Father, do what you are commanded; you will find me, if Allah wills, one of the steadfast.' *So when they both were resigned,* and he led him to the mountain,[17] we called to him, 'Abraham! You have indeed fulfilled the vision; ... verily this was a clear test!'" The verb in vs. 103, "they both submitted" (*aslamā*), marks the climax of the scene. Elsewhere in the Koran the verb means "embrace Islam"; here, it means simply "yield" to the will of Allah. Muhammad certainly had this supreme test in mind when he quoted the promise to the patriarch: "I make you an example for mankind to follow."

The Prophet must have had the scene before his eyes, and the all-important verb in his mind, long before he produced the thirty-seventh sura. And when he first began speaking of the "Muslims," it was the self-surrender of the two great ancestors of his people that led him to the use of the term. It required no more than ordinary foresight on the Prophet's part to see, at the very outset of his public service, that a struggle was coming; and that his followers, and perhaps he himself, would be called upon to give up every precious thing, even life itself, for the sake of the cause. Submission, absolute surrender to the divine will, was a fit designation of the faith revealed to Abraham, Ishmael, and the Arabs.

THE NARRATIVES OF THE KORAN[18]

We have seen in the preceding lectures that the Koran brings to view a rather long procession of biblical personages, some of them mentioned several times, and a few introduced and characterized repeatedly. The experiences of the chief among them are described in stereotyped phrases, usually with bits of dramatic dialogue. The two main reasons for this parade have been indicated: first, the wish to give the new Arabian religion a clear and firm connection with the previous "religions of the Book," and especially with the Hebrew scriptures; and second, the equally important purpose which Muhammad had of showing to his countrymen how the prophets had been received in the former time; and how the religion which they preached (namely Islam) was carried on from age to age, while the successive generations of men who rejected it were punished.

In all the earliest part of the Koran there is no sustained narrative; nothing like the stories and biographies which abound in the Old Testament. The ancient heroes are hardly more than names, which the ever-turning wheel of the Koran keeps bringing before us, each one laden with the same pious exhortations.

Muhammad certainly felt this lack. He was not so unlike his countrymen as not to know the difference between the interesting and the tiresome, even if he did not feel it very strongly. We know, not only from the tradition but also from the Koran itself, that his parade of Noah, Abraham, Jonah, and their fellows was received in Mecca with jeers. His colorless scraps of history were hooted at as "old stories"; and we happen to be told how on more than one occasion he suffered from competition with a real raconteur. The Meccans, like St. Paul's auditors at Athens (Acts 17:21), were ready to hear "some new thing," if only to laugh at it, but their patience was easily exhausted. One of Muhammad's neighbors, *an-Nadr ibn al-Harith*, took delight in tormenting the self-styled Prophet, and when the latter was holding forth to a circle of hearers, he would call out, "Come over here to me, and I will give you something more interesting than Muhammad's preaching!" and then he would tell them the stories of the Persian kings and heroes; while the Prophet saw his audience vanish, and was left to cherish the revenge which he took after the battle of Badr. For the too entertaining adversary, taken captive in the battle, paid for the stories with his life.

Muhammad of course knew, even without any such bitter lesson, what his countrymen would enjoy. It is quite evident, moreover, that he himself had been greatly impressed by the tales of patriarchs, prophets, and saints which had come within his knowledge; for he was in most respects a typical Arab. And while we know, especially from the introduction to his story of Joseph, that he eventually formed the purpose of adorning his Koran with some extended narratives in order to attract as well as to convince his hearers, it probably is true that an equally strong motive was his own lively interest in these famous personages and their wonderful deeds. There are certain incidents, or bits of folk-tale, which he elaborates merely because they delight him, not at all because of any religious teaching which might be squeezed out of them. This appears, for instance, in his tales of Solomon and the Queen of Sheba, of Dhu 'l-Qarnain (Alexander the Great), and of Joseph in Egypt. His imagination played upon these things until his mind was filled with them. Here was entertainment to which the people of Mecca would listen. Even stronger, doubtless, was the hope that the Jews and Christians, who had loved these tales for many generations, would be moved by this new recognition of their divine authority, and would acknowledge Islam as a new stage in their own religious history.

It is significant that all these more pretentious attempts at storytelling fall within a brief period, the last years in Mecca and the beginning of the career in Medina. They had a purpose beyond mere instruction or mere entertainment, and when that purpose failed, there was no further attempt in the same line. As to the relative proportions of Jewish and Christian material of this nature which Muhammad had in store, it will presently appear that the supply obtained from Jewish sources greatly predominates. Moreover, in the case of the only one of the longer legends which is distinctly of Christian origin there is good evidence that it came to Muhammad through the medium of a Jewish document.

But at the time when Muhammad began to put forth these few longer narratives, his Koran had grown to about one-third of the size which it ultimately attained. He must have taken satisfaction in the thought that it was beginning to have the dimensions of a sacred book, the scriptures of the new revelation in the Arabic tongue. The addition of a number of entertaining portions of history, anecdote, and biography would considerably increase its bulk, as well as its resemblance to the former sacred books.

Here appears obviously one very striking difference between the narratives of the Koran and those of the Bible. The latter were the product of consummate literary art, written at various times, for religious instruction, by men who were born storytellers. They were preserved and handed down by a process of selection, gradually recognized as the best of their kind, and ultimately incorporated in a great anthology. In the Koran, on the contrary, we see a totally new thing—a most forbidding undertaking: the production of narrative as divine revelation, to rate from the first as inspired scripture; narrative, moreover, which had already been given permanent form in the existing sacred books. Here was a dilemma which evidently gave the Arabian Prophet some trouble. If he should merely reproduce the story of Joseph, or of Jonah, wholly or in part, from the Jewish tradition, he would be charged with plagiarism. If he should tell the stories with any essential difference, he would be accused of falsifying.

A skillful narrator might have escaped this difficulty by his own literary art, producing something interesting and yet in keeping with the familiar tradition. But Muhammad was very far from being a skillful narrator. His imagination is vivid, but not creative. His characters are all alike, and they utter the same platitudes. He is fond of dramatic dialogue, but has very little sense of dramatic scene or action. The logical connection between successive episodes is often loose, sometimes wanting; and points of importance, necessary for the clear understanding of the story, are likely to be left out. There is also the inveterate habit of repetition, and a very defective sense of humor. In short, anyone familiar with the style of the Koran would be likely to predict that Muhammad's tales of ancient worthies would lack most of the qualities which the typical "short story" ought to have. And the fact would be found to justify the prediction.

In sura 11:27–57 is given a lengthy account of Noah's experiences; the building of the ark, the flood, the arrival on Mount Ararat, and God's promise for the future. It contains very little incident, but consists chiefly of the same religious harangues which are repeated scores of times throughout the Koran, uninspired and uniformly wearisome. We have the feeling that one of Noah's contemporaries who was confronted with the prospect of forty days and forty nights in the ark would prefer to take his chances with the deluge.

It must in fairness be reiterated, however, that this task of refashioning by divine afterthought would have been a problem for any narrator. Muhammad does slip out of the dilemma into which he had seemed to be forced; and the manner in which he does this is highly interesting—and instructive. The story, Jewish or Christian, is told by him in fragments; often with a repeated introductory formula that would seem to imply that the Prophet had not only received his information directly from heaven, but also had been given numerous details which had not been vouchsafed to the "people of the Book." The angel of revelation brings in rather abruptly an incident or scene in the history of this or that biblical hero with a simple introductory "And when...." It says, in effect: "You remember the occasion when Moses said to his servant, 'I will not halt until I reach the confluence of the two rivers'"; and the incident is narrated. "And then there was that time, Muhammad, when Abraham said to his people" thus and so. It is not intended, the formula implies, to tell the whole story; but more could be told, if it were necessary.

The more closely one studies the details of Muhammad's curious, and at first sight singularly ineffectual, manner of serving up these old narratives, the more clearly is gained the impression that underlying it all is the deliberate attempt to solve a problem.

The story of Joseph and his brethren is the only one in the Koran which is carried through with some semblance of completeness. It begins with the boy in the land of Canaan, and ends with the magnate in Pharaoh's kingdom, and the establishing of Jacob and his family in Egypt. It is the only instance in which an entire sura is given up to a single subject of this nature. The following extracts will give some idea of the mode of treatment.[19]

Gabriel says to Muhammad: "[Remember what occurred] when Joseph said to his father, 'O father! I saw eleven stars and the sun and the moon prostrating themselves before me!' He answered, 'O my boy, tell not your vision to your brothers, for they will plot against you; verily the devil is a manifest foe to mankind.'" After a verse or two of religious instruction the story proceeds:

The brethren said, "Surely Joseph and his brother are more beloved by our father than we; indeed he is in manifest error. Kill Joseph, or cast him away in some distant place; then we shall have our father to ourselves." One of them said, "Kill not Joseph, but throw him into the bottom of the pit; then some caravan will pluck him out." They said, "O father! what ails you that you will not trust us with Joseph, although we are his sincere helpers? Send him with us tomorrow to sport and play, and we will take good care of him." He said, "It would grieve me that you should take him away, and I fear that the wolf will devour him while you are neglecting him." They said, "If the wolf should devour him, while we are such a company, we should indeed be stupid!" And when they went away with him and agreed to put him in the bottom of the well, we gave him this revelation: "Thou shalt surely tell them of this deed of theirs when they are not aware."

They came to their father at eventide, weeping. They said, "O father! we went off to run races, and left Joseph with our things, and the wolf ate him up; and you will not believe us, though we are telling the truth."

Their father of course takes the broad hint given him, that they are lying; though they bring a shirt with blood on it as evidence. He accuses them of falsehood, and reproaches them bitterly. Then is told in a very few words how the caravan came, drew Joseph out of the well, and sold him for a few dirhems to a man in Egypt.

Thereupon follows the attempt of the man's wife to entice Joseph. Any episode in which women play a part is likely to be dwelt upon by Muhammad, and he gives full space to the scenes which follow. Joseph refused at first, but was at last ready to yield, when he saw a vision which deterred him. (The nature of this is not told in the Koran, but we know from the Jewish Midrash that it was the vision of his father, with Rachel and Leah.)[20] The Koran proceeds:

They raced to the door, and she tore his shirt from behind; and at the door they met her husband. She cried, "What is the penalty upon him who wished to do evil to your wife, imprisonment or a dreadful punishment?" Joseph said, "She enticed me." One of her family bore witness:[21] "If his shirt is torn in front, she tells the truth; if it is torn behind, she is lying." So when he saw that the shirt was torn from behind, he cried, "This is one of your woman-tricks; verily the tricks of you women are amazing! Joseph, turn aside from this! And do you, woman, ask forgiveness for your sin?"

Then certain women of the city said, "The wife of the prince tried to entice her young servant; she is utterly infatuated with him; verily we consider her in manifest error." So when she heard their treachery, she sent an invitation to them, and prepared for them a banquet,[22] and gave each one of them a knife, and said, "Come forth to them!" And when they saw him, they were struck with admiration and cut their hands and cried, "Good heavens! This is no human being, it is a glorious angel!" Then said she, "This is he concerning whom you blamed me. I did seek to entice him, but he held himself firm; and if he does not do what I command him, surely he shall be imprisoned, and be one of the ignominious." He said, "Lord, the prison is my choice instead of that to which they invite me. But if thou dost not turn their wiles away from me, I shall be smitten with love for them, and shall become one of the foolish." His Lord answered his prayer, and turned their wiles away from him; verily he is one who hears and knows.

This is characteristic of the angel Gabriel's manner of spoiling a good story. Aside from the fact that we are left in some uncertainty as to Joseph's firmness of character, it is not evident what the episode of the banquet had to do with the course of events; nor why the ladies were provided with knives; nor why Joseph, after all, was put in prison. These things are all made plain in the Midrash, however.[23]

The account of Joseph's two companions in the prison, and of his ultimate release, is given in very summary fashion. "There entered the prison with him two young men. One of them said, 'I see myself pressing out wine;' and the other said, 'I see myself carrying bread upon my head, and the birds eating from it. Tell us the interpretation of this.'" After a religious discourse of some length, Joseph gives them the interpretation; and it is implied, though not definitely said, that his prediction was completely fulfilled. The dream of Pharaoh is then introduced abruptly. "The king said, 'Verily I see seven fat cows which seven lean ones are devouring; and seven green ears of grain and others which are dry. O you princes, explain to me my vision, if you can interpret a vision.'" The princes naturally give it up. The king's butler remembers Joseph, though several years have elapsed, and he is summoned from the prison. He refuses to come out, however, until his question has been answered: "What was in the mind of those women who cut their hands? Verily my master knows their wiles." The women are questioned, and both the officer's wife and her companions attest Joseph's innocence. He is then brought out, demands to be set over the treasuries of all Egypt, and the king complies.

Joseph's brethren now enter the story again. Nothing is said about a famine in the land of Canaan, nor is any other reason given for their arrival; they simply appear. The remainder of the tale is in the main a straightforward, somewhat fanciful, condensation of the version given in the book of Genesis, with some lively dialogue. There are one or two touches from the Midrash. Jacob warns his sons not to enter the city by a single gate. The Midrash gives the reason;[24] the Koran leaves the Muslim commentators to guess—as of course they easily can. When the cup is found in Benjamin's sack, and he is proclaimed a thief, his brethren say, "If he has stolen, a brother of his stole before him." The commentators are at their wits' end to explain how Joseph could have been accused of stealing. The explanation is furnished by the Midrash, which remarks at this point that Benjamin's *mother* before him had stolen,[25] referring of course to the time when Rachel carried off her father's household gods (Gen 31 :19–35).

The occasion when Joseph makes himself known to his brethren is not an affecting scene in the Koran, as it is in the Hebrew story. The narrator's instinct which would cause him to work up to a climax was wanting in the Meccan Prophet's equipment. The brethren come to Egypt for the third time, appear before Joseph, and beg him to give them good measure. He replies, "'Do you know what you did to Joseph and his brother, in the time of your ignorance?' They said, 'Are you then Joseph?' He answered, 'I am Joseph, and this is my brother. God has been gracious to us. Whoever is pious and patient,—God will not suffer the righteous to lose their reward.'" This is simple routine; no one in the party appears to be excited.

Jacob wept for Joseph until the constant flow of tears destroyed his eyesight. Joseph, therefore, when the caravan bringing his parents to Egypt set out from Canaan, sent his shirt by a messenger, saying that it would restore his father's sight. Jacob recognizes the odor of the shirt while yet a long distance from it, and says, "Verily I perceive the smell of Joseph!" The messenger arrives, throws the shirt on Jacob's face, and the sight is restored. The story ends with the triumphant entrance into Egypt, and the fulfillment of the dream of Joseph's boyhood; they have all bowed down to him.

Before the impressive homily which closes the chapter, Gabriel says to Muhammad (verse 103): "This tale is one of the secrets which we reveal to you"; and he adds, referring to Joseph's brethren: "You were not with them when they agreed upon their plan and were treacherous."[26] This might seem to be a superfluous reminder; but its probable intent is to say here with especial emphasis, not only to Muhammad but also to others, that no

inspired prophet, Arabian or Hebrew, can narrate details, or record dia-
logues, other than those which have been revealed to him. Conversely,
every prophet has a right to his own story.

The tale of Solomon and the Queen of Sheba (27:16–45) gives further
illustration of Muhammad's manner of retelling in leaps and bounds. Here
also is shown, even more clearly than in the story of Joseph, his tendency
to be mysterious. The material of the narrative is taken from the Jewish
Haggada,[27] but much is omitted that is quite necessary for the understanding of the story. Change of scene is not indicated, and the progress of
events is often buried under little homilies delivered by the principal characters (I omit the homilies).

> Solomon was David's heir; and he said: "O you people! We have been
> taught the speech of birds, and we have been given everything. Verily.
> this is a manifest favor."
>
> There were assembled for Solomon his hosts of jinn, and men, and
> birds; and they proceeded together until they came to the Valley of the
> Ants.[28] An ant cried out: "O you ants! Get into your dwellings, lest
> Solomon and his armies crush you without knowing it." Solomon smiled,
> laughing at her speech, and said: "O Lord, arouse me to thankfulness for
> thy favor...."

Here follows a homily. We are left in some doubt as to whether the ants
suffered any damage; for the tale proceeds:

> He reviewed the birds, and said, "How is it that I do not see the hoopoe?
> Is he among the absent? I surely will torture him with severe tortures, or
> I will slaughter him, or else he shall bring me an authoritative excuse."
> He was not long absent, however; and he said: "I have learned something
> which you knew not. I bring you from Sheba sure information. I found a
> woman ruling over them; she has been given all things, and she has a
> mighty throne. I found her and her people worshiping the sun."
> Solomon said, "We shall see whether you have told the truth, or are one
> of the liars. Take this letter of mine, and throw it before them. Then
> return, and we will see what reply they make."
> She said: "O you chieftains! A noble letter has been thrown before
> me. It is from Solomon, and it says, 'In the name of God, the merciful
> Rahman; Do not resist me, but come to me resigned.' O you chieftains!
> Advise me in this matter." They said, "We are mighty men of valor, but

it is for you to command." She said, "When kings enter a city, they plunder it and humble its mighty men. I will send them a present, and see what my messenger brings back."

Solomon preaches to the messenger, threatens him and his people, and bids him return. Then he addresses his curious army: "Which of you will bring me her throne, before they come in submission?" (There was need of haste, for after the queen had once accepted Islam, Solomon would have no right to touch her property.) "A demon of the jinn said, 'I will bring it, before you can rise from your seat.' He who had the knowledge of the Book said, 'I will bring it, before your glance can turn.' So when he saw the throne set down before him, he said, 'This is of the favor of my Lord'" (and he adds some improving reflections of a general nature). The native commentators explain that the throne was brought to Solomon underground, the demons digging away the earth in front and filling it in behind; and all in the twinkling of an eye—according to the promise. The reader must not suppose, however, that this underground transit was from South Arabia to Palestine. Muhammad left out the part of the story which tells how Solomon's army was transported through the air to a place in the neighborhood of the queen's capital.

"He said, 'Disguise her throne! We shall see whether she is rightly guided, or not.' So when she came, it was said, 'Was your throne like this?' She replied, 'It might be the same.' Then they said to her, 'Enter the court!' And when she saw it, she supposed it to be a pool of water, and uncovered her legs to wade through. But Solomon (who was not absent) said: 'It is a court paved with glass!' She said, 'O Lord, verily I have been wrong; but I am now resigned, with Solomon, to Allah the Lord of the Worlds!'" That is, she became a Muslim. The Koran drops the story here, not concerned to tell that Solomon married her.

Of the queen's interest in the *wisdom* of Solomon, which plays such a part in the biblical narrative, and still more in the Jewish Midrash, not a word is said here. This feature must have been known to Muhammad, but it did not suit his purpose. His own quaintly disjointed sketch doubtless achieved the effect which he intended. The mystery of the half-told would certainly impress the Meccans; and the Jews would say, "We know these incidents, and there is much more of the story in our books!" So Muhammad would achieve a double triumph.

The account of Jonah and his experiences given in 37:139–148 is unique in the Koran. The whole biblical narrative, without any external features, is told in a single breath, a noteworthy example of condensation. Even the hymn of prayer and praise from the belly of the whale receives mention in vs. 143. As has already been observed, Jonah is the only one of all the fifteen *Nebiim Acharonim* to receive mention in the Koran. The name of the Hebrew prophet is given (here as elsewhere) in a form ultimately based on the Greek, seeming to indicate—as in so many other cases—an origin outside Arabia. The nutshell summary may have been made by Muhammad himself, after hearing the story read or repeated (though he nowhere else condenses in this headlong but complete fashion); or it may have been dictated to him, and then by him decorated, clause by clause, with his rhymed verse-endings.

> Verily, Jonah was one of the missionaries. When he fled to the laden ship, he cast lots, and was of those who lost. The whale swallowed him, for he was blameworthy; and had it not been that he celebrated God's praises, he surely would have remained in its belly until the day when men rise from the dead. So we cast him upon the barren shore; and he was sick; and we made a gourd to grow over him. And we sent him to a hundred thousand, or more; and they believed, and we gave them prosperity for a time.

The narrative of "Saul and Goliath" (Talut and Jalut) gives a good illustration of the way in which the Meccan Prophet's memory sometimes failed him.

The leaders of the children of Israel ask their prophet to give them a king (2:247). He argues with them, but eventually says:

> God has appointed Talut as your king. They said, "How shall he be king over us when we are more worthy to rule than he, and he has no abundance of wealth?" He answered, "God has chosen him over you, and has made him superior in knowledge and in stature (cf. I Sam. 9:2)...." So when Talut went forth with the armies, he said: "God will test you by a river: Whoever drinks of it is not of mine; those who do not taste of it, or who only sip it from the hand, are my army." So all but a few drank of it. When they had passed beyond it, some said, "We are powerless this day against Jalut and his forces." But those who believed that they must meet God said, "How often has a little band conquered a numerous army, by the will of God! He is with those who are steadfast." So they went forth

against the army,... and by the will of God they routed them; and David
slew Jalut, and God gave him the kingdom.

Here, obviously, is confusion with the tale of Gideon and his three
hundred picked men (Judg. 7:47). The casual way in which David finally
enters the narrative is also noteworthy.

The first half of the twenty-eighth sura (vss. 2–46) gives an interesting
outline of the early history of Moses, following closely the first four chapters of Exodus. It illustrates both the general trustworthiness of
Muhammad's memory, for it includes practically every item contained in
these chapters, often with reproduction of the very words; and also, a certain freedom in his treatment of the Hebrew material, for he introduces,
for his own convenience, some characteristic little changes and embellishments. This is the longest continuous extract from The Old Testament
which the Koran contains. Muhammad does not treat the story as an
episode in Hebrew history, but carries it through, in his cryptic fashion,
without any specific mention of the "children of Israel." The sura dealing
with Joseph and his brethren had already been put forth (it can hardly be
doubted), but he makes no allusion to it, nor to the entrance of Hebrews
into Egypt.

> Pharaoh exalted himself in the earth, and divided his people into parties.
> One portion of them he humbled, slaughtering their male children, and
> suffering their females to live; verily he was of those who deal wickedly.
> But we were purposing to show favor to those who were humbled in the
> land, and to make them leaders and heirs; to establish them in the earth,
> and to show Pharaoh and Haman and their hosts what they had to fear
> from them.

Haman appears consistently in the Koranic narrative (also in suras 29
and 40) as Pharaoh's vizier. Rabbinic legends mention several advisers of
Pharaoh (Geiger, 153), but Muhammad had in mind a more important
officer. He had heard the story of Esther (and of course retained it in
memory), and both name and character of the arch anti-Semite appealed
strongly to his imagination. That he transferred the person, as well as the
name, to Egypt is not at all likely. Gabriel knew that there were two
Hamans.

And we gave this revelation to Moses' mother: Give him suck; and when you fear for his life, put him into the river; and be not fearful, nor grieved; for we will restore him to you, and make him one of our apostles. So Pharaoh's family plucked him out, to be an enemy and a misfortune to them; verily Pharaoh and Haman and their hosts were sinners. Pharaoh's wife said, "Here is joy for me and thee! Slay him not, haply he may be of use to us, or we may adopt him as a son" (repeating the words which Potiphar uttered to his wife, in the case of Joseph). But they knew not what was impending.

Events develop as in the biblical narrative. Moses' mother is hindered by divine intervention from letting out the secret, in her anxiety. The child's sister follows him, keeping watch, unobserved, from a distance. The babe refuses the breast of Egyptian nurses, as the Talmud declares (*Sotah*, 12 b); so it comes about that he is restored to his mother. Arrived at manhood, Moses enters "the city" stealthily, and finds two men fighting: "The one, a member of his party; the other, of his enemies." He is called upon for help, and kills the "enemy" with his fist—the blow of an expert boxer. He repents of his deed, utters a prayer, and is forgiven; but on the following day, as he enters the city cautiously and in apprehension, the same scene is set: the same man is fighting with another of the hostile party, and cries out for help. Moses reproaches his comrade ("Verily you are a manifest scoundrel!"), but again intervenes. As he approaches, to deal another knock-out blow, the intended victim cries out: "O Moses, do you mean to kill me, as you killed a man yesterday? You are only aiming to be a tyrant in the land, not to be one of the virtuous!" Just then a man came running from the other end of the city, saying, "O Moses, the nobles are taking counsel to kill you! So be off; I am giving you good advice." Thereupon Moses starts for Midian.

The account of the happenings in Midian is given with characteristic improvement. Here again is illustrated the Prophet's lively interest in those scenes in which women figure prominently. He doubles the romance in the story, patterning it, in a general way, upon the account of Jacob and Rachel. *Seven* daughters at the well are too many; he recognizes only *two*; and Moses serves them gallantly, thereafter accompanying them home. "One of them came to him, walking bashfully, and said: 'My father is calling for you, to pay you for drawing water for us.' And when he came to him, and told him his story, he said, 'Fear not; you have escaped from an impious people.'" Muhammad neither names the father of the girls nor shows the least interest in him; he is merely a necessary property of the story. We could wish, however, that Muhammad (or Moses) had shown a more decided preference for the one or the other of the daughters.

> One of them said, "O father, hire him! The best that you hire are the strong and trusty." He said: "I wish to marry you to one of these two daughters of mine, on the condition that you work for me eight years;[29] and if you shall wish to make it a full ten years, that rests with you. I do not wish to be hard on you, and you will find me, if God wills, one of the upright." Moses replied: "So be it between thee and me; whichever of the two terms I fulfill, there will be no grudge against me; and God is the witness of what we say." So when Moses had completed the term [which term?], and journeyed away with his family [which daughter?], he became aware of a fire on the side of the mountain. He said to his family, "Wait here; I have discovered a fire. Perhaps I may bring you news from it, or a firebrand, so that you may warm yourselves." So when he came up to it, a voice called to him out of the tree, on the right side of the wady in the sacred valley, "O Moses! I am God, the Lord of the Worlds. Throw down your rod." And when he saw it move as though it were a serpent, he fled from it without turning back. "O Moses, draw nigh and fear not, for you are safe!"

The narrative then recounts the miracle of the leprous hand, the appointment of Aaron, and the first unsuccessful appearance before Pharaoh and his magicians. Instead of the story of the brickmaking task, which occupies the fifth chapter of Exodus, Muhammad introduces a feature which he adapts from the story of the Tower of Babel.

> Pharaoh said: "O you nobles! I know not that you have any god except myself. So now, Haman, burn for me bricks of clay, and build me a tower, so that I may mount up to the god of Moses; verily I consider him a liar." And he and his hosts behaved arrogantly and unjustly in the earth, nor considered that they shall be brought back to us. So we took him and his armies and cast them into the sea; behold therefore how the wicked are punished.

Gabriel concludes by saying to the Prophet (as at the end of the story of Joseph): "You were not on the west side when we decreed the matter for Moses, nor were you a witness; … nor were you dwelling among the people of Midian. . . . It is only by mercy from your Lord (that these things are revealed to you)."

This narrative of the early life of Moses is particularly instructive, not only as illustrating Muhammad's manner of retelling the biblical stories, but also as showing, better than any other part of the Koran, the freedom with which he could adorn his own account with properties deliberately taken over by him from other biblical stories with which he was familiar. That he felt himself to be quite within his rights, *as a prophet,* in so doing, may be considered certain.

The eighteenth sura holds a peculiar place in the Koran. The narratives of which it is mainly composed are at once seen to be different in character from the types which elsewhere are so familiar. While in every other part of the sacred book Muhammad draws either upon the biblical and rabbinic material or else upon Arabian lore, in sura 18 we are given a sheaf of legends from world literature. The stories have the characteristic Muhammadan flavor, it is true; yet the sura has distinctly an atmosphere of its own, and the Prophet makes no allusion elsewhere to any part of its narrative material.

First comes the famous legend of the Seven Sleepers of Ephesus. Certain youths fled to a cave in the mountains to escape the persecution of the Christians under Decius (c. 250 C.E.). Their pursuers found their hiding place, and walled it up. They were miraculously preserved in a Rip van Winkle sleep, and came forth some two hundred years later, in the reign of the emperor Theodosius II, when some workmen happened to take away the stones. The legend arose before the end of the fifth century, and soon made its way all over western Asia and Europe. Since it is a Christian tale, and since also there is particular mention of the Christians in the opening verses of the sura, some have drawn the conclusion that this little collection of stories was designed by the Prophet to attract the adherents of that faith especially. There is, however, nothing else in the chapter to give support to this theory, while on the other hand there is considerable evidence that even the opening legend came to Muhammad through the medium of a Jewish document. Aside from the fact that Muslim tradition represents the Jews of Mecca as interested in this tale (see Baidawi on vs. 23), and the additional fact that each of the following narratives in the sura appears to be derived from a Jewish recension, there is a bit of internal evidence here which should not be overlooked. In vs. 18 the speaker says, "Send someone . . . to the city, and *let him find out where the cleanest food is to be had,* and bring provision from it." This emphasized care as to the legal fitness of the food at once suggests a Jewish version of the legend. A Christian narrator, if the idea occurred to him at all, would have need to specify what he meant (e.g., food offered to idols). It is to be observed that this motive does not occur in the homily of Jacob of Sarug, nor is there anything corresponding to it in any of the early Christian versions which I have seen; those for instance published by Guidi, *I Sette Dormienti,* and Huber, *Die Wanderlegende.* There is no Christian element in the story, as it lies before us in the Koran; it might well be an account of the persecution of Israelite youths.

As usual, the narrative begins without scene or setting. Gabriel says to Muhammad:

> Do you not think, then, that the heroes of the story of the cave and of ar-Raqim[30] were of our marvellous signs? When the youths took refuge in the cave, they said, "Lord, show us thy mercy, and guide us aright in this affair of ours." So we sealed up their hearing in the cave for a number of years. Then at length we awakened them; and we would see which of the two parties made better calculation of the time which had elapsed.... You could see the sun, when it arose, pass to the right of their cave, and when it set, go by them on the left, while they were in a chamber within. ... You would have thought them awake, but they were asleep; and we turned them over, now to the right, now to the left; and their dog stretched out his paws at the entrance. If you had come upon them suddenly, you would have fled from them in fear. Then we awakened them, to let them question one another. One said, "How long have you tarried?" Some answered, "A day, or part of a day." Others said, "Your Lord knows best how long; but send one, with this money, into the city; let him find where the cleaner food is to be had, and bring back provision. Let him be courteous, and not make you known to anyone. If they get knowledge of you, they will stone you, or bring you back to their religion; then you will fare ill forever." So we made their story known; ... and the people of the city disputed about them. Some said, "Build a structure over them; their Lord knows best about them." Those whose opinion won the day said, "We will build over them a house of worship."

The verses which follow show that the Prophet was heckled about this tale, and felt that he had been incautious. The existing versions of the legend differed, or were noncommittal, as to the number of the sleepers.

Some of Muhammad's hearers were familiar with the story, and now asked him for exact information. It may be useless to conjecture who these hearers were, but the probability certainly inclines toward the Jews, who heckled Muhammad on other occasions, and of all the inhabitants of Mecca were those most likely to be acquainted with this literature. If, as otherwise seems probable, it came to the Prophet's knowledge through them, and in an anthology made for their use, they would very naturally be disposed to make trouble for him when he served out the legends as a part of his divine revelation. The Koran proceeds:

> They will say, "Three, and the fourth was their dog"; or they will say, "Five, and the sixth was their dog (guessing at the secret)"; others will say, "Seven, and their dog made eight." Say: "My Lord best knows their number, and there are few others who know." Do not dispute with them, unless as to what is certain; nor apply to any one of them for information. Say not in regard to a thing, "I will do it tomorrow"; but say, "If God wills." Remember your Lord, when you have forgotten, and say, "Mayhap my Lord will guide me, that I may draw near to the truth in this matter." They remained in their cave three hundred years, and nine more. Say: "God knows best how long they stayed."

After this comes (vss. 31–42) a parable of a familiar sort: the god-fearing poor man, and his arrogant neighbor, the impious rich man, upon whom punishment soon descends. This might be Jewish, or Christian, or (much less probably) native Arabic. It is not difficult to believe that Muhammad himself could have composed it entire, but more likely it is abbreviated by him from something which formed part of the (Aramaic?) anthology which was his main source in this sura.

Farther on (verse 59) begins the story of Moses and his attendant, journeying in search of the fountain of life. This is a well known episode in the legend of Alexander the Great, whose place is here taken by Moses. Muhammad certainly was not the author of the substitution, but received it with the rest of the story. To all appearance, we have here a Jewish popular adaptation of the legend. The opening words of the Koranic version, however, take us far back of Alexander the Great. Moses says to his attendant, "I will not halt until I reach the meeting-place of the two rivers, though I go on for many years!" Now this brings in a bit of very ancient mythology. In the old Babylonian epic of Gilgamesh the hero, after many labors and trials, goes forth in search of immortality. He hears of a favorite of the gods, Utnapishtim, who has been granted eternal life. After great exertions Gilgamesh arrives at the place where this ancient hero dwells, *"at the confluence of the streams."* Utnapishtim attempts to give some help, but Gilgamesh fails of his main purpose. The Koran proceeds:

> Now when they reached the confluence, they forgot their fish, and it made its way into the river in quick passage. After they had proceeded farther, Moses said to his attendant, "Bring out our luncheon, for we have suffered weariness in this journey of ours." He answered: "Do you see, when we halted at the rock I forgot the fish (and only Satan made me forget to mention the fact), and it took its way into the river marvelously." He cried, "That is the place which we were seeking!" And they turned about straightway on their track.

They had taken with them a dried fish for food, and the magical water restored it to life. This motive occurs in other legends, but the ultimate source of the main account here is plainly the narrative in Pseudo-Callisthenes, which in the forms known to us contains also this particular incident. Gilgamesh, Alexander, and Moses all find the place of which they were in search, but Moses' fish alone achieves immortality. It is important to observe, moreover, that Moses, like Gilgamesh, finds the ancient hero to whom God had granted eternal life. The Koran does not name him, but he is well known to Muslim legend by the name al-Khidr ("Evergreen"?).[31]

The story of Moses now enters a new phase. He becomes temporarily the peripatetic pupil of the immortal saint; the attendant who figured in the preceding narrative disappears from sight.

> So they found a servant of ours, to whom we had granted mercy, and whom we had taught our wisdom. Moses said to him, "May I follow you, with the understanding that you will impart to me of your wisdom?" He replied, "You will not be able to bear with me. For how can you restrain yourself in regard to matters which your knowledge does not compass?" He said, "You will find me patient (if God wills), and I will not oppose you in anything." "If then you will follow me," he said, "you must not question me about any matter, until I give you account of it."

The wise man who does strange things, ultimately explained by him, is well known to folklore. The amazement, or distress, of the onlooker is of course always an essential feature. The penalty of inquisitiveness, "If you question, we must part!" (as in the tale of Lohengrin), might naturally occur to any narrator—especially when the wise man is an immortal, who of necessity must soon disappear from mortal eyes. This feature, however, is not at all likely to have been Muhammad's own invention, but on the contrary is an essential part of the story which he repeats. Whoever the inquisitive mortal may have been in the legend's first estate, as it came to the Arabian prophet it was a Jewish tale told of Moses. More than this cannot be said at present.

The servant of God scuttles a boat which he and Moses had borrowed; kills a youth whom they happen to meet; and takes the trouble to rebuild a tottering wall in a city whose inhabitants had refused them shelter. On each of the three occasions Moses expresses his concern at the deed. Twice he is pardoned, but on his third failure to restrain himself the servant dismisses him, after giving him information which showed each of the three deeds to have been fully justified.

Last of all, in this sura, comes the narrative of the "Two-Horned" hero—again Alexander the Great. Verse 82 introduces the account with the words: "They will ask you about Dhu'l-Qarnain ('him of the two horns')". What interrogators did Gabriel have in mind? According to the Muslim tradition, the Jews were intended; and this is for every reason probable. The Koranic story, like its predecessor which told of the fountain of life, is based on Pseudo-Callisthenes; but it contains traits which point to a Jewish adaptation. Haggada and Midrash had dealt extensively with Alexander; and (as in the case of the story of the Seven Sleepers) no other of the Prophet's hearers would have been so likely to test his knowledge of great events and personages. What Muhammad had learned about Alexander seems in fact to have been very little. He tells how the hero journeyed, first to the setting of the sun, and then to the place of its rising, appearing in either place as an emissary of the one God. The major amount of space, however, is given to the account of the protection against Gog and Magog (Yajuj and Majuj), the great wall built by Alexander. This fantasy on traits of Hebrew mythology suggests the Haggada, and increases the probability, already established, that all of the varied folklore in this eighteenth sura was derived from a Jewish collection of stories and parables (probably a single document) designed for popular instruction and entertainment.

When to the longer narratives which have been described are added the many brief bits mentioned in the preceding lecture, and the fact is borne in mind that Muhammad's purpose is to give only a selection, or occasionally mere fragments, it is evident that he had imbibed a great amount of material of this nature. It included (1) biblical narrative more or less altered; (2) Jewish Haggada, in already fixed form; (3) a small amount of material of ultimately Christian origin; and (4) legends belonging to world literature, available at Mecca in the Aramaic language. The treatment is Muhammad's own, with abridgment in his characteristic manner, and embellishment mainly homiletic. For the chronological and other blunders he alone is responsible. Finally, it is to be borne in mind that the Prophet knew, better than we know, what he was trying to do. In the case of some habitual traits which we find amusing, such as the grasshopperlike mode of progressing, and the omission of essential features, we may well question to what extent they show shrewd calculation rather than childlike inconsequence. Since his purpose was not to reproduce the Jewish scriptures, but to give the Arabs a share in them, his method may be judged by the result. His hearers were not troubled by the violation of literary canons, for they felt themselves in the presence of a divine message intended for them especially. If they were mystified, they were also profoundly stirred and stimulated. Around all these Koranic narratives there is, and was from the first, the atmosphere of an Arabian revelation, and they form a very characteristic and important part of the Prophet's great achievement.

PART FOUR

Modern Textual Criticism of the Koran

14.

Literary Analysis of Koran, Tafsir, and Sira: The Methodologies of John Wansbrough

Andrew Rippin

*T*HAT JUDAISM AND CHRISTIANITY ARE religions "in history" seems to be a commonly accepted notion among many people today. The view is that history is the "'proving ground" of these religions, that the intervention of God in the historical sequence of events is the most significant truth attested by these religions. Whether or not this is theologically valid is a question that must he left for those who pursue such questions; what is of interest here are the implications which this view has had for "secular" historical studies and, most importantly here, for the historical study of religion. The idea that these are religions "in history" has led to an emphasis on the desire to discover "what really happened," ultimately, because of the underlying belief that this discovery would demonstrate the ultimate truth or falsity of the individual religion. Now that may or may not be an appropriate task depending on the particular view of history taken by the historian, but it has led to one important problem in the study of religion—the supposition that the sources available to us to describe the historical foundations of a given religion, most specifically the scriptures, contain within them discernible historical data which can be used to provide

Originally published in *Approaches to Islam in Religious Studies,* edited by Richard C. Martin (Tucson: University of Arizona Press, 1985), pp. 151–63, 227–32. Copyright © 1985 by The Arizona Board of Regents. Reprinted by permission of the University of Arizona Press.

positive historical results. In other words, the approach assumes that the
motivations of the writers of such sources were the same as the motivations
of present-day historians, namely, to record "what really happened."

Whether out of theological conviction or merely unconsciously
modern scholarship has approached Islam in the same way that it has traditionally treated Judaism and Christianity—as a religion of history, that
is as a religion that has a stake in history. Whether this approach is valid or
invalid is not the point here. What is relevant is that this view has led to the
same sort of attitude toward the sources available in the study of early
Islam as that which characterizes the attitude in the study of Judaism and
Christianity namely that these sources purport to record (and thus provide
us with) an account of "what real happened." The desire to know what
happened in the past is certainly not unreasonable nor is it theoretically an
impossible task; Islam most definitely has a history that needs to be recovered. But the desire to achieve positive results must not lead us to ignore
the literary qualities of the sources available to us.

Very little material of "neutral" testimonial quality is available for the
study of early Islam; sizable quantities of archeological data, numismatic
evidence, even datable documents are all very much wanting. Evidence
from sources external to the community itself are not plentiful either and
the reconstruction of such material into a historical framework is fraught
with difficulties. In *Hagarism,* Patricia Crone and Michael Cook have
attempted such a reconstruction and, although they successfully draw
attention to the problems involved in the study of Islam, they have not
been able to get beyond the limitations inherent in the sources, for they are
all of questionable historical authenticity and, more importantly, all are
treatises based in polemic. No one has yet expressed the problem better
than John Wansbrough. "[C]an a vocabulary of motives be freely extrapo-
lated from a discrete collection of literary stereotypes composed by alien
and mostly hostile observers and thereupon employed to describe, even
interpret, not merely the overt behavior but also the intellectual and spiritual development of helpless and almost innocent actors?"[1] The other
sources available to us—the Arabic texts internal to the Muslim community—consist of a limited mass of literature originating at least two centuries after the fact. Such information as this literature contains was written
in light of the passage of those two centuries and would indeed seem to
have a stake in that very history being recounted. These internal sources
intended, after all, to document the basis of faith, the validity of the sacred

book, and its evidence of God's plan for humankind. These sources recorded "Salvation History."

One brief example may help to clarify the exact dimensions of the problem. Nowhere has the attitude toward the historical character of the sources about the foundation of Islam proved to be more resilient than in the interpretation of the Koran. Muslim exegetes have a category of information available to them called *asbab al-nuzul,* commonly translated as the "occasions of revelation," which have been thought by Western students of the Koran to record the historical events concerning the revelation of individual verses of the Koran. Careful analysis of the individual uses of these *asbāb* in exegesis reveals that their actual significance in individual cases of trying to understand the Koran is limited: the anecdotes are adduced and thus recorded and transmitted in order to provide a narrative situation in which an interpretation of the Koran can be embodied. The material has been recorded within exegesis not for its historical value but for its exegetical value. Yet such basic literary facts about the material are frequently ignored within the study of Islam in the desire to find positive historical results. A good example of what I mean is found in a recent article on Muhammad's boycott of Mecca; a *sabab* (occasion) recorded in al-Tabari's *tafsir*[2] is used to defend and elaborate upon a complicated historical reconstruction about the life of Muhammad.[3] The desire for historical results has led to an entire glossing of the problems and limitations of the sources.

THE NATURE OF THE SOURCES

John Wansbrough of the School of Oriental and African Studies at the University of London has made a systematic attempt to get beyond the problems involved in trying to understand the beginnings of Islam. In two recent books Wansbrough argues for a critical assessment of the value of the sources from a literary point of view, in order to escape the inherent theological view of the history in the account of Islamic origins. The two works, *Quranic Studies: Sources and Methods of Scriptural Interpretation* (hereafter *QS*)[4] and *The Sectarian Milieu: Content and Composition of Islamic Salvation History* (hereafter *SM*),[5] fit together quite logically, although it should be noted that there is some progression of thought between the two works on some specific topics. *QS* was written between 1968 and 1971 although it was published in 1977; *SM* was written between 1973 and 1977, but published in 1978. Those following Wansbrough's numerous reviews will appreciate that his thought has not stopped there either.[6] Wansbrough emphasizes that the ideas he has put forth in his books are a tentative working out of the problems involved. *QS* deals primarily with the formation of the Koran along with the witness of exegetical writings (*tafsir*) to that formation; *SM* develops the theme of the evolution of Islam further through the traditional biographies of Muhammad (*sira* and *maghazi*), and then works through the process of the theological elaboration of Islam as a religious community, examining the questions of authority, identity, and epistemology.

The basic methodological point of Wansbrough's works is to ask the prime question not usually posed in the study of Islam: What is the evidence? Do we have witnesses to the Muslim accounts of the formation of their own community in any early disinterested sources? The Koran (in the form collected "between two covers" as we know it today) is a good example: What evidence is there for the historical accuracy of the traditional accounts of the compilation of that book shortly after the death of Muhammad? The earliest non-Islamic source testifying to the existence of the Koran appears to stem from the second/eighth century.[7] Indeed, early Islamic sources, at least those which do not seem to have as their prime purpose the defense of the integrity of the canon,[8] would seem to witness that the text of the Koran may not have been totally fixed until the early part of the third/ninth century.[9] Manuscript evidence does not allow for substantially earlier dating either.[10]

A question for many people still remains however (and the answer to it evidences Wansbrough's most basic and radical point): Why should we *not* trust the Muslim sources? Wansbrough's answer to this is substantially different from other expressions of similar skepticism, for example as argued by John Burton in *The Collection of the Koran,* where internal contradiction within the Muslim sources is emphasized and then that fact is combined with a postulated explanation of how such contradiction came about.[11] No, Wansbrough's point of departure is more radical: the entire corpus of early Islamic documentation must be viewed as "Salvation History." What the Koran is trying to evidence, what *tafsir, sira,* and theological writings are trying to explicate, is how the sequence of worldly events centered on the time of Muhammad was directed by God. All the components of Islamic salvation history are meant to witness the same point of faith, namely, an understanding of history that sees God's role in directing the affairs of humankind. And the difference that makes is substantial. To quote from a work that deals with the same problem but from the biblical perspective, "Salvation history is not an historical account of saving events open to the study of the historian. Salvation history did not happen; it is a literary form which has its own historical context."[12] Salvation history comes down to us in a literary form and must be approached by means appropriate to such: literary analysis.

At the outset it may be appropriate to pay attention to the use of the term "salvation history" in connection with Islam, especially in light of questions raised about its use outside the Christian context in general. Most recently H. W. F. Saggs has pointed to the fact that although the term "salvation" has a clear meaning in Christian thought—"it is the saving of the individual soul from destruction or damnation by sin for eternal life"— its application within Judaism would seem to mean "no more than that God maintained a particular religio-ethnic group in existence when the operation of normal political and social factors might have been expected to result in its extermination."[13] The term "salvation" is ambiguous at best and perhaps only rightfully applied in the Christian case. So that may lead to the question: Are we straitjacketing Islam into a Christian framework by using such a term as "salvation history?" Wansbrough has attempted to make reasonably clear what he means by the term and what it implies to him (e.g., *SM* ix, 31), making it evident that "salvation " as such is not the defining characteristic of this history. Indeed Wansbrough suggests (*SM* 147) that Islamic salvation history may perhaps be more accurately described as "election history" because of the very absence within its early formulation of an eschatological concern. Clearly Wansbrough does not conceive of "salvation" in the term "salvation history" as necessarily laden with its Christian connotations. But further "salvation history" may be taken on a different level simply as a technical term referring to literature involved in documenting what could just as easily be called "sacred history," that is, the "history" of man's relationship with God and vice versa. The intellectual baggage of *Heilsgeschichte* may simply be left behind in favor of reference to the literary genre.

Literary analysis of salvation history has been fully developed within biblical and Mishnaic studies; the works of Bultmann and Neusner are obvious prime examples.[14] All such works start from the proposition that the literary records of salvation history, although presenting themselves as being contemporary with the events they describe, actually belong to a period well after such events, which suggests that they have been written according to later points of view in order to fit the purposes of that later time. The actual "history" in the sense of "what really happened" has become totally subsumed within later interpretation and is virtually, if not totally, inextricable from it. The question of whether or not there is an underlying "grain of historical truth" may be thought to be of some concern here, namely, whether or not there must have been some sort of historical event or impetus out of which traditions grew and which therefore forms the kernel of the narrative. But the real problem here is that even if one admits the existence of such a "kernel" of history, is it ever possible to identify and extract that information? Wansbrough implies in his work that he feels that it is not, at least for the most part.[15] The records we have are the existential records of the thought and faith of later generations.

This basic insight into the nature of the sources is not totally new to the study of Islam. Goldziher, and Schacht even more so, understood that traditional sayings attributed to Muhammad and used to support a given legal or doctrinal position within Islam actually derived from a much later period, from times when these legal or doctrinal positions were searching for support with the body of material called the *sunna*. It has become characteristic of Islamic studies after Joseph Schacht, however, either to water down or to ignore totally the implications of such insights. This was clear to Schacht himself toward the end of his life.

> One thing disturbs me, however. That is the danger that the results achieved by the Islamic scholars, at a great effort, in the present generation, instead of being developed and being made the starting point for new scholarly progress might, by a kind of intellectual laziness, be gradually whittled down and deprived of their real significance, or even be turned inside out by those who themselves had taken no part in achieving them. This has happened in the past to the work of Goldziher ... and it has happened again, recently, with regard to the conclusions of the history of Islamic law achieved by critical scholarship.[16]

The "intellectual laziness" is, it seems to me, a counterpart to the desire to produce positive historical results—to satisfy that internal yearning to assert "what really happened."[17] The works of three people can be cited as the most obvious examples of the latter trend: in "The materials used by Ibn Isḥāq," W. M Watt distorts the work of Schacht and attempts to use

Schacht's results against the latter's own position,[18] and in the works of Sezgin[19] and Abbott[20] elaborate schemes are set forth to contradict the insights of Schacht, but are based on no *tangible* evidence. Sezgin especially displays an overt tendency to date works to the earliest possible historical period, with no apparent justification thereof, for example, in the case of the works of Ibn 'Abbas.[21]

Wansbrough's argument, however, is that we do *not* know and probably never can know what really happened; all we can know is what later people *believed* happened, as has been recorded in salvation history. Literary analysis of such sources will reveal to us the components with which those people worked in order to produce their accounts and define exactly what it was that they were arguing, but literary analysis will not tell us *what* happened (although the *possibility* of historical implications of such studies cannot be, and certainly are not within Wansbrough's work, totally ignored).

The point of Islamic salvation history as it has come down to us today, Wansbrough argues, is more specific than merely to evidence the belief in the reality of the theophany; it is to formulate, by adopting and adapting from a well-established pool of Judeo-Christian religious themes, a specifically Arabian religious identity, the inception of which could be placed in seventh-century Arabia. At the beginning of *QS* Wansbrough brings forth a multitude of evidences from the Koran which point to the idea that the very notions in that book demand that they be put within the total Judeo-Christian context, for example, the prophetic line ending in the Seal of the Prophets, the sequence of scriptures, the notion of the destroyed communities, and the common narrative motifs. This notion of extrapolation is, in a sense, the methodological presupposition that Wansbrough sets out to prove within his books by posing the question: If we assume this, does the data fit? At the same time he asks: What additional evidence appears in the process of the analysis to corroborate the presupposition and to define it more clearly?[22] This kind of approach to the material is similar to that of Harry A. Wolfson in his use of the scientific method of "conjecture and verification."[23] So the question raised by some critics concerning whether it is accurate to view Islam as an extension of the Judeo-Christian tradition cannot be considered valid until the evidence and the conclusions put forth in Wansbrough's works have been weighed. The point must always be: Is the presupposition supported by the analysis of the data? To attack the presupposition as invalid is to miss the entire point. To evaluate the work one must participate within its methodological presuppositions and evaluate the final results.

WANSBROUGH'S APPROACH TO THE SOURCES

Charles Adams has summed up the common feeling of many students of the Koran in the following words: "Such matters as the formation of the Koran text, the chronology of the materials assembled in the text, the history of the text, variant readings, the relation of the Koran to prior literature, and a host of other issues of this kind have been investigated thoroughly."[24] Wansbrough, however, has made it clear that we have really only scratched the surface of these studies. All previous studies, he states, have involved an acquiescence to the normative data of the tradition and are characterized by "a distinctly positivist method: serious concern to discover and to describe the state of affairs after the appearance of Islam among the Arabs..." (*SM* 2). What Wansbrough has done has been to bring to the study of Islam and the Koran the same healthy skepticism developed within modern biblical studies (and modern historical studies in general) in order to supplant such positivism. At this point it is worth noting that the highly praised work of Richard Bell,[25] although supposedly using the biblical methodology consequent on the Documentary Hypothesis, has, in fact, progressed not one iota beyond implicit notions in the traditional accounts of the revelation and the collection of the Koran; he took the ideas of serial revelation and the collection after the death of Muhammad (the common notions accepted by most Western students of the Koran) and applied them literally to the text of the Koran. However, the primary purpose of employing modern biblical methodologies must be to free oneself from age-old presuppositions and to apply new ones. This Bell did not do; in fact, he worked wholly within the presuppositions of the Islamic tradition. Wansbrough's claim that "as a document susceptible of analysis by the instruments and techniques of Biblical criticism [the Koran] is virtually unknown" (*QS* ix) can certainly not be questioned least of all by adducing the work of Bell.[26]

Wansbrough has also tried to show a way to free the study of the Koran from the uniquely fundamentalist[27] trend of the vast majority of modern treatments of the book in which the idea of an "original" meaning or intention is pursued relentlessly but ultimately meaninglessly. Such a position in scholarship has been reached especially because of two factors inherent in previous methodologies in the study of Islam. One, the basic historico-philological approach to Islam has become trapped by the consequence of narrow specialization on the part of its proponents. For the most part, there are few scholars active today who can move with equal agility throughout the entire Western religious framework and its necessary languages.[28] Scholars have come to feel that competent knowledge of Arabic and of seventh-century Arabia are sufficient in and of themselves to understand the rise of Islam.[29] No different are the views of such people as Serjeant, who attempt to champion the notion of the influence of pre-Islamic southern Arabia on Islam, but do so to the virtual exclusion of the Jewish element in the population there.[30]

The philological method has been affected also by a second method which within itself has produced the stagnation of Islamic studies within its fundamentalist framework. The irenic approach, which according to Charles Adams aims toward "the greater appreciation of Islamic religiousness and the fostering of a new attitude toward it,"[31] has led to the unfortunate result of a reluctance on the part of many scholars to follow all the way through with their insights and results. The basic problem of an approach to Islam that is concerned "to understand the faith of other men"[32] is confronted when that approach tries to come to grips with the historical dimensions of a faith that conceives itself as having a stake in that very history.[33] The irenic approach to Islam, it would seem, in order to remain true to the "faith of other men," is doomed most of all to avoid asking the basic question: How do we know?

Wansbrough's analysis of the basic character of the Koran reveals his assessment of the extent of the problem involved in the use of these two approaches to the Koran. Wansbrough isolates four major motifs of the Koranic message all from the "traditional stock of monotheistic imagery" (*QS* 1): divine retribution, sign, exile, and covenant. These motifs, Wansbrough notes, are "repeatedly signalled but seldom developed" (*QS* 1), a fact which leads him to emphasize throughout his works one of his major insights concerning the Koran: its "referential" style.[34] The audience of the Koran is presumed able to fill in the missing details of the narrative, much as is true of a work such as the Talmud, where knowledge of the appropriate biblical citation is assumed or supplied by only a few words. Only later when "Islam" as an entity with a fixed and stable identity (based on a political structure) comes into being after the Arabs' expansion out of their original home, does the Koranic material become detached from its original intellectual environment and need written explication—explication that is provided in *tafsir* and *sira*.

Two of the examples discussed by Wansbrough will clarify his notion of the referential character of the Koran. Most evident is the example of Joseph and the mention of the "other brother" in S. 12:59 (see *QS* 134, *SM* 24–25), parallel to the biblical account in Genesis 42:3–13; knowledge of this latter story is assumed on the part of the Koranic audience, for within the Koran no previous mention has been made of Benjamin and his being left at home due to Jacob's fears for his safety. Joseph's statement in the Koran, "Bring me a brother of yours from your father," comes out of nowhere within the context of the Koran, although not if one comes first with a knowledge of the biblical story. The second example is one which deals with Abraham's willingness to sacrifice his son and the removal within the Koran of the dramatic impact contained in the biblical story, where the son does not know that he is the one to be offered (*SM* 24). The question is far more complex because the Jewish exegetical tradition may play a role here; the study of Geza Vermes[35] makes it clear that many Jewish (and Christian) traditions adjust the story to let Isaac know he is to be sacrificed well before the actual event in order to emphasize the willingness of Isaac to offer himself. The Jewish exegetical tradition is referential as well; it already assumes that the basic story of the sacrifice is clear to its audience and that the significance of Abraham in the story will be evident to all who read the Bible; thus the emphasis is on Isaac but certainly not to the exclusion of the role of Abraham. The position of the Koran is similar. The knowledge of the biblical story is assumed; reference is made to developed traditions concerning the sacrifice. The referential character of the Koran should make clear the insufficiency of an approach to the Koran which looks at the so-called "exclusively Arabian" (whatever that may be!) character of the book and tries to ignore the total Judeo-Christian background.[36]

The notion of the referential style of the Koran also leads Wansbrough to the supposition that what we are dealing with in Islam is a sectarian movement fully within the Judeo-Christian "Sectarian Milieu" (*QS* 20, also *SM* 45). The parallels between Koranic and Qumranic literature, while not necessarily displaying an interdependency, *do* demonstrate a similar process of biblical-textual elaboration and adaptation to sectarian purposes.[37] The inner workings of the sectarian milieu are to be seen in both literary traditions.

The Koran as a document, according to Wansbrough, then, is composed of such referential passages developed within the framework of Judeo-Christian sectarian polemics, put together by means of literary convention (for example the use of *qul* ["say"] (*QS* 12 ff., also 47–48), narrative conventions (*QS* 18 ff.), and the conjunction of parallel versions of stories called by Wansbrough "variant traditions" (*QS* 20 ff.), which were perhaps produced from a single original tradition by means of variation through oral transmission within the context of liturgical usage (*QS* 17). Here, clearly enough, a variety of individual methods (e.g., form analysis, oral formulaic analysis) which have been worked out in fields outside Islam, primarily the Bible, are used by Wansbrough in his analysis of the nature of the Muslim scripture.

Significantly, Wansbrough's analysis reveals that the Koran is not merely "a calque of earlier fixed forms" (*QS* 33), that is, it does not merely seek to reproduce the Bible in Arabic, adapted to Arabia. For one thing, the Koran does not follow the fulfillment motif set as a precedent by the New Testament and its use of the Hebrew Bible. Rather, and, indeed, because of the situation of polemic from which the Koran derives, there is a clear attempt made to separate the Koran from the Mosaic revelation through such means as the mode of the revelation and the emphasis on the Arabian language of the Koran.

Canonization and stabilization of the text of the Koran go hand in hand with the formation of the community, according to Wansbrough (*QS* 51). A final fixed text of the scripture was not required, nor was it totally feasible, before political power was firmly controlled; thus the end of the second/eighth century becomes a likely historical moment for the gathering together of oral tradition and liturgical elements leading to the emergence of the fixed canon of scripture and the emergence of the actual concept "Islam."[38] This time period, Wansbrough several times points out, coincides with the recorded rise of literary Arabic.[39] Further evidence for this position is derived in *QS* from a "typological analysis" of *tafsir* (see *QS* 44 and ch. 4). The basic inspiration and thrust of Wansbrough's approach may once again perhaps be traced to modern biblical studies; such people as Geza Vermes and Raphael Loewe have been drawing attention to the need to stop plundering exegetical works, Greek and Aramaic translations of the Bible, and so forth, in order to find support, somewhere, for one's own argument. Rather, they suggest, such works must be studied as a whole with attention given to the historical context of their writing and to their literary context.[40] The analysis of Koranic *tafsir* literature into five genres—haggadic, halakhic, masoretic, rhetorical, and allegorical—once again sets the basic insight. The genres display an approximate chronological development in the above sequence and display a historically growing concern with the textual integrity of scripture and then with the community function of scripture.[41]

The *sira*, while partly exegetical as Wansbrough explains in *QS,* has a much greater role in Islam: it is the narrative witness to the Islamic version of salvation history. Most significant here is Wansbrough's analysis (*SM* ch. 1) of much of the contents of the *sira* into elaborations of twenty-three polemical motifs traditional to the Near Eastern sectarian milieu—items such as the prognosis of Muhammad in Jewish scripture, the Jewish rejection of that prognosis, the role of Abraham and Jesus in sectarian soteriology, and resurrection. All these themes are elaborated within a narrative framework set in seventh-century Arabia but yet all are themes that had been argued so many times before among sectarian groups in the Near East. The analysis of the *sira* underlines Wansbrough's main contention in both of his books that "by its own express testimony, the Islamic *kerygma* [is] an articulation . . . of the biblical dispensation, and can only thus be assessed" (*SM* 45).

It will be clear to any attentive reader of *QS* and *SM* that Wansbrough's work still leaves much to be done with the basic data in order to work out fully the implications of his kind of study. Close and detailed analyses of the many texts involved are still needed in order to demonstrate and, indeed, to assess the validity of his approach. What Wansbrough has accomplished, it seems to me, is to point to a new direction that Islamic studies could take in order to revitalize itself; Wansbrough has marked a path in broad outlines, but the road must still be cleared.[42]

Several reviewers have seized upon (and, indeed, Wansbrough himself has emphasized the point)[43] various statements in *QS* with regard to methods determining one's results. I. J. Boullata, in his review of *QS,* put the matter this way: "To quote him from page 91 'Results are, after all, as much conditioned by method as by material.' If this is true and his material is given credence in spite of its selectivity, there remains a big question about his method and the extent to which it conditioned his results."[44] Fazlur Rahman in his book *Major Themes of the Koran* makes a similar point about method.

My disagreements with Wansbrough are so numerous that they are probably best understood only by reading both this book and his. (I do, however, concur with at least one of his points: "The kind of analysis undertaken will in no small measure determine the results!" [p. 21]) I do believe that this kind of study [i.e., the comparison with Judaism and/or Christianity] can be enormously useful, though we have to return to Geiger and Hirschfeld [! not Speyer?!] to see just how useful it can be when done properly.[45]

What does Rahman mean here concerning method? Does he mean to imply: Well, Wansbrough has a method and that has been his downfall; I have no method so I have imposed nothing upon the material? I doubt that Rahman wants to urge methodological naiveté. More likely, perhaps, Rahman means: Wansbrough has his method and I have mine, but mine is right. That the methods which Rahman (and virtually every other student in the field) imposes upon his study happen to be, for the most part, the traditional theologico-historical methods is a fact that needs to be recognized, just as does the fact that Wansbrough imposes literary methods. If the study of Islam is to remain a scholarly endeavor and retain some sense of intellectual integrity, then it must, first, become methodologically aware and, second, be prepared to consider the validity of other methods of approach to the subject. This means that Islamic studies must differentiate between the truth claims of the religion itself and the intellectual claims of various methods, for ultimate "truth" is not susceptible to methodological procedures. To remain within the search for the "true" meaning of Islam and not to be prepared to free oneself from, for example, the priority of history[46] within the study of Islam, will surely sound the death-knell for a potentially vital and vibrant endeavor of human intellectual activity.

Notes

Chapter One: Introduction

1. A. Guillaume, *Islam* (Harmondsworth, 1978), p. 74.
2. E. Gibbon, *Decline and Fall of the Roman Empire,* 6 vols. (London, 1941), pp. 240ff.
3. T. Carlyle, *Sartor Resartus: On Heroes and Hero Worship* (London, 1973), p. 299.
4. S. Reinach, *Orpheus: A History of Religion* (New York, 1932), p. 176.
5. A. Jeffery, *Materials for the History of the Text of the Quran* (Leiden, 1937), p. 1.
6. J. Wansbrough, *Quranic Studies* (Oxford, 1977), p. ix.
7. A. Rippin, *Muslims: Their Religious Beliefs and Practices* (London, 1991), Vol. 1, p. ix.
8. C. J. Adams, "Quran: The Text and Its History," in *Encyclopedia of Religion,* Mircea Eliade, editor-in-chief (New York, London: Macmillan, 1987), pp. 157–76.
9. Ibid.
10. Ibid.
11. Ibid.
12. Ibid.
13. Guillaume, *Islam,* p. 189.
14. H. Hirschfeld, *New Researches into the Composition and Exegesis of the Qoran* (London, 1992), pp. 138ff.
15. R. Bell and W. M. Watt, *Introduction to the Quran* (Edinburgh, 1970), p. 93.
16. Al-Kindi quoted in A. Rippin, *Muslims,* p. 26.
17. S. Hurgronje, *Mohammedanism* (New York, 1916), p. 23.
18. R. S. Humphreys, *Islamic History: A Framework for Inquiry* (Princeton, 1991), p. 82.
19. C. Snouck Hurgronje, *Mohammedanism,* p. 24.
20. B. Lewis, *Islam, and the West* (New York, 1993), p. 94.

21. Hurgronje, *Mohammedanism,* p. 25.
22. Humphreys, *Islamic History,* p. 83.
23. Ibid.
24. I. Goldziher, *Muslim Studies,* trans., Barber and Stern, vol. 2 (London, 1967–1971), p. 19.
25. Ibid., p. 43.
26. Ibid., p. 44.
27. Ibid., p. 108.
28. Ibid., p. 169.
29. Ibid., p. 236.
30. Humphreys, *Islamic History,* p. 83.
31. J. Schacht, *The Origins of Muhammadan Jurisprudence* (Oxford, 1959), pp. 4–5.
32. Ibid., pp. 149–63.
33. P. Crone, *Roman, Provincial, and Islamic Law* (Cambridge, 1987), p. 7.
34. Humphreys, *Islamic History,* p. 84.
35. J. Wansbrough, *Quranic Studies* (Oxford, 1977), p. 20.
36. Ibid., p. 79.
37. Ibid., p. 51.
38. Ibid., p. 97.
39. Ibid., p. 44.
40. A. Jeffery, "The Quest of the Historical Mohammed," in *The Muslim World* 16 (1926): 342.
41. Wansbrough, p. 56.
42. Humphreys, *Islamic History,* pp. 84–85.
43. M. Cook, *Muhammad* (Oxford, 1983), p. 65.
44. Ibid., p. 74.
45. Ibid., pp. 75–76.
46. Ibid., pp. 76–82.
47. Ibid., p. 81.
48. Ibid., p. 82.
49. Humphreys, *Islamic History,* p. 85.
50. M. Cook and P. Crone, *Hagarism: The Making of the Islamic World* (Cambridge, 1977), p. 9.
51. Ibid., p. 8.
52. Ibid., pp. 14ff.
53. Ibid., p. 18.
54. Ibid., p. 21.
55. Cook, *Muhammad,* p. 86.
56. P. Crone, *Meccan Trade and the Rise of Islam* (Oxford, 1987), p. 215.
57. Ibid., p. 230.

Chapter Two: The Koran

1. Since in Arabic also the root *RHM* signifies "to have pity," the Arabs must have at once perceived the force of the new name.

Chapter Four: Three Ancient Korans

1. See a striking narration in the annalist *Ibn Hisham*, pp. 152, 1. 9f., who represents the Prophet as responding to his voice: "What shall I cry?" We cannot help thinking of the following words found in the prophet Isaiah (xl. 6): "The voice of (one) saying, '*Cry*,' and he said, 'What shall I cry?'" The very *qarā* which is used in both texts in the same sense will establish a curious and hardly accidental coincidence.

2. Palmer, *Sacred Books of the East*, vol. VI., pp. 55, 71, etc.

3. The question whether Muhammad could read and write is discussed but not decided by Nöldeke, *Geschichte des Qorâns*, pp. 7f.

4. A. Mingana, *Narsai Homiliae et Carmina*, 1905, vol. I. pp. 115–16 and 177 n. 1.

5. *Recueil des actes synodaux de l'Église de Perse*, edit. Chabot, in "Notice et extraits des manuscrits," t. XXXVII. pp. 532, 534, 536 *et passim*.

6. *Syn. Orient.*, p. 275. Cf. on this question Duchesne, *Les Églises séparées*, pp. 337–52: "Les Missions Chrétiennes au Sud de l'empire romain, les Arabes."

7. *Zeitschr. für Assyriologie*, XII, pp. 189–242.

8. Cf. a passage of Josephus (Ant. XI. 5) which tells his high repute (δόξα) with the people.

9. Muhammad often calls himself "the unlettered prophet." Cf. Nöldeke, ibid., p. 10.

10. G. Sale, *The Koran*, Preliminary discourse, p. 46.

11. He showed it to him twice in his last year.

12. See *Fihrist*, ed. by G. Flügel, p. 24.

13. The annalists know them to be 'Abdallah ibn Zubair, Sa'id ibn Al-'As, and 'Abdur-Rahman ibn al-Hareth, followers of the Prophet (*Fihrist*, p. 25).

14. Tabari, I. 2952, 10; 11, 516, 5; and Yakut, *Dictionary of Learned Men*, VI, 300, 499; see D. S. Margoliouth's *The Early Development of Mohammedanism* (1914), p. 37.

15. Margoliouth, *Mohammedanism*, pp. 69–70.

16. Muir, *Life of Mahomet* (1894), pp. xiv, xxi–xxii.

17. In Arabic *jahiliyya*.

18. Edit. of W. Ahlwardt, *The Divans of the Six Ancient Arabic Poets* (1870).

19. *Les poètes Arabes chrétiens* (1890); cf. another Arabic book of the same writer, *Le Christianisme et la littérature Chrétienne en Arabie avant l'Islâm* (1912). Everybody knows the conscientious studies of Sir Charles Lyall, on this subject.

20. Cf. S. Fraenkel, *De vocalibus in antiquis Arabum carminibus et in Corano peregrinis* (1880), p. 23 *et passim*.

21. Ita Geiger, *Oper. sup. laud.*, pp. 113–19.

22. This name is perhaps an echo of *Shelah*.

23. Ita M. Rodwell, *The Koran*, p. 109.

24. Cf. Maracci, Prodr. IV, p. 90.

25. In Niebuhr's *Travels*, II, p. 265.

26. The Perisan poet Sa'di calls him *the earth conquering horseman with his chestnut Buraq*.

27. Cf. A. Mingana, *Sources Syriaques*, vol. I, part II, pp. 182f.

28. *Chron. Syr.*, edit. Bruns, p. 120; and edit. Bedjan, p. 115.

29. Recently (1903) edited in Cairo, in 30 parts.

30. Edited in Calcutta (1859) by Nassau-Lees.

31. See A. Mingana, *Clef de la langue Araméenne* (1905), pp. 33–34.

32. Cf. M. Merx, *Historia artis grammaticae apud Syros* (Leipzig, 1889). Duval, *Littérature Syriaque*, 3me édit., pp. 285f.

33. Cf. Evod. Assemani, *Acta Martyr. Orient.*, vol. I, pp. 19, 54, etc. Nöldeke, *Geschichte der Perser und Araber zur Zeit der Sassaniden aus der Arabischen Chron. des Tabari*, p. 68, n. 1.

34. Quoted in Neubauer's *Géographie du Talmud*, p. 320.

35. Cf. Graetz, *Histoire des Juifs* (translated by Bloch), 1888, vol. III, p. 163 *et passim*.

36. See Brockelmann's *Geschichte, der Arabischen Litteratur*, I. (Weimar, 1898), p. 100.

37. Edited by H. Derenbourg, Paris, 1881–1889.

38. About the relations of the Mandaeans with Christianity, see Brandt, *Die Mandäische Religion, ihre Entwickelung und Geschichtliche Bedeutung*, pp. 140–45 *et passim*.

39. For a general view on Arabic Literature, the reader will find good information in R. A. Nicholson's *A Literary History of the Arabs* (1907); for some particular details several articles written, in Arabic, in the review *Al-Machriq* (Beirut), seem to be well documented and scientific.

40. See *Ibn Abi Usaibi'ah*, vol. I, p. 175 *et passim*. Bar Hebraeus, *Chron. Syr.*, pp. 134 and 162.

41. See Labourt, *Le Christianisme dans l'empire Perse* (1904), pp. 219f.

42. See B. Moritz's *Arabic Palaeography* (with 188 plates), Cairo, 1906; and L. Cheikho, *Spécimens d'écriture Arabe pour la lecture des manuscrits anciens et modernes* (Beirut, 1911).

43. *Facsimiles of Ancient Manuscripts etc.* Oriental Series, Part II, edited by W. Wright (London, 1877).

44. Cf. the valuable study of Prof. Brockelmann, in the *Encyclopaedia of Islâm*, vol. I, pp. 383f.

Chapter Five: The Transmission of the Koran

1. "No falsification; the Koran contains only genuine pieces." *Orientalische Skizzen*, p. 56.

2. "I agree, however, with Fischer that the possibility of interpolations in the Koran absolutely must be admitted." *Geschichte des Qorâns*, 2d ed. (1909) by Schwally, p. 99, no. 1.

3. The accusation very recently directed against the Arabists of this country by a well-known writer, that they are still living on Muir, is a meager tribute to the leading Arabist of Oxford and his colleagues of Cambridge; to take as examples some second-hand authors and scientifically worthless Islamizers is highly unjust.

4. *New Researches into the Composition and Exegesis of the Qoran*, p. 139.

5. *Mohammed et la fin du monde*, 2 ème fascicule, *Notes Complémentaires*, p. 149–56.

6. Cf. *The Moslem World* (1915), pp. 380f.

7. Edit. Schwally, II, pp. 112–14.

8. Cf. Casanova, Ibid, p. 109.

9. *Geschichte des Qorans* (1860), p. 193.

10. Bukhari III, p. 397 (edit. Krehl).

11. The same tradition is copied by "Muslim," II, p. 494 (edit. Dehli) and by "Tirmidhi," II, p. 309 (edit. Bulak).

12. *Leaves from three Ancient Qurâns* (1914). [See chapter 14 of this volume.]

13. The speaker is Zaid ibn Thabit mentioned in the foregoing traditions.

14. This same tradition is reported in III, 257, and in IV, 398.

15. This information has been copied by another traditionist ("Tirmidhi" II, 187) and by many subsequent writers.

16. Var. "torn up."

17. "As to admitting one tradition to be true to the detriment of the other, that seems to me impossible without falling into arbitrariness." Casanova, *Mohammed et la fin du monde*, II, 105.

18. "If they had assembled the whole Koran, why was so much effort needed later to bring the same thing together?" *Geschichte des Qorâns* (1860), p. 160.

19. "Criticism has highlighted the inadequacy as documentary evidence, if not of the earliest Islamic literature, of at least the rich later development represented by Bukhari's collection." R. Dussaud, in *Journal des Savants* (1913), p. 138.

20. "The details which surround the principal figure of Muhammad are really well-blurred and even end by becoming obliterated in a haze of uncertainty." Cl. Huart, in *Journal Asiatique* (1913), p. 215.

21. *J.R.A.S.* (1916), p. 397.

22. "As noted earlier, besides the poets, we possess the Sira [the biography of the Prophet], the Maghazi [the literature describing the war or raids on the infidels], the Sahih [the true or authentic traditions whose chain of transmitters is unassailable], the Musnad [the traditions supported by authorities resting on the Prophet], the Sunan [the deeds, utterances, and unspoken approval of the Prophet], a historical library, unique of its kind, in its extent and variety. To their combined evidence who would dare to deny all value?" Lammens's *Le berceau de l'Islam*, p. 130.

23. *Geschichte des Qorâns*, p. 189, *sq.*

24. p. 27 (edit. Flügel).

25. 2, 2, 836.

26. Ibid. I, 6, 2952.

27. Ibid. II, 1, 516.

28. *History of Muhammad's Campaigns* (1856), p. 68 (edit. Kremer).

29. Vol. I, p. 14.

30. *Chron. Arab*, p. 194 (edit. Beirut).

31. pp. 227 (edit. Jarrett).

32. Pt. I, 72–74.

33. II, 454 (noticed by Casanova, p. 124).

34. IV, 463 (noticed Périer, "vie d' al-Hadjdjadj," p. 257).

35. Vol. I, p. 183 (edit. Barone de Slane).

36. Cf. *Fihrist*, pp. 26–27.

37. VI, pp. 301–302 (edit. D. S. Margoliouth).

38. Mars-Avril, 1916, pp. 248f.

39. Genesis xix, 24.

40. Nau translates the Syriac expression *dla tubhaya* by "sans erreur possible," instead of "easily, without delay."

41. Lit. "the writings."

42. "Christian Arab tribes of Southern Syria.

43. It is very difficult to determine with exactitude the chronology of events at this period of Arab conquests.

44. Cf. W. Muir, *The Caliphate: Its Rise, Decline and Fall* (1915), pp. 153f.

45. Cf. in *Patrologia Orientalis*, V, p. 51, the Arabic text edited by B. Evetts.

46. These, however, might have been Jewish or Christian renegades.

47. Edit. Duval, *Corp. Script. Christ. Orient*, tomus LXIV, p. 97.

48. *Chronica Minora*, Ibid., tomus IV, pp. 30 and 38.

49. A. Mingana, *Sources Syriaques*, vol. I, pt. 2, pp. 146f.

50. Notice the Syriac word *Mashilmanutha* "tradition" in its rapport with "a written thing."

51. i.e., Monophysites.

52. i.e., Nestorians.

53. *Pol. und Apol. Literatur in Arab. Sprache* (1877).

54. Assemani, B. O. III, 1, 212.

55. 1901, p. 150.

56. *The Apology of al-Kindy Written at the Court of al-Mamun circa*, A.D. *830*. An excellent edition of this work has recently appeared in Egypt in the "Nile Mission Press," whose chairman is Dr. S. M. Zwemer.

57. "In the history of the criticism of the Koran, we must, I believe, place the Christian al-Kindi in the top rank." Ibid., p. 119.

58. Cf. Muir, ibid., pp. 70.

59. The predominant role of this monk will be carefully set forth in our future studies. The Arab authors who scarcely knew any other language besides Arabic confused his name with the title *Bhira* given by Aramaeans to every monk; see Nau, *Expansion Nestorienne en Asie* (1914), pp. 213–23, who showed how misleading was the practice of some scholars who simply availed themselves of the tardy Muslim Hadith.

60. These details will be studied in future.

61. Cf. *Geschichte des Qorans*, p. 255 (edit. Schwally).

62. This fact receives a direct confirmation from ibn Dukmak and Makrizi quoted on p. 33.

63. The work will be published for the Governors of the John Rylands Library by the Manchester University Press.

64. D. S. Margoliouth, in *Encyclopaedia of Religion and Ethics*, VIII, 879.

65. "In no way did Islam come into existence as a religious system, but rather as an

experiment of a sociological nature, designed to counter certain prevailing secular abuses."
H. Grimme, *Mohammed*, I., Münster, p. 14; München, p. 50.

66. *Mukaddimah*, p. 365 (edit. Beirut).

67. We cannot enter into details on this subject which is a digression from the Koranic theme.

68. *New Researches into the Composition and Exegesis of the Qoran*, p. 11.

69. "The Prophet was advised by Allah [Koran, lxxv. 16–17] not to be in a hurry to publish the Koran as a separate collection. The precaution was wise given the inconsistent character of certain revelations." *Fatima et les filles de Mahomet*, p. 113.

70. "But as to the fragments of bone, palm leaves, etc., on which were written, by the secretaries, the verses dictated by the Prophet, and which were used for the first recension under Abu Bakr, what happened to them? I refuse to believe that they would have been destroyed. What extraordinary sacrilege! How could one have treated in such a manner these witnesses, the most direct, of the revelation? In fact if they had existed, how does one explain the fear that 'Umar and Abu Bakr showed in seeing the Koran disappearing with the death of the reciters [of the Koran]? If they had not existed, all the passages (so numerous) where the Koran is designated (by the word *kitab*—a book or scriptures) must have been introduced after the event!

"Well, there you have the inherent contradictions in the traditional account, and all are resolved by the conclusion that I adopt: the Koran was put in written form for the first time thanks to al-Hajjaj who was probably relying on the legendary prototype due to 'Uthman. It is possible that there had been earlier transcriptions, but without any official character and consequently without unity." Ibid., pp. 141–42.

Chapter Six: Materials for the History of the Text of the Koran

1. *Fihrist* 36 mentions a number of works on *Ikhtilaf al-Masahif*, such as those by Ibn 'Amir (d. 118), al-Farra' (d. 207), Khalaf b. Hisham (d. 229), al-Mada'ini (d. 231), al-Warraq and one Muhammad b. 'Abd ar-Rahman. There was also a work with a similar title by Abu Hatim (d. 248); cf. *Fihrist* 59(2), a work derived from al-Kisa'i (d. 189) entitled *Kitab Ikhtilaf Masahif Ahl al-Madina wa Ahl al-Kufa wa Ahl al-Basra 'an al-Kisa'i*, and a *Kitab al-Masahif wa 'l-Hija'* by Muhammad b. 'Isa al-Isfahani (d. 253). Ibn Miqsam (d. 362) is also said to have composed a *Kitab al-Masahif* (*Fihrist* 33[6]), but the three famous *Masahif*-books were those of Ibn Abi Dawud (d. 316), Ibn al-Anbari (d. 327), and Ibn Ashta al-Isfahani (d. 360); cf. Itqan 13.

2. Vide Massignon's *al-Hallaj*, I, 241 and Bergsträsser, *Geschichte des Qorantexts*, 152ff. Some account of the man will be found in al-Khatib, *Tarikh Baghdad*, V, 144-148, Yaqut, *Irshad*, II, 116-119, and Ibn al-Jazari, *Tabaqat*, I, 139-142, No. 663.

3. On Ibn Miqsam see Yaqut, *Irshad*, VI, 499; Ibn al-Jazari, *Tabaqat*, No. 2945; Miskawaihi, *Tajarib* (ed. Amedroz), I, 285; and on Ibn Shanabudh see Ibn Khallikan (tr. de Slane), III, 16-18; Yaqut, *Irshad*, VI, 302-304 and Ibn al-Jazari, *Tabaqat*, No. 2707.

4. The seven were Nafi' of Madina (d. 169), Ibn Kathir of Mecca (d. 120), Ibn 'Amir of Damascus (d. 118), Abu 'Amr of Basra (d. 154), 'Asim of Kufa (d. 128), Hamza of Kufa (d. 158) and al-Kisa'i of Kufa (d. 189).

5. To the Seven were added Abu Ja'far of Madina (d. 130), Khalaf of Kufa (d. 229) and Ya'qub of Basra (d. 205) to make the Ten. Islamic scholarship is still divided over the question as to whether seven only or all ten are canonical.

6. To the Ten were added Ibn Muhaisin of Mecca (d. 123), al-Yazidi of Basra (d. 202), al-Hasan of Basra (d. 110), and al-A'mash of Kufa (d. 148) to make the Fourteen.

7. We hear of books composed on the Eight Readers, the Eleven Readers, the Thirteen Readers, and somtimes these included Readers not in the usual lists as given above. Thus the *Raudat al- Huffaz* of al-Mu'addil includes the readings of Humaid b. Qais, Ibn as-Samaifa' and Talha b. Musarrif (see Pretzl "Die Wissenschaft der Koranlesung" in *Islamica*, VI, p. 43). Also the Cairo MS of the *Suq al-'Arus* of Abu Ma'shar at-Tabari contains numerous *mukhtarat* beyond the canonical authorities, and the lost *Kamil* of al-Hudhali, though it is a work on the Ten, is said to have contained readings of forty extra Readers (*Nashr* I, 90).

8. A possible exception is the case of Abu Musa al-Qazwini to whom my attention has been drawn by Prof. Massignon, and who seems to have prepared a text in which varied colored dots represented alternative readings in the text. Some samples of this process are actually found in some Kufic codices of the third and fourth centuries, but so far as I know never consistently carried out.

9. The *Kashshaf*, ed. Nassau Lees, Calcutta, 1856.

10. *Al-Bahr al-Muhit*, 8 vols., Cairo, 1328 A.H. printed at the charges of the Sultan of Morocco, and unfortunately in the latter volumes printed in great haste and consequent inaccuracy.

11. *Fath al-Qadir*, 5 vols., Cairo 1349. In his MS the author used the text of Warsh 'an Nafi', i.e. the Madinan text tradition, but in the printing of this edition the publishers have stupidly changed it in every case to the Kufan text tradition of Hafs 'an 'Asim which is the one current in Egypt at the present day.

12. *At-Tibyan fi 'l-I'rab wa 'l-Qira'at fi Jami' al-Qur'an* on the margin of Jamal's supercommentary to Jalalain, 4 vols., Cairo 1348. (It was also printed separately at Cairo in 1302 and 1306, and with Jamal at Teheran in 1860 A.D.). Of his *I'rab al-Qira'at ash-Shadhdha* there is a broken MS in the possession of Dr. Yahuda of London and a complete MS discovered by the present writer in the East and now in the Mingana collection at Selly Oak.

13. *Ibn Halawaih's Sammlung nichtkanonischer Koranlesarten*, herausgegeben von G. Bergsträsser, Istanbul 1934 (*Bibliotheca Islamica*, VII). There are also variants recorded in his *I'rab Thalathin Suwar* of which three MSS are known.

14. *Nichtkanonische Koranlesarten in Muhtasab des Ibn Ginni*, von G. Bergsträsser, Munich 1933. (*Sitzungberichte der Bayerischen Akademie der Wissenschaften*, 1933, Heft 2). There are good MSS of the *Muhtasab* now available and it is hoped that the complete text may be published shortly. It is probable that other works of Ibn Jinni would repay examination for there are not a few uncanonical variants quoted in the commentaries from Ibn Jinni which do not figure in Bergsträsser's lists.

15. *Soyuti's Itqan on the Exegetical Sciences of the Qur'an*, ed. A. Sprenger, Calcutta 1857. (Bibliotheca Indica).

The recent work of az-Zanjani, *Tarikh al-Qur'an*, Cairo 1935, may perhaps represent the beginning of a new day. The author is visibly inspired by Western work on the Qur'an, and although bound hand and foot by the necessity of defending the orthodox position, he has made a useful assemblage of material from which others may start.

16. *Die Richtungen der islamischen Koranauslegung,* Leiden 1920, being the Olaus-Petri Lectures at Upsala, published as No. VI of the De-Goeje Foundation.

17. Erste Lieferung 1926; zweite Lieferung 1929: the third and concluding section has now been issued by his pupil and successor at Munich, Dr. O. Pretzl. Bergsträsser envisaged a much larger plan for a history of the text of the Koran based on an assemblage of materials on a vast scale, and of which the publication of a critical text of the Koran by the present writer was to form part. (See his preliminary statement, "Plan eines Apparatus Criticus zum Qoran" in the *Sitzungsberichte Bayer. Akad.,* 1930, Heft 7). The tragedy of the summer of 1933, which deprived Germany of one of her finest Arabists and the writer of a close personal friend, has necessarily delayed this project and somewhat changed it. Dr. Pretzl, however, has undertaken to continue with the plan and a new scheme for it is being elaborated. (See Pretzl, "Die Fortführung des apparatus criticus zum Koran" in *Sitzungsberichte Bayer. Akad.,* 1934, Heft 2).

18. E.g., the folio edition of 1857.

19. Bergsträsser has given an account of it in *Der Islam,* XX (1932), Heft I in his article "Koranlesung in Kairo."

20. Two of these older sources have been made available in careful editions in the *Bibliotheca Islamica* by Dr. Otto Pretzl, viz. The *Taisir* and the *Muqni* of ad-Dani (d. 444), the Spanish Muslim savant.— *Das Lehrbuch der Sieben Koranlesungen von Abu 'Amr ad-Dani,* 1930, and *Orthographie und Punktierung des Korans: Zwei Schriften von Abu 'Amr ad-Dani,* 1932. In the "Anmerkungen" to this latter text Pretzl notes a number of cases where the editors of the Egyptian standard text have deviated from the older tradition.

21. *Itqan,* 146.

22. Thus in the preface to the above-mentioned Egyptian Standard edition (student's edition of 1344) we read —

"Its consonantal text has been taken from what the Massoretes have handed down as to the codices which 'Uthman b. 'Affan sent to Basra, Kufa, Damascus and Mecca, the codex which he appointed for the people of Medina, and that which he kept for himself, and from the codices which have been copied from them."

23. There is a Shi'a tradition (Kashani, *Safi,* p. 9) that before his death the Prophet called 'Ali and told him that this material was hidden behind his couch written on leaves and silk and parchments, bidding him take it and publish it in codex form. It is also sometimes suggested that this material assembled by the Prophet was the nucleus of Abu Bakr's collection. In neither case, however, can we feel much confidence in the statements.

24. There are of course elaborate stories of the amanuenses of the Prophet, and there can be no doubt that he did employ amanuenses for his diplomatic correspondence. That certain of these amanuenses were at times called upon to write out special pieces of revelation is not at all impossible. It is difficult to take seriously, however, the theory that considers them as a body of prepared scribes waiting to take down revelations as they were uttered.

25. Ya'qubi (ed. Houtsma), II, 152; *Fihrist* 24; ad-Dani, *Muqni',* 4 ff. And cf. Nöldeke-Schwally II, 11 ff. There are many references to material that was lost at Yamama that should have formed part of the Koran.

26. Ibn al-Jazari, *Nashr* I, 6; *Fihrist,* 27; Bukhari (ed. Krehl) III, 397; Ibn Sa'd, *Tabaqat,* II ii, 112-114. See also Nöldeke-Schwally II, 8-11.

27. This name is probably a mistake for Mu'adh b. Jabal, as indeed Bergsträsser has noted, *Qorantext*, 173.

28. Assuming that there was a Medinan Codex. The stories of 'Uthman's committee in the *Muqni'* and in Ibn Abi Dawud certainly suggest that Medina had depended largely on oral tradition and that this committee of 'Uthman made a firsthand collection by taking down the material directly from the depositories and demanding two witnesses for every revelation accepted.

29. It will be remembered that the Ibadites made the charge against 'Uthman that he had tampered with God's word.

30. Ya'qubi, *Historiae* II, 197; Ibn al-Athir III, 86, 87; Qurtubi I, 53.

31. Ibn Abi Dawud, p. 83 quotes from Abu Bakr b. 'Ayyash (d. 194) the statement that many of the Companions of the Prophet had their own text of the Koran, but they had passed away and their texts had not survived. This same fact is evidenced by the recurring reference to *al-harf al- awwal* where what is meant is a reading from the time of the Prophet which is different from that in the 'Uthmanic text.

32. In the accounts of Ibn Shanabudh will be noticed the effort made to paint him as an ignoramus and a weak-minded person. This was the usual procedure with regard to all those suspected of unorthodox views and is not to be taken seriously. It is perfectly clear from the sources that he was a famous scholar and drew large numbers of students, who in those days as in these did not flock to listen to the ignorant and weak-minded.

33. An interesting modern example occurred during the last visit of the late Prof. Bergsträsser to Cairo. He was engaged in taking photographs for the Archive and had photographed a number of the early Kufic codices in the Egyptian Library when I drew his attention to one in the Azhar Library that possessed certain curious features. He sought permission to photograph that also, but permission was refused and the codex withdrawn from access, as it was not consistent with othodoxy to allow a Western scholar to have knowledge of such a text.

34. Cf. *Itqan* 428 and numerous quotations in *ad-Durr al-Manthur*.

35. Ibn al-Jazari, *Tabaqat* II, 184.

36. *Itqan* 13 and 428.

37. For his life see Ibn Khallikan (Eg. Ed.) I, 268, 269; Ibn al-Jazari, *Tabaqat*, No. 1779; Dhahabi, *Liber Class.*, II, 80; al-Khatib, *Tarikh Baghdad* IX, 464-468; Ibn al-'Imad, *Shadharat ad-Dhahab* II, 168, 273.

38. He is generally known as the pupil of Mhd b. Aslam at-Tusi and 'Isa b. Zaghba. Al-Khatib IX, 464, 465 gives a list of his various teachers, and the Readers from whom he drew his Koranic knowledge are listed by Ibn al-Jazari.

39. *Fihrist* 36 (11) attributes this book to his father Abu Dawud, the traditionist.

40. But see Ibn al-'Imad II, 273, and ad-Daraqutni in al-Khatib, IX, 468.

41. It was at first thought that Dr. Mingana's find in the palimpsest leaves published by him in 1914, *Leaves from Three Ancient Qurâns Possibly Pre-'Othmânic, with a List of Their Variants*, might provide us with fragments of one of these earlier codices. Closer examination, however, has shown that neither they nor the curious variants found by him in Syriac in a MS of Barsalibi (see *An ancient Syriac Translation of the Kur'an exhibiting new Verses and Variants*, Manchester, 1925), have any relation to the text of these old codices with which we are here concerned. See Bergsträsser, *Geschichte des Qorantexts*, pp. 53-57 and 97-102.

42. *Geschichte des Qorantexts*, pp. 60–96.

43. Sources for his life are— Nawawi, *Tahdhib*, 396 ff; Ibn al-Athir, *Usd al-Ghaba*, III, 256-260; Ibn Hajar, *Isaba* II, 890-893; *Tahdhib* VI, 27, 28; Ibn al-Jazari, *Tabaqat* No. 1914; Ibn Sa'd II, ii, 104 ff, III, i, 106 ff.

44. Nawawi, 372; Bukhari (ed. Krehl) III, 396.

45. Ibn Abi Dawud, p. 13 ff.

46. Ibn al-Athir, *Kamil* (ed. Tornberg) III, 86, 87.

47. On them see Nöldeke-Schwally I, 108 ff. The *Fatiha* was apparently added to some copies that gave Ibn Mas'ud's text. C.f. *Itqan*, 152, 187 and the statement of Ibn an-Nadim, *Fihrist*, 26.

48. This is the date he is said to have finished the *Fihrist*: the date of his death is uncertain.

49. In Tabari, *Annales*, I, 2963 the sura of Yunus which is the tenth sura in modern editions is called the seventh as here. Schwally suggests a misprint in the text of Tabari… but against this see Bauer in *ZDMG*, LXXV, 15.

50. *Fihrist* says that some gave 52 as coming before 51.

51. Ibn Hajar, *Tahdhib* II, 75-77.

52. There is a statement in the *Fihrist*, p. 26 from Mhd b. Ishaq, that there were many codices in existence purporting to be exemplars of Ibn Mas'ud's codex, but no two of them agreed with one another. Ibn an-Nadim claims to have seen a very old copy in which the *Fatiha* was included.

53. An alternative theory is that when the 'Uthmanic text was in general currency the material in Ibn Mas'ud's codex was arranged in new copies made thereof under the sura headings of the 'Uthmanic text, though not in the same order. It is obvious, of course, that later writers using material from one of these old codices would quote it according to sura and verse of the 'Uthmanic text.

54. Sources for his life are—Nawawi, 140, 141; Ibn al-Jazari, *Tabaqat*, No. 131; Ibu Sa'd III, ii, 59-62; *Usd al-Ghaba* I, 49, 50; Ibn Hajar *Isaba* I, 30-32; *Tahdhib at-Tahdhib* I, 187, 188.

55. One story going back to Abu' l-'Aliya (d. 90) is that in the caliphate of Abu Bakr an attempt was made to produce a codex, scribes writing to Ubai's dictation. This is usually told in connection with Abu Bakr's so-called recension (Ibn Abi Dawud, p. 9), but it might quite well describe the origin of Ubai's own codex (see Ibn Abi Dawud, p. 30).

56. *Fihrist* p. 28; Ya'qubi, *Historiae* II, 152; *Itqan*, 134 ff; Ibn Abi Dawud, p. 10. One finds the usual attempts to prove that 'Ali's assembling was only a memorizing, but on the face of it the story demands a written form.

57. A tradition from Ibn 'Abbas given in the *Manaqib* of Ibn Shahrashaub from ash-Shirazi's *Nuzul al-Quran*. Cf. Al-'Amili I, 150.

58. Al-'Amili I, 148.

59. *As-Safi*, pp. 9, 10.

60. Unfortunately the passage in the *Fihrist* which gave the sura order of 'Ali's codex is missing from the MS from which Flügel's edition was made.

61. There are numerous references to such codices in Arabic literature, and there are still in Shi'a hands portions of such codices said to have been written by members of Ahl al-Bait (see al-'Amili, *A'yan ash-Shia* I, 150 ff.) but in no case is the genuineness even arguable.

62. Goldziher, *Richtungen*, 272.

Chapter Seven: Progress in the Study of the Koran Text

1. There is a damning indictment of the commentaries from this point of view in the work of Muhammad Abu Zaid, *al-Hidaya wal'l-'Irfan* (Cairo, 1930), a work suppressed in Egypt by government order. See the account by the present writer in *Der Islam* XX, Heft 4.

2. Cf. Joh. Mich. Langii—*Dissertatio de Alcorani prima inter Europaeos editione Arabica, ante sesquesaeculum et quod excuvit in Italia per Paganinum Brixiensem facta, sed iussu Pontificis Romani abolita* (1703), and also Joh. Bern. de Rossi—*De Corano arabico Venetiis Paganini typis impresso sub saec. XVI. dissertatio* (Parmae, 1806).

3. *Alcoranus Muhammadis ad optimorum Codicum fidem edita* (Hamburg, 1694).

4. *Alcoranus textus universus, edidit Lud. Marraccio* (Paduae, 1698).

5. *Corani textus arabicus ad fidem librorum manu scriptorum et impressorum et ad praecipurum interpretum lectiones et auctoritatem recensuit Gustavus Flügel* (Lipsiae, 1834).

6. So I learned in conversation with sheikhs in Omdurman. Now, under the influence of Egypt, the Muslim youth in school use and learn the common system of Hafs.

7. Bergsträsser has given a full account of this edition in his article "Koranlesung in Kairo" in *Der Islam* XX (1932).

8. I suspect that this also is dependent on the Kazan lithographs, but as no exemplar of these Kazan editions is available to me here in Cairo it is impossible to check this.

9. On Dr. Mingana's palimpsest find—*Leaves from Three Ancient Qur'ā ns possibly pre-Othmanic* (Cambridge, 1914), see Bergsträsser, *Geschichte des Qorantexts*, pp. 97ff.

10. A preliminary collection of these was made by Bergsträsser in his *Geschichte des Qorantexts*, pp. 60–96, and a much larger collection has been made by the present writer to be published in the *JRAS*.

11. Later orthodoxy made desperate efforts to obliterate the memory of even these readings, as we can see in the cases of Ibn Shanabudh (Yaqut, *Irshad,* VI. 302–304; Ibn Khallikan. tr. de Slane. III 16–18; Ibn al-Jazari, *Tabaqat,* No. 2707), and Ibn Muqsim (Yaqut, *Irshad,* VI. 499; Ibn al-Jazari, *Tabaqat,* No. 2945; Miskawaihi, *Tajarib,* ed. Amedroz, I. 285.)

12. Cf. Bergsträsser, *Qorantexts,* pp. 2, 3.

13. We have an apt parallel in the enormous authority still exercised, particularly in orthodox circles, by the King James version of the Bible.

14. This number seven was connected with a well known tradition about the Koran having been revealed according to seven *ahruf,* a tradition which itself had obviously been invented to explain the variant readings of the text known to exist.

15. It should be noted that there is often wide difference of opinion as to the dates of some of these readers.

16. Bergsträsser gave some account of this plan in a paper, "Plan eines Apparatus Criticus zum Koran," published in *Sitzungsberichte* of the Bavarian Academy, 1930, Heft 7.

17. *Das Lehrbuch der sieben Koranlesungen von ad-Dani* (Istanbul, 1930).

18. *Orthographie und Punktierung des Koran, zwei Schriften von ad-Dani* (Istanbul, 1932).

19. This also will appear in the *Bibliotheca Islamica* very shortly.

20. The results appeared in an article, "Nichtkanonische Koranlesarten in Muhtasab des Ibn Ginni," in the *Sitzungsberichte Bayer. Akad.,* 1934, Heft 7. The readings are given there in transcription. It is hoped that it will be possible to publish the whole Arabic text of the *Muhtasab* some day.

21. Full accounts of the manuscript material brought to light there are given in section four of his article "Die Wissenschaft der Koranlesung" in *Islamica* VI (1933–34).

22. Bergsträsser has dealt with him and his writings in section three of his "Koranlesung in Kairo."

23. See his account of "Die Fortführung des Apparatus Criticus zum Koran" in the *Sitzungsberichte* of the Bavarian Academy, 1934, Heft 5.

Chapter Eight: A Variant Text of the Fatiha

1. Nöldeke-Schwally, *Geschichte des Qorâns*, I, 110.

2. *Mafatih al-Ghaib*, V, 281.

3. Ibn al-Jazari, *Tabaqat*, No. 3943 (vol. ii, p. 404). He was Imam of the mosque at Wasit, and a great authority on the *isnads* of the Kufan reader 'Asim, and one of the teachers of Abu Bakr an-Naqqash.

4. 'Abu 'Ubaid, *Fada'il*, fol. 434. That Ibn Mas'ud knew the *Fatiha* as used liturgically, however, is clear not only from the fact that we have several variants in it from him (see the present writer's *Materials for the History of the Text of the Qur'an*, p. 25), but also from the story coming from al-A'mash († 148) that Ibn Mas'ud was asked why he did not include the *Fatiha* in his codex, and he answered that if he had included it he would have put it in front of every sura (Qurtubi, *Al-Jami'li Ahkam al-Qur'an*, I, 115). This statement shows quite clearly that he considered it to be a liturgical piece to be recited before reading the Koran. Late copies of Ibn Mas'ud's codex, made in the next generation or two, added the *Fatiha* at the beginning (*Itqan*, 152, 187; *Fihrist*, 26).

Chapter Nine: Abu 'Ubaid on the Verses Missing from the Koran

1. On Abu 'Ubaid see Flügel, *Die grammat. Schulen der Araber*, p. 85 ff., and particularly Hans Gottschalk's essay "Abū 'Ubaid al-Qāsim b. Sallām: Studie zur Geschichte der arabischen Biographie," in *Der Islam* XXIII (1936): 245–89.

2. The Berlin MS is Or. Peterman 449, and an edition of the text is now being prepared by Dr. Anton Spitaler.

Chapter 10: Textual Variations of the Koran

1. *Umm* vii. 60.

2. Ed. Krehl ii. 209.

3. *Bulletin of the John Rylands Library*, p. 201.

4. Tabari iii. 2175, 7; 2176, 17.

5. *Irshad al-Arib* vi. 94. Cf. *Aghani* iv. 177 end (ea. 2).

6. Mubarrad, *Kamil* ii. 322 (Cairo ed.).

7. *Chronicle* iii. 211.

8. See *Fath al-Bari* vi, 342.

9. Al-Hasan b. 'Abdallah 'Askari, *Kitab al-tashif* (Cairo, 1908).

10. *Diwan* (Beirut, 1905), p. 215.

11. Ru'bah, ed. Ahlwardt. p. 149. Ahlwardt's translation, "Der Juden Bibel, drin der Kritzler malte die Züge die sein Griffel schrieb mit Tinte," most seriously misrepresents the meaning.

12. P. 144, 13. Ahlwardt is again misleading.

13. *Iqd Farid* ii. 166 (ed. 1).

14. *Aghani* vi. 101, et. 2.

15. *Diwan*, p. 418.

16. Comm. v. 165, ed. 1.

17. Her private copy is mentioned by Ibn Hanbal vi. 73.

18. *Kamil* ii. 91 (Cairo ed.).

19. i. 285, Cairo ed.

20. i. 252.

21. i. 422.

Chapter 11: What Did Muhammad Borrow from Judaism?

1. Sura XX. 39. Comp. Ex. II. 3.

2. Comp. Mishna Berachoth V. 4.

3. The Arabians sometimes use *tabut as-sakinat* also in the meaning of "Ark of the Covenant" (D'Herbelot, *Bibliotheque Orientale*, under "Aschmouil.")

4. Sura II. 249.

5. Hebrew *torah*, 'ο νόμος.

6. Later Arabians maintained just the opposite. Ahmad ben 'Abdu'l-Halim (Maracc. Prod. I. p. 5.) says: "If one says: Instruct me about the allusions to the Apostle of God in the Torah, one understands by that expression all revelaed scriptures, since they are all called Torah"; and further: "It is acknowledged that by the word Torah are meant revealed writings, particularly those which the possessors of the scriptures (Jews and Christians) alike read; therefore it includes the Psalms, the prophecy of Isaiah, and other prophecies, but not the Gospel."

However this does not alter the conviction which we have already expressed.

7. Arabic *al-injilu.* Comp. Suras III. 2, 43, 58, 86, V. 70, VII. 157, IX. 112, LXI. 6, LXII. 5.

8. The Arabic commentators give widely different meanings to the word, but they know nothing of that given by us just because it is foreign to the Arabic language. Elpherar seems to decide for the view that *adn* means permanence, as the pious will remain there forever.

9. Muhammad uses it thus in Suras IX. 73, XIII. 23, XVI. 33, XVIII. 30, XIX. 62, XX. 78, XXXV. 30, XXXVIII. 50, XL. 8, LXI. 12. See also V. 70, X. 9, XXII. 55, XXVI. 85, XXXI. 7, XXXVII. 42, LXVIII. 34, LVI. 88, LXX. 38.

10. Arabic *jannatu 'l-firdausi*, Greek ὁ παράδεισος.

11. Chagiga fol. 14. Compare Sura XVIII. 107, XXIII. 11.

Among many wrong explanations Elpherar gives the following correct one: "Mujahid says it means a garden in Greek, and Zajaj says it has passed into Arabic."

12. E.g., σύνοδος, i.e., Sunhadus and especially γέεννα, which is pronounced in Syriac, as Gíhano.

13. Suras II. 201; III. 10, 196; IV. 58, 95, 99, 115, 120, etc.

14. V. 48, 68; IX. 31, 34.

15. Hebrew *'am ha-aretz,* Greek λαϊκός from λαος.

16. Sura IX. 31, 34, *rubban.*

17. Suras III. 73, XXXIV. 43, LXVIII. 37, VII. 168.

18. Hebrew *shabbat.*

19. Suras II. 61, VII. 163.

20. Sura XVI. 125.

21. Hebrew *shekinah.*

22. Compare Greek λόγος τοῦ θεοῦ

23. Ex. XXV. 8; cf. Deut. XXXIII. 12, 16.

24. Ex. XXV. 22.

25. Arabic commentators do not seem willing to recognize this meaning. Elpherar on Sura IX. 26 says the word means security and rest; and on Sura XLVIII. 4 he says distinctly, "Ben 'Abbas says this word *sakinat* in the Koran always means rest except in the second Sura."

26. It is to be observed however that the Targums frequently use this word in the plural for the idols themselves, but not for idolatry.

27. Suras II. 257, 259, IV. 68, XVI. 38, XXXIX. 19.

28. Ibn Said according to Elpherar explains this word as follows: "*Furqan* is help against the enemy." Sura XXI. 49.

29. Sura VIII. 29.

30. Arabic *jahiliyya.*

31. Suras III. 2, XXV. title and verse 1.

32. Suras II. 50, XXI. 49.

33. Compare under *ahbar.*

34. Suras XV. 87, XXXIX. 24.

The Arabian commentators on Sura XV. 87 differ much in their explanation of this word, but one among them gives what seems to be the true meaning. Elpherar has: "Tawus says the whole Koran is called Masani." At the same time also a reference is made to the other passage cited by us, viz., Sura XXXIX. 24.

35. Hebrew *malkut shamayim,* Greek ἡ βασιλεια τῶν ουρανῶν.

36. Sura VI. 75, XII. 184, XXIII. 90, XXXVI. 83.

37. Suras X. 3, XI. 9, L. 37, LVII. 4.

38. Sura XLI. 8–11.

39. Sura L. 37.

40. Chagiga 9. 2.

41. Cf. Midrash on the Psalms at the end of Psalm xi.

42. Suras II. 27, XVII. 46, XXIII. 88, XLI. 11, LXV. 12, LXVII. 3, LXXI, 14.

43. Sura LXXVIII. 12.

44. Sura XXIII. 17.

45. Sura XI. 9.

46. Rashi on Gen. I. 2. Cf. Sura XXIII. 88, XXVII. 26, XXIII. 117, LXXXV. 15.

47. Taanith 10. Pesachim 94.

48. Sura III. 127.

49. See Erubin 19.1.

50. 2 Sam, xix. 1–5 (Sota 10).

51. Zohar II. 150.

52. Sura XV. 44.

53. Sukkah 32.

54. Suras XXXVII. 60, XLIV. 43.

55. Othioth Derabbi Akiba, 8. 1.

56. Concerning this intermediate place S'adi cleverly remarks that it seems to the blessed as hell, to the lost as paradise (D'Herbelot, *Bibliotheque Orientale,* under A'raf, p. 113).

57. Elpherar comments on this passages as follows:

"These are those whose good and evil deeds are so evenly balanced that the latter preclude them from paradise, while the former save them from hell; therefore they remain standing here until God has declared His pleasure concerning them." And later, when he gives our explanation of verse 45 in a long chain of traditions, he says:

"Those whose good and evil deeds are equal are the middle men and stand on the road. Thence they can see at once the inhabitants of paradise and those of hell; if they turn to the former, they cry 'Peace be unto you:' if to the latter," etc.

58. "They," i.e., the men between, not as Wahl and others explain it.

59. *Phaedon,* chap. 62.

60. Mishna Aboth, IV. 17.

61. Suras IX. 88, XIII. 26.

62. Matt. xix. 24; Mark x. 25; Luke xviii. 24.

63. Sura LXXV. 23.

64. Sura LXXXIX. 27 ff.

65. Take, e.g., the rabbinical saying: "Even in their death the righteous are called living;" and in Suras II. 149, III. 163, it is ordered that those who fall in holy war shall not be called dead, but living.

66. The view that by the expression *techiyath hammethim* the future world or the (spiritual) continued life of the (bodily) dead is meant is given clearly in the explanation which a Baraitha adds to the quoted utterance of the Mishna. To the words: "He who asserts that the belief in *techiyath hammethim* is no part of the Jewish religion has no part in the future world," he adds: "he denies the T. H., therefore he has no more a portion in it." Here the expression *techiyath hammethim* and "future world" are taken as identical in meaning. Compare too the Book Ikkarim, IV. 31.

67. Hebrew *yom ha-dın.*

68. Compare, e.g. Sura XXVI. 87. 88.

69. Suras XXI. 104, XXXIX. 67. Cf. Isaiah XXXIV. 4.

70. Sura XLIV. 9 ff.

71. Sura XVII. 60.

72. Sura XXII. 2. Comp. Suras XXVII. 89, XXXIX. 68, LXIX, 13 ff.

73. Ezekiel xxxviii. and xxxix.
74. Sura XXI. 96
75. Sura XVIII. 93.
76. Chagiga 16, Taanith 11.
77. Isaiah xliii. 12.
78. Cf. also Suras XXXVI. 65, XLI. 19.
79. Exodus xii. 12.
80. Sura XXI. 98.
81. Job viii. 7.
82. Proverbs xiv. 12. Kiddushin, 40.2. Compare Derech Erets; Sutta end of chap. II; Aboth of Rabbi Nathan, end of chap. IX; Erubin 26.2; also the Targums and their commentators on Deuteronomy vii. 10.
83. Sura III. 172.
84. Compare Sura IX. 55, 86, XXXI. 23. Elpherar says on IX. 55: "Mujahid and Ketada say that this verse has been transposed; it should run: 'Let not therefore their riches or their children in this world cause thee to marvel. Verily God intendeth only to punish them by these things in that world.'"
85. Psalm xc. 4.
86. Sanhedrin 96. 2. See also preface to Ben Ezra's commentary on the Pentateuch where he opposes this view.
87. Sura XXII. 46.
88. Sura XXXII. 4.
89. Cf. Sura C, 9.
90. Mishna Sanhedrin X.1.
91. Suras VI. 95, XXX. 49, XXXVI. 33, XLI. 30, XLIII. 10, etc.
92. Taanith at the beginning.
93. Sanhedrin 90. 2, and Kethubhoth III, 2.
94. Jebamoth 49.
95. Sura XLII. 50.
96. Commentators cite this verse as one in which the superiority of Moses is disputed; thus Elpherar says: "The Jews said to Muhammad; 'By God! if thou art a prophet, dost thou speak with God and see Him as Moses spoke with Him and saw Him?' Then he said: 'Moses did not see God.' And then came this verse: 'It was not granted to a man that God should speak to him, except in a vision, in a dream or through supernatural inspiration, or from behind a curtain, so that man hears His Voice, but does not see Him; He spoke thus to Moses also.'"
97. Arabic *ruh qudsi*, Hebrew *ruah ha-qodesh*, Greek τὸ πνεῦμα ἅγιον.
98. Suras LXXVIII. 38, XCVII. 4.
99. I Kings, xxii. 21.
100. Sanhedrin 44.
101. Sura XVII. 87.
102. Compare Suras XXXV. 1, XXXVII. 1, XL. 7, LXXVII. 1 ff., LXXIX. 11 ff.
103. Sura XXXII. 11.
104. Sura XV. 27.
105. "The genii are supposed to be a species of angels, and the devil is their father; he

has thus a posterity, which is mentioned with him; the (remaining) angels however have no posterity." Jalálu'ddin in Maracc. Prodr. II. 15.

106. Chagiga 16. 1.

107. Suras XV. 17, 34, XXXVIII. 78, LXXXI. 24.

108. The Muslim explanation of falling stars.

109. Sura LXVII. 5; compare Sura XXXVII. 7.

110. Sura LXXII. 19.

111. Fakihat Elcholefa, 94, proves that this is really the Arabic view: "A meritorious man says that in the sins of men there is nothing small, but whatever is done contrary to the Commandment is great with respect to Him who commands, who is exalted and holy."

112. Jebamoth 6.

113. Leviticus xix. 3.

114. Sura XXIX. 7.

115. Sura II. 240.

116. Sura III. 188.

117. Cf. also Sura IV. 46.

118. Cf. Berachoth X.

119. Mishna Berachoth IV. 5.

120. Sura IV. 102.

121. Mishna Berachoth IV. 4.

122. Sura XXIII. 3. Compare Ecclesiastes v. 1.

123. Sura IV. 46.

124. Berachoth 31. 2. Erubin 64.

125. Suras IV. 46, V. 9. Cf. Mishna Berachoth III. 4.

126. Sura V. 8. Berachoth 46.

127. Suras IV. 46, V. 9.

128. Sura XVII. 110.

129. 1 Samuel, i. 13. Berachoth 31. 2.

130. Cf. Sunna 86, 87, 88, 89.

131. Mishna Berachoth I. 2.

132. Sura II. 183. Compare the note in the first section for remarks on the Fast Day, 'Ashura.

133. Sura II. 228. Cf. Mishna Jabhamoth IV. 10.

134. Sura II. 233. Cf. XXXI. 13l.

135. Kethuboth 60.1. Compare Josephus Ant. 2. 9.

136. Sura XXIV. 31.

137. Sura III. 191. Cf. Numbers xxiii. 10.

138. Sura XVIII. 23.

139. Sura XLVI. 14. Cf. Aboth V. 21. That full understanding is not reached until the completion of the fortieth year is observed also by Philo (ἕκτη δὲ [ἑβδομάδι] συνέσεως ἀκμή), who here takes the forty-second year, only because he attaches particular virtue to the number 7, in which Solon also agrees with him (Vid. Philo, de Opificio Mundi, pp. 70–72, Ed. Pfeifer I).

140. Sura LXII. 5.

141. Sura IV. 87. Cf. Baba Kamma 92.

142. Pirke Rabbi Eliezer 34.

143. Ecclesiastes viii. 8.

144. Psalm xlix. 8.

145. Daniel xii. 13.

146. Proverbs xi. 4.

147. Isaiah lviii. 8.

148. Sura XVII, 4–8.

149. Sura II, 28–32.

150. Midrash Rabbah on Numbers, para. 19. Compare Midrash Rabbah on Genesis, para. 8 and 17, and also Sanhedrin 38.

151. Genesis i. 26.

152. Psalm viii. 5.

153. Suras VII. 10-18, XV. 28–44, XVII. 63–68, XVIII. 48, XX. 115, XXXVIII. 71–86.

154. Cf. Greek διάβολος.

155. The legend of the devil's refusal to worship Adam, given by me as a Christian one, was found by Zunz ("Die Gottesdienstlichen Vorträge der Juden," p. 291. Note.) in the MS. Midrash of Rabbi Moses Haddarshan, who however lived in the eleventh century.

156. Midrash Rabbah on Genesis, para. 8.

157. Arabic *Iblis* (διάβολος) instead of *Shaytān* (Hebrew *Shatan*).

158. This proper name is never used by Muhammad in this narrative; he uses throughout simply *janna* ("garden"), which shows that the Jews knew well the distinction between the home of our first parents and Paradise.

159. Suras VII. 18–25, XX. 115–27.

160. Arabic *Shaytān*.

161. Midrash Rabbah on Genesis, para. 17.

162. Genesis, ii. 21.

163. Pirke Rabbi Eliezer, xiii.

164. To the same effect Muhammad ben Kais (vide Elpherar on VII. 21): "His Lord called to him: 'O Adam, why hast thou eaten of that, when I had forbidden it to thee?' He replied, 'Lord, Eve gave it to me.' Then said He to Eve: 'Why didst thou give it to him?' She replied, 'The snake commanded me to do it.' Then said He to the snake: 'Why didst thou command it?' 'The devil ordered me to do it.'"

165. Genesis ii. 17, and iii. 5.

166. Genesis iii. 22.

167. Sura VII. 19.

168. Sura XX. 118.

169. Genesis iv. 3–9. Cf. Sura V. 30–36.

170. Commonly called Pseudo-Jonathan.

171. Pirke R. Eliezer, chapter xxi.

172. Sura V. 35.

173. Mishna Sanhedrin IV. 5.

174. Genesis iv. 10. Compare the translation of Onkelos.

175. Sura XLI. 92.

176. Suras XIX. 57, 58; XXI. 85, 86. Elpherar on Sura XIX. 57 says: "He is the grandfather of the father of Noah; his name is Enoch."

177. Sura XIX. 58. Compare Genesis v. 24 and the Tract Derech Erez cited in Midrash Yalkut, chap. XLII.

178. In Maraccio.

179. *Idris* is drived from *darasa*, "study." Elpherar on XIX. 57.

180. Suras XIX. 55, 56; XXI. 85.

181. Midr. Abhkhir quoted in Midr. Yalkut, chap. XLIV. Compare Yoma 67. 2. and Rashi, Zohar on Genesis i. 26.

182. Psalm viii. 5.

183. Sura II. 96.

184. This connection and comparison which might well appear very doubtful, and which seemed even to me at first nothing more than a conjecture, receives full corroboration from that which later Arabian authors, quite in harmony with the Mid. Yalkut, say about the angels. We find in Maraccius Prodromi iv, 82, the following: "Mujáhid says: The angels wondered at the wickedness of the sons of Adam, for apostles had already been sent to them; then their Lord (God) said to them: 'Choose out two of you, and I will send them that they may judge upon earth.' Then Harut and Marut were chosen, and they judged righteously, till Zahrah (the star Venus) came in the form of a most beautiful woman and complained about her husband. They were led astray by her and lusted after her, but she fled and went back to where she was before.... Muhammad says: 'Yahya states on another authority than that of Mujahid, that the woman through whom they were led astray was a human woman.' The union of these two views is to be found in the passages quoted from Midrash Yalkut.

185. Suras VII. 57–63, X. 72–75, XI. 27–50, XXII. 43, XXIII. 23–32, XXV. 39, XXVI. 105–121, XXIX. 13. 14, XXXVII. 73–81, LIV. 9–18, LXXI. 1–end.

186. Sanhedrin 108. (Comp. Midrash Rabban on Genesis, paras. 30 and 33, also on Ecclesiastes ix. 14.)

187. Sura XI. 40. Cf. Midr. Tanchuma, Section Noah.

188. Sura XI. 42, and XXIII. 27. Cf. Rosh Hashanah 16. 2, and Sanhedrin 108. The Arabic commentators seem to me to have quite misunderstood these passages, since they assume fabulous references. Our explanation, which is justified by a figurative interpretation of the words "And the oven glows," appears to me sufficiently confirmed by a comparison with the Talmudic utterance.

189. Sura XXIX. 18. Cf. Genesis, ix. 29.

190. Sura XI. 44, 45, 48.

191. Genesis, ix. 22 ff. The commentators actually call this son Canaan (compare Genesis, ix. 25 ff.) although they, like the Bible, do not reckon any son of this name in their enumeration of the sons, but count these three only.

192. Sura LXVI. 10.

193. The world "deliberate" is to be understood in the sense already sufficiently explained in the First Division, Third Section, so that we may use it from now on without further explanatory comment.

194. Sura XXXI. 11 ff.

195. Sura VII. 61.

196. Sura XI. 33.

197. Sura XI. 31, and XXVI. 109.

198. Arabic *qul.* XI. 37. Cf. XXIX. 19.

199. Compare Mid. Rabbah on Genesis para. 42. "Abram was called the Hebrew because he was descended from Eber." (Genesis xiv. 13).

200. *Yahudi.* Among the Arabs sometimes *Yahud,* more often *Hud.*

201. Suras VII. 63–71, XI. 52–64, XXII. 43, XXIII. 33–44, XXV. 40, XXVI. 123–141, XXIX. 37, XXXVIII. 11, XL. 32, XLI. 12–16, XLVI. 20–25, L. 13, LI. 41, 42, LIII. 50, LIV. 18–22, LXIX. 4–9, LXXXIX. 5–9.

202. Sura XXVI. 129.

203. Sura LXXXIX. 6. Cf. Genesis xi. 4.

204. Sura XI. 62. Compare Genesis x. 8, 9.

205. D'Herbelot, under the heading Nimrod, asserts that the Arabians connect Nimrod with the building of the Tower.

206. Midr. Rabbah on Genesis xi. 2, par. 38.

207. Sura XXVI. 128. Compare Exodus xxxii. 6.

208. Sura XI. 63.

209. Mishna Sanhedrin X. 3. Genesis xi. 8, 9.

210. Suras XLI. 15, XLVI. 23 ff., LI. 41, LIV. 19, LXIX. 6 ff.

211. Sura XXIII. 37.

212. Seder 'Olam quoted in Midrash Yalkut, chap. 62.

213. Genesis x. 25.

214. Genesis xxv. 22. Midr. Rabbah on Genesis, par. 68. Also par. 68. for Jacob's sojourn in the home of Eber.

215. Sura XI. 53, XXVI. 127.

216. Sura LXXXIX. 6.

217. Poc. Spec., p. 3.

218. Sura XVI. 28.

219. Maracc. on the passage.

220. *Hist. Anteislamica,* pp. 18 and 20.

221. Except in Suras L. 12, and LXIX. 4, where it precedes. In the former of these two passages it precedes the story of the Midianites also, and thus no chronological order is followed. In Suras LI. 43 and LIII. 51, it actually precedes the story of the Deluge, and in Sura LXXXV. 18, Pharoah is placed before Samud on account of the rhyme.

222. Poc. Spec., p. 3.

223. The passages which treat of this are the following:—Suras VII. 71–78, XI. 64–72, XXII. 43, XXV. 40, XXVI. 141–160, XXVII. 46–55, XXIX. 37, XXXVIII. 12, XL. 32, XLI. 12–18, L. 12, LI. 43–46, LIII. 51, LIV. 23–33, LXIX. 4–6, LXXXV. 18, LXXXIX. 8, XCI. 11–16.

224. Sura LIV. 28, XCI. 12.

225. Sura XXVII. 49.

226. See Genesis x. 24. This is also D'Herbelot's view. See his *Bib. Orient.* under Salih.

227. Isma'il ben 'Ali asserts however that Salih lived after Hud. (Maracc. Prodr., iv. 93).

228. Genesis xlix. 6.

229. Sura XVI. 124.

230. Arabic *hanif.* Sura II. 129, III. 60, VI. 79, XVI. 121, 124.

231. Sura II. 134.

232. On this Baidhawi has the following: "The Jews and the Christians disputed about Abraham, and each party believed they could count him on their side. They appealed to Muhammad and thereupon came this revelation. The meaning is that Judaism and Christianity first came into existence by the sending of the law through Moses and the gospel through Jesus." That this is the Jewish view is shown by the following passage:—"Our forefather Abraham observed the whole Law, for it is written (Genesis xxvi. 5.): 'Because Abraham obeyed My voice, and kept My charge, My commandments, My statutes and My laws.'" (Yoma xxviii. 2).

233. Sura IV. 124.

234. Sura II. 119 ff.

235. Sura XIV. 40.

236. Sura LXXXVII. 19.

237. Suras VI. 74–82, XIX. 42–51, XXI. 52–69, XXII. 43, XXVI. 69–105, XXIX. 15–23, XXXVII. 81–95, XLIII. 25–28, LX. 4–6.

238. Suras IX. 115, XXVI. 86–104, LX. 4. Sunna 395.

239. Suras II. 260, XXI. 69–74, XXIX. 23–27, XXXVII. 95–99.

240. Midrash Rabba on Genesis, para. 38.

241. Abulfeda (*Hist. Anteislamica,* p. 20) says: "Azar the father of Abraham made idols and served them and bade Abraham sell them, but Abraham said: 'Who would buy that which harms him and does him no good?'"

242. Sura IX. 115.

243. Midrash Rabba on Genesis, para. 38.

244. Sanhedrin 104.

245. Sura II. 128, 135.

246. Suras XXI. 71, XXIX. 25.

247. Sura XXVI. 88–104.

248. Sura XXIX. 17–23.

249. Compare above on Noah.

250. Suras II. 260, XXVI. 81.

251. Baidhawi says on Sura II. 262: "It is said that, after Nimrod had said: 'I make alive and I kill,' (II. 260), Abraham answered: 'Quickening is brought about by the return of the spirit to the body.' Nimrod replied: 'Hast thou then seen that?' Abraham could not answer in the affirmative and had to pass over to another argument. On this he prayed to the Lord for some revelation, in order that his mind might be easy about an answer to this question, if it were put to him again."

252. Genesis xv. 9. ff.

253. Sura II. 262.

254. Sura VI. 74.

255. Pointed out by Maracc. Prodr., iv. 90.

256. According to the Tarikh Muntakhab, Azar was the father of Tharah (D'Herbelot, *Bib. Orient.,* under Abraham, p. 11).

257. Vide Maracc. on the passage.

258. Sura XI. 72. Elpherar remarks: "By messengers he means angels."

259. Genesis xviii. Suras XI. 72–79, XV. 51–61, XXIX. 30–32, LI. 24–38.

260. Qiddushin 52.

261. Baba Mezia 86. 2.
262. Sura XV. 54 ff.
263. Genesis xvii. 17.
264. Sura XI. 74.
265. This is referred to in general terms in Sura II. 118; cf. Mishna Aboth, v. 3.
266. Sura XXXVII. 99–114.
267. Sura XXXVII. 112, 113.
268. Sura XI. 74; cf. two other passages, Sura XXXVII. 99 and 112.
269. Suras VII. 78–83, XI. 79–85, XV. 61–78, XXII. 43, XXVI. 160–176, XXVII. 55–60, XXIX. 27–35, XXXVII. 133–137, LIV. 33–39.
270. Compare especially Sura XXIX. 27–30.
271. Suras XXIX. 31, XV. 60.
272. Sura LXVI. 10.
273. Sura XXV. 42, and other passages.
274. Sura XXVI. 164.
275. On the passage quoted above (Sura XXXVII. 101) Elpherar remarks as follows: "The learned among the Muslims are divided about the lad whom Abraham was commanded to sacrifice; whereas the people of the Book on both sides (Jews and Christians) are agreed that he was Isaac, and common people are at one with them." Many commentators are then quoted, who also share this opinion. "Other however say that he was Ishmael," and for this opinion the authorities are not cited: "Both views are supported by the words of Muḥammad. Those who maintain that Isaac was the one sacrificed prove it from Sura XXXVII. 99: 'We brought him the joyful news that he should have a meek son.' And when he was grown up, then God commanded Abraham to offer up him who had been announced to him. But we do not read in the Koran that any son except Isaac was foretold to him, as it is written in the Sura entitled Hud: 'And we announced to him Isaac.'—Sura XI. 74. Those however who maintain that Ishmael was the one sacrificed prove it from the fact that the announcement of Isaac comes after the completion of the story of the sacrifice, when we read for the first time: 'And we rejoiced him with the promise of Isaac, a righteous prophet.'—Sura XXXVII. 112. This shows that the sacrificed person was another than Isaac. (The same view is given in detail by Jalalud-din as quoted by Maracc.) Further it is said in Sura Hud (XI. 74): 'We promised him Isaac and after Isaac's son Jacob. As he had announced Isaac, so he also announced to him Isaac's son Jacob.' How could he then have commanded the sacrifice of Isaac, when he had promised seed through him?" This last proof is truly not to be ranked very high, for a similar contradiction in Holy Scripture in the case of Genesis, xxi. 12, and Genesis, xxii. would then have to be explained. Beyond the first proof adduced, there is no necessity either for this argument, or for still another argument which immediately afterwards is cited in the commentary, viz., that the horns of the ram are preserved in Mecca, the dwelling-place of Ishmael. It will have been noted that in the text I have independently decided in favor of the view that Muḥammad believed that it was Ishmael whose sacrifice was ordered by God.

Doubtless all Arabian authorities would have come to this same conclusion, had not the Jews and Christians expressed their opinion so decidedly in favor of Isaac (in which they were followed by the common people). This fact prevented many from giving to the text of the Koran sufficiently impartial consideration, and hence led them to abandon

Muhammad's real view. The method by which these attempted to weaken the proof for the opposite opinion is clear from Elpherar's comment on Sura XXXVII. 112: "He who takes it that Ishmael was the one sacrificed explains that it was after this event that Isaac a prophet was promised to Abraham as a reward for his obedience; he who takes it that Isaac was the one sacrificed explains that it was only the prophetic gift of Isaac which was announced to Abraham. Akhrama in the name of Ibn 'Abbás explains that Isaac was announced to his father twice, once before his birth and again at the attainment of the prophetic gift." In the following verse, however, which upholds our view still more strongly, Elpherar gives an erroneous explanation of one part of the verse, and about the rest maintains a significant silence. In the legends of Islam, Isaac is almost without an exception spoken of as the one led to sacrifice. So also in Elpherar on Sura XII. 36, where Joseph relates his history to his fellow-prisoners, and on Sura XII. 86, where mention is made of a letter written by Jacob to the king who was keeping his son in prison. Here Isaac is always called "The sacrificed of God." And when Jacob in the course of the letter (quite according to the version of Sepher Hayyashar) alludes to the special protection of God enjoyed by his family he says: "As for my father, both his hands and his feet were bound, and the knife was put to his throat, but God ransomed him." Compare Abulfeda, *Hist. Anteislamica*, p. 22.

276. Suras XIX. 55, 56, XXI. 85, 86.

277. Suras II. 130, 134, III. 77, VI. 86, XXXVIII. 48.

278. Sura XIV. 41.

279. Sura II. 119.

280. Mid. Rab. on Genesis, para. 38.

281. Baba Bathra 16.

282. Sura II. 127.

283. Sura XI. 74.

284. The Arabic commentators, who may not and will not understand these words as we do, are obliged to seek some other reasons for the unsuitable allusion to Jacob. Thus Elpherar says: "It was announced to her that she would live till she saw her son's son."

285. Suras VI. 84, XIX. 50, XXI. 72, XXIX. 26.

286. Sunna 398 and 400.

287. Sura XII. 6, 38.

288. Sura II. 127.

289. On Sura XII. 4. See de Sacy, *Anthologie Grammaticale,* 125.

290. Elpherar has nearly the same words, with the addition however of a long chain of traditions.

291. Suras III. 87.

292. Israel is *Ja'qub,* Baidhawi.

293. Genesis xxxii. 33.

294. Sura II. 126–27.

295. Compare perhaps Genesis xviii. 19.

296. Midr. Rab. on Genesis, para. 98, and on Deuteronomy, para. 2.

297. Genesis xlix. 2.

298. Deuteronomy vi. 4.

299. Comp. the two recensions of the Jerusalem Targum on Deuteronomy vi. 4; also Tract Pesachim, p. 56.

300. Sura XL. 36.

301. Sura XII. 4–108.

302. Genesis xxxvii. 9–36 and chapters xxxix to xlvi.

303. Sura XII. 24.

304. Genesis xxxix. 11.

305. Sotah xxxvi. 2.

306. Elpherar in his comment on the verse quoted gives some of these particulars: "It is said on the authority of Ben 'Abbas that he said he had undone his girdle and approached her with a sinful purpose.

"Ketada and the greater number of the commentators say that he saw the form of Jacob, who said: 'O Joseph, though thy name is written among the prophets yet thou behavest like the fools.'"

307. Elpherar on xii. 31, agreeing with the Sepher Hayyashar, gives, contrary to Wahl's forced interpretation, the correct meaning as follows:

"They cut themselves with the knife which they had in their hands, thinking they were cutting the orange, but they did not feel the pain on account of their absorption in the contemplation of Joseph."

308. An allusion to this fable is found in a passage from the Midrash Abhkir quoted in the Midr. Yalkut, chapter 146.

309. Sura XII. 25.

310. Sura XII. 26.

311. So also Elpherar.

312. Sura XII. 42.

313. Midr. Rabbah on Genesis, para. 89.

314. Proverbs xiv. 23.

315. Genesis xl. 14.

316. Genesis xli. 1.

317. Elpherar has the following: "It is said that the butler did not remember to mention Joseph to the king. The virtual meaning of this is that Satan made him forget the mention of him to his Lord (Pharaoh). But Ben 'Abbas and most authorities after him say that Satan made Joseph forget the remembrance of his Lord, so that he sought help apart from Him and protection from a creature, and this was an omission to which Satan tempted Joseph." Then he quotes many other passages which represent this step of Joseph's as sinful.

318. Sura XII. 67.

319. Midr. Rabbah on Genesis, para. 91.

320. The same reason is given alike by the Arabic commentators and in the Midrash. (Cf. Elpherar on the verse "For fear of envious looks," which the ancients regarded as very disastrous in their consequences).

321. Sura XII. 77.

322. Mid. Rab., para. 92.

323. Genesis xxi. 19. The Arabian commentators give the most varying accounts. One of these confirms our view of an erroneous confusion with Rachel, viz., the following in Elpherar: "Sa'id Ben Jubair and Ketada say that his grandfather, his mother's father, had an image which he worshipped. This he stole secretly."

324. Sura XII. 86, 97.

325. Pirke Rabbi Eliezer, section 38.

326. Mid. Tanchuma quoted in Mid. Yalkut, chapter 143.

327. Genesis xxxvii. 35.

328. Sura XII. 69.

329. Sura XII. 11 ff.

330. Genesis xxxvii. 13 ff.

331. Genesis xxxvii. 24.

332. Sura XII. 47, 50.

333. Genesis xli. 14 ff.

334. Sura XII. 84, 93, 96. Cf. Genesis xlviii. 10.

335. Sura XII. 100, 101.

336. Genesis xxxv. 18 ff.

337. Sura XII. 4. Cf. Genesis xxxvii. 10.

338. On Sura XII. 4. De Sacy, *Anth. Gramm,* p. 127.

339. Sura XII. 100.

340. The Arabian commentators, who are quite conscious of this unsuitability, explain it away very cleverly by saying that Joseph made this digression, because it grieved him to be obliged to foretell evil to one of his fellow-prisoners. Elpherar comments on verse 37 as follows:

"After they had told him the dream, he was unwilling to give them the explanation for which they had asked him, because he recognized in it something that would be disagreeable to one of them. For this reason he put aside their question, and began a different discourse, in which he taught them about the gift of miracle-working and exhorted them to belief in the unity of God."

341. Suras XX. 37–44, XXVIII. 2–29.

342. Suras XX. 8–37, 44–51, XXVI. 9–17, XXVIII. 29–36, LXXIX. 15–20.

343. Suras VII. 101–25, X. 76–90, XI. 99–102, XX. 50–79, XXIII. 47–51, XXVI. 15–52, XXVII. 13–15, XXVIII. 36–40, XL. 24–49, XLIII. 45–54, LXXIX. 20–27.

344. Suras II. 46–47, VII. 127–39, X. 90–93, XX. 79–82, XXVI. 52–69, XXVIII. 40–43, XLIII. 55.

345. Suras II. 57, VII. 160.

346. Sura VII. 142 and 149. On the first passage Elpherar has: "Ben 'Abbas says that by Alwah he means the Torah;" and on the second passage he says more correctly: "Wherein is the Torah."

347. Suras VII. 135–47, 170, II. 52–55, 60, 87, IV. 152. In the Koran Mount Sinai is never mentioned in connection with the giving of the law, although it is so mentioned by commentators, e.g., Elpherar on VII. 140. But it was not unknown to Muhammad, seeing that it is mentioned on other occasions. Thus it is used as an oath in Sura XCV. 2. Again it is mentioned in the account of the creation of the olive tree (Sura XXIII. 20), in which passage the commentators cited by Elpherar take the name as an appellation. Among many diverging explanations one is adduced which appears to me right, viz., "It is said that in Syriac it means a place thickly planted with trees." It is to be noted that those mentioned above who take Sinai as an appellation do not regard it as identical with the mountain on which Moses received the law, which identification is merely cited as a possible view: "Ben Zaid says that this is the mountain from which Moses was addressed."

D'Herbelot (*Biblio. Orient.* under Sina, p. 793) says: "The Arabs sometimes call this mountain Sinaini (which however should be Sinani) with references to its two peaks Horeb and Sina; in this way Sinina might perhaps be taken as the genitive of the Arabic word Sinuna.

348. Suras II. 48–52, 87, VII. 148–55, XX. 82–99.
349. Sura VII. 154.
350. Sura V. 23–29.
351. Sura XXVIII. 76–88.
352. Sura XVIII. 59–81.
353. Suras XXVIII. 5, 7, 38, XXIX. 38, XL. 25.
354. Suras XXIX. 38, XL. 25.
355. Midr. Rabb. on Numbers, par. 14.
356. Compare Makarizi in De Sacy's *Chrest. Arabe.,* p. 143, line 9 of the first edition.
357. Sura XXVIII. 5.
358. Pirke Rabbi Eliezer, section 48.
359. Sura XXVIII. 8.
360. Sura LXVI. 11.
361. Exodus ii. 5.
362. 1 Chron. iv. 18.
363. Exodus ii. 7.
364. Sotah 12, 2.
365. There is an allusion to this also in Sura XXVIII. 11.
366. Suras XXVI. 19, XXVIII. 14.
367. Midr. Rabb. on Exodus, para. 5.
368. Sura XXVIII. 17 ff.
369. Sura XXVIII. 19.
370. Sura XXVIII. 23.
371. Exodus ii. 16.
372. Exodus iii.
373. Sura XXVIII. 29.
374. Sura XXVI. 17 ff.
375. Exodus ii. 23, iv. 19.
376. Midr. Rabb. on Exodus, para. 1.
377. Exodus ii. 23.
378. Midr. Rabb. on Exodus, para. 5.
379. According to Midr. Rabb. on Exodus, para 1, Dathan and Abiram were the two disputants, one of whom reproached Moses with the murder of the Egyptian.
380. Suras VII. 108, XXVI. 32.
381. Exodus vii. 8 ff.
382. Pirke Rabbi Eliezer, section 48.
383. Suras VII. 110, XXVI. 40.
384. Exodus viii. 15.
385. Sura X. 83. The suffix refers to Moses, as some Arabic commentators cited by Baidhawi (Henzii, *Fragm. Arab.,* p. 103) and by Elpherar take it.
386. Midr. Rabb. on Exodus, para. 5.

387. Suras XX. 74, XXVI. 48.
388. Midr. Yalkut, chapter 182.
389. Suras XXVI. 28, XXVIII. 38.
390. Midr. Rabb. on Exodus, para. 5.
391. Ezekiel, xxix. 3.
392. Sura XLIII. 50.
393. "Al-Hasan says by my command."
394. Sura XL. 29 ff.
395. Midr. Rabba on Exodus, para. 1.
396. Suras XVII. 103, XXVII. 12.
397. Sura VII. 130.
398. E.g., in Psalm, cv. 28 ff.
399. First mentioned in v. 132.
400. Exodus xiv. 10 ff.
401. Sura XXVI. 61. ff.
402. Sura X. 90 ff.
403. Not one Arabic commentator among those quoted in Elpherar appears to have had a suspicion of the explanation given above, which is so well suited to the words; still it is not a quote unknown to Baidhawi. Along with other explanations he gives (Henzii, *Fragm. Arab.,* p. 201) the following: "And today we save thee, i.e., we will bring thee back from where thy people are sunk—even from the depth of the sea, and we will put thee on dry land." And further on: "With thy body, i.e., whole and unharmed." But on the other hand the words "That thou mayest be a sign to those who shall come after thee" are explained by him only in the ordinary way, viz., that he should be a horror and a warning to them.
404. Pirke Rabbi Eliezer, Section 43. Comp. also Midrash on Psalm cvi. and Midr. Yalkut, chapter 238.
405. Exodus v. 2.
406. Exodus xv. 11.
407. Exodus ix. 15.
408. Exodus xvii. 6.
409. Exodus xv. 27. Comp. also the two recensions of Jerusalem Targum.
410. Suras II. 60, 87, VII. 170.
411. Abodah Zarah II. 2.
412. Sura II. 52 ff., IV. 152.
413. Deuteronomy v. 24 (Heb. v. 21).
414. Canticles v. 6.
415. Psalm xix. 8.
416. Sura VII. 150.
417. Sanhedrin 5. Rashi makes the same remark on Exodus xxxii. 4.
418. Sura XX. 87, 90, 96.
419. Sura XX. 97. Compare the wandering Jew in the Christian legend.
420. Judges xvii.
421. Rashi on Sanhedrin 101. 2.
422. Cf. Ahmad Ben Idris in Hottinger's *Hist. Orient.,* p. 84.

423. Cf. Makarizi (in De Sacy, *Chrest. Arabe,* i. 113 in the second edition, 189 in the first edition).

424. Suras VII. 147, XX. 90.

425. Exodus xxxii. 24.

426. Pirke Rabbi Eliezer, section 45.

427. Sura VII. 159.

428. Exodus xxxii. 26.

429. Pirke Rabbi Eliezer, section 45.

430. Sura XXVIII. 76.

431. Ecclesiastes v. 12.

432. Sura XXXIII. 69.

433. Cf. Abulfeda, *Hist. Anteislámica,* p. 32.

434. See Numbers xvi. 4.

435. Sanhedrin 110.

436. Numbers xx. 29.

437. Numbers xvi. 48. (Hebrews xvii. 13.)

438. Numbers xii. 1 ff.

439. Sura XVIII. 59–81.

440. Zunz (*Die Gottesdienstlichen Vorträge der Juden, Historisch Entwickelt,* 8. 130 u. Anm. d.) has pointed out the Jewish source of this story, in which the servant of God according to the Arabians is said to be Elias (cf. under Elias); only that, according to the Jewish source, the traveller is R. Joshua ben Levi, a man who plays a leading part in tales of marvel and adventure (cf. Zunz, pp. 140–41) and whom this adventure suits much better than it does Moses, who stands on too high a plane. We may easily recognize therefore the Jewish origin of this legend, which has been embellished quite after the manner of the Koran.

441. Sura XVIII. 82 ff.

442. Exodus xxxiv. 29 ff.

443. Numbers xix. 2 ff.

444. Sura II. 63 ff.

445. Sura II. 67.

446. Deuteronomy xxi. 2 ff.

447. Sura II. 68.

448. Sura II. 63.

449. Vid. Midr. Rabb. on Numbers, para. 19.

450. Baba Bathra, 17.

451. Suras LXIV. 12, VII. 138.

452. Cf. Sura III. title and verse 30 ff.; Sura XIX. particularly verse 29; Sura LXVI. 12, and Sunna 405.

453. Sura XXVIII. 10.

454. Sura XXVIII. 28 ff.

455. Elpherar on Sura XXVIII. 23.

456. *Hist. Anteislamica,* p. 30.

457. Exodus ii. 17.

458. Suras VII. 83–92, XI. 85–98, XXII. 43, XXV. 40, XXVI. 176–92, XXIX. 35–36, XXXVIII. 12, L. 12–13.

459. Midr. Rabb. on Exodus, para. 1.
460. Exodus ii. 16.
461. Exodus ii. 17.
462. Suras VII. 83, XI. 86.
463. It seems as though Muhammad had confounded the Midianites with the inhabitants of Sodom, to whom such things are imputed by the rabbis.
464. Sura XXIX. 35.
465. Sura XXVI. 180.
466. Sura XXVI. 186, 187.
467. Suras VII. 83, XI. 85, XXIX. 85, XXII. 43.
468. Suras VII. 83–92, XI. 85–98.
469. It is all very well for Ahmad ben as-Salim (quoted by Maracc. on Sura VII. 83) to assert that this is the opinion of "a heap of fools." Some regard Jethro as the father of Shu'aib (as Elpherar on Sura VII. 83); others, as his nephew (cf. the passage quoted above from Elpherar on Sura XXVIII. 23). The difference in the names confuses the commentators, and also their ignorance of the source from which here, as often, Muhammad drew.
470. That Moses obtained the staff from Jethro is asserted also by D'Herb., *B. O.,* under the word Shu'aib, p. 722, according to the Muhammadan view.
471. E.g. Sura XXVI. 176 ff.
472. Suras XXV. 40, L. 12.
473. Sura L. 12.
474. On Sura XXV. 40.
475. On Sura XXV. 40 (vid. Maracc.).
476. Sura VII. 174–75.
477. Sura II. 247.
478. Sura II. 247–53.
479. Samuel viii. 20.
480. Samuel x. 27.
481. Sura II. 249 must be thus understood.
482. Judges vii. 5 ff.
483. 1 Samuel xiv. 24 ff.
484. *Ṭālūt* probably derived from *ṭāla,* to be tall.
485. 1 Samuel ix. 2, x. 23.
486. Sura II. 248.
487. Sura XXXVIII. 16
488. Samuel xii. 1 ff.
489. Sura XXXVIII. 20–23.
490. Sura XXXVIII. 23–26.
491. Sura XXI. 78.
492. Suras XXI. 79, XXXIV. 10, XXXVIII. 16–20.
493. Sura XXI. 80.
494. Sura XXVII. 15.
495. Sunna 148.
496. On Sura XXXVIII. 16.
497. Psalms cxix. 62.

498. Berachoth.
499. Suras IV. 161, XVII. 57.
500. Suras II. 61, IV. 50, V. 65, VII. 166.
501. Sura XXVII. 15, 16.
502. 1 Kings v. 13.
503. Suras XXI. 81, 82, XXXIV. 11, 12, XXXVIII. 35–39.
504. On Esther i. 2.
505. Ecclesiastes ii. 8.
506. Sura XXVII. 20–46.
507. Second Targum on the Book of Esther.
508. 1 Kings, x. 9.
509. Sura XXVII. 30.
510. Sura XXXIV. 13. Cf. on this point Gittin, 68.
511. Sura XXXVIII. 33–35.
512. Sanhedrin 20.
513. 1 Chronicles xxix. 23.
514. Ecclesiastes i. 3.
515. Ecclesiastes ii. 10.
516. Cf. also Midr. Rabba on Numbers par. 11; on Canticles iii. 4; and on Ruth ii. 14.
517. Sura XXXVIII. 29–32.
518. Sanhedrin 21.
519. Deuteronomy xvii. 16.
520. 1 Kings x. 29.
521. Sura II. 96.
522. Sura XXVII. 18–19.
523. Proverbs vi. 6 ff.
524. Chullin 57. 2.
525. P. 91.
526. *Ilyas:* Suras VI. 85, XXXVII. 123. In one place he is called *Ilyasin* (Sura XXXVII. 80) on account of the rhyme. We find among other opinions in Elpherar the following:
"It is said that Ilyasin is a dialectic change for Elyas, as Ism'ail for Ism'ain and Mikhayil for Mikhayin." These examples are certainly unsuitable, for in them the change is only from "l" to "n," while here the complete addition of the syllable *in* takes place. This the Arabs, in spite of the similar *sinina* mentioned before, seem to shrink from explaining as a change deliberately made on account of the rhyme.
527. Sura XVIII. 59–82.
528. Suras VI. 86, X. 98, XXXVII. 139, XXI. 87, LXVIII. 48.
529. Suras X. 98, XXI. 87–88, XXXVII. 139–49, LXVIII. 48–51.
530. Suras XXI. 83–84, XXXVIII. 40–45.
531. Sura LXXXV. 4 ff.
532. Daniel iii. 8 ff.
533. An intimation that this passage refers to this circumstance is given by the Arabian commentator Muqatil (cited by Elpherar), in that he asserts that there were in fact three "people of the burning fiery pit"; and of the pits one was in *Fars,* i.e., Persia, and indeed under Nebuchadnezzar; but he adds:

"God revealed nothing in the Sura about this or about the other event which took place in Syria, but only revealed about the one under Dhu-nawas. But this intimation is enough for the strengthening of our opinion."

534. Ezekiel xxxvii.

535. Sura II. 244.

536. The Arabian commentators know of this but dimly, for Ismail Ben 'Ali gives out in the name of Ibn Talib that this event took place in the time of the Judge (?), i.e., Ezekiel, who came after the son of Caleb, in this office. (Maracc. Prodr. IV. 83.)

537. Sanhedrin. 92.

538. Sura XXV. 47–48

539. 2 Kings xx. 9–12.

540. Sura IX. 30. Sunna, 462.

In D'Herbelot (under the word "Ozair," p. 691) much is adduced from Muslim commentators and historians to explain this passage, which however, in harmony with the Talmud, only asserts Ezra's renewing of the law.

541. Sanhedrin 21. 2.

542. *Prod.* iv. 85.

543. Sura II. 261.

544. Nehemiah ii. 12 ff.

545. Suras VI. 86, XXXVIII. 48.

546. Suras XXI. 85, XXXVIII. 48.

547. 1 Kings xviii, 4.

548. *Reisebeschreibung* II, 265.

549. According to Khondemir (D'Herbelot, *Bibl. Orient.,* under Elisha ben Akhthob) Dhu'l-Kifl was a follower of Elisha, but Obadiah was contemporary with Elijah.

550. Pocock, *Notre Misc.,* chap. 9, p. 369.

551. Sura V. 85.

552. Suras II. 58, V. 74.

553. Sura V. 21.

554. Suras II. 88, LXII. 6.

555. Sura IX. 30. Sunna 462.

556. Sura II. 128, 135.

557. Sura II. 73, and other passages.

558. Sunna 70 ff.

559. Sunna 97 ff.

560. Sura II. 183.

561. Sura II. 229 ff.

562. Sura II. 230.

563. Deuteronomy xxiv. 1 ff.

564. Sunna 460.

565. Sura II. 223.

566. Sura IV. 158.

567. Matthew xix. 8.

568. Suras III. 44, 87, IV. 158, V. 89, 90.

569. Suras V. 4, VI. 146, XVI. 116.

570. Acts xv. 19–28.
571. Sura VI. 147.
572. Leviticus xi. 3, 7, 27 ff., and 39 ff.
573. Sura V. 49.
574. Exodus xxi. 23 ff.
575. Mishna Baba, Ramma viii. 1.

Chapter 12: The Sources of Islam

1. Sura lxxxv. 21; vi. 19.
2. S. xcvii. 1. Sent down, then, as they say, to the lowest heaven, and thence by Gabriel communicated to the Prophet, bit by bit, as occasion required.
3. "What think ye of Allat and al-Uzza and Monat, the other third?... They are but empty names which ye and your fathers have named goddesses." S. liii. 19.
4. The story arises out of the strange mistake of Ur of the Chaldees (Gen. xv. 7) for the same word signifying an oven or fire.
5. It is worth the while of anyone not familiar with the Koran to read this at length, as given in Surah xviii. 8-24.
6. Aaron's sister Maryam is curiously confused with Mary of the Gospel.
7. S. iii. 41; v. 19.
8. S. v. 121.
9. S. lxi. 6.
10. S. iv. 156.
11. S. xlii. 16; ci. 5 and 6: "He whose balance is heavy shall live in pleasure; but whose balance is light, his dwelling-place shall be hell fire."
12. S. xvi. 103: "They say a certain man teacheth him; but the tongue of him whom they mention is foreign, while this is simple Arabic"—hardly an answer in point!
13. I learn, however, from the author that he is not of this opinion, but thinks that the originals, in whatever language, ancient or difficult to decipher and understand, should be printed in full, as otherwise the Orientalist will suspect the translation as an invention of the author; or if not in the text of the work, they might, he thinks, be lithographed and placed at the end of the volume.
14. See also sura vi. 19 and xcvii. 1. Also Ibn Khaldun, i. 194 and ii. 458.
15. Job xxxi. 26-28.
16. Bk. iii. 8.
17. To these the Koran replies, sura L. 14: "Is our power exhausted by the first creation; for these are in perplexity as to a first creation."
18. Our author pithily remarks that the Muslims of today who seek forgiveness through the intercession of their holy men are as much polytheists as those old Arabs were.
19. Some say there were 360 around the Ka'aba. But Ibn Ishaq gives authorities for only fifteen generations of idolators before the Prophet's time.
20. The two passages given by our author from the *Sabaa Mu'allaqat* contain several verses, more or less similar to the following texts in the Koran: sura liv.1, xxix.31 and 46, xxxvii.69, xxi.96,

xciii. 1; this last: "By the brightness of the morning; *and by the night when it groweth dark.*" The passages noted are the same in both, with occasionally a few verbal differences.

21. What follows is from Abul Feda, who quotes from Abu Isa al-Maghrabi.

22. Sura vii. 156. The word used for illiterate is *Ummy.* R. Geiger's view is that this word has an altogether different meaning—viz., that Muhammad held he was of the *Ummat* or Arab people, and not an *Ajemy* or non-Arab, as a Jew would be held to be. But seeing that the word has been universally held to mean unlearned (and unable to read), I think we must accept that interpretation. It does not, however, much matter in the present argument.

23. Targum of Jonathan ben Uzziah; also the Targum of Jerusalem. In Arabic Cain is called Cabil.

24. Gen. iv. 10, "Bloods" in the margin for blood.

25. Sura ii. 260, vi. 74-84, xxi. 52-72, xix. 42-50, xxvi. 69-79, xxix. 15, 16, xxxvii. 81-95, xliii. 25-27, lx. 4, and other passages.

26. Such as the *Qissas al-Anbia* and *Araish al-Majalis.*

27. *Ancient History from the Mukhtasar fi Akhbar il Bashar.*

28. Sura vi. 76, etc.; all from the Koran so far is in italic; and so also in the next two pages.

29. Sura vi. 80-85.

30. Sura xix. 40.

31. Sura xxvi. 75-77.

32. Sura ii. 260.

33. Sura ii. 260.

34. xxxvii. 90.

35. Here the text is quoted: "He broke them all in pieces except the biggest, that they might lay the blame on it" (sura xxi. 59).

36. Cotada and al-Sidy are quoted here; and it is added from al-Dzahhak, "Perhaps they may give evidence as to what we should do, and punish him."

37. A note here added to the following purport: Muhammad on this remarked that Abraham in all told three lies, all on behalf of the Lord, namely, "I am sick"; "the big one hath done this"; and what he said to the king regarding Sarah, "She is my sister."

38. In the last few pages the quotations from the Koran are all from suras xxi. and xxxvii., and the verses being so numerous and detached are not numbered in detail; but they will be found in passages succeeding verse 52 of the former, and verse 84 of the latter sura. The Koran passages are throughout printed in italics.

39. Sura vi. 74.

40. Same as the present town, Mugheyr.

41. Jonathan ben Uzziel.

42. Sura xxvii. 20-45.

43. See also 2 Chronicles ix. 1-9.

44. Meaning "a lady and ladies," in Ecclesiastes ii. 8.

45. Sura ii. 96.

46. Cap 44.

47. The origin of the name is traced still further east to the ancient Sanskrit wind-gods the *Maruts.*

48. The original Babylonian text is here given as indeed the author does in most of

the original quotations. A close translation is also given, but only the general purport is here attempted.

49. Genesis vi. 2 and 4: "The sons of God saw the daughters of men that they were fair, and took them wives of all which they chose.... There were giants in these days,... when the sons of God came in unto the daughters of men, and they bare children unto them, the same became mighty men which were of old, men of renown." The "sons of God," according to our author, mean righteous men of the seed of Seth. The commentator quoted is Jonathan, son of Uzziel. There is a Sanskrit story of the similar ascent of two angels, and a Houri like Zohra, from which the Armenians may possibly have taken their tale; and from this idolatrous source the Jews no doubt received it, and from them, the Muslims.

50. The term *Nefilim*, i.e., persons who fell upon the helpless around them and committed violence and oppression on the earth.

51. Sura ii. 96.

52. From the Jewish story in the Abodah Sarah.

53. Sura xx. 90.

54. Pirke Rabbi Eleazer.

55. No doubt the Prophet thought that the Jews said "Sameri" (Samaritan) when they said "Sammael." They regarded Sammael as the angel of death.

56. Sura ii. 28; iv. 152.

57. Such as, the Garden of Eden, *taghut, furqan, sakina, tabut, hibr,* etc., all from one or other of the Hebrew, Syriac, or Chaldean tongues.

58. Sura xv. 44; xvii. 46. Jewish books, Hagigah, and Zohar.

59. Sura xv. 17 and 34; xxxvii. 7; lxvii. 5.

60. Mishnah Berakhoth.

61. Matth. vi. 5.

62. Sura lxxxv. 21 and 22.

63. *Qissas al-Anbia.*

64. Exodus xxiv. 12; 1 Kings viii. 9; Hebrews ix. 3, 4.

65. From Pirke Aboth, v. 6.

66. *Araish al-Majalis.*

67. Sura xviii. 8-26: Dost thou consider that the companions of the cave, and al-Rakim, were one of our signs and a great miracle? When the young men took refuge in the cave, they said, "O Lord, grant us mercy from before Thee, and dispose our business for us to a right issue." Wherefore we struck their ears so that they slept in the cave for a great number of years: then we awaked them.... We will relate unto thee their history with truth. They were young men who had believed in their Lord; and we had abundantly directed them; and we fortified their hearts with constancy when they stood before the judge; and they said, "Our Lord is the Lord of heaven and earth; we will by no means call on any god besides him; for then we should surely utter an extravagance...." And they said to one another, "When ye shall separate yourselves from them, and from that which they worship besides God, then fly into the cave: your Lord will pour his mercy upon you abundantly and dispose your business to advantage." And thou mightest have seen the sun, when it had risen to decline from their cave to the right hand, and when it went down, to leave them on the left hand: and they were in the spacious part of the cave. This was one of the signs of God.... And thou wouldest have judged them to have been awake, while they were sleeping;

and we caused them to turn themselves to the right hand and to the left. And their dog stretched forth his forelegs in the mouth of the cave; if thou hadst come suddenly upon them, verily thou wouldst have turned thy back and fled from them, and thou wouldst have been filled with fear at the sight of them. And so we awaked them out of their sleep, that they might ask questions of one another. One of them said, "How long have ye tarried here?" They answered, "We have tarried a day, or part of a day." Others said: "Your Lord best knoweth the time ye have tarried. And now send one of you with this your money into the city, and let him see which of its people hath the best and cheapest food, and let him bring you provision from him; and let him behave circumspectively, and not discover you to anyone. Verily, if they come up against you, they will stone you, or force you to return to their religion; and then shall you not prosper forever." And so we made their people acquainted with what had happened to them.... And they said, "Erect a chapel over them; their Lord best knoweth their condition.... Some say the sleepers were three, and their dog was the fourth; others say they were five, and their dog the sixth, guessing at a secret matter; and others say they were seven and their dog the eighth. Say, "My Lord best knoweth their numbers; none shall know them except a few." Wherefore dispute not concerning them, unless with a clear disputation, and ask not any (of the Christians) concerning them. ... And they remained in their cave three hundred years and nine years over.

68. "Story of Martyrs," i. 95.

69. Sura xix. 28, 29.

70. Sura lxvi. 12 and iii. 31.

71. Sura xxv. 37.

72. Coptic *History of the Virgin.*

73. Story of Joseph's dream.

74. Protevangelium.

75. Protevangelium. It is remarkable that we have the same story repeated in the *Rauzat al-Ahbab* regarding the birth of Muhammad himself!

76. Sura iii. 41 and 43.

77. Sura v. 119.

78. Matthew xxvi. 20-20; Mark xiv. 17-25; Luke xxvi. 14-17; John xiii, 1-30.

79. It is also possible that the dream of Peter in which food was sent down to him in a sheet may have originated the idea of the table descending from heaven. It was, however, but a dream. Acts x. 9-16.

80. John xiv. 16, 26, xv. 26, xvi. 7. Called also the *Faraclete.*

81. Our author exemplifies this by words begun with two Arabic letters sounding very similar, and liable to be mistaken one for the other.

82. *Manes*, and hence the Manichaeans.

83. *Araish al-Majalis.*

84. The argument might have been strengthened by a reference to Ephesians v. concerning the marriage of Christ and the Church.

85. *History of Joseph the Carpenter.*

86. Sura xxix. 57, and iii. 182.

87. *Qissas al-Anbia.*

88. John xiv. 30. The Muslims apply the name "Prince of the World" to their Prophet, not understanding its true meaning.

89. Mark ix. 49; 1 Corinthians iii. 13.

90. Matthew xix. 24; Mark x. 25; Luke xviii. 25.

91. Sura xxv. 6,7.

92. Sura lxviii. 15.

93. Sura xlv. 6, 7.

94. *Sirat al-Rasul.*

95. *Sirat* Ibn Hisham.

96. At each ascent the same salutation is repeated, but it has been left out here in all but the first.

97. Mishkat al-Masabih.

98. One of the angels noticed above is said to have led Arta aloft, just as we are told that Gabriel guided Muhammad upwards.

99. This resembles a tree called by the Arabs *Tuba*, as well as a marvellous tree of the Zoroastrians, similarly named as if from it flowed sweet water.

100. The Targum of Jonathan.

101. Genesis ii. 8-17.

102. Suras lv. 72; lvi. 22.

103. The author gives an interesting passage on the derivation of the name Houri or *Huri*, from the Pahlavi word *Hur*, or Sun, the same as *Khur*, still used in Persia with a similar meaing. The Arabs not knowing this, trace the word to *hur*, or black-eyed.

104. *Zarrat i Kainat* called in the Avesta *Fravashiyo.*

105. I.e., victory of God.

106. The *Bundahishnih*, capp. I. and II.

107. *Qissas al-Anbia.*

108. *Rauzat al-Ahbab.*

109. *Qissas al-Anbia.*

110. The Minukhirad, as old as the Sassanides.

111. Yesht xix. 31-37.

112. *Desatir-i Asmani.*

113. It is difficult to explain in English how Chinavad became *Sirat*, but it comes from the varied sound of the letters—*ch* being turned into sharp *s.*

114. *Dinkart*, an ancient Zoroastrian book.

115. The *Dasatir-i Asmani.*

116. It has been published both in the original and in the Dari translation.

117. Excepting only the ninth.

118. *Dinkart.*

119. *Rauzat al-Ahbab.*

120. *Sirat al-Rasul*, by Ibn Hisham and Ibn Ishaq.

121. *Sirat al-Rasul*, or Life of the Prophet.

122. Ibn Ishaq tells us that Muhammad, while believing himself forbidden to pray for his own mother, yet when asked by a female relative of Zaid whether she might pray for him, said: "Yes, for he will be raised as a separate religious community at the last day."

123. Sura xxxiii. 37.

124. Sura v. 48, 50.

125. Genesis xvii. 19.

126. Genesis xxii. 18.

127. John viii. 56.

128. Galatians iii. 16 and 29.

Chapter 13: The Jewish Foundation of Islam

1. Formally these words are said by the angel Gabriel to Muhammad.

2. See Axel Moberg, *The Book of the Himyarites* (Lund, 1924).

3. See the references in Horovitz, *Untersuchungen*, p. 129

4. See the *Zeitschrift der deutschen morgenländischen Gesellschaft*, vol. 41, p. 720, and the *Encyclopedia of Islam*, s.v. " 'Isā".

5. This explanation is at least as old as the year 1861 (see Rudolph, p. 67, note 25). See also the references in Horovitz, *Untersuchungen*, 128 f. Rudolph would explain the supposed pairing of Jesus with Moses on the ground that each of the two was the founder of the religion. But Muhammad did not by any means regard Moses as a *Religionsstifter,* he was a lawgiver—which Jesus was not. A more plausible ground might be seen in the simple fact that both were members of the family of 'Imran.

6. See Lammens, *L'Arabic Occidentale avant l'Hégire,* p. 80, top.

7. This refers to the Prophet's admonition to pray and (especially) recite the Koran *at night*—probably the only time when the most of his converts had opportunity to learn the ritual prescribed for them. (The nocturnal prayer was soon superseded, as no longer necessary, by the increased number of daily prayers; see the fifth lecture.) The need of private devotions in the night season was always felt by the especially devout in Israel, from the Psalter onwards; and even public services at certain times were the rule in some medieval Jewish communities, as at Qairawan in the time of Hai Gaon (I owe this reference to Professor Obermann). In *Berachoth* 14a (bottom) the devotee who spends the night reading the Torah is commended. Muhammad had seen something of the sort at Mecca; see Sura 3: 109, mentioned in the preceding lecture. On the general subject of Jewish asceticism, see now especially Montgomery, "Ascetic Strains in Early Judaism," *Journal of Biblical Literature*, vol. 51 (1932), pp. 183–213.

8. Probably the fast Ramadan should be excepted, but even this is by no means certain.

9. That is, the Hijaz.

10. The orthodox Muhammadan tradition supplies this lack, to be sure. See for instance Krehl's *Bokhari* II, 78, below.

11. *Bokhari,* ed. Krehl, II, 78, below.

12. *Too* mild, as the event proved, to make his own children follow the right way!

13. In the oriental texts of the Koran this forms a single verse. In Fluegel's edition it occupies vss. 31–34, as far as the word *huwa.*

14. Here, as in the following examples, I refer to the Nöldeke-Schwally, *Geschichte,* as the standard and by far the most influential work.

15. Hence the now customary assignment of sura 98, plainly a Meccan composition to the Medina period.

16. Interpolations and transpositions have often been postulated by interpreters of the Koran because of failure to take full account of Muhammad's very individual literary habits. Thus Nöldeke-Schwally, p. 144, will have the words: "So be not in doubt of meeting Him!" an interpolation, "da sie sich auf keine Weise in einen Zusammenhang bringen lassen." ["because they (the words) in no way fit the context."] The words are thrown in as the summary of Moses' teaching; and those who heard the prophet *recite* the passage can have been in no doubt as to its meaning.

17. I regard the word *jebin* as a variation of *jebel* for the sake of the rhyme, according to the license which Muhammad allows himself in several other places in the older part of the Koran. The verb *talla* is used of "leading" a beast; see the dictionaries of Hava, Wahrmund, and Dozy.

18. Weil's *Biblische Legenden der Muselmänner* (1845) contains both Koranic legends and those of later origin. Dr. Alexander Kohut gave an English translation of a number of them, with notes, in the N.Y. *Independent,* Jan. 8, 15, 22, and 29, 1891, under the title "Haggadic Elements in Arabic Legends").

19. On the Jewish and Muhammadan embellishment of the story of Joseph, see especially Israel Schapiro, *Die haggadischen Elemente im erzählenden Teil des Korans* (1907).

20. Sotah 36 b; Jer. Horayoth 2, 46 d; Tanhuma wayyesheb, 9.

21. According to the Jewish Midrash this was a baby in the cradle; Yashar, wayyesheb 86a-: 89a; see Ginsberg's note in his *Legends of the Jews.*

22. Yashar, l.c., 87a–87b; Tanhuma wayyesheb, 5. The former may have used the Koran (Ginsberg).

23. Yalkut I, 146; Midrash Hag-Gadol (ed. Schechter), I, 590.

24. Ber. Rab. 91, 6; Tan. B. I, 193 f., 195; Midrash Hag-Gadol I, 635.

25. Ber. Rab. 102, 8; Tan. B, I 198; Midrash Hag-Gadol I, 653.

26. Observe also the use of this formula in 3: 39 and 28: 44, 46.

27. I omit the references, which are given by Geiger, pp. 181–86.

28 This episode is probably Muhammad's own creation, based on his hearing of Prov. 6: 6–8.

29. Muhammad of course avoids the number given in the biblical story of Jacob.

30. This curious name, as has already been said (see p. 46), is the result of an easy misreading of the *Decinus* written in the Aramaic script.

31. For the literature dealing with these ancient folktales and their use in the Koran, see the notes in Nöldeke-Schwally, 140 ff., and Horovitz, *Koranische Untersuchtungen,* 141 ff. See also what was said, in regard to the probable form in which these legends were available at Mecca, in the second lecture, p. 36.

Chapter 14: Literary Analysis of Koran, Tafsir, and Sira

1. John Wansbrough, *The Sectarian Milieu: Content and Composition of Islamic Salvation History* (Oxford: Oxford University Press, 1978), pp. 116–17; also see his review of Patricia Crone and Michael Cook, *Hagarism: the Making of the Islamic World* (Cambridge: Cambridge University Press, 1977) in *Bulletin of the School of Oriental and African Studies* [hereafter,

BSOAS] 41 (1978): 155–56. Other interesting reviews of *Hagarism* are J. van Ess in *The Times Literary Supplement* Sept. 8, 1978, pp. 997–98 and N. Daniels in *Journal of Semitic Studies* [hereafter, *JSS*] 24 (1979): 296–304. Cf. M. A. Cook, "The Origins of *Kalam*," *BSOAS* 43 (1980): 32–43 for a good example of what *can* be demonstrated by external sources. Also see Patricia Crone, *Slaves on Horses: The Evolution of the Islamic Polity* (Cambridge: Cambridge University Press, 1980) especially ch. 1; Michael Cook, *Early Muslim Dogma: A Source-Critical Study* (Cambridge: Cambridge University Press, 1981), and his *Muhammad* (Oxford: Oxford University Press, 1983).

2. This *sabab*, the author admits (see note 3 below), is not found in al-Tabari's *Ta'rikh*; this fact should have raised the curiosity of the author about the literary qualities of the material with which he was dealing. It should be noted in this regard that al-Ṭabarī indeed recognized the difference between exegesis and history.

3. Fred McGraw Donner, "Mecca's Food Supply and Muhammad's Boycott," *Journal of the Economic and Social History of the Orient* 20 (1977): 249–66; another, slightly different example is found in Uri Rubin, "Abū Lahab and Sūra CXI," *BSOAS* 42 (1979): 13-28, esp. pp. 13–15. On the *asbāb al-nuzūl* see A. Rippin, "The exegetical genre *asbāb al-nuzūl*: a bibliographical and terminological survey," *BSOAS* 48/1 (1985).

4. *Quranic Studies: Sources anl Methods of Scriptural Interpretation* (Oxford: Oxford University Press, 1977). Reviews of *QS* are as follows: *Bibliotheca Orientalis* [hereafter *BO*] 35 (1978): 349–53 (van Ess); *BSOAS* 40 (1977): 609–12 (Ullendorf); *Der Islam* 55 (1978): 354–56 (Paret); *Journal of the American Oriental Society* [*JAOS*] 100 (1980): 137–41 (Graham); *Jewish Quarterly Review* [*JQR*] 68 (1978): 18–84 (Nemoy); *Journal of the Royal Asiatic Society* [*JRAS*] (1978): 76–78 (Serjeant); *JSS* 24 (1979): 293–96 (Juynboll); *Muslim World* [*MW*] 47 (1977): 306–307 (Boullata); *Zeitschrift der deutschen morganländischen Gesellschaft* [*ZDMG*] 128 (1978): 411 (Wagner); *Theologische Literaturzeitung* 105 (1980): 1–19 (Rudolph).

5. Major reviews of *SM* are as follows: *BSOAS* 43 (1980): 137–39 (van *Ess*); *Journal of the American Academy of Religion* [*JAAR*] 47 (1979): 459–60 (Martin); *JSS* 26 (1980): 121–23 (Rippin); *Der Islam* 57 (1980): 354–55 (Madelung); *BO* 37 (1981): 97–98 (Juynboll); *JRAS* (1980): 180–82 (Cook); *ZDMG* 130 (1980): 178 (Nagel).

6. See esp. his review of Josef van Ess, *Anfänge muslimischer Theologie*, *BSOAS* 43 (1980): 361–63.

7. See *SM* 58–59; Crone and Cook, *Hagarism*, pp. 17–18.

8. An example would be the *tafsīrs* ascribed to al-Kalbī and Muqātil; for a variety of reasons which he outlines in QS, Wansbrough concludes that the form in which the texts are found today probably stems from a period later than the date of the supposed authors.

9. Examples would be *Fiqh Akbar I*, and the *Risāla* of al-Ḥasan al-Baṣrī; see *QS*, 160–63.

10. See Wansbrough's review of Nabia Abbott, *Studies in Arabic Literary Papyri, II, Qur'ānic Commentary and Tradition*, in *BSOAS* 31 (1968): 613–16; cf. A. Grohmann, "The Problem of Dating Early Qur'āns," *Der Islam* 33 (1957): 213–31; Grohmann's whole point, of course, is to emphasize the difficulty involved in dating Koranic manuscripts.

11. John Burton, *The Collection of the Qur'ān* (Cambridge: Cambridge University Press, '977). See Wansbrough's review in *BSOAS* 41 (1978): 370–71.

12. Thomas L. Thompson, *The Historicity of the Patriarchal Narratives: The Quest for the Historical Abraham* (Berlin and New York: Walter de Gruyter, 1974), p. 328.

13. H. W. F. Saggs, *The Encounter with the Divine in Mesopotamia and Israel* (London: Athlone Press, 1978), pp. 65–66.

14. See Wansbrough's review of Neusner's work *BSOAS* 39 (1976): 438–39 and 43 (1980): 591–92 and of Neusner's students, *BSOAS* 41 (1978): 368–69 (Zahavy); 42 (1979): 140–41 (Green); 43 (1980): 592–93 (Gereboff). The most important work of Rudolf Bultmann is *The History of the Synoptic Tradition*, trans. John Marsh, 2d ed. (Oxford: Blackwell, 1968). Neusner has published so much it is virtually impossible to select any one writing; his paper, "The Study of Religion as the Study of Tradition in Judaism," in *Methodological Issues in Religious Studies*, ed. Robert D. Baird (Chico, Calif.: New Horizons Press, 1975), pp. 31–48, is most useful.

15. Neusner's work, on the other hand, seems to imply that a certain amount of historical information is extricable. Implicitly the debate is over basic concerns of interpretational theory, e.g., H. G. Gadamer, *Truth and Method* (New York: Seabury, 1978) *vs.* E. D. Hirsch Jr., *Validity in Interpretation* (New Haven: Yale University Press, 1967).

16. Joseph Schacht, "The Present State of Studies in Islamic Law," *Atti dei terzo Congresso di Studi Arabi e Islamici* (Naples: Instituto Universitario Orientale, 1967), p. 622. Schacht concludes: "I have too strong a confidence in the scholarly competence of the workers in the field of Islamic law, both lawyers and orientalists, to regard this as anything but a passing aberration." If only that were true!

17. Also out of the common desire (need?) to provide "endings," i.e., to eliminate ambiguity; see F. Kermode, *The Genesis of Secrecy* (Cambridge, Mass.: Harvard University Press, 1979), chapter 3; idem, *The Sense of an Ending* (New York: Oxford University Press, 1967).

18. W. M. Watt, "The Materials Used by Ibn Isḥāq," in *Historians of the Middle East*, ed. Bernard Lewis and P. M. Holt (London and New York: Oxford University Press, 1962), pp. 23–24. Watt quotes C. H. Becker (agreeing with Lammens), "... the *Sīra* is not an independent historical source. It is merely *hadīth*—material arranged in biographical order," (p. 23) to which Watt retorts: "Since Becker wrote, there has been the important work of Joseph Schacht on legal *hadīth*. ... Professor Schacht holds that it was not until the time of al-Shāfi'ī (d. 820) that it became the regular practice for legal rules to be justified by a *hadīth* reporting a saying or action of Muhammad. ... If this theory is correct ... then *hadīth* as they are found in the canonical collections were not in existence in the time of Ibn Isḥāq (d. 768)" (pp. 23–24). Thus, for Watt, the historical validity of Ibn Isḥāq's material is proven since it was written before the fabrication of legal *hadīth!* Cf. P. Crone, *Slaves on Horses*, p. 211, nt. 88: "Watt disposes of Schacht by casuistry."

19. Fuat Sezgin, *Geschichte des arabischen Schrifttums* (Leiden: E. J. Brill, 1967), vol. 1.

20. Nabia Abbott, *Studies in Arabic Literary Papyri*, II, *Qur'ānic Commentary and Tradition* (Chicago: University of Chicago Press, 1967); cf. Wansbrough's review (nt. 10 above).

21. See Sezgin, *GAS* 1:32; cf. A. Rippin, "Ibn 'Abbās's *Al-Lughāt fi'l-Qur'ān*," *BSOAS* 44 (1981): 15–25; also "Al-Zuhrī, *naskh al-Qur'ān* and the problem of early *tafsīr* texts," *BSOAS* 47 (1984): 22–43, and Wansbrough, *QS*, chapter 4.

22. An example of such "additional evidence" appears in *QS* and *SM* in the notion of "terminological transfer."

23. Harry Austryn Wolfson, *The Philosophy of the Kalam* (Cambridge, Mass.: Harvard University Press, 1976), p. 72; see Wansbrough's review of the work, *BSOAS* 41 (1978): 156–57.

24. "Islamic Religious Tradition" in *The Study of the Middle East,* ed. L. Binder (New York: Wiley, 1976), p. 61.

25. Specifically *The Qur'ān, Translated,* 2 vols. (Edinburgh: T. & T. Clark, 1937–39), and *Introduction to the Qur'ān* (Edinburgh: University Press, 1963 [1953]).

26. Cf. Serjeant's review of *QS* in *JRAS* (1978): 78, and also van Ess's review in *BO* 35 (1978): 349.

27. The term is not meant as one of derision but rather as one descriptive of textual method; see James Barr, *Fundamentalism* (Philadelphia: Westminster Press, 1978), esp. pp. 11–89. Modern scholarship on the Qur'ān treats that book as textually (if not theologically) inerrant and, more basically, lacking in contradiction. The latter point is nowhere more clearly illustrated than in attempts to understand prayer and almsgiving in the Qur'ān in terms of a (reconstructable!) historical progression; the alternative view that the various passages on these topics represent variant traditions of different localized communities which have been brought into conjunction seems far more plausible in light of our knowledge of Judeo-Christian tradition and its establishment. But to assert this is to contradict the typical Western approach to the Qur'ān.

28. See the well-phrased statements of Franz Rosenthal in the introduction to the reprint of Charles C. Torrey, *The Jewish Foundation of Islam* (New York: KTAV, 1967 [1933]).

29. M. Hodgson's emphasis on the Irano-Semitic background of Islamic culture may prove an honorable exception to this general statement; see Marshall G. S. Hodgson, *The Venture of Islam,* 3 vols. (Chicago: University of Chicago Press, 1974), esp. vol. 1.

30. For modern studies of South Arabia, see, for example, the following recent works: Jacques Ryckmans, *Les inscriptions anciennes de l'Arabie du Sud: Points de vue et problèmes actuels* (Leiden: E. J. Brill, 1973); and J. Pirenne, "La religion des Arabes préislamiques d'après trois sites rupestres et leurs inscriptions" in *Al-Bahit: Festschrift Joseph Henninger zum 70. Geburtstag am 12. Mai 1976* (St. Augustin bei Bonn: Anthropos-Instituts, 1976), pp. 177–217 and cf. the use Serjeant makes of such works in his review of *QS, JRAS* (1978): 76–77.

31. Adams, "Islamic Religious Tradition," in *The Study of the Middle East* (see nt. 24 above), p. 38.

32. Adams, p. 4o, in reference to the "irenic" approach to Islamic studies advocated by W. C. Smith.

33. Jane Smith, in "Islamic Understanding of the Afterlife" [paper presented at the symposium on Islam and the History of Religions (see preface to the present volume)], points directly to the problem very explicitly but seems not to see the solution: "Does the asking of 'wrong' questions necessarily mean that answers will be unrelated to the truths about actual Muslim faith and practice?" If the study of Islam continues to be confronted in terms of "actual Muslim faith and practice" then the problem will continue to exist. The question must be asked: "Is that what we are after?" "Are we studying sociology or intellectual history?" We can do either, and both are without a doubt important, but one cannot ask intellectual-historical questions of sociological data.

34. See *SM* 24–25; *QS* 1, 40–43, 47–48, 51–52, 57–58 as well as the analysis of haggadic *tafsīr* in chapter 4 of *QS* which Wansbrough conceives of as illustrating the point (see *SM* 24).

35. Geza Vermes, "Redemption and Genesis xxii—The Binding of Isaac and the Sacrifice of Jesus," in his *Scripture and Tradition in Judaism: Haggadic Studies,* 2d rev. ed. (Leiden:

E. J. Brill, 1973), pp. 193–227. Also see P. R. Davies and B. D. Chilton, "The Aqedah: A Revised Tradition History," *Catholic Biblical Quarterly* 40 (2978): 514–46.

36. And this would include those who attempt to postulate some sort of aberrant Judaism and/or Christianity known specifically to Arabia.

37. This procedure within Qumran is perhaps most clearly enunciated in Bleddyn J. Roberts, "Biblical Exegesis and Fulfillment in Qumran," in *Words and Meaning: Essays Presented to David Winton Thomas,* ed. Peter R. Akroyd and Barnabas Lindars (Cambridge: Cambridge University Press, 1968), pp. 195–207, although such an interpretation goes against the mainstream of Qumranic scholarship where the trend to try to identify characters such as the Wicked Priest and Teacher of Righteousness predominate as in, e.g., Vermes (see nt. 35 above). Also see *SM* esp. 52–54

38. See *QS* 49; *SM* 58, 139, where the notion of the lack of eschatology in the *Sīra* indicates a secure political position.

39. "An historical circumstance so public [as the emergence of the Qur'ān] cannot have been invented": see Serjeant's review of *QS* in *JRAS* (1978): 77. The notion that a "conspiracy" (!) is involved in such a historical reconstruction becomes a rallying point for many objections; see N. Daniel's review of *Hagarism* in *JSS* 24 (1979): 296–304. Contrary to Daniel (p. 298), one could claim that one hundred years is a long time, especially when one is dealing not with newspaper headlines and printing presses but the gradual emergence of a text at first within a select circle, then into ever widening circles. One could point to similar instances of "conspiracies" in the canonization of other scriptures, for example the identification of John the disciple with the Gospel of John in well less than a century after the emergence of the text. Besides, as in so many things, it all depends on which conspiracies one likes or does not like; Serjeant says of John Burton [*The Collection of the Qur'ān* (Cambridge: Cambridge University Press, 1977)] that he "argues vastly more cogently than Wansbrough's unsustantiable assertions, that the consonantal text of the Qur'ān before us is the Prophet's own recension," but involved in Burton's book—if one bothers to read it carefully and not get carried away by its conclusion—is a "conspiracy" to which Serjeant's objection to Wansbrough's theory should apply as well. But obviously the conclusions are what count for Serjeant, not the method by which they are reached. (See his review of *QS, JRAS* [1978]: 76). Cf. also Angelika Neuwirth, *Studien zur Komposition der mekkanischen Suren* (Berlin and New York: Walter de Gruyter, 1981) and my review *BSOAS* 45 (1982): 149–50.

40. See, for example, Raphael Loewe, "Divine Frustration Exegetically Frustrated— Numbers 14: 34 *tenū'ātī,*" in *Words and Meanings,* ed. Lindars and Akroyd, esp. pp. 137–38; G. Vermes, *Scripture and Tradition,* introduction.

41. The historical appearance of exegetical "lists" of scriptural passages, whether of (apparent) scriptural contradiction, semantic aspects, or legal rulings (see *QS,* chapter 4 for these types of lists) indicate the emergence of a fixed text of scripture. Note M. R. Waldman's observation in chapter 6 of this book: "As the Qur'ān itself became 'listed,' i.e., arranged in fixed order according to some fixed criteria of listing, further listing of the contents of the Qur'ān according to other principles of listing followed naturally." Precisely, Wansbrough would perhaps say; the earliest evidence of "listing" according to other criteria indicates the likely historical moment of the emergence of the fixed Qur'ānic canon.

42. See my review of *SM, JSS* 26 (1981): 121–23.

43. See his review of van Ess, *Anfänge muslimischer Theologie*, in *BSOAS* 43 (1980): 361–63.

44. *MW* 67 (1977): 307; the quote from *QS* is somewhat out of context, although cf. Wansbrough's review of van Ess, *Anfänge* in *BSOAS* 43 (1980): 361.

45. Fazlur Rahman, *Major Themes of the Qur'ān* (Chicago: Bibliotheca Islamica, 1980), p. xiv; see my review in *BSOAS* 44 (1981): 360–63. Rahman incorrectly quotes *QS*; it should read "...the kind...", there is also no explanation point (!) in Wansbrough's text. The possibility that there could be a difference of opinion over the value of literary analysis *per se* cannot be overlooked but Rahman's statements hardly are sufficient to urge such a position; cf. however, van Ess's review of *SM, BSOAS* 43 (1980): 137–39, where precisely that argument is attempted; one needs to look no further than, for example, Frank Kermode, *The Genesis of Secrecy* (see nt. 17 above) to see the continued vitality of literary analysis, however.

46. G. H. A. Juynboll, in his review of *QS* in *JSS* 24 (1979): 293–96, expresses this inability perfectly: "What makes W.'s theories so hard to swallow is the obvious disparity in style and contents of Meccan and Medinan *sūras*" (p. 294). Similar to this are Rahman's comments in chapter 12, and in *Major Themes*, p. xvi, about chronological necessity due to the doctrine of *naskh* (which he conceives of as "removal" of verses alone, not as legal abrogation). The possibility that *naskh* refers to replaced Jewish practices (Burton) or to abrogated earlier dispensation (Wansbrough) is not even entertained by Rahman; both these alternate solutions obviate the chronological "necessity."

Contributors

THEODOR NÖLDEKE (1836–1930). The growing interest in Islamic studies in Europe led the Parisian Academie des Inscriptions et Belles-Lettres in 1857 to propose as the subject for a prize monography "a critical history of the text of the Coran." The subject attracted the young German scholar Nöldeke, who had already published the year before a Latin disquisition on the origin and composition of the Koran. Nöldeke won the prize, and an enlarged German version of the prize-winning work was published in Göttingen in 1860 as *Geschichte des Qorâns.* It became the foundation of *all* later Koranic studies. It is still referred to and is considered an indispensable tool for further research on the Koran. Some of his essays were gathered and published as *Sketches from Eastern History.*

LEONE CAETANI (1869–1935). Caetani was born into one of the most illustrious families in Italy. His father was the Prince of Teano, and Duke of Sermoneta. Many members of the family distinguished themselves in politics and the world of scholarship. Leone was largely self-taught in Oriental languages. The first volume of his monumental work, *Annali dell' Islam* appeared in 1904 in Milan, and the tenth and final volume came out in 1926. Caetani brought a highly critical mind to the study of Islam; indeed his radical criticism of the sources led him to dismiss the authenticity of a large part of the traditions for the first part of the life of Muhammad.
Caetani also served as a deputy in Parliament between 1909 and 1913.

ALPHONSE MINGANA (1881–1937). Mingana was a great scholar of Arabic, especially Syriac. He was a member of the Chaldaean Church in Iraq, where he was also professor of Semitic Languages and Literature in the Syro-Chaldaean Seminary at Mosul. He collected invaluable Arabic and Syriac manuscripts that became the foundation for the famous Mingana Collection, now housed in Birmingham, U.K. The last twenty years of his life were spent in England where he taught Semitic Languages. His essays were collected in *Woodbrooke Studies: Christian Documents in Syriac, Arabic, Garshuni* (1927).

ARTHUR JEFFERY (18??–1952). Arthur Jeffery, professor of Semitic Languages at Columbia University and at Union Theological Seminary, was one of the great scholars of Islamic Studies.

Apart from numerous articles in learned journals, Jeffery wrote two works that are considered definitive in their respective domain, in 1937 *Materials for the History of the Text of the Qur'ān: The Old Codices,* and in 1938 *The Foreign Vocabulary of the Qur'ān.* The latter was a tour de force that reviewed about 275 words in the Koran that were regarded as foreign. This survey led Jeffery to examine texts in Ethiopic, Aramaic, Hebrew, Syriac, Greek, Latin, and Middle Persian, among other languages. His research led him to look for and at manuscripts in the Middle East, including Cairo. Other works include *The Qur'ān as Scripture* (1952).

DAVID S. MARGOLIOUTH (1858–1940). Margoliouth was professor of Arabic at the University of Oxford, and a member of the Council of the Royal Asiatic Society. He was the author of numerous artiles and books on Islam, including *Muhammad and the Rise of Islam* (London, 1905) and *The Early Development of Mohammedanism* (London, 1914). His research into the history of early Islam led him to compare the life of Joseph Smith, the founder of Mormonism, to that of the Prophet of Islam, and forced him to conclude that human beings with unusual powers fall easily into dishonesty.

ABRAHAM GEIGER (1810–1874). Geiger's study on the Jewish foundations of Islam was originally composed in Latin and submitted to the University of Bonn in 1832, in response to a contest set by the philosophy faculty. He won, and the University of Marburg later accepted his essay as a thesis and awarded him a doctorate. Geiger was but twenty-two years old when he wrote this little masterpiece. He later distinguished himself in the rabbinate as one of the founders of Reform Judaism, and as a Judaic scholar and theologian of great perception and power. Geiger was born into a very strict orthodox family in Frankfurt, and by the age of three was already receiving instruction on the Bible, and studying the Talmud by the age of six. He began his career as a rabbi in 1833, serving in Wiesbaden, Breslau, Frankfurt, and Berlin. He wrote numerous works, edited a journal, and taught until his death in Berlin in 1874.

W. St. Clair-Tisdall (1859–1928). The Reverend W. St. Clair-Tisdall was the secretary of the Church Missionary Society, an organ of the Church of England for missions, in Isfahan, Persia. A brilliant linguist, he spent much time researching the sources of Islam in their original languages. He wrote, among other works, *The Religion of the Crescent*, *The Noble Eightfold Path*, and *The Original Sources of the Qur'ān* (1905).

C. C. Torrey (1863–1956). Torrey was professor of Semitic Languages at Yale University. He worked with the American Schools of Oriental Research in the Near East, helping to excavate a Phoenician necropolis at Sidon. He was an expert on Palestinian antiquities in general and a formidable biblical scholar with more than fifteen works to his credit, such as *The Four Gospels* (1947), *The Apocryphal Literature* (1945), and *The Second Isaiah* (1928).

A. Rippin (1950–   ). Andrew Rippin is associate professor of Religious Studies, University of Calgary, Alberta, Canada. He has written numerous articles, and coedited with Jan Knappert a work that has become a standard textbook, *Textual Sources for the Study of Islam* (1986).